Cromwell and Scotland

Source: A Fight at Dunin in Scotland, Between the Scots Women and the Presbyterian Kirkmen (Edinburgh, 1652).

Cromwell and Scotland

Conquest and Religion, 1650–1660

R. SCOTT SPURLOCK

JOHN DONALD

First published in Great Britain in 2007 by
John Donald, an imprint of Birlinn Ltd

West Newington House
10 Newington Road
Edinburgh
EH9 1QS

www.birlinn.co.uk

ISBN 10: 1 904607 77 2
ISBN 13: 978 1 904607 77 9

British Library Cataloguing-in-Publication Data
A catalogue record for this book is available on request
from the British Library

Typeset in Sabon by
Koinonia, Manchester
Printed and bound in Britain
by Bell and Bain Ltd, Glasgow

To my parents
and the unyielding faithfulness and friendship
of Manders

Contents

Acknowledgements

I would like to offer my heartfelt thanks to all those who have supported me over the past four years during the production of this thesis, particularly the following: my supervisors, Dr Susan Hardman Moore and Dr Jane Dawson, who have shown exceptional support, encouragement and patience; Professor David F. Wright, for his great kindness and guidance during my studies at New College; the staff of New College Library, Edinburgh, for their many trips to special collections; the staff of the National Library of Scotland; and the congregation of Morningside United Church, to whom I owe a special debt of appreciation. Portions of this book were revised and added thanks to the generosity of the Institute for Advanced Studies in the Humanities at the University of Edinburgh where I received a postdoctoral fellowship in 2006–7: grateful appreciation to Professor Susan Manning, Anthea Taylor and Donald Ferguson. Sincere thanks and a great debt of gratitude are owed to both Dr Frances Dow and Professor John Morrill, whose guidance and feedback were immeasurably beneficial in the transformation of this work from a PhD thesis into its present form. More than just examiners, they have been advisors and friends. Thanks are also extended to the Strathmartine Trust, whose generous grant advanced the publication of this book. Finally, my heartfelt gratitude and appreciation to Amber, Cliff and Karen for nearly a decade of kindness and support.

Conventions and Abbreviations

Conventions

All dates given in this work have been adjusted to the modern calendar, with 1 January marking the beginning of a new year. Additionally, publishers are only given for seventeenth-century works printed in Scotland during the Interregnum.

Abbreviations

AGA Church of Scotland, General Assembly, *Acts of the General Assembly of the Church of Scotland, 1638–1842*, ed., Pitcairn, T., (Edinburgh, 1843).

APS Innes, C. and Thomson, T., eds, *The Acts of the Parliament of Scotland*, 11 vols (Edinburgh, 1814–44).

Abbott, *Cromwell* Abbott, W.C., ed., *The Writings and Speeches of Oliver Cromwell*, 4 vols (Cambridge, MA, 1937–47).

Baillie, *L & J* Baillie, Robert, *Letters and Journals*, ed., Laing, D., 3 vols (Edinburgh, 1841–2).

Balfour Balfour, Sir James, *The Historical Works of James Balfour*, 4 vols (Edinburgh, 1824).

Baxter, *Synod of Fife* Baxter, C., ed., *Ecclesiastical Records. Selections from the Minutes of the Synod of Fife, 1611–1687* (Edinburgh, 1837).

Blairs Papers Hay, M.V., *The Blairs Papers, 1603–1660* (London, 1929).

BQ *Baptist Quarterly*

Brodie Brodie, Sir Alexander, *Diary of Alexander Brodie of Brodie (1652–80)* (Aberdeen, 1863).

COS Church of Scotland

COSGAC Church of Scotland, General Assembly, Commission

CSPD Green, M.A.E., ed., *Calendar of State Papers, Domestic Series 1651–1660*, 13 vols (London,1877–86).

Clarke MSS Microfilm copy of the William Clarke Manuscripts held in Worcester College, Oxford and NLS, ed., Aylmer, G.E., Brighton Harvester Microfilm, 1977–9. Listed by volume number.

Clarke Papers   Firth, C.H., ed., *The Clarke Papers*, 4 vols (London, 1891–1901).

Clarke Papers V   Henderson, F., ed., *The Clark Papers: Further Selections from the Papers of William Clarke*, Camden Fifth Series, vol. 27 (Cambridge, 2005).

Cramond, *Elgin*   Cramond, W., ed., *The Records of Elgin, 1234–1800* (Aberdeen, 1898).

Cramond, *Moray*   Cramond, W., ed., *Extracts from the Records of the Synod of Moray* (Elgin, 1906).

Donaldson, 'Schism'   Donaldson, G., 'The Emergence of Schism in Seventeenth-Century Scotland', *Scottish Church History* (Edinburgh, 1985), 204–19.

Dow   Dow, Frances, *Cromwellian Scotland: 1651–1660* (Edinburgh, 1979; 1999).

EUL   Edinburgh University Library

FES   Scott, H., ed., *Fasti Ecclesiae Scoticanae*, 7 vols (Edinburgh, 1915–1928).

Fox   Fox, George, *The Journal*, ed., Smith, N. (London, 1998).

Gardiner, *C & P*   Gardiner, S.R., ed., *History of the Commonwealth and Protectorate 1649–1656*, 4 vols (London, 1903).

Henderson, *RLSCS*   Henderson, G.D., *Religious Life in Seventeenth Century Scotland* (Cambridge, 1937).

Holfelder   Holfelder, K.D., 'Factionalism in the Kirk during the Cromwellian Invasion and Occupation of Scotland, 1650 to 1660: The Protester–Resolutioner Controversy' (PhD Thesis, University of Edinburgh, 1998).

JEH   *Journal of Ecclesiastical History*

JFHS   *Journal of the Friends Historical Society*

JPHSE   *Journal of the Presbyterian Historical Society of England*

Kinloch, *St Andrews & Cupar*   Kinloch, G.R., ed., *Ecclesiastical Records. Selections from the Minutes of the Presbyteries of St. Andrews and Cupar, 1641–1698* (Edinburgh, 1837).

Lamont   Lamont, John, *The Diary of Mr John Lamont of Newton, 1649–1671*, ed., Kinloch, G.R. (Edinburgh, 1830).

Nickolls   Nickolls, J., ed., *The Original Letters and Papers of State, Addressed to Oliver Cromwell; Concerning the Affairs of Great Britain* (London, 1743).

Nickalls, *Fox*   Fox, George, *The Journal of George Fox*, ed., Nickalls, J.L. (Cambridge, 1952).

Nicoll   Nicoll, John, *A Diary of Public Transactions and Other Occurrences, Chiefly in Scotland, 1650–67*, ed., Laing, D., (Edinburgh, 1836).

NLS   National Library of Scotland

ODNB   *Oxford Dictionary of National Biography*

Penney, *Fox*   Fox, George, *The Journal of George Fox*, ed., Penney, N., 2 vols (Cambridge, 1911).

RCGA   Mitchell, A.F. and Christie, J., eds, *Records of the Commission of the General Assembly*, 3 vols (Edinburgh, 1890–1909).

RCME   Stephen, W., ed., *Register of the Consultations of the Ministers of Edinburgh and Some Other Brethren of the Ministry*, 2 vols (Edinburgh, 1921–30).

RHCA   Firth, C.H. and Davies, G., eds, *The Regimental History of Cromwell's Army*, 2 vols (Oxford, 1940).

RSCHS   *Records of the Scottish Church History Society*

Robertson, *Lanark*   Robertson, J., ed., *Ecclesiastical Records. Selections from the Registers of the Presbytery of Lanark, 1623–1709* (Edinburgh, 1839).

Row, *History of the Kirk*   Row, John, *The History of the Kirk of Scotland* (Edinburgh, 1842).

Rutherford, *Letters*   Rutherford, Samuel, *Letters of Samuel Rutherford*, ed., Bonar, A.A. (Edinburgh, 1863; 1984).

S & C   Firth, C.H., ed., *Scotland and the Commonwealth* (Edinburgh, 1895).

S & P   Firth, C.H., ed., *Scotland and the Protectorate* (Edinburgh, 1899).

SHR   *Scottish Historical Review*

SHS   Scottish History Society

Stevenson, *Counter-Revolution*   Stevenson, D., *Revolution and Counter-Revolution in Scotland, 1644–1651* (London, 1977; Edinburgh, 2003).

Stuart, *Aberdeen*   Stuart, J., ed., *Selections from the Records of the Kirk Session, Presbytery, and Synod of Aberdeen* (Aberdeen, 1846).

Stuart, *Strathbogie*   Stuart, J., ed., *Extracts from the Presbytery Book of Strathbogie. 1631–1654* (Aberdeen, 1843).

TRHS   *Transactions of the Royal Historical Society*

TCHS   *Transactions of the Congregational Historical Society*

Underhill, *Records*   Underhill, E.B., ed., *Records of the Churches of Christ Gathered in Fenstanton, Warboys and Hexham, 1644–1720* (London, 1854).

Wariston, ii   Johnston, Sir Archibald, of Wariston, *Diary of Sir Archibald Johnston of Wariston*, ed., Flemming, D.H., vol. 2 (Edinburgh, 1919).

Wariston, iii   Johnston, Sir Archibald, of Wariston, *Diary of Sir Archibald Johnston of Wariston*, ed., Ogilvie, J.D., vol. 3 (Edinburgh, 1940).

Citadel
Garrison
Loch Ness Frigate

1. Kilcreggan(?) Castle
2. Dumbarton Castle
3. Craigbarnet (Campsie)(?)
4. House of Kilsyth
5. Kinneil House

6. South Queensferry
7. Craighouse
8. Dunfermline
9. Burntisland
10. Kirkcaldy

11. Wemyss
12. Struthers Castle
13. Inchkeith
14. Inchgarvie
15. Anstruther

16. Crail

?- denotes uncertainty
of Location.

Map of Cromwellian Garrisons
Cromwellian Garrisons Occupied for at Least Three Months

Introduction

In 1982, John Morrill reviewed three recently published works which together he lauded for their great strides in charting the religious history of seventeenth-century Scotland. Two of the works primarily focused on the religion of the country, while the third did not. Frances Dow's *Cromwellian Scotland* is an academic study par excellence dealing with the political and military history of Interregnum Scotland. The focus of her work meant she dealt with the religious issues of the period in so far as they related directly to the political climate. So in terms of ecclesiastical history, Morrill professed 'there is still a thesis to be written on the Scottish Church in the 1650s'.[1] K.D. Holfelder's 1998 PhD thesis took steps in this direction by deciphering the complexities of Presbyterian polity during a turbulent decade which witnessed a dramatic schism within the Kirk.[2] Yet, while this work addressed the internal Presbyterian religious discourse within the Kirk, a large gap in the story of Interregnum Scottish religion and its most distinctive aspect remains untold. The intention of this book is to help fill the void in studies of seventeenth-century Scottish religion in one of its most dynamic decades.

Ecclesiastical studies of seventeenth-century Scotland have often focused (perhaps over-focused) primarily on the Covenanters' struggle against Episcopacy. Such an interpretation has understandably been forged by the persecution and martyrdom of Presbyterians during the 'Killing Times'. Unfortunately, however, this has tended to overshadow the earlier part of the seventeenth century and resulted in the subscription of the covenants in 1638 and 1643 being viewed primarily as setting the stage for the brave stand against the king later in the century. As a result, historians have often treated the Interregnum 'as little more than a parenthetical break' in an otherwise seamless struggle.[3] Such a perspective has meant the modest research produced on Scottish religion of the 1650s, like James Beattie's *History of the Church of Scotland during the Interregnum*, explore little beyond the Protester–Resolutioner schism.[4] Other more general histories of Scotland have tended to merely gloss over the decade altogether, focusing instead on the covenanting periods before and after. There are some noticeable exceptions to this generalisation, which will be discussed below, but the traditional emphasis on how a national covenanted presbytery should interact and engage with secular authorities has tended to overshadow the degree to which Presbyterianism and its covenants came under the scrutiny of a growing number of Scots during the Interregnum.

In contrast to previous works on the Interregnum, this study will focus on the backlash against the Kirk and the covenants brought about by Scotland's engagements with the English parliament and subsequently with the king during the English civil wars. The policies of the Kirk during the 1640s engendered a deep seated antipathy among nonconformist religious groups in England who anxiously embraced the 1650 invasion of Scotland as a crusade against a domineering national church. For this reason the English army that crossed the Tweed into Scotland on 22 July 1650 was in general more religiously radical in its disposition than any in the preceding decade. Their conquest and occupation led to the introduction of an unprecedented degree of Protestant variations into Scotland, all of which desired to proselytise Scots away from an intolerant Kirk. It is the motivation of the invading English, the success of their missionary endeavours and the reaction of the Scottish populace that are the focus of this book.

What is most exceptional about Interregnum Scotland, from the religious perspective, is that for the first time religious toleration became the official policy of the Scottish government.[5] In turn, the debate between Presbyterians and Independents that took place in England during the 1640s penetrated the popular Scottish consciousness for the first time. Although Kirk ministers like Robert Baillie and Samuel Rutherford fired volleys against English Independents and sects from the presses in London during the 1640s, prior to the Interregnum the dialogue between Presbyterians and Independents had been tightly censored in Scotland. From December 1638 the General Assembly strictly controlled the religious products of Scotland's presses by requiring that all works referring to the Kirk or religion receive pre-publication approval from the fiery clerk of the assembly and advocate for the Kirk, Sir Archibald Johnston of Wariston.[6] In August 1643 the assembly ordered ministers, 'especially ... upon the coasts', to 'search for all books tending to separation'. All such works and their distributors were to be referred to the local presbyteries in an effort to 'hinder the dispersing thereof'.[7] By 1647 the censorship of the Presbyterian–Independent debate further escalated when the General Assembly passed an act prohibiting the printing, importing or distribution of literature 'maintaining Independencie or Separation'.[8] This act, prompted by what Scottish representatives to the Westminster Assembly had witnessed in London, intended to prevent 'the errours [which] ... have (in our neighbour kingdome of England) spread as a gangraen' from doing the same in

Scotland.[9] This strict censorship efficiently prevented the general populace of Scotland from any familiarity with the nuts and bolts of the debate taking place England, but they may have done even more than that.

Although some ministers and intellectuals in Scotland kept abreast of the developing dialogue, especially those directly involved in it, there is evidence suggesting the bans may have prevented Scotland's universities from attaining Independent works. In 1653 John Row, the principal of King's College Aberdeen who signed a declaration in favour of Independency, not only denied being influenced by the writings of John Cotton but claimed never to have seen any of Cotton's works. As a result of the General Assembly's strict censorship, the arrival of Cromwell's forces in 1650 initiated a fresh controversy in Scotland. Irrespective of the fact that the content of the religious debates was not new, as its rhetoric reflected the recycled debates of the previous decade in England, for the people of Scotland the presence of English troops inititiated an utterly new discussion.

The scholarship of Anne Hughes demonstrates that a religious 'fluid marketplace' existed in England during the 1640s and 1650s wherein alternative forms of Protestantism vied for popular support. In this atmosphere of religious competition the growth of radical sects forced 'Orthodox' ministers to engage in public debates with radical opponents in an attempt to curb sectarian growth and to defend their parishioners. This study will explore how the introduction of sects into Scotland, under sweeping toleration imposed by the English Commonwealth regime, created a similar dynamic in Scotland, drawing ministers of the Kirk into a struggle for the hearts and souls of Scotland's population against an occupying army with an evangelical agenda.

Older studies addressing different aspects of the religious diversity during the period predominantly focus only on particular sects.[10] Only two attempts have been made to analyse the overall breadth of what took place and provide an overview of how the various sects engaged with the Scottish populace.[11] G.D. Henderson's 'Some Early Scottish Independents' offers a deluge of citations providing snapshots of particular individuals or places, while briefly touching on the presence of the English army and making a few observations about the existence of Quakers in Scotland.[12] The bulk of the article focuses on the personas of the leading figures among the Aberdeen Independents. Although it provides good information, it does little to tie events together. W.I. Hoy's 'Entry of Sects into Scotland' is significantly more holistic in its approach and brings to light important sources that provided a welcome jumping-off point for beginning this work.[13] However, Hoy also presents additional challenges resulting from inaccurate and incorrect citations.[14] Beyond these exploratory works, little has been done to draw the various strands together.

This book will set out to establish the fundamental role of religion as a motive for England's conquest and occupation of Scotland from 1650 to 1660. From the outset of their campaign the English army, largely comprising Independents, Baptists and members of other nonconformist religious groups (or sects), rallied behind the task of bringing down the intolerant national Church of Scotland, which under the guise of the Solemn League and Covenant had intervened in both English civil wars. The resentment English nonconformists felt towards the rigid Presbyterians north of the border is not difficult to understand when Scotland's sole stipulation for involvement in each war was that religious uniformity be agreed upon by both nations in the form of the presbytery. The Scots fought with the parliament in the First Civil War, believing parliament had agreed that the uniform pattern of ecclesiastical government for the two kingdoms would be the presbytery. When this expectation failed to be met, the Scots joined the king in the Second Civil War on the condition he impose, for a trial period, a national Presbyterian church in England. As a result, Scottish meddling set the stage for Cromwell's 1650 invasion of Scotland.

This study falls into two parts. The first focuses on the motives for England's invasion of Scotland and enquires to what degree an anti-Presbyterian sentiment existed within the English regime and army. Chapter 1 evaluates the literature produced by both sides in order to establish that Scotland's state Church and its narrow interpretation of the covenants were among the most important, if not indeed the most important, motivations for England's campaign against Scotland. Furthermore, it establishes that the Scots understood the threat posed to the Kirk by an 'army of sectaries' entering Scotland. Hence the invasion represented a battle for the souls of the Scottish people and the outcome would resound as a providential declaration of God's favoured form of church government. Chapter 2 explores the efforts and means of Englishmen to promulgate their own particular religious views in Scotland. Under the religious toleration imposed by the regime in February 1652 many religiously radical members of England's army viewed the country as 'a field white with harvest'.[15] The third chapter gauges, by analysing the use of Scotland's strictly controlled presses, the regime's changing policy regarding religious settlement, the promotion of congregational autonomy over that of national hierarchies, and the establishment of religious toleration in Scotland in the manner exhibited in England.

The second part of this study addresses the results of different religious groups planting themselves among the Scots. Chapter 4 investigates the separation of Scots from the Kirk by means of forming wholly indigenous Independent congregations. Moreover, it inquires into the Kirk's own culpability for this schism. The testimony of Scots who left the Kirk demonstrates how events of the 1640s not only antagonised their southern neighbours but sowed seeds of discontent among some parishioners and clergy.

As a result, the policies of the Kirk prepared the way for the message of separation preached by English missionaries during the Interregnum. The fifth and final chapter compares the experiences of Baptists and Quakers in Scotland and seeks to establish why they experienced varying degrees of success. It considers the factors that enabled the Friends to be the sole sectarian religious group introduced during the Interregnum to survive and grow through the Restoration period.

In order to avoid being sidetracked from the purpose of this study, the Protester–Resolutioner conflict is not directly discussed in what follows.[16] However, where divisions between the Protesters and Resolutioners were fostered or indeed engendered by the English as part of their efforts for achieving a religious settlement, it will be addressed, or, as is the case discussed in chapter 4, when the distinction between particular groups of Protesters and Independents became blurred. Essentially this book is an attempt to bring to light the oft-forgotten and dynamic religious open market instituted by the Commonwealth/Protectorate in Scotland in the wake of what many contemporaries considered to be the reign of an oppressive Presbyterian Kirk. The Interregnum represents a decade in which formerly rigid supporters of the covenants and opponents to toleration came to heed Cromwell's desire that God would 'make all Christians of one heart'.[17]

A number of the sources used in this study have been utilised in previous works, such as the letters of Archibald Johnston of Wariston to the Aberdeen Independents[18] and the debate between James Guthrie and the General Baptist James Brown.[19] In these cases this study delves deeper into these works as source material than they have previously been used. For example, Wariston's extensive replies to Aberdeen, which he produced after multiple private conferences with Alexander Jaffray and John Menzies, are drawn heavily upon as important sources for identifying the particular doctrinal position of the Aberdeen Independents. This is important because previous studies have relied almost completely upon the Aberdonians' initial declaration in favour of Independency which they produced months before separating.[20] Likewise, the debate between Guthrie and Brown is not used just to identify the doctrines disputed between the two ministers, but also as a case study for how public disputes were carried out and how they fit into the overall policy of the English regime.[21] In other cases material is reanalysed to produce wholly new information neglected by earlier studies. For instance, I have identified several of the signatories to a Scottish petition for religious toleration and subsequently been able to ascribe to them their proper religious affiliation. As a result, this study demonstrates how Scottish Baptists, Independents and Quakers joined together in the closing months of the Interregnum to request mutual toleration for one another at a time when their English counterparts had little sympathy for one another.[22] Additional material in this study is utilised for the first time. Where this occurs it is duly noted, but probably the most intriguing instance is the identification of an anonymous manuscript as a forgotten work of Samuel Rutherford.[23] Consequently, this book identifies the context of the paper and ascribes a relatively precise date for an important, but long-ignored, manuscript.

Finally, a word about the terminology used in this book. The term 'sectarian' is a loaded phrase within modern Scotland in relation to Protestant–Catholic bigotry. This is not the sense in which it is used here. For our purpose, a sect 'is a subdivision or splintering off from an already established religion'; for the present study Protestant Christianity.[24] Or more specifically, 'the independence of the church or group from the state, coupled with the freedom of the individual from coercion in matters of conscience and religion'.[25] Perhaps an important distinction to keep in mind in relation to the political situation in which sects were introduced into Scotland is provided by Benton Johnston. He defines a church as 'a religious group that accepts the social environment in which it exists' while 'a sect ... rejects the social environment in which it exists'.[26] Werner Stark took this argument one step further and declared that often sectarians 'are *in* their country rather than *of* their country ... they are even, as a rule, *against* it'.[27] It is by this definition that the religious groups who entered Scotland as part of Cromwell's army and their Scots proselytes are referred to as 'sectarian', because they stood against and were a response to the expansionist policies of the established Church of Scotland. More importantly, the use of the word sectarian rests not on a modern interpolation thrust into the seventeenth century, but rather upon the prevalent use of the term in the period of study itself. Repeatedly Scottish writers referred not to an 'English' army invading, but to an 'army of sectaries' or to the army of 'the publicke enemy Cromwell, and the sectarian traitorous rebels of England'.[28] The journal *Perfect Passages* stated that Scots clergy continued to preach against the 'English as Sectaries and Schismaticks' long after their arrival.[29] Consequently, Scots who accepted the religious alternatives advocated by the English army were termed 'sectaries'. William Dundas lamented, when looking back upon the Interregnum, that the Kirk labelled him a 'sectary' for 'my looking one step further then their publick Faith'.[30] Thus the Scots defined their enemy less by nationality and more by their divergent religious practices. Yet more importantly, in its contemporary context the term 'sect' was embraced by many who rejected national churches and instead joined gathered congregations in England.[31] As a result, the government and Kirk of Scotland naturally identified the introduction of radical Protestant groups as 'sects' and Scottish proselytes as 'sectarians'.

1 'The Covenant' vs 'The Lord of Hosts'

A Struggle for Public Opinion through the Printed Propaganda of War

> Nor must it be forgotten what hazard our own nation hath run of late, through the malice, falshood, and Factions of the late *Presbiterian Drivers*. He that will remember what they did in the year 1647, 48. 49. 50. and 51. must needs confesse, that great hath been the deliverance of this Commonweal, and the manner of it almost incredible, considering the waies and meanes whereby we have been rescued out of the Claws of the old Tyranny; which (through their faction and fury) was at the very point of returning in again upon us. From hence therefore let us conclude, that no Error is more dangerous, no Treason more pernicious to a Commonweal then the driving of Faction.[1]
>
> *Mercurius Politicus*, July 1652.

Even before the English army crossed into Scotland on 22 July 1650, a war of propaganda raged between the Scottish Kirk and the English parliamentary army. The intensity of this clash led J.D. Ogilvie to dub it 'a combat in itself, although one in which only ink was spilled'.[2] As the inevitability of conflict became increasingly apparent, polemical works took on a fundamentally important role as both nations strove to galvanise support. In Scotland, the imposing threat of the battle-hardened and well-oiled military machine of the parliamentary army made Scottish national unity essential for any successful defence against an English invasion. With the nation's religion, monarchy and sovereignty at stake Scotland's civil and ecclesiastical governments (who were largely the same group)[3] rallied the nation under the banner of the covenant and published against the evils of the English 'Sectarian army'. They hoped by convincing Scotland's populace of the blasphemous and heretical nature of the English they would ensure a unified defence. Yet the Scots were not alone in their urgency to rally supporters. Many of those who backed the English parliament during their campaigns against Charles I in England and their invasion of Ireland needed reassurance before they would take part in any invasion of Scotland, forcing parliament and the army to justify their invasion of an independent nation which practised a 'rightly reformed religion' to the significant number of moderates and Presbyterians among their own ranks.[4] While initially both the English and Scots focused their propaganda on rallying allies, as the English invaders approached the Tweed, their attentions turned towards under-mining support for the rigid covenanting government of the Scots. Thus the propaganda of both nations served a twofold purpose: first, to rally popular support for their own cause; and second, to wage a war of propaganda against their opponents both at home and abroad.

The Role of Religion in the Conflict

Between 25 June 1650, and the autumn of 1651, polemical works were produced by both English and Scots to establish the political stability of their positions, but the language that predominated in these works was religious. The reason for this is simple. Although a military and political conflict, the underpinning ideological issues were rooted deeply in the religious issues of the day. Although Scotland had proclaimed Charles II as king of all of Great Britain and Ireland on 5 February 1649, Charles' presence in Scotland the following year can only be seen to be at best partially responsible for the English invasion. In fact even this declaration of temporal authority had an underlying religious function recognised by the English regime. Scotland's declaration of Charles II as king of all Great Britain did not represent simply a pro-monarchy sentiment, but a declaration of Scotland's intention to pursue the archetypal models of both ecclesiological and secular government illustrated in the Kirk's interpretation of the Solemn League and Covenant.[5] Hence the invasion of Scotland by the English parliament represented a backlash against the pattern of religious and secular society plotted by the Kirk.

So while England's invasion had clearly political and secular motivations (preventing further Scottish incursions into England) the Commonwealth identified the ideological enemy who fostered Scotland's interference into English politics and society to be the Kirk and its covenants. Certainly, many Scots recognised this to be the case. 'This pairtie,' wrote the diarist John Nicoll, 'eftir thai haif actitit such thinges in England and Yreland, conceaving that thai can not be establisched and eat the fruit of thair awin devyces without contradictioun, als long as the Kirk of Scotland standis in thair way.'[6] Nicoll rightly recognised that by 1650 the Kirk represented the greatest obstacle to the Commonwealth, not the king. The English army knew the score as well. Cromwell had declared in 1648 that 'our brothers of Scotland – sincerely Presbyterian – were our greatest Enemies'.[7] In that year he attempted to solidify the relationship between the English Independents and the Scottish Kirk by aiding the settlement of the extreme party of the Kirk into power through the Whiggamore Raid. He hoped they would be more amenable to his own Independent party in England.[8] However, the Scots Kirk had proven on more than one occasion they would only settle for one arrangement and it would have to be wholly on their terms. Throughout the 1640s Scotland, under the guise of the National Covenant (1638) and the Solemn League and Covenant (1643), repeatedly intervened in English affairs solely on the basis of establishing Presbyterianism in England through 'a religious union' in order to secure the Kirk.[9] As a result, the English invasion of Scotland must be viewed as the result of a series of events stretching back to the ascendancy of Presbyterianism in Scotland with the signing of the National Covenant, wherein Scotland's attitude to the presbytery became 'imperialistic'. That is to say, the preservation of presbytery at home, as well as the exportation of presbytery abroad, came to dominate both Scottish politics and policy.

When Charles I attempted to secure a semblance of religious uniformity throughout his kingdoms by imposing a Book of Common Prayer on the Scottish Kirk in 1637, a backlash took place, challenging royal authority and opening the door for the civil wars throughout the three kingdoms.[10] Popular resistance to royal interference in ecclesiastical affairs prompted the production of the National Covenant in 1638. Later in the year the General Assembly convened, denounced the king's interference in religion, deposed the bishops, deposed the high commission and restored Presbyterianism as the governmental structure of the Kirk. Although the covenant affirmed the role of the king, from Charles' perspective it undermined the divinely sanctioned authority of his royal prerogative. As a result, two brief conflicts ensued, deemed the 'Bishop's Wars', which set a precedent for armed resistance to royal absolutism and hence may be seen as a precursor to all the British civil wars that followed. Thanks to Swedish military strategies, innovations and experience gained by Scots mercenaries serving in the army of Gustavus Adolphus in the Thirty Years War, the Covenanters quickly forced the king to capitulate in the first 'war' in 1639 and routed the royalist forces near Newcastle in August 1640 in what came to be known as the Second Bishop's War.

The following year Scot representatives travelled to London to negotiate terms with the king. In addition, they approached the recently appointed 'Long Parliament' requesting a policy of religious uniformity between the two kingdoms. The Scots argued that the king's tyranny, particular in respect to religion, represented a threat to the wishes of both nations' legislative bodies and argued a uniformity of religion would protect the wishes of the godly throughout the Stuart kingdoms. This proposal represents the first in a series of events demonstrating Covenanted Scotland's refusal to function independently of affairs in England. Scotland, if not desirous of a union, at least refused to be independent of the political and ecclesiastical process in England.[11] The Long Parliament refused this proposal, but circumstances soon changed. In 1642 the civil war broke out between the king and England's parliament. In outlining its primary aims to Scotland's General Assembly, parliament proclaimed the advancement of 'the Truth and Purity of the Reformed Religion, not only against Popery but against all other superstitious sects and innovations whatsoever'.[12] After a series of one-sided defeats at the hand of royalist forces, parliament approached the Scots for military support. According to Robert Baillie the English sought a 'civil league', but the Scots held out for 'a religious Covenant'. Desperate for military assistance, the English acquiesced and the Solemn League and Covenant was drawn up in Edinburgh in June 1643. The document pledged in its first clause to strive to

> sincerely, really, and constantly, through the Grace of God ... the preservation of the Reformed Religion in the Church of Scotland, in Doctrine Worship, Discipline, and Government, against our common Enemies, the reformation of Religion in the Kingdoms of England and Ireland, in Doctrine, Worship, Discipline, and Government, according to the Word of God, and the Example of the best Reformed Churches. *And shall endeavour to bring the Churches of God in the three Kingdoms to the nearest conjunction and Uniformity in Religion, confession of Faith, Form of Church-government.*[13]

Only in the latter clauses did the covenant speak of monarchy, although it preserved the divinely ordained role of the monarch. Both sides felt as though they had attained what they sought. The English assured Scottish support in their war against the king by pledging to pursue 'reformed religion', while the Scots had, they believed, attained what they sought in 1641 by reaching an agreement for religious uniformity. Although no particular form of church government is defined, the Scots certainly believed that 'the preservation of the Reformed Religion in the Church of Scotland' represented the penultimate 'example of the best Reformed Churches'. The Scots understood this agreement as an assurance by parliament that England would adopt a Presbyterian form of national church government.

The First Civil War ended in 1646 with the English parliament–Scottish coalition victorious. However, during the three years they fought together a mutual distrust began to develop. Part of this stemmed from Scottish involvement in the Westminster Assembly of Divines. Although not constituent members, the Scots, who had been invited to join the newly formed assembly by the English representatives in Edinburgh who had helped to draw up the Solemn League and Covenant in 1643, took a leading role and demonstrated a single aim throughout: the establishment of a Presbyterian church government in England. English Independents and other non-conformists, who predominated in the parliamentary army, resented this foreign intervention in religious affairs and accordingly grew wary of Scotland's ultimate aims. Likewise, the Scots and English Presbyterians increasingly questioned the orthodoxy of their English cohorts. Already in 1644 Robert Baillie worried that young impressionable Scots serving alongside English parliamentary soldiers ran a great risk of heretical infection.[14] By 1646, the final year of the First Civil War, Presbyterians began making concerted efforts to name and shame heretics. Foremost in this endeavour was Thomas Edwards, who produced a three-part publication entitled *Gangraena*. According to Edwards, the whole New Model Army might be labelled 'Independent', but in reality it served as a breeding ground for ever-evolving heresies. So although they had served as allies for three years in a shared struggle against the king, Presbyterians, both English and Scot alike, came to view the New Model Army as a dangerous liability, while the New Model Army and much of parliament perceived the Scots as singularly minded in their unjustified intervention in English affairs.[15] Henry Marten reminded the commissioners that their input regarding religion should be at best humble advice; in other matters the Scots should stay out of English affairs.[16]

The smouldering distrust between the Scots and the English army found further credence in the events of 1647. Both treated with the king, vying to secure their own desired settlements. In May the Scots treated with Presbyterian MPs over moving the king to Scotland and sending a Scottish army into England. Recognising the threat, English soldiers abducted the king, keeping him at the New Model Army's leisure. The Scots perceived this as an underhanded move and further evidence of the sectarian, heretical and dangerous disposition of the army. The Committee of Estates received advice from the Kirk denouncing the influence of sectarians in England and advocated the necessity of religious uniformity throughout Great Britain along Presbyterian lines before any lasting settlement between the two nations.[17] However, the New Model Army experienced internal dissensions threatening the coherence and solidarity of their cause. During the summer Cromwell and Ireton sought to secure a settlement on terms amenable to the New Model Army, but more radical elements fuelled by Leveller principles refused proposals resulting in any compromise of their burgeoning republican principles. Opposition to the status quo of government rose up within the New Model Army, which found expression in *The Case of the Armie Truly Stated*. In October and November, debates between the commanders of the New Model Army and elected 'agitators' took place at Putney. It became increasingly clear what these elements would require in a settlement with the king: religious liberty and widespread toleration.

Prompted by disappointment in the failure of Presbyterian ecclesiastical government materialising in England, the increasing tolerance of parliament towards sects and the overwhelming 'sectarian' nature of the English army, the Scots approached the king. Late in December 1647, the Scots entered into an Engagement with the King, agreeing to aid him in opposition to the parliament on the sole condition he impose a three-year trial period of national presbytery in England and take all expedient action 'for suppressing the opinions and practices of Anti-Trinitarians, Anabaptists, Antinomians, Arminians, Familists, Brownists, Separatists, Independents, Libertines, and Seekers, and generally for suppressing all blasphemy'.[18] Although extremely controversial in Scotland, as it ultimately led to the division of the Kirk into two parties, the engagement represented a widely held sense of urgency that England needed to be Presbyterian. Under this Engagement with the King, Scotland entered the Second English Civil War despite covenanted commitments to parliament.

The war was short, and the king and his allies lost. Charles sought refuge with the withdrawing Scots army, but for £400,000 sterling the Scots sold the king back to parliament. Meanwhile, a dynamic shift of power took place in Scotland. In 1648 the radical party of the Kirk seized power in what has come to be known as the Whiggamore Raid, and established its rule with the aid of Oliver Cromwell's army, which entered Scotland for this purpose on 21 September. This radical party perceived the Engagement with the King to have been a compromise to their covenanted principles. Cromwell assisted the Kirk Party to consolidate their power, believing it would meddle no further in English affairs. He was wrong. The execution of the king met with outcry in Scotland, where it was widely believed that the covenants upheld the divine right of monarchy. With the death of Charles I, Scotland, believing it to be its covenanted duty, sent representatives to the Prince of Wales at Breda in the Netherlands to broker an agreement for his return. Once again, Scotland's sole stipulation for crowning Charles II was that he sign the covenants with the clear understanding that they implicitly supported Presbyterianism.

The commissioners of the General Assembly openly declared against the 'army of sectaries' in 1648 and sent the parliament of England a testimony to Scottish abhorrence of religious toleration in February 1649.[19] In light of events transpiring since 1647, the English parliament and army believed that the Scots, having invested so much wealth and blood in promoting Presbyterianism (under the guise of the covenants), would be unlikely to sit idly by and watch England lie either under a vast religious toleration or under a 'sectarian' parliament and army. For England's Independents, explains Allan Macinnes, the defeat of the Scots became imperative for the security of a free state.[20] As a result, proponents of religious toleration and liberty construed the invasion of Scotland as a defensive campaign, which may go some way towards explaining why the army received orders to invade Scotland with great exuberance. It became *esprit de corps*, and letters abounded from English officers expressing an unusual enthusiasm within their ranks and 'a spirit of prayer and piety not usual in camps'.[21]

There can be little doubt that the invading English army viewed the Presbyterian Church of Scotland as paramount an enemy as Scottish support for the crown. Several contemporary sources affirm the widely held anti-Presbyterian intentions of Cromwell's invasion. The Welsh-born Presbyterian Christopher Love (although clearly not impartial) declared the primacy of anti-Presbyterian motives for the invasion of Scotland shortly before his execution for treason in 1651. According to Love, the Scots' passion for 'a scriptural presbytery ... [and] sound doctrine' constituted in a national Presbyterian church, as well as zealous opposition to any compromise in this respect, fuelled parliamentarian fears that the Kirk would inevitably lead to further Scottish interventions in English affairs.[22] Importantly, however, Presbyterians were not alone in branding opposition to the Kirk as a primary motivation for the English invasion of Scotland. In 1654 an anonymous veteran of Dunbar wrote to the Protector in defence of Baptists, and cited their anti-Presbyterian motives as evidence of their piety and a common thread shared among all the English combatants who took part in the campaign. 'I confess they [the Baptists] have been enemies to the Presbyterian church, and so were you when at Dunbar,' writes the author, 'or at least you seemed to be so by your words and actions ... and made this an argument why we should fight stoutly, because we had the prayers of the Independent and baptised churches.'[23] This is the reason for the prominence of religion in the tracts produced in the run-up to Dunbar. Religion was fundamentally at the root of the conflict between the two nations. In fact, on the eve of the war English newsprints persisted in conveying the message 'that on the Scottish part you may call this third War *Bellum Presbyteriale*'.[24]

Polemic as Self-Definition

Through the use of terms such as covenant, providence and election, both sides set out, in internally and externally directed polemics, to paint a partisan picture of God's divine will and to defend the religious validity of their positions in a manner closely related to the disputes within the Westminster Assembly. For example, Cromwell's press spun the conflict as a battle between those who advocated religious freedom, toleration and the preservation of Protestant diversity against the Scottish Kirk and establishment seeking to impose a largely 'unwanted' religious conformity on England in the form of a national Presbyterian model of ecclesiastical government. The Church of Scotland, in contrast, painted itself as the champion of Reformed religion, defending Protestantism against the 'sectaries' and 'heretics' who had overthrown the English Church, killed the king and assailed Reformed orthodoxy in the Assembly of Divines. In this light, the struggle between Scotland and England in 1650–1 might be seen as a socio-political manifestation of the heady theological debates of the Westminster Assembly. With this in mind, this chapter seeks to demonstrate how the propaganda used to influence domestic religion in England during the 1640s, especially in the struggle between Presbyterianism and Independency during the Westminster Assembly, continued to be used in the international political conflict of the 1650s between England and Scotland.

Two aspects in particular are crucial for understanding the polemical dialogue between the Kirk and Cromwell's troops. First, both sides believed that their propaganda would actually have an effect on popular opinion and swing public support. The Kirk certainly believed that by lambasting its opponents as heretical it would secure public opposition of the Scottish populace against the English army of 'blasphemous sectaries', heartening them to defend their nation and religion.[25] They also believed lower-ranking English soldiers could be convinced of their grievous error in invading a 'rightly reformed' and independent kingdom. Likewise, the English supposed their cause would awaken dormant desires for drastic social and religious change among the Scottish populace. Given the chance, the Scottish masses would jump at the opportunity to be liberated from systems that oppressed them, both politically and religiously. Hence, the English identified their role as providential, believing they entered Scotland to 'deliver them from slavery' rather than 'bring them to misery'.[26] Motivated by this self-perception as providential liberators as opposed to conquerors, the English addressed the common people of Scotland in the language of Christian fraternity in an attempt to befriend them.

The second important aspect of the propaganda that works itself out in the texts and is fundamental to the conflict between the Scots and the English (and also to their differing interpretations of the events of 1650–1) are the different ways in which they understood the operation of God's divine will in the world. The importance of this cannot be overemphasised, as some scholars have noted that both the Kirk party in Scotland and the English parliament verged on theocracies.[27] Scotland depended heavily on its covenanted status with God, while England depended on the guidance of God's providential blessings. Basic to every event and action taken by the Kirk and government of Scotland (especially after the signing of the Solemn League and Covenant in 1643) was adherence to the covenants. Their relation to the covenants served to create a largely consistent and static framework for them to work from. As Margo Todd explains, Scotland was 'a nation bonded together by a religious conviction, ready to take up arms'.[28] The covenants created a largely united vision and way of interpreting God's will, and represented the penultimate expression of God's providence by placing Scotland in the same sort of relationship with God that Israel had experienced in the Old Testament. For this reason, men like Archibald Johnston of Wariston believed that 'the making of the National Covenant was the wedding day of Christ the bridegroom with Scotland his bride', and as a result, 'the Israel parallel came more and more to the fore' in the months following its signing in 1638.[29] Within this covenanted relationship, clear guidelines existed: obedience ensured blessing and protection for God's people, while disobedience and sin brought divine punishment in order to restore the relationship. Consequently the Kirk interpreted everything that occurred in terms of its covenanted status with God, either as affirmation or as correction. As part of its covenant, the nation pledged to maintain Presbyterianism, promote it whenever possible and uphold the monarchy. These obligations of covenant narrowed the Kirk's view of providence, because of the need to preserve both the monarchy and what it perceived to be the most perfect form of church government, the Presbytery.[30] What could not be reconciled with the covenant and the preservation of Presbyterianism was outside the Kirk's field of vision in interpreting God's providence.

In contrast, the Commonwealth's primary interest in God's unrestrictable providence meant a much more dynamic conception of God's workings in the world than could be confined to a static framework of interpretation, like that of the Kirk. The interpretation of providence influenced every aspect of life in Puritan England.[31] And while the Commonwealth believed providence to be consistent and lead in a linear direction, it need not necessarily follow the course of fallen human wisdom, nor could it be defined by a penultimate expression or definition such as a National Covenant. Therefore fervent prayer and devotion from the elect is necessary to understand God's perpetually revealing providence, since it must be continually reinterpreted. In the case of the Scottish Kirk, it was not that it held the covenants so high that it disregarded providence as something less than a continual revealing of God's will, but in the Kirk's estimation providence had to be consistent with, and interpreted in relation to, the Covenant. The English also held the covenant as being important, but viewed it as a product of God's providence for a particular point in time. As a product of providence, the covenant could not limit the scope of providential interpretation in England like it did in Scotland. Owing to these different understandings of God's workings, the two nations had different understandings of the events of 1650, and differing interpretations of their obligations and roles in the unfolding of God's divine will. Because both nations believed themselves to be in a special relationship with God, it became important to convince the general public of the divine right and blessing upon their religious preferences, political establishments and military campaigns. The pre-invasion propaganda produced by both sides expresses the dynamic and symbiotic relationship between religion and politics within mid-seventeenth-century Britain, and the political importance of religious propaganda. As much as the conflict of 1650 was a struggle between nation–states, it equally represented a conflict over political and religious ideologies. In other words, for Scotland the religion and form of government set forth in the covenants served as the yardstick by which to measure God's will, while in England there was a growing sense that a radical break with the past was at hand and that God's providence would lead beyond covenants and historical precedents to the establishment of Christ's kingdom in this world. Both sides agreed that the outcome of war would be the vindication of one of their interpretations.[32]

Polemical Models for the Kirk

In her studies of seventeenth-century England Ann Hughes has focused on the practice of using polemics as a tool for gaining popular support for denominations within a 'fluid marketplace' for religion. In particular she asserts that English Presbyterians of the 1640s and 1650s, although not anything like a majority party in England, were 'far from writing off the mass of the people as prone to profanity or to radical heresy' and well aware of the importance of popular support for their cause. Accordingly, some English Presbyterians spent 'their careers competing for public support and influence in the pulpit and in the press'.[33] By exaggerating the excesses of their sectarian opponents they sought to polarise religious positions and make their own Presbyterian position seem much more moderate and appropriate.[34] Scots Presbyterians, like Robert Baillie, warmly received their works, praising the manner in which Thomas Edwards' treatises painted dangerous factions 'in clearer colours than yet they [had] appeared'.[35] Baillie's enthusiastic support for this sort of publication is evidenced by multiple references in his letters between 1644 and 1646 to his excited anticipation for the works of Edwards and others to be published.[36]

Prompted by the impending invasion of Scotland by an army comprised largely of sectarians, fuelling fears that the sort of religious 'fluid marketplace' existing in England loomed dangerously on the horizon for Scotland, the polemics published by the Kirk in the 1650s represent the continuation and combination of two different propaganda traditions, as well as an altogether new endeavour. David Stevenson has shown how the Kirk first began to use mass printing as a tool for influencing public opinion and defending Presbyterianism during the 1638 General Assembly in Glasgow when the Covenanters produced both a *Protestation* against the king's dissolution of the assembly and the acts of that assembly. So effectively did the Kirk use propaganda against Charles I the following year in an effort to secure the support of the English people, the king had to respond with his own publications. Again in 1640 the Kirk published *The Intentions of the Army of the Kingdome of Scotland* and *The Lawfulnesse of our Expedition into England Manifested* to persuade the English public that the entry of Scottish forces into England should not be interpreted as a Scottish invasion of England, but an attack on the tyrant Charles I.[37]

However, by 1650 the threat to Scotland's national church came not from Rome, bishops or a tyrannical king, but rather from forms of Protestantism lacking the degree of discipline desired by the Presbyterian Kirk. Drawing upon the example established by Edwards a decade earlier in England, and faced with an unprecedented threat to the recently re-established Presbyterian Kirk, the Church of Scotland produced tracts directed at the general public using popular imagery intended to sway public support. Although some Scots also wrote against English sectarians in the 1640s – such as Samuel Rutherford and Robert Baillie – their works were intended for other intellectuals and not to woo popular opinion in the way that Thomas Edwards and Thomas Hall had in England. The polemics produced by the Kirk through the summer of 1650 show the Kirk, in the manner exhibited by Edwards and Hall, making a concerted effort to sustain popular (public) support by putting the excesses of their opponents into print. Just as Ann Hughes explained Edwards' intentions in *Gangraena*, the Kirk sought to polarise 'orthodox ... Presbyterians' against 'radical sectaries, soldiers and Independents'. They hoped their publications would have the same significant impact in the summer of 1650 as *Gangraena* had in England in the late 1640s.[38]

The Kirk drew upon the images of a 'Sectarian army' used by Edwards in *Gangraena*, wherein he wrote 'I do not thinke there are 50 pure Independents in the whole English Army.' In his estimation the religious composition of the English army was an amalgam of every sect and heresy present in England, with the soldiers perpetually cross-fertilising one another with new varieties of error. 'In one word,' wrote an army chaplain who provided him with information, 'the great Religion of that sort of men in the army, is liberty of conscience, and liberty of preaching.'[39] With these examples at hand, the Kirk set out to portray the dark heretical and covenant-breaking nature of the approaching army in the same clear and colourful way that Edwards had done in England. For the Church of Scotland, the approaching English were not just a temporal foe but 'sectaries' who held 'monstrous blasphemies and strange opinions in Religion', suffered from 'a spirit of Delusion and Rashness' and had shown 'themselves playne enemies' of true religion by maintaining 'that impious monster of Toleration'. Unlike Hall and Edwards, who in England represented a minority trying to gain popular support, the Kirk worked from a majority position aiming to maintain popular support rather than muster it. While Edwards' and Hall's works might have been read aloud to gatherings or congregations, they were largely dependent upon the literacy of their intended audience. The Kirk, on the other hand, benefited from the ability to have its tracts read out in every parish church across Scotland by order of the General Assembly. This represented an important advantage in Scotland, where as late as the 1630s only 50 per cent of the population could read, while in the countryside the figures dropped to between 10–20 per cent for men and less than 10 per cent for women.[40] Accordingly, the Kirk worked from a privileged position for two reasons. First, it read its own tracts to the populace of Scotland in the parish, while English tracts were left to be pondered only by those who could read or had them read aloud. Second, they were attempting to maintain popular support rather than create it.

Polemical Warfare

As the inevitability of conflict became apparent by late June 1650, the first publications were produced. On 25 June 1650 the commissioners of the General Assembly of the Church of Scotland published *A Seasonable and Necessary Warning Concerning Present Dangers and Duties*. The work followed just days after the commissioners proclaimed a Day of Humiliation and Fasting to be observed by every congregation on the last day of June.[41] This corporate action was intended to cleanse the nation and ensure that Scotland was just and pure in the sight of God in light of the three great dangers facing the nation: first, the 'sudden and unexpected approachings of the Sectarian forces in our Neighbour Kingdom of England'; second, the oppression of the godly in England and Ireland 'now groaning under the tiranny' of England's parliament, which 'if providence doe not otherwise dispose, ere we our selves may be brought to the like or worse extremity'; and third, Scotland's own Malignant party.

The commissioners of the General Assembly produced *A Seasonable and Necessary Warning* in order to explicate the present danger facing the country, and ordered it to be read in every parish church.[42] In addition to the 'snares' of the Scottish Malignants who reared their ugly heads under Montrose earlier in the year, a new threat lurked south of the border in the form of an army of 'Sectaries', which threatened not only the sovereignty of Scotland, but also its properly reformed religion. Largely ignoring the political reasons for the invasion, the Kirk argued the fundamental cause to be the devious intentions of the English army to bring the same social disorder to Scotland that their distorted religious views had produced in England.

> All that concerns Religion, lye in the dust altogether forgotten and despised by those men, and instead of the beauty and order that should be in the house of God, a vast toleration of many grosse errors is allowed, whereby so many and so monstrous blasphemies and strange opinions in Religion have been broached and are vented in England, as the like hath not been heard of almost in any generation.[43]

Although written against both internal and external threats, the primary thrust of the work framed the English army as a dark and blasphemous entity. The Kirk reiterated this overwhelming concern for the subversive threat of sectarian religion by republishing several earlier declarations, one of which forbade allowing 'idler(s) who hath no particular calling, or vagrant person(s) under pretence of a calling' to perform 'Worship in Families … Seeing persons tainted with errours or aiming at divisions, may … creep into houses and lead captive silly and unstable souls'.[44] According to the commissioners, the survival of the church and kingdom of Scotland depended upon the unity of the nation through adherence to the Kirk and the covenants. *A Seasonable and Necessary Warning* represented the first in a series of publications produced by the Kirk and the approaching English which gradually developed into a polemical dialogue leading up to the battle of Dunbar.

On 26 June 1650, the day after the Kirk published *A Seasonable and Necessary Warning*, England's parliament produced its declaration of war. Although the *Declaration of the Parliament of England, upon the Marching of the Armie into Scotland* listed several political motives for invading Scotland, such as lack of reparations for the damages caused by Scotland's invasion of England in 1648, their rejection of a treaty with the English and the proclamation of Charles II as king of England and Ireland, parliament immediately followed them with the pertinent religious issues, citing slanderous allegations by the Scots, who in the wake of hostilities within the Westminster Assembly 'declar'd against Us as Sectaries', as one of the fundamental grounds for their invasion of Scotland. The Kirk's slanders, they argued, fostered division among Christians by subordinating the importance of Christian unity to their own strict and narrow interpretation of the covenant. In contrast to this policy of division, the English framed their venture into Scotland as an attempt at unifying the godly 'to meet together in the power of true Religion and Holiness'.[45] Accordingly, parliament claimed promotion of right religion and the gathering of the godly as political motives for its invasion of Scotland. Thus from the outset religion played a paramount role in both England and Scotland's public declarations.

Two religious themes in particular ran throughout the propaganda. First, the nature of the Solemn League and Covenant, what it required for civil government and who had been the initial breaker of this shared covenant, thus freeing the other side to legitimately act out in force. Second, the issue of church polity, which also remained closely linked to the issue of covenant, in that the promotion of a uniform standard of worship and doctrine throughout Britain remained one of the primary issues of interpreting the document. The Scots had assumed Presbyterianism would be the model of uniformity. As a result, they viewed the toleration of great variations in both doctrine and worship amongst the English Independents as a violation of the covenant. This prompted allegations from the Kirk that the English tolerated a milieu of heresy, with the English counter-charging the Scots presbytery of being tyrannical. Although the *political* entity of the English parliament had published its declaration of why its army marched on Scotland and the Scottish Committee of Estates produced a response, the dialogue that followed flowed from the commissioners of the Kirk and the English army marching north.

It is worth noting why the commissioners of the Kirk and the invading English forces produced the bulk of the propaganda, rather than the official political institutions of the Committee of Estates and the English parliament. For a nation that overwhelmingly believed itself to be in a covenanted relationship with God, it appeared natural for the religious branch, the Kirk, to defend the nation's covenanted position. A further motivation for the Kirk's involvement undoubtedly rested upon the fear of losing the religious monopoly for which it had struggled so hard in the 1630s and '40s if parliament's army should triumph. Hence the Kirk viewed ideological opposition to the English army as imperative. For the English army, the production of propaganda arose out of necessity. According to M.J. Seymour, the parliamentarian regime had no official propaganda facility or office. The closest thing to officially published propaganda came through the mutually beneficial relationship between the Interregnum regimes and the independent publishers producing 'newsbooks' for economic gain.[46] With no programme in place, propaganda by the parliamentarian regime had to be produced in an ad hoc way. However, Cromwell's forces were not unprepared for the publication of polemics. When they marched for Scotland in 1650, Cromwell had his own printer and printing press in tow, 'expecting either to convince by its reasoning, or to delude by its falsehood'.[47] With a printing press and skilled men such as Oliver Cromwell, John Owen and the professional propagandist John Hall, the army had the potentially devastating weapon of propaganda at its disposal.[48]

The English army published three tracts during its initial invasion of Scotland, all of which were fundamentally religious in nature and directed at the general populace of Scotland. The papers argued for a distinction between being members of the Kirk and being God's elect, contending that election made them brethren in Christ with the English and that this took priority over membership in the Kirk, or even citizenship in a temporal kingdom.[49] The commissioners responded with tracts directed at the lower ranks of the English army, under the pretext of being appeals from the Scottish people, urging the soldiers to understand that they risked their salvation by breaking England's covenant with Scotland. Despite the three primary political reasons for the English invasion being clearly spelled out in parliament's declaration of war, religious themes dominated the literature.[50]

The publications of the Kirk and the army in July and August created an exchange of propaganda directed not only at their political opponents but to the whole population of both nations, which Cromwell called 'these great transactions'.[51] The English army produced its first tract, entitled *A Declaration of the Army of England upon their March into Scotland*, while camped at Newcastle-upon-Tyne.[52] Cromwell had at least 800 copies of the declaration printed. Five hundred copies were sent into Scotland with his trumpeter (Bret), a duty that carried the title 'hope forlorn', while the other 300 went to Carlisle.[53] According to one of the soldiers in Newcastle, two days were spent composing a draft document, of which

1,000 copies were printed. Four days later every copy was burned and production started all over again, suggesting the great care taken in the tract's composition. This also indicates the importance Cromwell ascribed to propaganda.[54] Unlike later tracts produced by the army on the portable press carried in their train, the tract produced in Newcastle came off the press of the ardent Royalist Stephen Bulkley, who had been persuaded to cooperate.[55] During this time of preparation in Newcastle, the soldiers held a fast and heard sermons preached by five of the ministers who accompanied them.[56]

While *A Declaration of the Army of England upon their March into Scotland* is signed in Cromwell's name by his secretary John Rushworth, its authorship, as well as that of the other religiously worded tracts produced by the army on its march north, probably rests with the army's chaplains as much as with any of the officers. Cromwell acknowledged as much in a letter to the General Assembly in August, when he attributed the authorship of a later tract to the soldiers 'and some godly ministers with us'.[57] Among the ministers accompanying Cromwell into Scotland was the great John Owen. While Peter Toon rightly suggests Owen's ideas significantly shaped the work, Owen's influence may have been far greater than simply providing the ideology that lay behind it.[58] In the opinion of the early nineteenth-century biographer William Orme, a number of the works bearing the signature of Cromwell likely originated from the pen of John Owen.[59] Yet in the case of this declaration, there has been some discrepancy of view between historians as to when Owen joined with the northward-marching army. According to Orme, Owen did not rendezvous with the army until Berwick, yet both Anne Laurence and Peter Toon believe Owen made the entire march north from London and preached while the army stayed in Newcastle.[60] If Owen was in Newcastle when the declaration was written, which appears to be the case, then the man that Toon has called the 'Architect of Independency' would have been present to aid in the important and careful composition of the army's declaration.

As the editions later printed in London and Edinburgh suggest, the army directed its declaration to the general populace of Scotland and not to the General Assembly or any other institution of the Scottish Kirk or state.[61] Written to 'satisfie them (the Scottish Brethren) of the grounds of our present Ingagement' it represents an endeavour reminiscent of the Covenanter work produced to justify the Scottish invasion of England in 1640, mentioned above.[62] For this reason the authors addressed it to 'whom we look upon as our brethren', and expressed their 'desire to make a distinction and separation of you from the rest'. Although expressing satisfaction with parliament's reasons for invading Scotland as 'agreeable to the principles of religion, nature and nations' and therefore sufficient, the soldiers in the English army desired to write to their 'brethren' in Scotland to explain 'the great and wonderful transactions wrought' amongst them 'by the mere finger of ... God'.[63] This introduction made two theological claims about the English campaign. First, the tract's repeated references to the brethren, elect and saints in Scotland and its humble references to the fraternal links they had with the pious English army made Cromwell's intentions in producing the work clear. He was bypassing the central religious hub of Scotland and making his case directly to the godly people in Scotland who were God's 'Elect'. This is why he had 800 copies printed for distribution within Scotland. He sought to establish that unity between God's elect transcends political or even ecclesiastical allegiances. Second, 'the great and wonderful transactions wrought by the mere finger of ... God' were invoked as evidence of God's providential blessings upon the English army. Not only were the English the Christian brethren of the elect in Scotland, they were also God's chosen instrument of imposing the divine will of God.

The paper's claims of affinity between the army and the elect in Scotland and their role as God's instruments were made even clearer in the tract by its differentiation between the elect and the rest of Scotland. Far from wanting to bring any harm to God's elect, the letter warned it would be sinful and foolish for any godly individual in Scotland to stand in opposition to the divinely chosen mechanism for imposing the will of God. 'Nothing is so predominant in us,' they stated, 'as the love we have towards those that fear God there, who may possibly suffer through their own mistakes, or our disability to distinguish in a common calamity.'[64] The message was clear: opposition to the English army is opposition to God's divine will; take up arms with the reprobates in Scotland against the English army at your own peril. In militarily resisting the English army, the godly in Scotland would force them to shed the blood of fellow members of the elect body of Christ. However, the burden of responsibility rested with the elect in Scotland. Not only would resistance to God's providence be suicidal, it would also be sinful. In this way, Cromwell attempted to create bonds of fraternal compassion with his audience in Scotland.

As part of this appeal to the people of Scotland, *A Declaration of the Army* gave three primary justifications for the invasion of Scotland. The first was political. The guilt of breaking the covenant lay with the Scots for imposing Charles II upon England and Ireland, and upon the Scots' earlier invasion of England.[65] The second was religious. The tract argued that accusations made by the Scots (such as those in *A Seasonable and Necessary Warning*) that the English were complacent towards heresy were slanderous and uninformed.[66] In contrast, Cromwell labelled the Kirk's domination of religion overzealous, its singular devotion to the presbytery unchristian, and its intended imposition of Presbyterianism on England against the spirit of the Covenant.

As for the Presbyterian, or any other form of church-government, they are not by the Covenant to be imposed by force ... Doth that name, or thing, give the difference between those that are the members of Christ and those that are not? We think not so. We say, faith working by love is the true character of a Christian; and, God is our witness, in whomsoever we see any thing of Christ to be, their we reckon our duty to love.[67]

According to Cromwell, the English government did not oppose Presbyterianism, since 'we are desirous that those who are for the Presbyterian government, should have all freedom to enjoy it', but it was not to be imposed on anyone.[68] The third reason was moral. According to the tract, Charles II was an unscrupulous man set against all right religion, a man who would associate with the darkest sorts of people in order to regain his throne. The king's associations with Malignants and Papists in Ireland clearly proved this. While the underhand and oppressive intentions of the Kirk and the king threatened their religious freedom, the English yearned to provide tolerant religion and freedom of conscience for all the elect. These succinct aims intended to justify to the people of Scotland the political (although religiously charged) and pious reasons underpinning the invasion. Yet the 'saints' of Scotland were not the only target of this work of propaganda. Establishing the providential nature of their war and the fundamental causes behind it was also intended to reassure Cromwell's own troops of the justness of their cause, that it had been prompted by the sordid actions of the politicians of Scotland and tyranny of the Kirk, and above all that it was the will of God to free the elect in Scotland from the forces that threatened to suffocate their religious freedom.[69] Additionally, affirming the just nature of the invasion to English civilians of either moderate or Presbyterian leanings became imperative, for which reason printers republished the papers in London.

The commissioners of the General Assembly did not miss any of the implications of the English propaganda. Uninterested in the position of the national church, the English army sought solidarity with the common pious people of Scotland. Moreover, addressing the tract to the 'Saints' or 'Elect' rather than the Kirk implied that the Kirk was not synonymous with the people of God in Scotland, and that God's elect were a minority not limited to or even indicated by the Kirk. The commissioners quickly picked up on the subversive nature of the tract. Recognising the urgent need to reply they produced *A Short Reply unto a Declaration*. While the English appealed to the people of Scotland to view toleration towards the English army as a sign of election, the Kirk made the counter-claim. According to the *Reply*, 'all the Saints that are in Scotland' would naturally abhor everything taught by the sectarians, their ways being so 'grievous' the elect would 'cry ... to Heaven against their present oppression', preferring to 'indure any affliction, then to involve themselves in the guilt' of the unjust English invasion.[70] Thus both sides alleged solidarity with their position to be indicative of election and appealed to pious people that their own position represented the proper Christian allegiance. The Kirk's *Reply*, which was distributed throughout the presbyteries of Scotland, closed by speaking not to the English but to Scots, warning them to recognise the English as 'high-handed' covenant breakers, subverters of ancient forms of government, and more concerned with liberty than with religion as they 'let people do what ever they want in Religion if they help them'.[71]

The commissioners contrasted the criticisms of the Kirk's Presbyterian form with the lack of a functioning church government in England. They denied that the Kirk equated Presbyterianism with the totality of Christ's church or that being Presbyterian was tantamount to being elect. Instead they turned back to the familiar accusations that the English were far too tolerant towards heresy and suggested their supposed toleration prevented the existence of a proper presbytery in England or any other form of church government that maintained purity and opposed error. They labeled claims by Cromwell 'that those who are for Presbyterial Government, should have all freedom to enjoy it' as ridiculous in light of the parliament's refusal to instigate ecclesiastical courts or the imposition of censures.[72] By neglecting to prescribe a church government with the ability to confront and remove heresy, the commissioners asserted that the English parliament and army threatened to make impotent all churches over which they had influence. By linking the English to heresy and representing them as opponents to proper church discipline, the commissioners hoped to drive a wedge between the invading enemy and anyone in Scotland who might harbour sympathy for their religious pleadings.

As Cromwell's forces approached the Tweed they composed a second paper, entitled *A Declaration of the Army of the Commonwealth of England to the People of Scotland*, while camped near Berwick-upon-Tweed.[73] The declaration, wrote Ogilvie, was 'wholly intended to be a lure to win over the common people to the side of Cromwell', an endeavour 'not without some success'.[74] Yet its necessity was owed to the Kirk's own successful propaganda campaign. According to Whitelocke, when the English crossed the border they found that the people had been told horrific stories by Scots ministers, 'that the English Army intends to put all the men to the sword, and to thrust hot irons through the women's breasts'.[75] Other reports claimed that 'the English would cut the throats of all men, cut off the right hands of boys between six and sixteen, burn women's breasts, and destroy everything'.[76] These stories put great fear into the occupants of the Borders until, according to Whitelocke, they were abated by Cromwell's own publications.[77]

The army's second declaration decries the 'groundles and unjust Reproaches, and most false Slanders [spread by the Kirk], to make the Army odious, and to render us unto the people [of Scotland], as such that are to be abhorred of all pious, peaceable, and sober Spirits, and to be rather Monsters then Men'.[78] It posits that the unjustness of the Kirk's accusations should be evident to the people of Scotland who were able to remember the well-behaved and pious conduct of the English soldiers in the country in 1648. Moreover, the English army did not enter Scotland for personal profit, but only to secure a 'firm peace between two nations', to prevent 'the destruction of the godly and well-affected' and to preserve the 'power of Godliness and holiness in both nations'.[79] In light of the army's clear purpose, it urges the people of the Borders to ignore the craft and subtelty of the Kirk's declarations and to remain in their homes, since 'the Gentry and Commonalty of ... Scotland ... are not the Persons, who ... laid the certain foundations of a second unrighteous and unjust Invasion of England'.[80]

Despite English assurances of civility, the Borders were largely empty when the parliamentary army crossed the Tweed.[81] Upon orders of the Committee of Estates, every male aged between sixteen and sixty was commanded to collect all available provisions and gather in Edinburgh to make preparations for a unified defense of the nation.[82] Accordingly, the English army reported having seen no more than ten Scotsmen between Berwick and Edinburgh, leading them to believe that those few able men left behind were spies.[83] Of 'the wives [that] stay behind,' wrote White-locke, '... some of them do bake and brew, to provide bread and drink for the English Army.'[84] This mild cooperation can be accounted for by the desolation of the border country after all food and supplies had been taken away by the retreating male population. Compliance in baking and brewing allowed these women (and their families) to avoid starvation. The barrenness and depopulation of the Borders gave witness to the successful propaganda campaign by the Kirk.

An official response to Cromwell's second appeal to the people of Scotland came from the Committee of Estates. Although produced by a political body (the civil governing body of Scotland), it persisted in the language of religion.

> We do therefore desire the Officers and Souldiers of the Army under Lieuetenant Generall Cromwell, to lay to heart the great guiltinesse and misery that followes upon an unjust Invasive War, especially, of Gods Covenanted people ... The cry of the Church and Kingdom of Scotland, the Virgin forced in the fields crying against her ravisher, is loud and shrill in the ears of God.[85]

For Scotland, purely political language could not adequately address the situation at hand. For both the Committee of Estates (who were almost totally under the influence of the 'Kirk Party'[86]) and the commissioners of the Kirk, the only language sufficient to define the situation was that of the covenants, because the problems facing Scotland were believed to stem from England's betrayal of the Solemn League and Covenant.

The commissioners of the Kirk did not remain silent either. Besides defending the Kirk's position to the people of Scotland, they also directed propaganda at the English soldiers. *For the Under-Officers and Souldiers of the English Army, from the People of Scotland* represents an attempt to subvert the English attack from within the army and is framed as an appeal out of concern for the salvation of the English troops led astray by the more sinister officers. The various political reasons enumerated in the English parliament's declaration of war are again systematically refuted, but the penultimate shot stressed each soldier's personal accountability for participating in an invasion of Scotland: 'Those among you shall be wise, who shall take Warning to proceed no farther in an evil way, lest God, who is the Judge of all things, look upon such Injustice, and Ingratitude, and Breach of Covenant, and require it.'[87] Some solid evidence exists to support the legitimacy of this polemical angle. Before the army began its march north, several incidents demonstrate parliamentary soldiers having reservations about participating in an invasion of Scotland. Lord Fairfax represents the most notable example. He stepped down as commander-in-chief of the English forces when parliament made the decision to invade Scotland. His conscience prevented him from initiating a war against a nation engaged in the Solemn League and Covenant with England. In order to avoid controversy or further qualms of conscience within the army, the official reason for Fairfax's resignation was attributed to health rather than conscience.[88]

Yet withdrawals from the army for reasons of conscience were not limited to the time before the army started marching north. Although the troops declared they would live and die with Cromwell while camped at Newcastle, some soldiers continued to struggle with conscience.[89] Shortly before the army crossed the Tweed several lower-ranking officers were removed and others resigned, including Colonel Bright, whose resignation brought about the creation of the Coldstream Guards.[90] Bright had requested two weeks' leave, which would have allowed his absence when the army entered Scotland. The refusal of this request prompted his resignation. According to Grainger, 'qualms of conscience' regarding the justness of invading England's jointly covenanted neighbour probably lay at the root of Bright's actions.[91] It was to individuals who shared such reservations that the Kirk directed *For the Under-Officers and Souldiers*: individuals whose consciences teetered on the brink. By the time of the tract's publication (30 July), however, the English had already crossed the Tweed, and so the document probably came too late to have any wide-ranging affect. Morally and psychologically, the Scottish Borders had been the final obstacle to the conscience of the English soldier. Once across the border, invasion had irrevocably been acted out. Those remaining in the English ranks after the final conscience-driven withdrawals at Berwick were predominantly the more extreme Independents, Baptists and antiroyalists, or more moderate individuals who had wrestled with the issues involved and cast in their lot with Cromwell's forces.

After they crossed the Tweed, the English forces seemed largely unhindered by the Kirk's publications, and their officers apparently made no attempts to prevent soldiers from reading Scottish propaganda. Cromwell wrote to the commissioners of the General Assembly shortly after receiving *For the Under-Officers and Souldiers of the English Army*, exclaiming 'send as many of your papers as you please amongst ours, they have free passage, I feare them not; what is of God in them would it might be embraced and received'.[92] Yet, Cromwell did not feel that the Scots treated the products of English presses so freely. In the same letter promising free distribution of Scottish tracts among his troops, he accused the Kirk of censoring English declarations and preventing them from reaching the Scottish people, a charge which the Kirk vehemently denied. Cromwell accused the Kirk of poisoning the minds of the Scottish people: 'And by your hard and subtle words,' he wrote to the General Assembly, 'you have begotten prejudice in those who do too much (in matters of conscience, wherin every soul is to answer for itself to God) depend upon you.'[93] Cromwell desired free distribution of the propaganda by both sides, the Kirk did not. For the Kirk, a successful defense to the ideological attacks of the English depended on three endeavours: first, prevention of sectarian ideologies spreading amongst the Scottish people (by censorship if necessary); second, vilification of Independency as 'sectarian' and 'blasphemous'; and third, undermining the English attack by playing upon fears of covenant breaking or displacing a 'rightly' Reformed church. All three of these they did with a good deal of success. The English, however, strategically used polemics as well.

By early August the English army was well aware of the factions forming within the Scottish forces, and it used this chink in the Scottish armour as a basis for its own propaganda. Within Scotland, accusations of Malignancy swarmed around those showing loyalty to the king. On 13 August, the Kirk composed a declaration known as the 'West Kirk' declaration, intended to embrace the new king while at the same time distancing the nation from the guilt of his personal sins.[94] This, the Kirk hoped, would free those fighting for the kingdom of Scotland from any stigma of Malignancy and in turn undercut the English claim that their invasion was a stand against Malignancy rather than the covenant. Published on 14 August 1650, the commissioners of the General Assembly sent the 'West Kirk' declaration to Cromwell along with a letter from General Leslie (the commander of the Scottish forces) requesting that the paper be given the free distribution promised.[95]

Complying with the Scots' request, Cromwell 'caused [the West Kirk declaration] to be read in the presence of so many officers as could well be gotten together on a sudden' and immediately penned responses to both the declaration and Leslie's letter.[96] The Kirk believed the West Kirk decla-ration put to rest the matter of Malignancy versus covenanted protec-tion of the monarchy, taking away some of the impetus of the English campaign by separating the sovereignty of the Scottish crown from the person of Charles II. They identified the Scottish cause as the promo-tion of God's chosen form of government for Scotland as defined in the covenant rather than political support for the person of Charles Stuart. Although Archibald Johnston of Wariston decreed the declaration 'vexed many of [the English] and hindred ... [their] intended merch', the official English response showed no sign of abeyance.[97] Rather than justifying the Scottish cause, Cromwell argued that the West Kirk declaration affirmed the English accusations of Malignancy. By placing a king on the throne who had ties with Catholics both in Ireland and on the continent 'under pretence of the Covenant', Cromwell maintained Scotland could not possibly be acting according to the covenant. Hence they were political Malignants rather than religious Covenanters.[98]

Cromwell's accusations deeply affected the Scottish Kirk and govern-ment. Although Wariston slighted Cromwell's reply as 'a rapsodik aunsuer to our paper, shewing that he could not separat our conjunction with the King from Malignancy', he went on to report that several ministers 'pressed on our consciences the guilt of not purging and setling the King's family'.[99] Shortly thereafter, three important events provoked by Cromwell's criti-cism occurred. First, some officers within the Scottish army composed a remonstrance affirming the West Kirk declaration and effectively giving their assent for the implementation of drastic measures, including purging the army.[100] Second, on 16 August the king finally signed a declaration proclaiming his personal guilt, rejecting the errors of his parents and declaring himself to 'have no enemies but the enemies of the Covenant, and ... no friends but the friends of the Covenant'.[101] For several months the king persistently refused to sign such a declaration, which included an explicit denial of both his mother and father, but Cromwell's accusa-tions of Malignancy and the presence of his army on Scottish soil forced the king's hand. In signing the declaration, Charles II set aside everything but the covenant, including his claim to the throne outwith the covenant's sworn upholding of the Scottish monarchy, and gave tacit approval for the removal of all Malignant individuals from both his personal court and the army. As a result, all Scotland's interests, including the king's, were publicly and ostensibly consigned to the covenant, and it was for the covenant alone that the army would take up arms. On the same day that Charles signed the declaration, the Scots also set about heavy purging within the army.[102] This represented the third important event prompted by Cromwell's letter and the culmination of the West Kirk declaration, the army's remonstrance and Charles II's declaration. Cromwell's accusations alone were not responsible for initiating the purges, as some significant purging took place earlier in the month. However, his charge that separation of the covenant cause from Malignancy was indiscernible as long as Malignants persisted among their ranks hastened the process and goaded the Scots to purge their forces to the most extreme ends.

Preparations for purging began at the beginning of August. Scottish Covenanters had developed a belief that a small, pure army comprised of godly soliders could defeat a much larger foe, like Gideon's army in Judges 6–8. Gideon's army, although outnumbered, were nonetheless blessed by God for their purity attained through purging, and empowered to defeat their heathen adversaries. A precedent for this belief had been established in 1649, when Gilbert Ker's small Covenanter force of 360 soldiers defeated a royalist force of 1,100 at the battle of Balvenie.[103] On 1 August the commissioners of the General Assembly ordered the ministers assigned to the various regiments of the Scottish army to begin compiling lists of 'officers or volunteers' who had been engagers in the unlawful invasion of England, as well as those persons the ministers deemed scandalous in order that they might be removed.[104] Between 2 and 5 August, purges took place throughout the army, but the commissioners complained on 6 August that obstruction of the purging further fomented God's anger against Scotland.[105] However, once the commanders in the army and the king had given their consent in the forms of the army's remonstrance and the king's declaration, the purges could be taken to the extreme. On 16 August, just two days after Cromwell's letter, the most stringent purging occurred.[106] By the end of the month, thousands of officers and soldiers had been removed from the Scots army, significantly weakening their forces. Some estimates suggest a reduction of the army by as much as one third. One report put the number of soldiers removed at 5,000, while another recorded the expulsion of over eighty officers.[107] Thus the events of 13–16 August provide a significant example of successful English propaganda, in that Cromwell's response to the West Kirk declaration altered (or at least hastened and intensified) the policy and actions of Scotland.

The pre-Dunbar propaganda battle came to a head with a declaration produced by the English army while camped at Musselburgh on 1 August 1650, in direct response to the Kirk's *For the Under-Officers and Souldiers of the English Army*.[108] *A Declaration of the English Army Now in Scotland* set out the purely religious and pious desires lying at the heart of their invasion of Scotland:

> We value the Churches of Jesus Christ, who are the lot of Gods inheritance Ten thousand times above our own lives; yea, we do bless the Lord we are not onely a Rod of Iron to dash the common enemies in pieces, but also a hedge (though very unworthy) about Christs Vineyard; and if we know our own hearts, where ever the lot of Gods inheritance shall appear to be found in Scotland, we shall think it our duty, to the utmost hazzard of our lives

to preserve the same ... We desire it may be known to you our Brethren in Scotland, That we are not Soldiers of Fortune, we are not meerly the servants of men, we have not onely proclaimed Jesus Christ, the King of Saints, to be our King by profession, but desire to submit to him upon his own terms ... and it is our prayer daily, That those that fear the Lord in England and Scotland may become one in the hand of the Lord, and joyn together in the advancement of the Kingdom of Jesus Christ, and throwing down, and tramping upon the Seat of the Beast. And thus we have in the naked plainness of our souls opened our hearts unto you our dear Brethren that fear the Lord in Scotland, where-ever you be found, whether in the highest Councils or the poorest Cottages, who though you now lie scattered, the Lord will in his due time bring you together, and binde you up as his Jewels, and make you one with those that fear the Lord amongst us.[109]

From the outset of the English army's march north, the government and clergy of Scotland recognised the potential danger posed by several thousand English soldiers maintaining varying degrees of sectarian doctrine entering Scotland. In the previous decade Robert Baillie had expressed concerns that young Scottish soldiers fighting in England ran the risk of being infected by English doctrines simply by serving alongside parliamentary soldiers, but those concerns paled significantly in comparison to the new situation.[110] The declaration of the English on 1 August exacerbated the worst fears of individuals like Baillie. Not only were these 'blasphemers' and 'heretics' already present in Scotland, but they openly boasted of their intentions to promote their own theological positions to the residents of Scotland, to gather them together and to oppose the Kirk both physically and ideologically.

According to the declaration, the Scots had brought war upon themselves, because the covenant had become an idol for Scotland and because Scotland had, in the person of Charles II, chosen a supporter of the Throne of the Beast. Now, Scotland faced the potential loss of its political freedom through military conquest as well as subversion of its recently reacquired presbytery through the active intervention of the English Independents and nonconformists, and all because those in power in Scotland had tried to impose these things on both its English neighbours and on the innocent people of Scotland. 'When Scotland chose new gods, and would have a King out of a Family that God had rejected, then was war in the Gates.'[111] The language of this tract gives a good indication of the radical nature of the English army. As Tai Liu points out, it smacks of millenarianism and provides as justification for its actions the 'destruction of antichrist, the advancement of the Kingdom of Jesus Christ, the Deliverance and Reformation of his church'.[112] Once again, this third declaration represented the English as a force intent on liberating Scotland. However, unlike earlier declarations, by the beginning of August the parliamentary army proclaimed liberation from religious oppression as the primary motivation for the invasion, rather than being merely a by-product. The army declared its intentions to gather and protect all God's people in Scotland. Yet who did the godly require protection from? In this third tract the army clearly set its invasion of Scotland within the context of the Commonwealth's larger self-appointed task of liberating Europe from the grip of the antichrist and defeating him once and for all. In fact, the religious radicals in the English army perceived the antichrist not just in the office of Charles II, but also in the ecclesiastical structures of Presbyterianism.[113]

In the past the parliamentary army had used the language of slaying the beast of the antichrist when referring to Papacy or Episcopacy, but now there was no Episcopal threat in Scotland. The English army had taken the language formerly used to attack Prelacy and levelled it against the Presbyterian Kirk: this was the institution that welcomed the new king, 'one of the ten horns of the beast'.[114] The tracts launched a smear campaign against the Kirk and a plea to the Scottish people to 'joyn together in the advancement of the Kingdom of Jesus Christ, and throwing down ... the Seat of the Beast'.[115] To justify its publication, the army declared it to be a sincere response to a Scottish request for the grounds of the invasion; however, no such Scottish paper survives.[116] Although both religion and politics had been the original language of the propaganda produced by the Scots and the English, as the penultimate showdown at Dunbar approached, religion moved even more to the fore.

Covenant versus Providence

The nature of Scotland's devotion to the covenants served as a prominent theme throughout the papers produced before Dunbar. In a letter to the General Assembly on 3 August 1650, Cromwell famously requested the Kirk to re-evaluate its position, urging the commissioners of the Kirk to reflect upon Isaiah 28:5–15 – 'The priest and the prophet reel with strong drink ... they err in vision, they stumble in giving judgement' (28:7) – and with regard to covenant, 'because you have said, "We have made a covenant with death, and with Sheol we have an agreement; when the overwhelming scourge passes through it will not come to us; for we have made lies our refuge, and in falsehood we have taken shelter"' (28:15).[117] In directly quoting the prophet Isaiah, Cromwell places the purpose of the English army in prophetic terms. He identifies Scotland as a nation in covenant not with God but with death and hell, and labels the Kirk as the unclean, drunken priests who 'error in vision ... stumble in judgement' and wallow, intoxicating themselves, at tables 'full of vomit and filthiness'. Thus the English campaign represents the 'overwhelming scourge' that Isaiah prophesies will pass through the land to free the nation from its captivity to a blind clergy and misguided covenant. In such terms, Cromwell declared the inevitability of English victory as prophetically pre-ordained, and the army's role to be that of the providentially blessed liberators of God's people.

In their reply, composed by James Guthrie, the commissioners of the General Assembly played what has been called their trump card in defending their adherence to the Solemn League and Covenant.[118] Guthrie reminded his English audience that the Kirk was not alone in signing it.[119] This charge served as the impetus for the republication of John Vicars' broadsheet *A Caveat for Covenant-Contemners and Covenant-Breakers*.[120] The paper had originally been published in London in 1648, in opposition to those who had signed the Solemn League and Covenant, and catalysed the Scots' march south against the king. The Kirk had *A Caveat* re-published in 1650, with a list of 222 members of the House of Commons who had signed the Solemn League, including Scotland's most prominent enemy, Oliver Cromwell. The broadsheet also provided lists of Scripture supporting the making and upholding of covenants, scriptural warnings against covenant breaking and examples of divine condemnation against those who break their covenants.

This leads to the question: if Cromwell and other Englishmen had signed the covenant, then who were they to demonise it? Did they not also have a responsibility to uphold a covenant that they had sworn to? It became evident through their publications and their interpretation of events that the English were far less interested in the covenant than they were in providence. While the Scots equated adherence to the covenant with receiving God's blessing, the English viewed their continuing military successes as clear evidence that they were following God's providential plans. Even before the battle of Dunbar, many in the English force were confident of their providential favour. According to one soldier's account, even in the barren and stripped Scottish Borders he found unequalled peace and contentment:

> Although I have been without many things of delight and superfluity which your southerne parts and most parts of England afford: yet I cannot say that I ever was in want of anything that was necessary to preserve life, for a good conscience is a continuall feast, and I have found as much content in a peice of rye bread, or a hard bisket, and a cup of water, as ever I did in the most dainty cakes or delitious wines. I have laid down to rest with as much content upon a board, or on the ground with a bundle of straw, as ever I did into the best fetherbed in England. God hath indeed prepared a table in the wilderness, such a table as is full of rich and good things, ful of marrow, wine on the lees refined. The comforts of his spirit, and a sweet communion with him, which surpasses all other injoyments whatsoever, and farre better than all kindes of services of sacrifices which can be performed by us, while we are here in this earthly tabernacle.[121]

Such a claim of providential contentment is quite astonishing in light of other contemporary reports of the short supply and often poor state of supplies.[122]

For the English, their victory over the Scots at Dunbar when they were outnumbered by at least 4,000 soldiers and held the weaker ground reaffirmed their belief that God's providential blessings were upon them.[123] On the day before the battle, Cromwell lamented the depletion of his army through illness and remarked that merely escaping Scotland would entail a 'miracle'.[124] Victory, however, was absolute. While 3,000 Scots were killed and another 10,000 taken prisoner, only twenty English soldiers died on the day.[125] The English soldiers interpreted this as an indisputable evidence of providential deliverance. The importance of this belief in providentialism cannot be overestimated, as it came to bear on every aspect of seventeenth-century life, not only for individual Puritan minds but also English political 'tactics and action'.[126] God's hand was seen in every occurrence, from menial things like changes in the weather to more miraculous events, such as the victory at Dunbar, 'where triumph was snatched from defeat'.[127] According to Worden, the Commonwealth viewed Dunbar 'as an especially significant declaration of God's favour' upon the English enterprise.[128] For this reason, Cromwell wrote to parliament requesting that instead of feeling pride for the momentous victory it should thank God for His providence through acts of charity.[129]

Whether providential or not, Cromwell certainly viewed his successes as having divine origin.[130] Despite the fact that his superior military tactics and disciplined forces were sufficient in themselves to deliver victory, Gardiner maintains Cromwell utterly attributed the victory at Dunbar 'to the direct intervention of Providence against a hypocritical nation'.[131] The account of the battle he prepared for parliament drips with the language of providential deliverance, declaring that the army overcame 'meerly with the courage the Lord was pleased to give'. Despite being outnumbered, the enemy was 'made by the Lord of Hosts as stubble to [our] swords'.[132] Later in September, when reporting the movements of his army to parliament, he wrote 'Whereas it hath pleased God by his gracious Providence and Goodnesse, to put the City of Edenburgh, and the Town of Leith under my power'.[133] For Cromwell, as long as his army continued to win, he felt sure that the hand of God directed him. As one critic wrote, Cromwell wrongly equated his army's military supremacy with 'a providential power'.[134]

Covenant or no covenant, the 'providential' victories of the English over their opponents were leading them towards their goals and taken as evidence of divine direction. Throughout the accounts of their victories over the Scots at Dunbar, Inverkeithing and Worcester, the English contrasted the Scots' battle cry of 'the Covenant', 'for the faith of the Covenant' or 'Scotland' with their own 'Lord of Hosts' or 'Providence'.[135] The implication drawn from their differing battle cries and the multiple defeats of the Scots was that the English were affirmed in their constant availability to the leading of God's providence, while the Scots' deifying of the covenant served to bring God's punishment upon them. John Owen confirmed this belief in his report of three Scots ministers who received 'the lot of war' at a skirmish near Musselburgh on 30 August 1650. The Scottish army marched out with the ministers in the fore like a righteous shield or a righteous guarantee of victory, similar to the Israelites' use of the Ark of the Covenant. Had God favoured them, Owen declared, they should have been unscathed.[136] Other reports of English victories sent to London also stress the providence of God as the source of the English successes over and against the cause of the covenant. In a work entitled *Emanuel, or, God with us*, the English Independent minister John Canne proclaimed the victory at Dunbar as evidence 'That the Lord of Hosts was against the Covenant, the Scots Cause ... for if we will take the Presbyterian sence of it, the Covenant enjoynes men to destroy the Church of God, and to suppresse the gifts of God, and the Spirit of Christ in his Saints, and Servants'.[137] Likewise, when news of the victory at Dunbar reached Massachusetts, John Cotton preached a sermon of thanksgiving for the providential advancement of God's cause, and later wrote to Cromwell congratulating him on the victory.[138] Cromwell replied, thanking the clergyman for the support and prayer of the godly in New England, only lamenting that the victory entailed the suffering of some godly Scots who foolishly opposed them, and branding the victory as a fulfilment of prophecy.[139] By framing the outcome of Dunbar in such terms, Independents in both old and New England heralded Cromwell's victory as unequivocally the dispensation of God's judgement in their favour, and a condemnation of tyrannical state churches.

As a result, the battle of Dunbar served as a twofold triumph for the English. Militarily they scattered the bulk of Scotland's forces and took nearly 10,000 prisoners. But of even greater importance, psychologically (in terms of their propaganda war) the routing of the Scots by a numerically inferior English force fighting on foreign soil served as a huge providential boost for a parliamentary army that faced military opposition in Scotland and some political opposition at home. By the storming of Dundee on 1 September 1651, the English army no longer proclaimed 'For the Lord of Hosts', but the much more definitive 'God with us!' Reports of English victories therefore helped to galvanise support for the army back in England, to abate fears that may still have been festering in the backs of the soldiers' minds and, most importantly of all, to challenge the claims of the Kirk. For Gardiner, the great victory at Dunbar was as much over the Solemn League and Covenant as it was over the Scots. The trouncing of the Scottish army and the subsequent conquest of the country over the following months ensured that the Kirk could no longer impose political or ecclesiastical governments upon England.[140] Cromwell himself perceived the religious ramifications of his victory over the Scots, declaring 'Surely it's probable the Kirk had done their do'.[141] Yet the religious importance of the campaign did not fade away after Dunbar and the battle of Worcester exactly one year later; instead it became increasingly apparent in the regime's occupation of Scotland. Opposition to the Kirk continued as a fundamental part of Commonwealth policy. The settling of a civil magistrate in Commonwealth Edinburgh required candidates to publicly denounce the tyranny and oppression of both the Scottish state and, more exceptionally, the Kirk.[142]

Presbyterian Interpretations in the Wake of Dunbar

After the Scots' shambolic defeat at Dunbar, the English easily overran the rest of Scotland south of the Clyde–Forth line. Although not uncontested, the army maintained stable control and could move through the Lothians and as far as Glasgow with little opposition. The Scots government withdrew to Perth and faced the difficult task of trying to keep its supporters loyal and eager to sustain opposition against the invaders. To do this it had to explain the crushing defeat at Dunbar in a manner that ensured God remained with it, which it did in two ways. On the whole the Presbyterian interpretation both north and south of the Tweed held that, like Israel before them, God's chosen people were suffering for their hidden sins, but they had not lost their favoured status ensured by the covenants.[143] Cromwell challenged the Scots ministers who sought refuge in Edinburgh Castle when the English entered the city to see God's providence in what had occurred at Dunbar: 'And shal we after all these our Prayers, Fastings, Tears, Expectations, and solemn Appeals, call these bare Events?'[144] The Kirk rejected Cromwell's interpretation in favour of an Old Testament allusion to the relationship between God and Israel. If God could use the Babylonians and Assyrians to correct the Israelites, then could the English not be used to correct the Scots? In response to this interpretation of events, fasts and public repentance were ordered to be held throughout Scotland on 12 September 1650 in order to purge the nation of its sin, while the Kirk published confessions of the sins of the ministry.[145] Bound together with the order for fasting was *A Shorte Declaration and Warning to all the Congregations of the Kirke of Scotland*, also composed by the commissioners of the General Assembly. The commissioners ordered both documents to be read in every congregation at the earliest opportunity.[146] The tract urged Scots to ignore rumours which interpreted the demise of the Scots army as a judgement against the covenant. Instead, it instructed the soldiers in the army to look deeply at their own lives and repent of carnal activities and secular hopes. Finally, it conveyed the idea that the error rested not in their covenant with God, but in their adherence to it. The primary causes cited for holding a national day of public humiliation were the 'manifest provocations of the King's house', neglect to purge the king's household, laxness and ignorance among the people, divisions in the army and the seeking of personal preferment rather than defence of the covenant.[147] The urgency of dealing with hidden sins, particularly failures in adhering to the covenants, featured as the theme of Patrick Gillespie's fast-day sermon on 26 December 1650 in Glasgow.[148] The Protester minister preached on 2 Kings 23, explaining Scotland suffered specifically for the sins of its king. For Gillespie, the sins of the king laid equally with the kingdom, because 'the King's sin becomes the Kingdom's sin, in so far as it is not mourned for, and repented of'. Incorporation of kingship in a covenant between God and a nation makes the nation culpable for the personal sins of the monarch. In other words, Scotland had controverted God's ideal and made the same mistake as Israel in pursuing a king in 1 Samuel 8.

A second explanation for Scotland's plight laid complete blame for the scourge that had befallen them upon the English. Those who favoured this explanation would eventually become Resolutioners. Rather than a sign that God had turned against them, or was correcting them, these individuals labelled the defeat at Dunbar a betrayal by the English, with whom they were supposed to be in covenant. Their breaking of the covenant with Scotland, according to the commissioners of the General Assembly, amply proved that the Commonwealth was not 'in subordination to Religion'.[149] As a result, the Scottish defeats at Dunbar and Worcester could not be blamed on a failure by the Scots, but rather wholly upon the English betrayal of the Solemn League and Covenant.

The Kirk made several proclamations to prevent compliance with the English now comfortably entrenched on Scottish soil, declaring that any Scot who assisted, joined or even spoke positively of the conquering army ran the risk of extreme censure or even excommunication.[150] The commissioners of the General Assembly passed their first act against compliance on 1 November 1650, and distributed it in manuscript form before eventually publishing it on James Brown's press in Aberdeen. The act required presbyteries to note any persons either complying or corresponding with the 'sectaries' or the 'army of the sectaries' and to report them to the commissioners.[151] In March 1651, another declaration entitled *A Short Declaration and Warning to the Ministers and Professors of this Kirk* proclaimed:

> The Adversaries roaring making a strange noise in the midst of some Congregations, the Inevitable hazard of our dear brethren, to bee seduced into pernicious Heresies and Errours, by the deceatfull practises and speaches of Sectaries, that are cunning to deceave, & speak lies in hypocrisie; The Innocent blood of our brethren murthered by the Sword of a mercilesse enemie; the sighing of the Prisoners, Inhumanelie and cruelly used by these who keep them captive; The care of preserving our posterity from being sunk in the dark dungeons of Errours ... Doe cry so lowd in the ears of all who have ears to hear, and a heart to understand to bee awake and quickened unto the necessarie Duetie of the tyme.[152]

This paper, also produced by the commissioners, warned the people not to be 'carried about with the wynde of Strange Doctrine' and to recognise the clear opposition to true religion represented by the English upholding that 'impious monster of Toleration'.[153] Moreover, it urged continued adherence to the cause of the covenants, declared that those who did not unite with them scattered God's people and 'risked themselves under the hazard of the displeasure of GOD and the censures of the Kirk' as well as civil punishment from the state.[154]

However, not everyone in Scotland found the Kirk's explanations convincing. The town clerk of Glasgow, hearing of Scotland's defeat at Dunbar, declared 'our way in that business [the covenant and engagement against England] was not what it ought to have been; and after some getting it laid to heart, I was challenged for my implicit engaging therein' and resolved to never again adhere to a course of action based upon the judgement of others.[155] Similarly, Alexander Jaffray began to look at the dispensation of events and Scotland's multiple defeats as signs of a more specific fault than just failure to adhere to the covenants.[156] For him, it was a short step from viewing the defeat at Dunbar as a punishment from God to labelling Scotland's adherence to the covenant as the cause of this punishment. He extracted the fundamental error of the Solemn League and Covenant as the Kirk's unwarrantable devotion to Presbytery:

> And finding that the maintaining of Presbytery was one, if not the main and chief end proposed, by those that were most honest and single-hearted, in contriving and carrying on the Covenant – (others, as statesmen and politicians, had other ends; but I speak of the godly,) – thus having found that we were so engaged to Presbytery, as the only way of Christ, I was necessarily led on to inquire about the thing itself – if indeed it was truly so. This was the true occasion and rise of my inquiry in these matters; and not, as some have conceived, that I was thereto engaged and insnared by men's persuasions, or other base and corrupt ends.[157]

However, such questioning of the Presbyterian Kirk was not widespread immediately after the defeat at Dunbar. On the whole, support for the Kirk and covenants remained high even after Worcester, although cracks began to show and the splintering of Presbyterian factions that would occur in 1652 began to become apparent. The Kirk had largely withstood the initial storm of English propaganda and had delayed the potentially disastrous religious ramifications of the defeat at Dunbar.

The religious vigour that underpinned the English soldiers' invasion of Scotland was corroborated during their occupation of the country. The English soldiers' attitude towards the Kirk, as Frances Dow explains, was tempered by a 'belief that the church had been largely responsible for promoting the late war against England'.[158] Symbols of both the monarchy and the intolerant presbytery were legitimate targets for the frustration of the soldiers.[159] During the closing months of 1650 several churches in

Edinburgh were damaged or destroyed. Holyrood Palace was set alight
and the University of Edinburgh ransacked. In other parts of the country,
Kirk services were interrupted, and stools of repentance, which became
a symbol of what the soldiers despised in Presbyterianism, were derided
or destroyed.[160] Subsequently the policy of the English towards Scotland
reflected their distrust of an overtly powerful Scottish clergy.

What became a greater concern for Scotland's rigid Presbyterians was
the settlement of English troops in garrisons throughout Scotland. With a
largely non-literate population in rural areas, the parishioners of the Kirk
were much more susceptible to verbal persuasion than they had been to
the printed tracts produced in 1650. Once English garrisons – many with
resident chaplains – had been established in remote areas of the country,
two new forms of polemic came into practice: public preaching and
public disputing. For the first time ever, the populace of Scotland found
themselves exposed to new forms of Protestantism that had never before
reached the heart of the countryside. Sectarian teaching was far-flung,
with Baptist churches in Leith, Edinburgh, Ayr, Perth, Cupar, Aberdeen
and Inverness, not to mention the high proportion of Independents within
the forces. Regiments were migratory and manned garrisons throughout
the country. As a result, Englishmen preached in the most remote corners
of Scotland. By 1655 even the remote garrison at Inverlochy, established
by the arrival of 1,000 troops from Ireland in June 1654, had its own
chaplain.[161] Isolated parish ministers were forced to minimise the impact
of sectarian public preaching in any way possible. At times, this meant
they had little choice but to acquiesce to challenges for public disputes.
Thus a new chapter began in the struggle between the Kirk and the English
sectarians for the heart and souls of the Scottish people.

2 'Go not to Gilgal nor Bethaven!'
Presbyterian Resistance to the Polemics of Sectarian Occupation[1]

It was after that through a Boundless Tolleration, a deludge of Errors had broken in upon England, and the Sectarian Army having Subdued Scotland, and dispersed themselves in all the Parts of it, Corrupt Men and Seducers among Them, did endeavour to pervert the People from the Truth.[2]

George Meldrum, 1692

Anne Laurence has argued that the English forces made little religious impact on Scotland during the Interregnum for two reasons: first, Presbyterians were so embroiled in their own internal divisions they paid little attention to the English sects; second, 'there was no serious missionary activity by the English'.[3] This chapter will argue that in light of contemporary evidence both these assertions are unequivocally false. Instead, Interregnum Scotland represented a hotbed of religious discourse in which all parties involved were forced to participate in some degree of missionary activity, if for no other reason than to stave off the attempts of rivals. Moreover, in direct contrast to Laurence's claim, it was the English chaplains and soldiers who most ardently pursued proselytising activities.

After the battle of Dunbar, the English ceased to be simply an invading army and became an occupying force capable of pursuing their desired objectives. That their objectives had religious implications should not be surprising in view of their initial propaganda. As the first chapter has demonstrated, both Scots clergy and English sectarians defined the conflict between the nations as both a temporal military clash as well as a struggle for the souls of Scotland's populace. In England during the 1640s and on into the 1650s religious radicals, in opposition to the established clergy, invaded pulpits, preached in the open air and goaded their opponents into public disputes.[4] With their conquest of Scotland the English radicals within Cromwell's army introduced these practices into Scotland and employed them against the Kirk. The sectarian presence in Scotland reaffirmed old fears among Presbyterians 'that the gangrene of thair errouris may tak hold upone sum ignorant and unstable myndis' among their parishioners.[5] Although ministers of the Kirk initially rejected the prospect of disputing points of religion publicly, they were eventually compelled to enter into public disputes with English sectarians and to compete for the adherence of their parishioners in what they perceived to be an increasingly open religious contest.

Ann Hughes has done much to explain the importance and role of public disputations in England during the Civil War period. Her work is also of great significance for understanding public religious disputes in Cromwellian Scotland, as it provides a clear model for both the motivations behind these events and general profiles of the participants. According to Hughes, the importance of public religious disputes did not rest wholly in the rhetorical exchanges over dogmatic positions, but equally in the motives of the participants. The radical religious ideas surfacing in the freedom of the Civil War and Interregnum no longer subscribed to what had previously been held as indisputable dogmatic facts. The 'radical' representatives in England's public disputes of the 1640s and 1650s were described by Thomas Edwards in *Gangraena* precisely for their opposition to 'Orthodox' parish ministers. While the accuracy of his descriptions of radicals and their activities may be dubious, it is interesting to note that many of those Edwards described as taking over pulpits, arguing in the streets and participating in slightly more organised public disputes were soldiers of the parliamentary army and, according to Hughes, 'rigid separatists and often also Baptists'.[6] These radical elements made up a significant portion of the parliamentary army. When they arrived in Scotland they became missionaries for sectarian religion and introduced both radical new doctrines and revolutionary methods of evangelism. As disputants they not only threw out the accepted framework of dogmatics, but also refused the staunch rules of debate that were central to academicians.[7] This posed a significant problem for parish ministers who felt bound by these rules, because the power of public persuasion cannot be limited to well-reasoned theological arguments. This is particulary true when disputes were intended to influence the opinion of the general public, rather than to dialectically determine the truth.

In Hughes' English model, these public debates generally took place between ministers of the established or orthodox churches and religious radicals. Radical disputants tended to be more disruptive and frequently appealed to the audience for support, while their orthodox counterparts methodically adhered to set rules of academic debating. When radicals brought about disputes they employed anarchic strategies to dominate these sometimes raucous encounters. One tactic that greatly threatened the orthodox disputants was the intervention of 'radicals' planted in the audience, a ruse employed in England by the Baptist minister Thomas Collier. He would appeal to his adherents, pretending to be unbiased auditors in the crowd, who on command would become riled and shout down Collier's opponent.[8] An effective tactic, it gave the impression that

Collier's arguments swayed a large portion of the audience. A second aspect of radical disputing was unwillingness to concede to proofs contrary to their position. Free to refuse systematic arguments, they were also free from conceding their positions, even when opponents clearly laid out logical proofs against them. Even well-educated 'radicals' would evade difficulties through uncouthly violating the proper etiquette of academic disputation. Hughes relates the shock of Richard Baxter at John Tombes' (a Baptist) inability to adhere to the rules of logic: 'When he was stuck he "breaks over the hedge, and turns all the dispute into a discourse and goes up and down at pleasure".'[9] Such behaviour eventually led the Presbyterian John Ley to warn fellow orthodox ministers to avoid these situations by ensuring, first, that rules for the dispute be agreed beforehand; second, that opponents were credible and worthy; and third, that the occasion be edifying to all that attended.[10] However, when radicals provoked disputations, orthodox ministers had a difficult time rejecting them without losing face by appearing afraid or lacking in confidence about the certainty of their position. It was, in fact, orthodox ministers who had the most at stake in public encounters. They faced the prospect of defending orthodox faith in front of their own parishioners, against antagonists of unknown repute who were free from the bounds of order and reason that they themselves were obliged to follow. With so much at risk, why did the orthodox ministers of England enter into these debates in the 1640s and 1650s? According to Hughes, their willingness to engage their sectarian opponents is indicative 'of the fluid marketplace that religion in England had become and of the willingness of orthodox Puritans to compete in it'.[11]

Hughes' work significantly aids an understanding of what took place in Scotland during the Cromwellian occupation. It provides insight into the reasons why ministers of the Kirk might have entered into public disputes with their sectarian conquerors, as well as the motives of the English chaplains in pursuing them. According to Hughes, orthodox clergy became involved in disputes with their radical opponents when they felt it necessary to vie for the hearts of their parishioners. That Scottish clergy became involved in public disputes with English sectarians suggests they, like their Presbyterian brethren in England, were being forced to compete for the adherence and devotion of the public. The catalyst for this fear within the Scottish clergy was primarily the drawing power of English preaching and its widespread presence.

A Widespread Sectarian Presence

With Charles II's defeat at Worcester (3 September 1651) and the subsequent fall of the major population centres of Scotland, Cromwell's forces rapidly gained a stranglehold on most of the country. What they could not conquer, they simply contained. By December 1651 a garrison at Inverness controlled the north of the country, all of the north-east including

Aberdeen had been secured and everything south of the River Tay firmly rested under English domination.[12] In order to maintain control and keep restless Highlanders at bay, the English established garrisons and citadels throughout the country. From September 1650 English soldiers were garrisoned in and around Edinburgh, including Holyrood palace, Canongate and Leith, where in total nearly 5,000 English soldiers resided through the winter.[13] As early as April 1651 'the English had garrisons at Douglas, Evandale Castle (Avondale) in Strathaven, Linlithgow, Kilmarnock and Hamilton'.[14] By the spring of 1652 the construction of citadels had begun at Ayr, Inverness and Perth (St Johnston).[15] The following year garrisons were posted in Edinburgh, Dundee, Aberdeen, Inchgarvie, Linlithgow, Dumbarton, Stirling, Burntisland, Tantallon Castle, Bass Island, Inchkeith, Ruthven Castle (Badenoch), Braemar, Blair Atholl, Dunkeld, Brodick Castle, Dunstaffnage, Dunnolly, Dunnottar Castle, Duart Castle, Orkney, Peebles, Cupar and Falkland.[16] Construction of a citadel at remote Inverlochy began in 1654 and garrisons were reported at Inverary and Drummond Castle near Crieff.[17] As the decade progressed, it seems that the normative pattern established by the army was an increasing number of garrisons with fewer troops in each location. Especially after the suppression of Glencairn's Rising, Monck deemed it valuable to have a wider distribution of troops to observe possible discontent and preserve law and order by containing the clans.[18] Although the historian Malcolm Laing suggested that the number of garrisons in Scotland diminished to twenty-eight by 1656, regimental rolls in the Clarke Manuscripts confirm that English soldiers were garrisoned or quartered in over sixty different locations.[19] Although this is the earliest surviving compilation of regiments and quarters, additional lists for 1658 and 1659 are also extant. None of these lists, however, should be viewed as being complete, since a list of 'minor garrisons' in June 1658 records a dozen additional locations not contained in the main corpus.[20]

Due to the nature of the army's composition and its wide distribution, it is likely that even the most remote corners of Scotland were exposed to 'sectarian' doctrines and the English message of toleration. Moreover, it is plausible that each of the garrisons and citadels stretching from the southern border north to Shetland, and from Brodick Castle, Inverlochy and Stornoway in the west to Aberdeen and Dunbar in the east, held gathered religious meetings. Reports from across the country indicate that these gathereings had an early and intentional religious impact upon their immediate localities. One English report dated 8 January 1651 relays the information that 'there is a very precious people who seek the face of God in Sutherland and divers other parts beyond Invernesse … the people in those parts will rather leave their owne Ministers and come to private houses where our officers and souldiers meete together'.[21] Another report from Tarbet (Argyll) in the summer further supports the dissemination of

English religion to the edges of Scotland: 'Some of the Highlanders have heard our preaching with great attention and groanings, and seeming affection to it.'[22] Yet sectarian interference was not limited to the vicinity of garrisons. In 1653 the synod of Argyll found it necessary to send a minister to investigate reports of lay English sailors performing marriages and baptisms on the island of Jura.[23] While Scots living near an English garrison were perhaps more likely to come into direct contact with English ideas, even people living in more remote parts might experience English sectarianism at first hand with regiments passing through isolated areas or English ships making landfall. In some ways Scots in remote areas may have been more susceptible to English notions of sectarian religion, especially in places like Jura, where the local parish charge had lain vacant since 1649.[24] Unfortunately, for many of the remote parts of Scotland few records from the Interregnum period have survived.

With the English presence so widely spread throughout Scotland, they were in an excellent position to maintain their control over the country, promulgate their ideologies and impose their will. This represented a dangerous time for the Kirk, especially because the English often success-fully befriended or at least achieved a high level of interaction, with the native populace.[25] For example, in March 1653 the inhabitants of Lewis took up arms with English soldiers garrisoned at Stornoway against the Earl of Seaforth.[26] At Inverlochy, Lochiel and Clan Cameron entered into a 'strict league and friendship' with the English that lasted to the Restoration, despite the clan's initial slaughter of seventy English troops.[27] Similarly, an account from the minister of Kirkhill dated 1655 reveals a high level of interaction between the garrison and the population of Inverness. According to his report the garrison, which began constructing its citadel on 16 May 1652, provided a wide range of English luxuries, including 'a great long tavern with all manner of wines, viands, beer, ale and cider'. It also meant a large financial boost for Inverness. The fir logs needed for construction were purchased from a local laird named Hugh Fraser of 'Struey's woods', who received 30,000 merks in one transac-tion. Lured by exceptional pay, a great number of Scots laboured in the building work. In fact, so many Scots laboured on the project that the minister declared 'hardly could you get one to serve you' in some other work. In total the project cost £80,000, much of the cost going toward the payment of masons, carpenters and other skilled labourers. However, the benefits were not merely pecuniary.

> They brought such store of all wares and conveniences to Inverness that English cloth was sold near as cheap here as in England: the pint of claret went for a shilling. They set up an apothecary's shop with a druggist's: Mr. Miller was their chirurgeon, and Dr. Andrew Moore their physician. They not only civilised but enriched the place. It were vain to relate what advantage the country had by this regiment.[28]

This interaction built relationships and provided the ministers and soldiers of the English forces with opportunities to advocate their own beliefs, doctrines, and forms of Christianity. Among the forces garrisoned at Inverness during the decade there is evidence of numerous 'Sectarian' groups, including 'Anabaptists', Independents and Quakers.[29]

A more astonishing link between the English army and the Scottish populace is alluded to in the Kirk Session records of Ayr. Early in 1653 several unfortunate Scotswomen found themselves before the session for having 'fallen' pregnant to soldiers from the Cromwellian garrison. Among those cited for fathering children were three Scots: William Cockburne 'Scotchman ... in Captain Ponson's regiment ... borne in Edinburgh'; Andrew Woddhill 'a soldier with the Englishmen', possibly from Paisley; and Charles Stewart 'Scotisman ... in Capt. Pontson's regiment.'[30] There is also some evidence to suggest that a Scot by the name of 'Glengarrie' served Cromwell's forces in Canisbay (near John O'Groats) sometime between 1652 and 1655.[31] When these soldiers enlisted in the English ranks is uncertain, but their participation would presumably have required some degree of acceptance of the ideological rationale for the invasion. As a result, Scots serving in the Commonwealth army might be the upshot of early English attempts to foster Commonwealth principles among the people of Scotland. Through propaganda, governance, the use of Scottish labour in construction and supply of provisions, and even by enlisting Scots soldiers, the English regime made significant strides towards establishing friendly relations with the general populace of Scotland. The Kirk certainly recognised the threat posed by the presence of English troops. When the English garrison at Elgin temporarily withdrew from the burgh, the Kirk Session ordered ministers to carry out a systematic examination of all the burgh's residents. They began by producing a list of residents to ensure that no one would be overlooked, but this so delayed the examination process that their plans were eventually scuppered when the soldiers returned a month later.[32]

An Evangelical Occupation

In contrast to Anne Laurence's claims, England's occupation of Scotland can not be disregarded as religiously benign. In the closing months of 1651 an English journal purported the possible benefits to be had if some Kirk ministers were removed and replaced by able English preachers in order to 'draw the people off the leaven of their Pharisaical and rigid Presbyterian Teachers'.[33] This comment came from William Clarke, secretary to the English army in Scotland, and reflected the commonly held perception within the English regime that Scottish Presbyterianism fundamentally opposed the basic republican and religiously tolerant principles underpinning the Commonwealth. Clarke's comments indicate that the Commonwealth's plan in Scotland required not only well-trained soldiers but also well-prepared preachers. Clarke later suggested that an honest preaching soldier should replace every parish minister in Scotland.[34] A week after his plea for clergy, the English Council of State appointed four ministers to accompany the parliament's commissioners for Scotland as chaplains.[35] In March 1652 the Commissioners for Ordering and Managing the Affairs of Scotland debated sending an additional 'twelve or more' ministers into Scotland to garrisons and 'other convenient places' and approved the funds later in the month.[36] Accordingly, the Commissioners for Ordering and Managing the Affairs of Scotland employed ten ministers to serve in Scotland, some of whom ministered to civilian congregations.[37] The propagation of toleration and religious Independency served as integral aspects of establishing a lasting settlement in Scotland and were advocated through the pulpits by English chaplains and ministers serving in Scotland. These men preached publicly on a regular basis, sometimes to large gatherings, where Scots in attendance 'were much taken with the doctrine'.[38]

Two sermons preached in Scotland by English chaplains early in the decade survive in print, one by Nicholas Lockyer and one by John Owen.[39] That these sermons were preached in Scotland and subsequently printed in Leith by the English-controlled press single them out as exemplary models of what the Commonwealth desired from preachers. Owen based his sermon on Isaiah 56:7, 'For mine House shall be called an House of Prayer for all People'. He used the passage as a metaphor for how Christ built his church, which is the house of God. In particular, Owen made four claims about the church: first, he spoke not only of the universal church but of individual congregations, for example, 'every particular Church of his Saints, inasmuch as they partake the nature of the whole'; second, as the sole designer and builder of his church, 'Christ doth all alone'; third, only the elect could be the 'living stones' required for its construction; and fourth, Christ alone was the watchman capable of maintaining his church.[40] These four claims about the church made up part of an intricate and subtle attack against national churches, and therefore Scotland's Presbytery. In his preface to the work, Owen described this agenda as pouring out 'a savour of the gospel on the sons of peace in Scotland'.

Owen's definition of what the church is creates an equally clear picture of what the church is not. It cannot be a national institution that includes the masses, because only the elect can be part of the true church. It cannot be controlled or watched over by humans on a national level, because national rulers are detached from the congregations and so are unable to know who should be admitted and who should not. Equally, according to Owen, those who have historically proclaimed themselves as watchmen over Christ's church 'have watched onely for their own advantage' and have been 'the very worst of dogs'.[41] The sermon clearly sets forth Owen's theology of Independency, which supports particular congregations, made up of the elect and gathered by Christ, 'which are usefull Partitions in the great mysticall House', the universal body and church of Christ.[42] Owen's espousal of Independent thinking is consistent with his preaching in England and indicative of why Cromwell brought him to Scotland. In other words, Cromwell felt Owen's ideologies and message had a fundamental place in the English plan for Scotland. The centrality of Independency in the campaign against Scotland may also explain why so many New Englanders (both chaplains and soldiers) who had returned to Britain during the civil wars took part in the war against Scotland, and indicate why the Council of State sent Samuel Mather, eldest son of Richard Mather and brother of Increase, to Leith where he resided from 1652 until 1654.[43] Although Owen left Scotland in October 1651, his sermons continued to serve a fundamental role in the Commonwealth's agenda. Just a few months after his departure, Robert Lilburne wrote to Cromwell appealing for more able ministers to preach publicly and for some of Owen's printed sermons for distribution. Importantly, Lilburne suggests that the need for these prints stems from a desire among Scots to be more 'truly informed concerning our (the English Army's) proceedings'.[44] In other words, the writings of John Owen would aid in defining the English purpose in invading Scotland. Lilburne's request may have been the motivation for Owen's sermon *The Advantage of the Kingdom of Christ* being printed by the English-run Evan Tyler print house in Leith the following year.[45]

Nicholas Lockyer's *A Litle Stone Out of the Mountain* is the only other surviving English sermon. Although equally tailored to the purpose of the occupying sectarians, Lockyer approached the task far less subtly than Owen. While Owen's sermon was pro-Independent, Lockyer's sermon was openly anti-Kirk. Preached sometime in 1651, he elaborated and published it in Leith in 1652 at the behest of his superiors. The epistle dedicatory, signed by Joseph Caryl, John Oxenbridge and Cuthbert Sydenham, the chaplains to the Commissioners for the Affairs of Scotland, served to further affirm that the message of the sermon fitted well into the regime's policy. *A Litle Stone Out of the Mountain* attacked what Lockyer claimed to be the inherently corrupt nature of national churches, which included the sinful masses, and declared the Presbyterian Kirk to be beyond hope of regeneration. Although some Presbyterians suggested that stringent purging of congregations, similar to the purges of the Scottish army prior to Dunbar, would restore the Kirk, Lockyer flatly rejected any possibility that a national church could be purged, declaring 'how impossible it is, that the far lesser number (retaining their present constitution) should regularly cast out the greater part there from'.[46] He also asserted that external authority over a congregation, such as bishops or presbytery, was an invention of mankind.[47] For Lockyer, the only authority over a congregation was Christ and the elders of that particular congregation. In reference to the condition of the Kirk, he wrote: 'All that I have heavy upon my heart, respecting both the one and the other, is, that as to Church order, they are in an ill vessell, which cannot possibly live, in such stormes as now beat upon it, from Heaven and from the Saints, and therefore I could wish that all the godly were out on't.'[48] In Lockyer's estimation, the only way forward for the church in Scotland would be through gathering individual congregations of devout Christians out of the ailing national church: like the gathering of the first churches out of synagogues (Gal. 1:22).[49] Once again, this represented the promotion of Independency and the toleration of gathered churches, ideals that the Commonwealth believed necessary for securing stability between the two nations.

While these works espoused an anti-Presbyterian hypothesis in opposing external power over congregations, they did not advocate ideologies particularly Baptist, Arminian or Libertarian in nature. They stopped short of supporting any particular sects other than Independency in its broadest context. Instead they limited their scope to ecclesiological arguments over the 'corrupt nature' of state churches and the purity of independently gathered congregations of the elect. The publication of these sermons, coupled with the government's appointment of men like John Owen, Nicholas Lockyer, Cuthbert Sydenham, John Oxenbridge and Joseph Caryl as chaplains to the council, and Samuel Mather's appointment to Leith, suggest that the regime supported the promulgation of Independency and toleration but not necessarily particular doctrines beyond these of a broad ecclesiological nature.

While it caused the commissioners of the Kirk great distress that anti-Presbyterian sermons were being preached by English divines like Owen and Lockyer, it caused even greater anxiety that Cromwell allowed men who were not ordained to preach publicly. It was the soldiers within the regiments who harboured the more radical doctrines. From the time that Cromwell arrived in Edinburgh in early September 1650 he made it clear through a famous series of letters exchanged between himself and Walter Dundas, governor of Edinburgh Castle, that his soldiers would not only be permitted but encouraged to preach. When the English army arrived in the capital Cromwell invited the ministers of the city seeking refuge in the castle to withdraw and return to their pulpits. Although offered free liberty to preach they refused the invitation, citing lack of assurance for their safety. According to the clergymen, they had heard reports of Cromwell's troops persecuting, and even martyring, ministers in England, Ireland and the Borders of Scotland. Cromwell adamantly denied that any ministers had ever suffered at the hands of his soldiers, and counter-charged the Scots ministers of being more concerned with their own well-being than with the service of their 'Master'.[50]

The letters then turned to the role of the minister and the right to preach. In response to Scots accusations that the Commonwealth silenced ministers in England, Cromwell declared that English ministers had 'liberty to preach the Gospel, though not to Rail, nor under pretence thereof to over

top the Civil Power, or debase it as they please'.[51] In this way he made
a distinction between the spiritual preaching of the Gospel and the use
of the pulpit as a political soapbox. However, as the sermons of Owen
and Lockyer show, spiritual preaching could serve a political purpose. He
continued: 'No man [ordained or layman] hath been troubled in England
or Ireland for preaching the Gospel.'[52] This is precisely what worried
the General Assembly and the rigid Presbyterians of Scotland, for they
disagreed with their English counterparts with regard to what constituted rightful 'Gospel' preaching. The Scots would have preferred to err
on the side of stringency in matters of preaching discipline rather than
to open the pulpits to anyone who felt they had something to say. The
ministers accused Cromwell, because of his allowing laymen to preach in
Edinburgh's pulpits, with opening their pulpits 'that men of meer Civil
place and employment, should usurp the calling and employment of the
Ministry, to the scandal of the Reformed Kirks'.[53] In response, Cromwell
struck thunderously against the notion of an elevated clergy, branding
ministers as 'helpers' rather than 'Lords over the faith of Gods people'.[54]
To the ministers' criticism of soldiers preaching in their vacated pulpits,
Cromwell famously retorted:

> Are you troubled that Christ is preached? Is preaching so inclusive in your
> function? Doth it scandalize the Reformed Kirks, and Scotland in particular?
> Is it against the Covenant? Away with the Covenant, if this be so, I thought
> the Covenant and these could have been willing that any should speak good
> of the name of Christ; if not, it is no Covenant of God's approving, nor the
> Kirks you mention, in so much the Spouse of Christ. Where do you finde in the
> Scripture a ground to warrant such an assertion, That preaching is included in
> your function though an approbation from men hath order in it, and may do
> well, yet he that hath not a better warrant then that, hath none at all. I hope
> he that ascended up on high, may give his gifts to whom he please ... indeed
> you erre through the mistake of the Scriptures: approbation is an act of conve-
> niency in respect of order, not of necessity to give faculty to preach the Gospel,
> Your pretended fear lest error should step in, is like the man that would keep
> all the wine out of the country, lest men should be drunk. It will be found an
> unjust and unwise jealousie, to deny a man the liberty he hath by nature, upon
> a supposition he may abuse it, when he doth abuse it, judge.[55]

The position of Cromwell terrified the commissioners of the Kirk. While
it was undesirable to have English ministers and chaplains preach, at
least they were ordained and finite in number. Allowing the soldiers to
preach, however, meant that not only were men who possessed 'heretical'
beliefs overrunning the country, they were allowed to preach their heresy
at leisure.

   The widespread distribution of the English and their close proximity to
the people made the penchant of the English soldiers to preach a primary
threat to the established religion of Scotland. That the English troopers
would preach publicly was unavoidable. Many of the soldiers were keen

preachers, and they preached whenever the opportunity arose. James Nayler, for instance, began to preach to a crowd so soon after the battle of Dunbar that the smoke probably still hung heavily in the air.[56] Nayler is a particularly important example of the English soldiers' propensity for preaching. While some scholars have incorrectly identified him as a chaplain to Cromwell's forces,[57] he was not even ordained. When Nayler preached along the roadside after the battle of Dunbar, he was a quartermaster in Lambert's regiment of horse,[58] a layman with Independent leanings and not yet convinced as a Quaker.

Other examples of English laymen preaching publicly are easily found. According to eighteenth-century ecclesiastical historian Matthew Craufurd, many of Cromwell's officers and soldiers did regularly 'preach and distill their errors to the people'.[59] There are accounts that they preached regularly in Aberdeen and Edinburgh, and also in various parts of Fife and Stirling, where Scots contemporaries described them as being 'gifted men' who 'preached as they were moved'.[60] James Burns, the bailie of Glasgow, recorded that both English ministers and officers 'preached daily' in the city in 1651.[61] In Edinburgh, General Lambert preached frequently at both the 'East Kirk'[62] and the West Kirk (St Cuthbert's),[63] while Cromwell preached in both St Giles' and the Tron Kirk.[64] According to Bulstrode Whitelocke, while the Kirk's ministers remained in hiding in Edinburgh Castle in October, preaching continued in St Giles': 'The general and his officers met at the great church in Edinburgh on the Lord's-day, where many Scots were, and expressed much affection to the doctrine preached.' And, even more boldly, 'divers of the Scots come to hear the ministers of the army, and seem to be much converted by them, and offer to be employed by the general'.[65]

General Lambert 'urged' Edinburgh's city council to appropriate to him the East Kirk of the city 'for his exercise at sermound'. The church, which Nicoll described as both 'speciall ... the best in the toun'[66] and as 'the new kirk', was the eastern portion of St Giles', which had been separated from the Old Kirk sometime between 1639 and 1642.[67] By December 1651 the city council had given Lambert control of the church, and it became a place where English ministers and soldiers, both officers and troops, preached regularly.[68] This prompted Protesters to complain to Cromwell of the irregularity in allowing 'officers and souldiers to stepp into pulpits and to speake there what they list'.[69] The commissioners of the General Assembly responded to this widespread broaching of sectarian doctrine in January 1651 by urging the people of Edinburgh (who had been under the control of the English since early September 1650) to avoid sectarians: 'We earnestly exhort yow ... above all, that yow beware to joyne with them (the sectaries) in any publict worship or any private exercise of religion. Who ever will venture to toutch pitch may be defyled before they be awaire.'[70]

This exhuberant penchant for lay preaching should not be allocated merely to the early enthusiastic days of the occupation. Nicoll reported that several English soldiers taught openly in the public places of Edinburgh in May 1652.[71] Neither should the phenomenon be viewed simply as an activity occurring in Scotland's burghs. The kirk session records of Alyth recorded an English trooper commandeered the pulpit of their kirk in March 1652.[72] In Elgin, the English did not prevent the local minister from preaching, but following the minister's sermon on 16 December 1651, Colonel Thomas Fitch entered the pulpit and offered his own sermon.[73] It was a shrewd move by Fitch; by waiting for the minister to complete his sermon Fitch probably ensured a good attendance for his own exposition. Around this time, William Falconer, minister of Dyke, complained of members leaving his church to hear others preach.[74] English preaching represented a difficulty facing Kirk ministers across the country.

Religious Toleration

The threat of sectarian preaching was further magnified by the official imposition of religious toleration in February 1652.[75] A *Declaration of the Parliament of the Commonwealth of England, Concerning the Settlement of Scotland* laid out the terms under which a Tender of Union would be established. Although approved by parliament on 28 October 1651, they kept plans of how they intended to settle affairs in Scotland a closely guarded secret until 31 January 1652 when the commissioners for Scotland enumerated the details. In matters of religion, parliament vaguely declared:

> As to what concerns the advancement of the glory of God, that their [parliament and its commissioners in Scotland] constant endeavours shall be, to promote the Preaching of the Gospel there, and to advance the power of true Religion and Holinesse, and that God may be served and worshipped according to his mind revealed in his Word, with protection, and all due countenance and encouragement therein to the people of that Nation, from those in authority under the Parliament.[76]

How this vague declaration would be put into practice depended on the parliament's commissioners in Scotland. The commissioners, unbeknownst to the people of Scotland, had been sent with instructions to promote the preaching of the Gospel in Scotland, but to provide financial support only for ministers known to be pious and well affected to the Commonwealth.[77] On 11 February 1652 the commissioners produced an 'Explanation' intended to clarify, among other things, the regime's position on religious toleration.[78] It explained that

> care shall be taken for removing of scandalous persons, who have intruded into the work of the Ministry, and placing of others fitly qualified with gifts, for the instructing of the people in their stead. And that such Ministers whose

consciences oblige them to wait upon God in the administration of spiritual Ordinances, according to the order of the Scottish Churches, with any that shall voluntarily joyn in the practice therof, shal receive protection and encouragement from all in Authority, in their peaceable and in-offensive exercise of the same.[79]

This in itself would have been undesirable to the Presbyterians of Scotland, since they rejected the notion that temporal governments had any rights to remove or to plant ministers, but the explanation continued, extending the same protection to those 'who not being satisfied in conscience to use that Form [Presbyterianism], shal serve and worship God in other Gospel way, and behave themselves peaceably and in-offensively therein'.[80] Toleration was imposed and the Kirk's domination of Scottish religion broken by the commissioners' interpretation of the act.

The commissioners extended civil protection to anyone, explains Frances Dow, 'who could prove himself to be worshipping God in a "Gospel Way" – a vague term which implied a serious threat to the monopoly of the Church of Scotland'.[81] The Kirk already knew what wide-ranging forms of religion were encapsulated in a mid-seventeenth-century English definition of 'Gospel Way' through the debates of the Westminster Assembly, where the Kirk's representatives had stringently opposed Independency, nonconformity and toleration. Parliament's declaration introduced a degree of religious liberty previously unknown in Scotland.[82] Alexander Brodie of Brodie amply summarised the trepidation felt by fellow Presbyterians when he wrote in his diary: 'I conceive the word Gospel-way may include all, and be extended to all, if the magistrate so please, for he makes himself judge.'[83] Within months of the completed conquest of Scotland, the Presbyterian Kirk faced what it perceived to be the grave consequences of an imposed religious toleration in Scotland. The ministry adamantly preached against the declaration, decreeing it opposed to the covenants and warning of judgement against those who supported it.[84] It was, as the biographer of Samuel Rutherford put it, 'as unwelcome to a portion of the Presbyterians, and as much an object of reprobation and censure, as persecution itself would have been'.[85]

Despite the imposition of toleration, the Kirk attempted to enforce censures upon those who fraternised too closely with sectarians. However, even before passing legislation the English army had pursued a policy of inhibiting the censures of the Kirk, as is demonstrated in the case of Sir Alexander Irving of Drum. In December 1651 the presbytery of Aberdeen summoned Irving to appear for asserting that 'no Sectary is so much to be abhorred as a Presbyterian', for publicly declaring after the fall of the monarchy 'let the Devil take Presbytery, and the Covenant, it came from hell, let it go back to it again' and for tending towards Roman Catholicism.[86] Irving's response resounded as a shattering blow to the authority of the Kirk. Notwithstanding a complete denial of any leanings towards popery, he refused to appear before a Presbyterian inquisition. Irving appealed to two English proclamations produced in previous months. The first was a proclamation against the imposition of oaths produced by General Monck in October 1651, which Irving claimed to be directed specifically to all 'Ministers and other Kirk Officers'.[87] The second (no longer extant) 'Warrant' dated 2 December would not allow civil magistrates to 'seize upon, meddle with, or any ways molest the persons or estates of any excommunicated person, or any ways to discharge any other persons whatsoever; to desist from dealing or trading with the said excommunicated persons, without order from the commonwealth of England or their commissioners'.[88] These declarations effectually removed all temporal sting from the Kirk's censures, providing anyone disaffected with Presbyterianism a reason to cleave to the new government. Irving subsequently petitioned Colonel Overton, commander of the English forces in Aberdeen, to mediate the situation and challenged John Row (the moderator) and rest of the presbytery of Aberdeen to appear before Overton at his lodgings in Aberdeen on the day they had appointed to try him. His brazen riposte to the presbytery included a warning that if they proceeded any further against him they would, by the previous proclamations of General Monck, be presumed to be enemies of the Commonwealth.

Irving praised General Monck for his 'pious enclination towards those that are the highly oppressed in their consciences'. He implored Monck to intervene against the 'animocity of our church judicature' asserting, rather obsequiously, that he could not in good conscience submit to the presbytery of Aberdeen because it was not sanctioned by the Commonwealth of England, and it was the Commonwealth that he now looked to for protection 'from the fury of a superstitious clergy'.[89] In response to Row, Irving taunted the presbytery by branding them a court in opposition to the interest of the Commonwealth, 'which by the Providence of God is now our Soveraign Lords and Masters'. He jeered at them by asking to be pardoned from 'any such businesse of a Presbyterian Judicatory' until such time as the Commonwealth ordered him to do so. Turning from mocking jibes to a more aggressive critique, he battered the 'Hierarchical hedge' of the presbytery for doing more to stifle God's Vineyard than to keep out the wild boars of the antichrist, suggesting that their time would be better spent preaching the Word of God to all nations rather than oppressing the people through their ambitious desires of 'unwarrantable obedience'.[90] The sentence of excommunication was carried out on 26 January 1652, but Irving posited that it carried no weight with either God or man since it came from men rather than from God's 'church'.[91] According to Irving, the presbytery of Aberdeen was

> mor full of fyery zeall, to advance thair awn ambitious and wordlie interests than the gospell of Jesus Christ … urging me this twelve moneth bygone with threatening of excommunication, and of temporall losses, to swear and

subscryue thair solemn league and covenant, as gif it had been a matter of saluatione for me to sweare to establische by armes Presbiteriane governament in England.[92]

Athough excommunicated, no temporal actions could be taken against him. The irony is that Irving was probably a Roman Catholic. Reports sent from William Bannantyne, apostolic prefect of Scotland, in 1654 list Drum and his family among the faithful. Moreover, it has been argued that he had assistance in his paper deluge against the presbytery by a Jesuit named John Walker.[93] Whether or not this is the case, we can see the extent to which toleration would be extended to opponents of the Kirk so long as individuals affirmed fundamental values of the Commonwealth's policies, even if ambiguously.

Intriguingly, the moderator of the presbytery of Aberdeen who pushed so hard for Irving to come back into the fold was one of the men who just four months later would vent similar concerns over the motives of Scotland's covenant and Presbyterianism and declare their own separation from the Kirk. Alexander Irving's audacious refusal to comply with the wishes of the presbytery of Aberdeen and his appeal to the English regime for protection set a precedent essentially establishing tolerance, or at least preventing persecution, before any official legislation from the English parliament did so. *Mercurius Politicus* praised Irving's refusal to bow to the Presbyterians and claimed that his protection by the English caused the Kirk to look upon Monck and Overton as 'great Antagonists'.[94] These events in Aberdeenshire foreshadowed the Commonwealth's changing method of dealing with the Kirk and provided an indication of how the English intended to settle affairs in Scotland. The imposition of toleration in February 1652 reiterated this policy of supporting individuals willing to stand against the Kirk.

In addition to diminishing the effect of Kirk censures under the umbrella of toleration, the regime also established means for dealing with Scots ministers unwilling to comply with the new order of ecclesiastical affairs. On 4 June the Commissioners for Visiting and Regulating Universities declared they would remove and replace ministers who were found to be scandalous in their lives or conversation.[95] This legislation forced Kirk ministers to adhere to the rules set forth by the new English regime or risk losing their stipends. Protesters labelled this an incursion upon the 'liberties and privileges of the Church of Christ' and denounced any intervention by secular authorities into the planting or deposing of ministers to be 'contrarie to the discipline and government of this church and the civile lawes of the land', which until such time as Scots law was overturned continued to be the law of the land.[96]

Public Disputes

A dilemma began to unfold for Scots ministers whose parishioners attended the English sermons on a regular basis. With religious toleration in place they could do little to oppose the sectarians other than attempt to discredit their theology, especially since church censures carried little weight and would only drive parishioners into the open arms of the English. When the English arrived, they had attempted to dispute with the Scots publicly, but this practice was rejected. Public disputing over religious truths was a foreign and undesired practice in Scotland. Yet with little other opportunity to confute their opponents and with the momentum of sectarian preaching swelling, individual ministers, and perhaps presbyteries, were eventually forced into the realisation that the choice to debate had to be seized in order to protect their congregations. There is some evidence to support the idea that presbyteries or synods may have sanctioned the participation of Scots ministers on these occasions. At a dispute between James Wood and the English chaplain James Brown in which the Englishman exasperated his opponent by his evasion of arguments, Brown asked if anyone else would take up the dispute. Andrew Hinniman (Honyman),[97] a minister from St. Andrews, stood up and replied that many in Scotland would as God's servants be willing to defend the truth, but not without a public calling from the Kirk.[98] On other occasions ministers seem to have taken part wholly of their own volition. Just as Hughes suggests that in England the orthodox clergy's participation in public religious disputes stemmed from a developing religious 'open market', in Scotland the weakening of church censures through toleration and the persistent preaching of English sectarians forced some Scottish ministers, likewise, to engage in disputation for the preservation of their parishioners.

The idea of publicly disputing doctrine to ascertain its truth in the presence of the laity was completely unheard of in Scotland's ecclesiastical experience. Since the Reformation, important issues of religion were worked out through being openly debated within the hierarchical structure of Presbyterianism: that is, in the presbyteries, synods and General Assemblies. Even under Episcopacy, during the first third of the seventeenth century, when controversial questions were discussed by those in prominent places, it occurred behind closed doors rather than as a public dispute in front of the general public.[99] Although common in England, Scotland's drastically different social situation made public disputes an unusual and somewhat impractical notion. Throughout the 1640s and 1650s an atmosphere of political tension and a widespread desire for radical change in both the structures of religion and government permeated England, wrought through civil war and religious upheaval. In that atmosphere of upheaval, public disputes represented a good way to kindle popular support in bustling urban England. Scotland, however, was not an urban nation like England, and people were far less interested in drastic political or religious change. In the words of H.R. Trevor-Roper, 'England and Scotland were poles apart'. England was wealthy, Scotland was poor; England was under going great changes, Scotland had already experienced its great 'religious revolution'.[100] This is not to deny that the Commonwealth's pleas for political and religious change greatly moved some Scots; however, such desires were not pervasive and remained unpronounced before the arrival of the English army. Yet there existed among the English a widespread belief that many Scots wanted to see change in political and religious structures.[101] Although a misinterpretation of the situation, this provided soldiers desiring public disputes a legitimate rationale for pursuing possible opponents among the Scottish clergy.

As a result, public disputes became part of the fabric of Scotland's life during the Interregnum. Several reports of disputations survive. The clergy of Glasgow, along with James Guthrie and Hugh Binning, held a private dispute with Cromwell and his chaplains in April 1651.[102] Wariston, the leading lay member of the Protester party, entertained two disputes with English ministers: the first with Thomas Smallwood and William Good over the legality of the invasion of Scotland in May 1651, and the second with Good in June over the covenant.[103] Numerous public disputes occurred between the Scots clergy and Quakers, including George Fox.[104] Some names can be given, while other disputants cannot be identified, yet contemporary sources attest that disputes occurred frequently. One English newspaper reported rather optimistically: 'The great and vehement disputes, causeth many of the presbyterian party to tremble, and many hundreds fall off from the old tyrannical way, and with great alacrity embrace the new light of freedom.'[105] Another identified the primary participants as 'ministers of regiments' and 'Scotch ministers', and further intimated the hopes of many English that the disputes 'may end to the discovery of the truth'.[106] These accounts not only relay the fact that they occurred, but also their regularity and purpose.

> There are many vehement and great disputes in Edinburgh, Glasgow, and several other places of eminency, touching Church-government, and the Doctrine and Discipline of these times. Our Ministers have entertained their challenges several times; and their pains have wrought so well, that hundreds forsake the old tyrannical Presbytery, and cleave to our party.[107]

Whether lay or ordained, John Nicoll declared, 'men war not aschamed to tak upone thame the functioun of the ministrie ... and [offer] publict disputes'.[108] The Fife diarist John Lamont reported that troops from Colonel Fairfax's regiment interrupted the church service at Pittenweem on Sunday 24 May 1653 and demanded that the minister dispute with them publicly. George Hamilton, the minister, cut his sermon short due to the ruckus, but the soldiers swore they would continue to pester him until 'he made good his promise ... to dispute with' them.[109]

James Brown, in particular, repeatedly sought public disputes wherever he went with the intention of winning popular support for his Baptist beliefs. While in Scotland he publicly disputed with Samuel Rutherford, James Wood (professor of theology at the University of St Andrews) and James Guthrie.[110] When Brown's dispute with Rutherford took place is uncertain, but his disputes with Wood and Guthrie are the best attested of any disputes in Interregnum Scotland.[111] A graduate of Oriel College, Oxford in 1638, Brown soon took the parish charge of Tenbury, Worcestershire. At an unspecified date he found himself convinced of the errors of the state church through a public dispute with a Baptist minister. Rejecting Episcopacy, he became 'through mercy a Preacher of the faith which once he destroyed'.[112] Probably due to this conversion experience Brown became an eager disputant. Eventually he joined the parliamentary army as a chaplain and in 1652 began serving Colonel Fairfax's regiment of foot soldiers, a regiment which gained a notorious reputation for disrupting ministers of the Kirk.[113] Brown had an active ministry in Scotland. According to the Baptist historian R.B. Hannen, Brown started preaching publicly in Cupar as soon as the regiment arrived, and numerous baptisms took place during their stay.[114] In September and October 1652 'the said Mr Browne did rebaptize severall of Coll. Fairfax foot regim[ent] in the water of Eden, near to Erdries lodging, by dipping them in the water over head and eares, many of the inhabitants looking on'.[115] During that first year in Fife a handful of Scots in and around Cupar also joined the Baptist fellowship. Three sisters named Elspet, Isobel and Christin Millar were all baptised in the River Eden.[116] In addition, when William Thomson, an English soldier, married Isobel Webster, a Scotswoman, James Brown officiated as minister.[117] Yet Brown did not limit his energies to ministry: he also sought to dispute with the indigenous clergy.

On 12 and 14 October 1652 Brown publicly disputed with James Wood in St Andrews over the doctrines of paedo-baptism, the severity of the Fall, and the nature of atonement. Two separate accounts survive. The English version, which appeared in several journals, reported no clear winner but relayed hopes that 'a good seed had been planted' through the advocacy of English doctrines.[118] The Scottish account, in contrast, spoke disparagingly of Brown's debating skills. His arguments were allegedly so poor that an English soldier stood up and declared that Brown seemed a little confused.[119] 'Mr. Wood had the far best of both dayes, bot Browne wold not be convinced,' wrote the eyewitness John Lamont.[120] In the summer of 1653, Colonel Fairfax's regiment moved from Fife to Stirling, which meant new ministers with whom Brown could dispute. He spoke with both ministers in Stirling, David Bennett and James Guthrie, but must have identified Guthrie as a more desirable opponent and began to pester him for a public dispute. Besides simply being the local minister, it is likely that Brown desired to dispute with Guthrie because he had become one of the foremost members of the Protester party. Brown's choice of opponents in Scotland shows he preferred high-profile opponents, perhaps because they might ensure a larger audience. Despite claims in the introduction to *Scripture-Redemption Freed* that he never instigated public disputations, the evidence contradicts this assertion. Brown wrote in his introduction:

> I never challenged any Minister of Christ to dispute, but once as I remember, and that was when I was a Parish-Priest and Minister of Antichrist (as many now are) and the Lord in mercy made that man an instrument to reveal to me the principles of the doctrine of Christ; and the beginnings of that blessed Gospel-light, which I now through grace walk in. I could wish that all the Parish-Ministers would seek to dispute with those they count Hereticks. (I mean such as walk in obedience to the commands of Christ) till they sped no worse then I did.[121]

In contrast to the first part of this statement, Brown enthusiastically endeavoured to procure public disputes. His own testimony expresses how life-changing such an encounter had been for him. It should not be surprising if he desired to provide the same revelatory experience for some other poor minister lost in an anti-Christian church. It was Brown, according to Guthrie, that requested their public dispute.[122] Likewise, after his dispute with James Wood it was Brown who essentially challenged all comers.[123] Although Hannen claims the presbytery of Cupar instigated the debate between Wood and Guthrie in 1652, there is no corroborating evidence to support his claim.[124] Overwhelmingly the data indicates Brown actively provoked the public disputes in which he participated during his stay in Scotland, a point supported by Guthrie's assertion to Brown: 'I have heard it to be your way in England, and have known it to be your way in Scotland to go about from place to place, provoking to publick disputs.'[125]

As the best documented dispute from beginning to end of any during this period, the contest between James Guthrie and James Brown serves as an excellent case study of the provocating circumstances, topics discussed and aftermath of a public religious dispute in Interregnum Scotland. Although Guthrie gives no express reasons for why he succumbed to Brown's challenges, the Scottish church historian Robert Wodrow reports episodes illustrating why Guthrie, as well as other ministers, might have acquiesced to requests for disputation: first, the regular interruption of Kirk services by English soldiers; and second, the drawing power of English preachers. English intrusions upon services represented an important issue across Scotland.[126] Besides the disruption at Pittenweem mentioned above, the presbytery of Peebles and Biggar complained on 26 May 1651 of bitter and violent intrusions:

> They have in many partes disturbed divyne worshippe, impeding our coming together, scattering us when we were mett, contradicting us in performing

of the worshippe of God; and some of us have been assaulted by them with charged pistolls and uther weapons when we were in pulpit and at our houses, and others of us have been caryed away in our persons and detained for a time. Neither hes their rage stinted here, nor are we so much troubled with their oppression against us, but that which breaks our hearts and exceeds all the rest (becaus done more immediatly against God) is their cruell mocking of his worshippe, constant profaneing his Sabboths, and ther horrid blasphemies of his holie name.[127]

Guthrie faced similar obstruction to his ministry. One Sabbath, while on his way to the Kirk, a mob of 'Sectarians' and 'Malignants' confronted him and physically prevented his passing. Unable to reach the Kirk he instead preached in his home.[128] Such an account explains why one of Guthrie's stipulations for agreeing to a dispute with Brown was that English soldiers cease harassing Stirling's ministers and interrupting divine worship.[129]

A second reason that Guthrie acquiesced to disputing with Brown was the risk sectarian preaching posed to his congregation. Guthrie and several other Protesters wrote to Cromwell in March 1653 about 'the English actings amongst us', seven months before his debate with Brown, complaining of the 'errours daylie vented in this land ... by some in the Army' and the intrusion of English soldiers into Scottish pulpits.[130] Yet in Guthrie's case the threat posed by this preaching struck exception-ally close to home in an incident involving Guthrie's friend and servant James Couie.[131] In all accounts James Couie served as a faithful friend and servant to Guthrie, even transcribing the final letters dictated by Guthrie from his prison cell in Edinburgh before his execution in 1660. Despite his loyal friendship, the following story provides an intriguing insight into the attraction of the English preachers and the struggle faced by the Scottish clergy to impede their success.

> James Couie went one evening and heard one of the Sectarie's Ministers preach in Stirling. Mr Guthrie missed James out of the house, and he very narrowly enquired where he had been? James did a while conceal where he was, but at length Mr Guthrie importuning him to tell, he at length told that he was hearing one of the English Ministers preach; at which Mr Guthrie seemed to be very displeased, and said, 'James, go not to Gilgal nor to Bethaven! Whatever these men be, they have nothing to do here!'[132]

Couie's sneaking out to hear English ministers preach must have shocked Guthrie into a realisation the Presbyterian influence in Scotland was not unassailable. In acquiescing to the persistent requests of James Brown for a debate, Guthrie probably hoped that his ministry would cease to be pestered and he could once and for all stop the preacher attempting to steal away converts from his congregation and from his own household!

The details of the dialogue between Brown and Guthrie survive through Guthrie's own meticulous record of both the dispute and the correspondence. No doubt this represents his own wish for the debate to be carried out in writing, in order that it might be made available to a wider audience. Two copies of his collection survive: one in Guthrie's own hand, and a copy made from the original by Robert Wodrow.[133] The question naturally arises: if all the records of the dialogue between Brown and Guthrie are the product of Guthrie, how reliable or non-partisan can they be, especially since Ann Hughes points out that the manner in which disputants published their own version of events served as a polemical form in itself.[134] Two basic points support the legitimacy of Guthrie's account. First, what survives is a long, consistent and chronological collection of all but three of the letters between the two men as well as a transcription of the debate (missing just two pages). In total the corpus comprises nearly 60,000 words. It seems very unlikely that Guthrie altered the letters, as they provide a nearly audible dialogue in which the authors respond to questions arising in previous letters. Hence, the only question-able material is to be found in the transcript of the debate itself. It is impossible to know whether Guthrie wrote it down from memory, or if he acquired it from someone who had taken it down at the time of the debate. In either case it brings us to the second point in support of the accuracy of Guthrie's account: the behaviour and theology of Brown recorded in his debate with Guthrie are consistent with the various accounts of his earlier dispute with James Wood and his own comments regarding a disputation with Rutherford.[135] Brown chose the same subjects for the debates and used very similar arguments.

Before the dispute Guthrie sought to ensure that it would proceed in an orderly fashion. He requested that Brown subscribe in writing to the orderly practices of proper academic disputing, including the use of syllo-gisms, argument based only on the strength of Scripture and reason, and a promise to 'forbear passions and reproachfull reviling expressions'.[136] Probably already aware of sectarian disputing in general through English writers like Thomas Edwards, Guthrie also seems to have already known about Brown in particular: 'I did desire you to forbear reproaches and revilings, because … I have heard of your manner.'[137] Additionally, he added the stipulation that neither Brown nor the troops under his care interrupt worship in any of Stirling's kirks. Although Brown agreed to the terms he did so with sarcasm:

> I shall endeavour to keep to the form of sound words in all our reasonings, not digressing from the point in hand: I shall by Gods grace wit meekness, love and holy zeal for God carry on our discourse none shall speak (by my consent) in relation to our reasoning but you and I … But that I should undertake that none shall ever do it is to require an impossibility; for I have but a short space to stay here 2dly: my time is not to be forever in this world: 3dly I cannot command mens consciences.[138]

Clearly Guthrie never intended Brown to ensure that no one would ever interrupt his ministry, and as such Brown's response seems somewhat acerbic. Yet this serves as an indication of the divergences that separated the two men's approaches to public disputing. Guthrie sought concise answers and definitions, while Brown tended to go to extremes. Guthrie disregarded the sarcastic response and reasserted his expectations for an orderly disputation, asking: 'Will [you] debate syllogistically, and without long rhetoricall discourses, yea or not?'[139] His repeated pressing for the proper use of syllogisms and arguments reaffirms that Guthrie had knowledge of Brown's past refusals to employ them. Besides awareness of his practice, Guthrie also prepared to confute Brown's theology by requesting a copy of the chaplain's recently published *Scripture-Redemption Freed from Men's Restrictions*.[140]

When the two men finally met at 10 o'clock on the morning of Friday, 21 October 1653, it immediately became apparent that Guthrie had been correct in his efforts to ensure the debate would have rules to prevent it from becoming a spectacle. From the outset, issues of procedure arose. Although the topics, order and structure of the day were arranged in advance, they began by disagreeing over which topic to address first. Guthrie expressed his intention to refute Brown's doctrine that Christ died for everyone. Brown disagreed, and the differences multiplied from there. When finally allowed to begin against universal atonement, Guthrie opened by stating 'whosoever is not given of the Father to Jesus Christ, these Jesus Christ did not dy for, But all men are not given of the Father to Jesus Christ: therefore Jesus Christ did not dy for all and every man'.[141] He made the traditional predestinarian argument: not everyone is elect, and Christ died only for the elect. Brown rejected this statement as unscriptural. The Scot made several attempts to explain the Scriptural foundation of his position, but Brown continued to oppose his rival's line of argument.

BROWN: I know no truth in Scripture by argument Sir I shall shou you Scripture for what I say, if you have no Scripture for it than nothing can be said.

GUTHRIE: Is this truth or falshood which I have said.

BROWN: I desire Scriptur = truth and no syllogisms.

GUTHRIE: The Lord Jesus Christ did use syllogisms himself; and if you speak against it you [sheu] yourself a[n] irrational man; according to the Scripture this is either truth or falshood I have said, your answers Sir I desire in the affirmative or in the negative.

BROWN: Friends mark a[n] irrational man he takes me to be.

GUTHRIE: What else can I take you to be if you will not grant the argument to be either truth or falsehood.

BROWN: Bring Scripture for what you say.

GUTHRIE: Sir I say Scripture sayed this, whom soever Christ dyed for are given to him of the Father.

BROWN: Scripture does not say so many words.

GUTHRIE: Does it say the thing it self?[142]

Guthrie maintained the traditional Calvinistic view that atonement was limited to the elect. Yet Brown refused to accept anything other than verbatim Scripture as proof. This led Guthrie to ask if his opponent would only accept truth if found in Scripture in 'so many letters, syllables and words'.[143] Although both men agreed before the dispute to use syllogisms as a way of proving their arguments, Brown flatly denied them on the day. Eventually Guthrie challenged him as to whether he accepted 'Scripture consequences'. Brown responded 'not in that nature', at which point Guthrie raised the question: if there is no Scripture in the New Testament giving a warrant for a Christian to be a magistrate or a soldier, then 'by Mr Browns divinity' there is no warrant under the New Testament for a Christian to be a soldier or a magistrate. 'I pray you where you and your powers are,' asked Guthrie. 'I put you to it before all whom you serve Mr Brown to answer.'[144] In reply, Brown accused Guthrie of changing the subject, but increasingly it became clear who was being evasive.

Repeatedly Brown turned from his opponent to the crowd gathered in Holy Trinity Church, at one point proclaiming in response to Guthrie's syllogism, 'ye that understand consider this falsity and deceit, it is nothing but Sophistry'.[145] On at least seven different occasions Brown turned to the crowd rather than answer his opponent's challenges. Often this resulted from Brown being dumbfounded by Guthrie. At times Brown seemed unable to see the full implications of his own theology. Guthrie, who proved to have a very sharp wit and a deeper understanding of Brown's theology than Brown did, on several occasions had to answer questions he had posed to his opponent when Brown proved unable to do so. When discussing atonement, Guthrie asked, based on Romans 8:32, whether God gives the saints 'all things' because of their belief, because they are members of the church, or whether it is because Christ died for them? Essentially Guthrie asked: who gets the inheritance bought through Christ's death and why? Brown could not satisfy Guthrie with an answer, because he could not differentiate between those various aspects of atonement within his theological construct. He believed in a sort of universal atonement in which Christ died to pay for the sins of the 'first covenant', or for Adam's sin but not for the rest of humanity's sins. However, Brown could not verbalise his position sufficiently adequately to engage Guthrie in a discussion of it. After asking the question eight times, Guthrie answered for Brown, explaining that the saints get all things because Christ died for them, and he did this because they are elect.[146] Later, when discussing the implications of universal atonement, Guthrie again silenced the Englishman. Brown argued that since Christ's death had freed humanity from any responsibility for original sin, people need only to repent of their own personal sins and cast them away. This did not sit well with the strongly Calvinist Guthrie and led him to ask to whom the 'word of reconciliation' should be preached. When pressed as to the ramifications of his doctrine and being unable to satisfy the Scotsman, Guthrie again spoke for Brown: 'Since you labour to argue instead of answering my argument I give you a clear answer thus, God is reconciled by the death of Christ in regard of purchase or price there being now a ransom laid down by which the justice of God is satisfied for the sins of the elect ... I pray all the hearers to consider the argument: If Christ died for all sins then the Gospel need not be preached to any.'[147] While Brown disagreed with this assertion, because he believed the Gospel taught that repentance was necessary in order to 'cast away' sin and be redeemed, he was unable to clarify his position.

The debate continued to pursue the nature of atonement. Guthrie pushed the point that only those who are given by the Father (the elect) are saved by the blood of the Son. It was evident from early in the debate that a fundamental chasm separated the two men's theologies. When faced with the predestinarian concept of God's giving the elect to Christ, Brown tried to skirt the issue by suggesting a twofold giving, the first being the giving of all of creation to Christ, the second being conditional on an individual's faith in Christ.[148] In Guthrie's estimation, this in no way hampered his argument. He believed that faith was given by the Father to the elect; therefore it did not matter if there was a twofold giving, because the second giving was still dependent on the Father. Hence, he perceived his proof to be sound. Eventually Brown had to define his understanding of the nature and scope of Christ's death and in so doing shocked Guthrie. According to Brown, Christ did not die to save anyone from spiritual death, but rather His death saved all of humanity from the temporal death caused by Adam's sin. One day, explained Brown, all of the dead will rise from the grave to be judged, not for the sin of Adam but for their own sins, which they will be personably responsible for, because according to Brown, 'all have so much means of grace as leaves them without excuse'.[149] He believed that those who repented of their sins would be saved and those who did not would be damned. Guthrie described this not only to be 'strange divinity' but declared it contrary to both Independents, such as Thomas Goodwin and John Cotton, and the doctrines of the Anabaptists. He called Brown's doctrine the 'grossest part and the very dregs of pelagianism ... condemned and exploded by all the Christian churches and contrary to the confessions of faith of all the protestant churches in the world'.[150] The implication of Brown's theology was clear to Guthrie: if Christ's death freed all humanity only from a mere temporal death brought about by Adam's sin, then Brown rejected the Reformed doctrines (e.g., Lutheran or Calvinist) of original sin, Predestination and maybe, most importantly to the Scottish mentality, covenant. It also diminished Christ's role in redemption and removed him completely from the salvation of the individual, since according to Brown salvation was dependent wholly on the repentance and casting off of one's own sins.

In an attempt to regain control of the debate, Brown returned to his original proposition that Christ died for all. The brunt of his argument laid on five Scriptures – Isaiah 53:6, 1 John 1:23, 1 Thes 2:6, 2 Cor 5:14–15 and Heb 2:9 – all of which he believed clearly stated that Christ died for all.[151] Brown must have momentarily felt confident, having presented what he felt were five solid verbatim portions of Scripture explicitly declaring that Christ died for 'all' or 'every man' or 'the world'. Guthrie coolly replied that the use of the term 'all' did not refer to every individual and that even the use of globalised terms such as 'the world' as it is used in John 6:33 refer only to the saints: 'For the bread of God is he who cometh down from heaven and gives life to the world.'[152] Brown protested and claimed that 2 Thes 2:10 supported his belief that those who perished did so because they wilfully refused to love the truth and so be saved. Guthrie discounted this use of the Scripture, explaining that those spoken of were damned not because they did not choose to love the truth but because they could not choose to love the truth.[153] Brown simply could not grasp double predestination, it being contrary to everything he held to be true. 'Sir … I do not judge it blasphemy,' stated Brown, 'to say that through Christ all men may have power or are inabled to believe.' And again later he asserted: 'I conceive if so be there is a spirit of wisdom in the hearers this day, they will need no proof of this, I beleive you cannot but see and know it is the duty of the creatures to do only so much as God enables them to do.'[154]

In a last effort to confute predestinarian election, Brown cited Heb 10:29: 'How much more severely do you think a man deserves to be punished who has trampled the Son of God under foot, who has treated as an unholy thing the blood of the Covenant that sanctified him, and who has insulted the Spirit of Grace?'[155] Essentially, the question he posed was how could Guthrie explain that only the elect are sanctified through the blood of Christ, if Paul states that some of those who are sanctified reject Christ? This probably, as W.I. Hoy suggests, represents Brown's strongest argument of the day.[156] However, Guthrie quickly countered the danger by explaining that those referred to in the verse were only sanctified externally, that is to say, they had not been fully sanctified. While they had made a public profession, they were not in fact actually elect. He used the example of Simon Magus, who professed outwardly to love Christ but inwardly remained a reprobate. This left Brown with little else to say but that Guthrie's gloss was 'exceeding[ly] dark … a dark gloss on a clear text'.[157]

Unable to establish his own views of universal atonement in the face of Guthrie's well-defended theology of predestination, Brown turned to the second issue of the day, the practice of infant baptism. In the tradition of covenant theology that shaped the thinking of the Church of Scotland, and in the tradition of the continental Reformers, Guthrie maintained that because circumcision had been the seal of God's covenant with the Jews, and because it had been extended to both those in covenant with God as well as their children, baptism, the sign of the new covenant, was available to all who are in covenant with God. Brown agreed with Guthrie that God was in covenant with children, and even infants. However, in the case of infants he argued that, since they were unable verbally to accept the covenant for themselves, God was in covenant with them but they were incapable of being in covenant with God. Bemused by this logic, Guthrie retorted 'an unheard of distinction … all these with whom God is in covenant … they are in covenant with Him', and he cited Deut 29:10–12 and Ezek 37:21 as proof that God was not only in covenant with the children of the Jews but also their children's children.[158] The debate ended with neither side giving any ground in their discussion of paedo-baptism, and with Guthrie charging 'I get nothing from you but words and strange divinity'.[159] Through the dispute it became increasingly apparent that the two men were fundamentally separated by their understandings of original sin, atonement, predestination, election and covenant.

Although Robert Wodrow's *Analecta* praises Guthrie's immense patience in disputing, James Brown clearly agitated the Scots minister.[160] What seems to have aggravated him most was Brown's inability to follow the rules of academic debate, declaring near the end of their dispute: 'Mr Brown you have printed you[r]self a fellow in Oxford; but surely you do not keep the laws of dispute!'[161] This accusation that Brown knew the rules of academic disputing but refused to use them validates Hughes' thesis that many educated 'radicals' rejected the use of an academic or 'orthodox' framework of disputing, rather than being unfamiliar with them. Guthrie closed the dispute by making it known to Brown and all in attendance that he felt his time had been wasted. In terms reminiscent of Baxter's complaint about Tombes, Guthrie told Brown: 'I perceive when [in] many thing[s] you are straited and knows not how to answer, you make diversions and turns you to your friends; Therefore the day being spent, and it now growing dark I leave you with your friends since I can get no clear satisfying answer from you to any thing that I propound.'[162] Despite Brown's best efforts at evasion and his attempts to engage the crowd, Guthrie maintained both his composure and control of the debate, and refused to give into his opponent's 'radical' approach.

Less than a week after their public dispute, Brown started hounding the Scots minister for a second dispute, alleging: 'I find that publick disputts are very profitable for the hearers … I desire that another day may be sett apart for the finishing of what was then begun' as well as the justification of national churches.[163] Guthrie was away in Edinburgh when the letter arrived at his house. Informed of Guthrie's whereabouts by the messenger, Brown sent a second letter to him in the capital. Upon returning from Edinburgh, just two days after the initial letter was sent, he informed

Brown that despite receiving two letters in less than twenty-four hours he held 'little or no inclination' for further public disputes, but inquired whether Brown continued in his 'former importunity concerning a new disput'. He expressed his utter bewilderment at both the intentions of Brown and the roots of his theology:

> I confess that to me it is unknown what you mean or intend by such impor-
> tunat and frequent provocations for venting such strang and uncouth opinions
> which are contrary to the whole tenor and current of the Scriptures, and to the
> judgment of all sound divines in all ages, yea, many of them to the judgment
> not only to the congregationall divines in old and new England but also to the
> confession of the faith of many of the Anabaptists churches.[164]

Brown explained that his desire for a second 'fuller conference' stemmed wholly from a desire to 'advance the glory of the Lord in the manifesta-tion of truth either by you or me no humble sober heart was ever a loser by free and fair reasoning out of the Scriptures'.[165] To this request Guthrie offered five reasons why a second public dispute was unwarranted: first, Brown held 'many uncouth and strange opinions contrary to the tenor of the Scriptures'; second, 'indifferent men' may be led astray by Brown's heretical teachings; third, the English chaplain deferred to the crowd in the previous dispute rather than answering his inquiries; fourth, he failed to allow the Scripture consequences he had promised to; fifth and finally, Brown's reputation preceded him as one who goes 'from place to place, provoking to publick disputs'.[166] Yet in spite of these good reasons not to enter into a second debate, Guthrie left the possibility open by offering his opponent four conditions that might clear the way for a further dispute. Guthrie demanded that Brown provide in writing: first, a scriptural defence of his position on original sin and magistrates restraining heretics; second, evidence that the officers and soldiers of the English garrison actually desired a second dispute in order to prove that others than Brown alone desired it; third, an agreement for allowing argument by Scripture consequences and acknowledgement that divine truth could be proven by clear deductions and inferences from Scripture; and fourth, an assurance that Brown would not evade questions or engage in long discourses which tended to 'darken a disput'.[167] Only on completion of all four conditions would the Scots minister even consider a second conference.

Continuing in his usual manner, Brown's response did little to appease his would-be opponent. Replying on the same day (31 October) that he received Guthrie's conditions, he showed no signs of wishing to change his former ways. 'Surely if I maintain any corrupt doctrine,' wrote Brown, 'if you were a minister of the Lord Jesus you should take every opportu-nity to oppose me in my publick exercises knowing that I give liberty to all men to ask a reason of any thing that I deliver, I should willingly so deal with you if you were free to it, but knowing you are unfree to such debates I have endeavoured to prevail with you for a fixed conference.'[168]

He arrogantly ended the letter 'in your next I desire your positive answer whether you disput or not? and what day it shall be' after only paying lip service to Guthrie's required conditions.[169] Hardly a humble response from the man requesting a second debate.

Yet again Guthrie, reputed for his patience, was pushed beyond his ability to restrain himself. 'My soul is weary of your importunity,' he wrote. 'It is not from any fear either of you[r] strength, or jealousie that ... I have not hitherto condescended to allow you any more publick dispute; indifferent men who were wittnesses to our last debate, and I suspect your own conscience also, doth bear record that I have no cause to decline it upon that accompt.'[170] He explained that being a minister of Jesus Christ did not necessarily entail debating the corrupt doctrine of another in public. In response to the doctrine that Brown put forward, Guthrie made it clear that he saw nothing new in it:

> Mr. Brown I again desire to tell you that your opinions are the very dregs and grossest part of Pelagianisme, Popery and Armenianisme[171] and that Pellagius, [Robert] Bellar[mine] and Armenius did plead these causes much more strongly than you do, and that the arguments of your book are but little of their stuff borrowed from them and published in a worse frame, and therefore they be errors I do see little advantage in debating with you for refutations of them because you bring nothing for strengthening thereof but what hath been abundantly refused already.

Despite all these reasons not to give Brown his much-desired second debate, he offered his would-be opponent one final chance. In a letter dated 2 November, Guthrie stated he would entertain a second encounter over the issue of paedo-baptism (or 'baby sprinkling' as Brown called it) on two conditions: first, that Brown submitted in writing to following the 'ordinary known received rules of disputation'; and second, that referees be appointed to officiate the dispute and keep it on track. Guthrie even went so far as to suggest two Englishmen to serve as the referees, Major John Cloberry, the commander of the garrison at Stirling, and Samuel Bryan, a minister associated with the garrison in Stirling. It is up to the judges, he wrote, to 'prescrib to us both that method and ways of arguing which we shall be obliged to follow'.[172] After making these immense concessions for a dispute that he claimed little desire to take part in, Guthrie understandably added the ultimatum, 'which if you do refuse I beseech you to be silent and trouble me no more'.[173]

Up to this point the lines of communication remained open, but from here they took a turn for the worse and were irreconcilably damaged. Rather than accepting this beneficial set of conditions, Brown rejected the need for referees, arguing he had always agreed to follow the rules of proper academic debating and so the services of Major Cloberry and Mr Bryan were not required. He then made the ill-advised mistake of claiming that Cloberry and Bryan judged being named as referees without their prior consent 'a kind of an affront'.[174] Guthrie immediately sent letters to both men enquiring whether they had taken offence at their nomination, and to guage whether the troops of the garrison were even interested in a second dispute. Major Cloberry professed to have been accused of a 'gross disingenuity' by Brown's accusation. Far from being insulted, he praised Guthrie for his compromise, claiming never to have met 'with greater ingenuity and candor' than the Scots minister had shown by putting his trust in them. Samuel Bryan, likewise, denied any insult in being nominated and further attested that he and the Major were impressed with the self-denial of Guthrie in asking Englishmen to be judges when 'the antagonist' was 'our friend, acquaintance, countreyman and member of the army'.[175] It also came to light that besides falsely putting words into the mouth of the garrison commander, Brown had seemingly exaggerated the interest within his regiment for further disputes. Cloberry told Guthrie he had heard little discussion among his troops about a further dispute.

Contrary to Brown's avowal of adherence to rules of academic disputing, both Major Cloberry and Samuel Bryan questioned the value of the first encounter. Unless a subsequent dispute be 'orderly and methodicall', wrote Bryan, it would once again be time 'vainly spent'. With regards to prescribing a rule for a second dispute, Major Cloberry explained that both he and Bryan were wary of the task, being ignorant of how a legitimate disputation could take place without the allowance of logical arguments. Bryan also assured Guthrie that if a second dispute did come about both he and Major Cloberry would perform faithfully in the trust Guthrie placed in them and act as just referees, 'if Mr Brown will not wave or decline the way of arguing by consequences methodically digested unto syllogisms according to the known and common law of disputation'.[176]

Armed with letters from the commander and the minister, Guthrie wasted no time in letting Brown know that he had been caught out as a liar on two counts. It was Brown's false accusations that insulted the two men rather than Guthrie's gracious suggestion that they would be suitable judges. In addition, he informed Brown of the lack of truth in his claims that many English soldiers desired to attend a second dispute. In the light of these two fabrications, Guthrie resolutely refused to take part in any further public disputes with Brown, leaving the English chaplain with only one option. Any further discourse would have to be in writing in order for it to be published for the 'view and judgement of others'.[177] Rather than being apologetic, Brown responded in his typically barbed manner: 'I am sure that some others with my self were more than confident that you never intended another publick disput.'[178] Unwilling to accept that opportunity had slipped past him, he even offered to submit a list of officers who wished to observe further disputes, but Brown had missed his chance. There would be no futher public disputes between them. In response to Brown's arrogant letter, Guthrie lost his patience for the third time:

You may have confidence more then enough that you do great things in disput and I have heard of your boasting ... . If you can be entreated to do yourself so much favour as to enquire and hearken to the judgment of discerning and unbyassed men you'll happily hear that in publick disput you have often been put to silence and shame and brought to such straits that you could neither grant nor deny nor distinguish and have been forced to run upon contradictions not only to the truth but even to your self and have shewn such weekness *as even your own friends have been ashamed of you* ... It is not from any thing I have found or do fear of your strength or the strength of your cause that I shun more publick disput with you and therfore be not puffed up in mind ... *many able and gracious men, ministers and Professors of the Gospell in several parts of the land, do not judge you worthy to be disputed with in such away as you call for*; which I speak not for preferring of my self nor vilifying of your person, but to give you an ingenuous account of the things that makes me so little inclinable to hearken to your desire and to convince you (if possibly) of the error of your way.[179]

Despite the disappointment of being denied a second public dispute, Brown agreed to carry on in correspondence if Guthrie would prepare a written defence of paedo-baptism. Guthrie produced a treatise of nearly 10,000 words. Although Brown had been transferred to Burntisland Guthrie still expected a response, since the two had agreed to continue their discourse via letters, but he never received one. Instead, the dialogue sputtered out. Brown's failure to provide an adequate response suggests that he had little interest in discourse, only in gathering an audience.

Guthrie's successful dispute with Brown and his management of Brown's subsequent requests for a further dispute may be attributed to three factors. First and foremost, Brown could not employ the 'radical' tactics, described by Edwards and mentioned by Hughes, available to his counterparts in England. It would have been impossible for Brown's supporters from the regiment to infiltrate the meeting posing as Scots and shout down Guthrie, as Collier's followers had done to his opponents in England, or to act out a mass conversion. In relation to the bustling streets of London, Stirling was a small place and strangers were quickly recognised. Had Brown's followers attempted any disruptive antics they would only have served to undermine his efforts by depicting the English, at least in the eyes of reserved Presbyterians, as brash hooligans rather than pious Christians interested in conferring over the truths of the Christian faith. This meant that Brown received no support from the crowd to distract or shout down his opponent. In turning to the crowd, Brown found no relief from Guthrie's probing questions. The second factor aiding Guthrie's success was the unsuitability of public disputation as a means of winning over the populace of Scotland. Scotland lacked England's intense atmosphere of revolution and radical religious change. The vast majority of Scotland's populace held no resentment for the religious form of their national church. Certainly, tensions between Protesters and Resolutioners

ran high, but the value of Presbyterianism as a viable form of ecclesiastical government was not the issue.[180] Most Scots did not perceive the
Kirk as being overly intellectualised, nor did they view the predestinarian Calvinism as oppressive. Those who attended the dispute between
Guthrie and Brown did so out of curiosity rather than out of a yearning
for religious liberation or change. In essence, the lack of a revolutionary
atmosphere at these disputes neutered the tactics of the English 'radicals'.
For this reason, the strategies developed by the radical groups that formed
in England in the 1640s were ill suited to wooing the Scottish people. Both
of these first two factors significantly aided the third: Guthrie's ability
to manage the direction of the dispute. Guthrie initiated the topics and
unrelentingly kept his opponent to the questions at hand. Guthrie never
allowed Brown to stray, while his questions continually put Brown to the
test. Being in a position to keep a tight reign on the dispute, combined
with Brown's radical ploys being neutralised, the Scots clergyman easily
refuted his opponent's theology.

What this case study seems to suggest – and this may have been the
pattern across Scotland – is that the ability of English preachers attracted
curious Scots to hear them lecture. Initially the Scots clergy would have had
little need or desire to enter into public disputes with the English, despite
the continual prompting of the English chaplains and soldiers. However,
as the Scots clergy saw the threat of sectarian preaching increase, particularly after the imposition of toleration in February 1652, they weighed up
the threat and decided that taking part in disputes might be necessary to
curb the threat. Guthrie's experience of his close friend and servant James
Couie attending the sermons of an English preacher must have been a
startling revelation. Warnings alone did not seem to impede attendance
at English sermons. Coupled with the need to put an end to the English
disruption of Kirk services, the risks were weighed up and participation
in public disputes was deemed necessary. Fortunately for the Scots, when
they entered into disputes with 'sectaries' in Scotland they were on home
soil. Their English opponents, unable to employ radical and distracting
tactics, faced the prospect of being locked into an unavoidably academic
dispute. In this situation, with an audience largely curious rather than
revolutionary, they failed to sway the masses. While English preaching
may have been magnetic, attempts to proselytise through disputes were
thwarted by tenacious and well-educated Scots clergy. Perhaps the efforts
of men like James Brown might have been more effective if they had stuck
to public preaching rather than picking oratorical fights with opponents
who outmatched them in the intellectual arenas in which these disputes
took place.

While many individuals within the English forces were motivated to be
missionaries for their own religious groups, the incident between Guthrie
and Brown suggests that the Commonwealth regime did not support the

promotion of particular doctrines, only the promotion of toleration and the right of autonomously gathered congregations to form and govern themselves. Evidence for a policy of maintaining moderation in religion is supported by the sermons chosen for publication in Scotland by the English regime, and also by Whitelocke's report dating from July 1652 that 'the independents endeavour to settle a freedom there from the tyranny of the presbyterian classes and prelatical high commissioners, not excluding moderate dissenters from church government from a share in the advantages of government'.[181] The English regime sought to facilitate an alternative to a national church that enforced conformity or 'formality', just as they had in the previous decade in England.[182]

Some Englishmen, however, like Brown, used the opportunity of a public dispute to promote their own views rather than promoting the Congregationalism advocated in the sermons of Owen and Lockyer. This may explain why Brown's superior, Major Cloberry, when given the opportunity to support a second dispute between the two ministers, chose not to encourage it. Perhaps he recognised that slight profit had come from the first dispute in contrast to the positive response towards English preaching. The promotion of toleration and the gathering of congregations remained the regime's primary interest, not the spreading of particular doctrines. This perspective seems to have been dominant within Cloberry's regiment, which C.H. Firth praised for its non-partisan stance and ability to avoid becoming embroiled in the doctrines of radical sects like the Quakers or Levellers.[183] Instead, they supported the position of Cromwell and other moderate Independents in the government, that toleration was necessary for a successful and stable union.[184] A public dispute over paedo-baptism, atonement or even predestination did little to establish the toleration necessary for an adequate union of Christian nations. The only dispute in which there is record of a key member of the English regime participating occurred between Cromwell, his chaplains and the Scots clergy of Glasgow. On this occasion they did not debate doctrine or practice, but whether the invasion of Scotland had been a violation of the Solemn League and Covenant.[185] Cromwell advocated that the Solemn League and Covenant had not been broken in the English invasion of Scotland, because it had already been nullified by Scotland's invasion of England in 1648. Furthermore, he argued that the covenant which had bound both nations did not exclude all Protestant forms other than Presbyterianism. For Cromwell and his fellow members of the Commonwealth government, the religious questions to be discussed with Scotland's clergy were not those regarding baptism or atonement, but rather the unity of Protestant Christians through the toleration of differing doctrines.

Contrary to claims that the English occupation intended to make little religious impact on Scotland, this chapter has demonstrated the evangelical intentions of the soldiers and chaplains to advocate their personal religious ideologies. Moreover, the regime maintained a policy of supporting their endeavours as long as they served to advance the core ideologies of independently gathered congregations and toleration. While this chapter has dealt primarily with the endeavours of individuals to promote their own doctrines among the Scots, and the regime's support of these activities, the following chapter will focus on an aspect of Commonwealth/Protectorate policy that provides a clear indication of the regime's changing strategy regarding religion: the use of the printing press in Interregnum Scotland.

3   *The Dead-Man's Testament* and *A Litle Stone*

The Commonwealth's Campaign against the Scottish Presbytery[1]

What the wise observing King uttered long agoe, that of making of Books there is no end, was never more verified in any then it is in the present age wherein, *scribunt docti indoctique*, every smatterer and every fancie-full head must have the Presse travel to bring forth their froathy conceptions: And Presses by many are made use of as engines to discharge revylings, reproaches, and blasphemies against the God of Heaven, his blessed Truths, wayes and Ordinances.[2]

James Wood, 1654

One of the most indicative forms of evidence to support the Common-wealth's true intentions regarding the Kirk is its use of the printing press in Scotland. It has been argued that England's government during the Interregnum was rather impotent in its control of English printing presses. Despite the passage of strict laws to regulate printing by the Common-wealth, printers were largely left alone as long as they did not rant against the government or print blatant heresy.[3] While complaints of leniency in controlling the press in England may have rung true, especially to London's Presbyterian printers, in Scotland the English mastery of the presses created a very different situation. There can be no doubt over who controlled what was printed during the Interregnum in Scotland, particularly in the early years. After the English entered Edinburgh on 7 September 1650, they quickly seized control of the capital's presses, and only one of the city's three major printing houses continued to operate.[4] Although the regime did not impose strict laws regulating the presses of Scotland as it had in England, the martial nature of its rule enabled it to maintain strict control over Scotland's small number of presses with little difficulty. During the Interregnum, authority to print rested entirely with the English army. As A.J. Mann describes it, 'put most simply "*cum privi-legio*" replaced "*cum privilegio regali*".'[5]

Throughout the Interregnum the English-controlled presses of Scotland produced declarations and newsbooks for the benefit of the regime. In addition they also produced various forms of polemics aimed against the opposition. While a handful of tracts were produced against monarchical government and the person of the king, the vast majority of polemical works continued to be aimed at the Scottish presbytery. According to Frances Dow, the Kirk, with its strict interpretations of the Covenant, although internally divided, represented the greatest sustained opposition to the plans of the 'sectarian' presence in Scotland.[6] But even more importantly, the Kirk represented the greatest sustained opposition to the religious toleration and pattern of government fundamental to the Commonwealth. This ideological opposition to a republican state that promulgated the practice of sectarian religion was magnified by the Kirk's unquenchable desire to interfere in English affairs. In this respect, H.R. Trevor-Roper was largely correct when he explained the occupation of Scotland by the English as a reactionary endeavour by which the 'new English Revolution' imposed itself upon Scotland as a counter-action to the continued pressing of the 'old Scottish revolution' (Presbyterianism) upon England.[7] Dow similarly interprets the long-term aim of England's policy as safeguarding 'the revolution in England by exporting some elements of it into Scotland'.[8] Since many Englishmen believed the stability of their regime to be forged in religious ideology, the intolerant presbytery continued to be the Commonwealth's primary opponent. For this reason the English regime used Scotland's own printing presses to produce propaganda for undermining Presbyterianism and for promoting gathered churches in its place. The initial works of propaganda were fairly subtle: the regime did not attack the Kirk overtly, but rather the degree of reformation that had taken place in Scotland. By the second year of the occupation some papers were so officiously anti-Presbyterian that the Protester party complained to Cromwell: 'By many, severall pamphlets are printed and vented full of scorne and reproaches, not only against the whole Ministrie, but against sundrie of the ordinances of God.'[9] And again in 1653: 'Wee read and hear many things that are industriously printed and spread for loosing the bond of the covenant or placing the performance of the articles thereof in things that to our best understanding are contrarie unto and destructive of the dueties contained therein.'[10]

Before Cromwell entered Scotland in July 1650 he had already established that the printing press would be an important tool in his campaign, and its importance did not diminish during the occupation. From the outset printed material produced in Scotland served as a primary channel through which the English regime communicated with the populace. Immediately upon his arrival in Edinburgh (7 September 1650), in an endeavour to ingratiate himself with the residents, Cromwell produced a printed declaration granting protection for anyone who wished to bring goods to market.[11] Permission for markets to take place was welcome news to the residents of Edinburgh, who had complained early in August that food, drink and other provisions were so scarce they could hardly be purchased, and when they could be found prices had risen to twice their normal rates.[12] Cromwell almost certainly printed his declaration on the

Edinburgh press of Evan Tyler, the king's printer in Scotland. Although Cromwell had a portable press in his military train, he had already shown that when available he preferred to use a permanent press: it was faster, more efficient and produced better-quality text. But how could Cromwell have had access to the king's printing press in Edinburgh on the very day that he arrived in the city? While the English forces were in Newcastle, they had persuaded the 'unbending Royalist' Stephen Bulkley to print the *Declaration of the Army of England, Upon their March into Scotland.* In Scotland, however, the use of Evan Tyler's press did not represent the one-off production of a single document but the beginning of a decade-long English ascendancy over Scotland's presses.

In 1647 the London Stationers Company purchased both Evan Tyler's Edinburgh printing house and his patent as the king's printer in Scotland that had been granted to him in 1641. They made the purchase to stop cheap offprints inundating the English market, which Tyler had been able to produce under his charter. By 1650 an Englishman named John Twyn resided in Edinburgh and ran the print house along with seven English servants, but the stationers kept the imprint of Evan Tyler. David Stevenson identified the value of a London-based printing cooperative maintaining the imprint of 'Evan Tyler' from 1647 into the Interregnum:

> At a time when relations between the kingdoms were frequently strained and sometimes led to war, for the (London Stationers') Company to have advertised through its imprint its ownership of the Scottish state printer could have led in Scotland to demands for a Scottish take-over, and in England demands that the Company stop its Scottish branch printing anti-English propaganda. The problems of the multi-national company in times of international tension are nothing new![13]

It is because the printers working under the name of Evan Tyler were English and employed by the London Stationers Company that such a seamless transition occurred in September 1650 between the printing of Scottish propaganda and English propaganda. Stevenson notes that this must have been a relief to the English printers working there.[14] An entry in the Calendar of State Papers records the English control of the press and notes a lack of desire for using it to produce anything for the English market.[15] Instead the regime continued to use the press purely for producing texts for distribution in Scotland. The centrality of the press in English plans is evidenced by the relocation of the press to the heavily garrisoned town of Leith sometime before mid-March 1651. Effectively this moved the press into the heart of the Commonwealth's regime: Leith would become the largest of England's citadels in Scotland and an important hub from which Interregnum government in Scotland operated. Within months the press started printing Scotland's first multi-issue newspaper entitled *Mercurius Scoticus* (produced from 22 July 1651 to 13 January 1652), to satiate the desires of 'many Forreigne expectants eyes' and the English soldiers in Scotland who desired to be kept abreast of news from England and Ireland.[16] The English regime's intention to use the printing press as a chief means of communication, coupled with the willing compliance of Scotland's greatest printing press, enabled the new English regime to print at its leisure.

During the first month of the English occupation of Edinburgh, Evan Tyler's press produced three works, all of which favoured the cause of the Commonwealth and set the tone for the Commonwealth's early use of propaganda: first, befriend Scotland's poor; second, vilify the king; and most importantly, third, undermine the Kirk. The first work published in Edinburgh has already been mentioned: Cromwell's declaration allowing much-needed markets to take place in the capital. Second, the regime reprinted *The King of Scotlands Negociations at Rome for Assistance Against the Common-Wealth of England* intended to alienate the 'papist' Charles II from the fervent Presbyterians who supported the covenants' position on monarchy.[17] This edition included the text from the earlier version printed in London as well as some additional letters between the lord chancellor of Scotland and the king taken at Dunbar. Even in these polemics against monarchy, religion prevailed as a fundamental reason for opposing Charles II. The third of these early publications was *Several Letters and Passages*, comprising correspondence between Cromwell and Walter Dundas, the governor of Edinburgh Castle. Already discussed in chapter 2, these letters focus on the differences between Presbyterian and Independent thinking over the interpretation of providence, the liberty of Christians, the right of laymen to preach and the continuing process of reformation. The letters served as a forerunner of the bulk of the Commonwealth's propaganda that would follow.

External Calls for Reform

In the closing months of 1650 Tyler's press produced general reports of news pertaining to the Commonwealth, proclamations by the government and polemics aimed at the established Presbyterian status quo: questioning the degree of reformation in Scotland and the prevailing form of church government. The republication of William Dell's sermon preached before the parliament in 1646 and entitled *Right Reformation* fits into this last category. The work pleads for the internal nature of 'Gospel Reformation' which is contrasted against simple 'Civil-Ecclesiastical Reformation'.[18] Although written four years earlier for an English audience, its reproduction in a Scottish setting implied that Scotland's Reformation merely occurred in the structure, hierarchy and liturgy of the Kirk rather than in the hearts of the people. In contrast to a superficial reformation forcefully imposed by men, true inward Gospel reformation, explained Dell, is brought about by Christ (the only true reformer) and must be peaceful, because the Gospel is peaceful. This represented a great complaint that

Independents had against the presbytery. For English Independents, civil magistrates have no place in imposing reformation or religious conformity upon individuals, because reformation does not come from human will but rather from the will of God.[19] Proper reformation begins in the Word and produces changes in the heart, unlike civil-ecclesiastical reformation, which is an imposed reformation and 'reforms by breathing out threatnings, punishments, prisons, fire, and death'.[20] While civil-ecclesiastical reformation initially makes a 'great noise and tumult', it eventually cools 'and after lies as still as a stone'.[21] The differentiation between 'Right reformation' and 'Civil-Ecclesiastical reformation', presented in the contemporary context of Scotland's occupation by a sectarian army, could not be viewed by the Kirk as encouraging to their position. Without ever mentioning the Kirk directly, the message of the work in its new publication was clear: the English regime sought the promotion of further religious change that it hoped would carry those receptive in Scotland beyond both Presbyterianism and an intolerant state church. From the Kirk's perspective, the publication of the work on a Scottish press did not bode well for the future use of Scotland's printing presses.

In late November or early December 1650 another work with similar intentions emerged from Tyler's press.[22] John Owen's *The Branch of the Lord* (already discussed in chapter 2) comprised a compilation of two sermons preached by the English chaplain at Berwick-upon-Tweed and Edinburgh. He dedicated the published work to Cromwell, whose solitary intention in these 'great under-takings' was, according to Owen, the gathering together and unifying of God's elect. Now indistinguishable from each other, the sermons professed Jesus Christ as the sole owner, builder, inhabitant, watchman and avenger of the Church. Christ alone could perform these functions and only the elect were chosen to be the building material of the church: 'dead stones' turned into the 'children of Abraham'.[23] Intended 'to poure out a savour of the Gospel upon the Sons of Peace' in Scotland, the sermons actually called for the elect in the country to abandon their assemblies 'resting on outward Church privileges' and made up of 'dead rubbish' and gather into a 'spiritual Estate where men are living stones'.[24] Once again the Kirk was not attacked overtly, but Owen challenged the composition of a church that included the profane masses, and proposed further reform beyond the outward forms that inhibited the proper gathering of Christ's church in Scotland.

By early 1651 the English began to take a more subversive approach to the Church of Scotland. Part of this process was to help facilitate the Protester–Resolutioner division within the Kirk. When the English took Edinburgh, the Resolutioner-controlled commissioners of the General Assembly withdrew to Aberdeen, where they printed their works on the press of James Brown. This gave one party of the Kirk a voice in print, but not the other. The English took the stance that allowing the factions within the Kirk to 'vent their spleen on one another', as Frances Dow explains, served to weaken the Kirk as a whole.[25] As a result, the English regime printed Protester works in order to foster the divisions within the Kirk. These works made up the bulk of the corpus relating to the Kirk produced by Tyler's press during 1651. However, after the battle of Worcester on 3 September 1651, the threat posed by Charles II diminished significantly, leaving the Kirk unrivalled as the single greatest enemy of the Commonwealth in Scotland. The regime stopped its tacit support of the Protesters and levelled its attacks at all strands of the Kirk.

Mysterious Voices from Within

After Charles II's flight to the continent, the Kirk remained uncontested as the prime obstacle to the regime's plans. The Presbyterian stranglehold on Scottish religion and the Kirk's railing against compliance with the English prompted some Englishmen to call for the complete removal of the Presbyterian hierarchy.

> The truth is, *if you give them an Inch, they will take an Ell*, and be like Thorns in your sides, when you think to have more quiet and security. Therefore, you must demolish the whole structure of that Hierarchy if you will bee at rest: For, the Assembly leads the Classes; the Classes the Parochial Priests, and these all (more or less) lead the Common people by the nose upon any expedition; so that if the State shall have need to levy men, little will be done, upon any occasion, without the consent of the Soveraign Kirk Authority.[26]

As a means of combating this threat, and with absolute control of all of Scotland's presses, the English printed a series of works either written by Scots or penned in a manner to give the impression that they were written by Scots, contesting the covenanted status of both the Kirk and the kingdom of Scotland. These works are extremely important for two reasons. First, they indicate a growing discontent within Scotland towards the aims and means of a national covenant so bound up with maintaining a Presbyterian church. Second, they demonstrate an English desire to foster these feelings by using the mechanism of propaganda in order to diminish the threat of Scotland's intrusive national Kirk.

A Word of Advertisement & Advice to the Godly in Scotland was among the first of these papers. The original Edinburgh edition simply identified the author as 'A Scotch man ... a cordiall wel-wisher to the interest of the godly in Scotland, both in civils and spirituals', but the preface to the later London edition provides additional information about the author and the purpose of reprinting it in England.[27] The preface explains that Cromwell sent the paper to the printers in London along with a letter instructing them to reproduce the work so that those 'that truly fear God' and who continued to be unsatisfied with the war in Scotland might be persuaded of its just nature. The paper's power for swaying public opinion rested in Cromwell's claims that the author, who pleaded for a union between the godly in both countries, 'was lately one of the Committee of Estates in Scotland, and at the first entrance of our Army a Lieutenant Colonel against us'.[28] Who exactly wrote the work is uncertain. If Cromwell's description of the author as being both a lieutenant-colonel and a member of the Committee of Estates is correct, it could have been any one of seventeen different men who held both positions.[29]

The work represents a significant shift in English polemical tactics. Unlike previous works of propaganda written by Englishmen, or Scots advocating a particular strain of Presbyterianism, this document represents an appeal from a Scotsman to his fellow Scots urging them to cast off their misconceptions of the covenants, to recognise the malignant intentions of those in positions of influence, and to seek Christian unity with the godly in England. For the author, Scotland falsely believes that overturning Episcopacy and reinstating the presbytery is the penultimate fulfilment of God's will. However, the greatest threat to God's people is never open enemies who are easily identifiable, but rather internal enemies: profane men who detest the godly and godliness. As an example, he cites the actions of the Kirk Party in 1648 who preached against the 'Sectarians' in England, but then welcomed their assistance when the opportunity arose for a *coup d'état* against the established 'malignant' government of Scotland.[30] Once their own aims were achieved and the English withdrew from Scotland 'there was nothing almost to be heard in Pulpits but the Army of Sectaries, the persideous Murtherers, filthy Dreamers, Contemners of Authority, Razers of the foundations of Government, Alterers thereof contrary to the Covenant, and therefore perfidious Covenant-breakers'.[31] As a result, the author claims that their actions were carried out 'under the pretence of good Patriots', making it evident that 'their interest is worldly, and not Spirituall, and hath the Mark of the Beast upon it'.[32] Yet far from intending to justify the actions of the English, the author endeavours to show how those in power in Scotland created division between the godly in both countries in order to satiate their own personal greed. It was this hypocritical manipulation of the covenants to advance a hidden agenda that brought heightened tensions and mistrust between the two countries, and ultimately war.[33]

In addition, the author entreats the people of Scotland to take notice of two things: first, the source of their contempt for England's 'sects'; and second, the actions taken by Scotland's church and government that made Cromwell's invasion unavoidable. Rather than denounce the godly in England based merely upon the slander of the Kirk, he pleads for the Scottish people to take notice of the deception and liberate themselves from ignorance:

> [The Kirk's] naming all the English Army Sectaries and Blasphemous, without exceptions, Enemies to the People of God and to godliness, Their bitter way of expressing of this, without ... refuting their Error, or shewing what they held,

their laboring to wrest every thing to the worst sence ... yet I appeal to one and all of you, if their hath not been, and is such a spirit even amongst you, that you could not, nor cannot bear any thing differeing from your own opinion (or rather the opinion of the Kirk) whether in Doctrine, Discipline, or the business of the time, notwithstanding the most of you ... could not give a reason for what you held or practised, especially in these things relating to the times, but were implicitly led by other men's judgements, which is your reproach, your sin and your snare this day.[34]

While not excusing the English invasion, the author points out that the Scots had several opportunities to prevent it. Scotland's refusal to sign a treaty with the Commonwealth, its continual treating with the king (and proclamation of Charles II as king of Great Britain and Ireland) and its own invasion of England in 1648 for the advancement of Presbyterianism all played their part in bringing about the invasion.[35] All three actions were taken in the interest of covenant and promulgated by the Kirk.

Finally, there is an appeal for his fellow Scots to look beyond their present suffering and recognise the great work that God had begun in bringing the godly in both nations together. Although it might seem that the godliest in Scotland suffered the most during the invasion, God's providence works in inexplicable ways. 'Perhaps,' he explains, 'the Lords designe is to make each of you usefull in convincing one another in the extreams that either of you (it may be) hath been inclining to ... Sure I am it is the Designe of God, to have his People one, & to cause them follow him together with one heart.'[36] Rather than a trial or a punishment for some failure in keeping the Covenant, *A Word of Advertisement* urges fellow Scots to consider the possibility that the present situation might instead be God's way of bringing together His people in the two nations for them to correct each other's excesses and errors, thereby promoting the kingdom of God over and above the kingdoms of the world.

In late November 1651 Evan Tyler's Leith-based press printed the most dubious of the English polemics against the Kirk and the second by a Scottish author. As its title suggests, *The Dead-Man's Testament* was the posthumous publication of a letter written by a poor, blind 'sometimes inhabitant of Leith' named Thomas Wood.[37] Prefixed to the work is a letter from the lieutenant-governor of Leith verifying the Commonwealth's approval of its publication:

Having perused this Book, Intituled, *The Dead-Mans Testament*; I do finde it to be Orthodox and sound, and likewise usefull for the Lords People, namely, those to whom it is directed, I do therefore allow it forthwith to be Printed and Published. Given under my hand at Leith, Novemb. 25. 1651. Timo[thy] Wilkes

If by 'Orthodox and sound' Wilkes, an Independent, meant derisive against the Kirk and the covenant then this is an entirely orthodox work.[38] It is intriguing that the first work to appear by authority is nowhere near being the first publication produced by the regime in Scotland. Neither is it the first publication from Tyler's press after the move to Leith. Perhaps the inclusion of a letter sanctioning the publication of the work signifies the changing role of the English army. By November 1651 the conquest of Scotland had largely been completed, and the army set about the task of maintaining order in Scotland by martial law. More importantly, perhaps, Cromwell had returned to England in pursuit of Charles II's army when it marched south at the end of July and was never to return to Scotland. In the absence of the commander-in-chief of the parliament's forces, the letter provided a record of why and by whom the publication had been authorised. Wilkes' certification demonstrates that this production was part of the Commonwealth's continuing struggle to separate the people of Scotland from the Kirk and was for this reason 'usefull for the Lords People'.

Whether the author of *A Dead-Man's Testament* really was Thomas Wood, or whether it was even a Scot, is open to debate. Thomas Wood can only be described as an enigmatic figure at best. According to William Dundas, Wood held a position in the 'Custom-house' in Leith. On several occasions he found himself at odds with the Presbyterian authorities for advocating 'that Christ was the Word, and that the Letter was not the Word' and 'that the Word was made Flesh, and dwelt among us'.[39] As early as 1646 the commissioners of the General Assembly ordered a trial and censure of Wood by the presbytery of Edinburgh.[40] This does not represent the only conflict between Wood and the Kirk, but by 1649 Wood bowed 'to the Assembly against his Light' in order to avoid excommunication, which would have meant losing his job.[41] These events may have been what led the Edinburgh antiquarian Robert Mylne (1643?– 1747) to include the work in a collection of Quaker pamphlets. That Mylne believed Wood to be a Quaker is clearly evidenced in the table of contents: 'Wood that quaker Indweller in Leith his dead mans testament 1651.'[42] This assertion is profoundly important, since the earliest Scottish Quakers are believed to have appeared in 1653.[43] If accurate, this demonstrates missionary success by the Friends in convincing native Scots at least two years earlier than has been traditionally believed. No matter what his actual religious affiliation, Wood certainly held little love for the covenanted Presbyterianism of the Kirk.

Evidently a number of questions linger about the authorship of the work. However, concrete answers about Wood are largely irrelevant, because even if he is the source of *A Dead-Man's Testament* others were involved. A postscript informs the reader that Wood was blind, which means that someone else transcribed the work, and additionally that a mystery Scot completed the tract and delivered it into the hands of the English.[44] Perhaps this person served as the scribe who took down the blind man's words, or perhaps he simply put his own words into the dead man's mouth. According to the postscript, only the first eleven pages of

the paper were finished at the time of Wood's death. The final four pages
pertaining to the assemblies of the Kirk, and the postscript itself, were
completed by the unnamed Scot 'at the desire of a Religious Officer of the
English Army'.[45] Why he gave this work to the English and why he added
to it are both questions that cannot now be answered. What is clear is
why the English printed the work. *A Dead-Man's Testament* is a direct
attack on the national Kirk by a deceased Scotsman, and as such served
as a perfect critique of the Kirk for two reasons. First, coming from a
Scotsman its accusations had the immediacy of someone familiar with the
Kirk. Second, a dead author could not be drawn into a dialogue over his
position or shamed into recanting his views, nor could he be confuted or
cross-examined. Its voice from beyond the grave gave it a mystical appeal
and sense of authority far beyond what Owen or Nicholas Lockyer could
produce. The work stood as the final testament of a Scotsman discontented
with the national Kirk. Although the persuasion of the author is uncertain,
his intentions become secondary to those who printed it.

Wood addressed his letter to 'all the Saints of Scotland, Fellow-Heirs
of the Blessing with those in England'. First, his mellifluous words
implored his compatriots to recognise the true causes of their present
distress; second, he struck out at what he claimed to be the five errors that
plagued the Kirk: its constitution, doctrine, worship, errant covenants and
National Assemblies. For too long the Kirk had been put upon a pedestal
to be overly glorified 'as did the Jewes in the Temple', all the while being
overrun and polluted by 'all the prophane multitude of ignorant Atheists,
Witches, Blasphemers, Drunkards, Scolders, and Mockers of Godlines in
the Land, under the name of a true Reformed Church of Christ, and a
communion of the Faithful'.[46] This mixing of the multitudes took place,
according to Wood, because of the greed of the rulers of the Kirk. In their
desire for power they sought to join civil and ecclesiastical powers, and
in so doing compelled sinners to appear before kirk sessions and synods,
'although not to God (who approveth no compelled service)'.[47] Simply
put, the Kirk made the same error as the Roman Church. By forcing all
within their sphere of influence to conform to the Kirk they created a
mass pollution in both local congregations and in the national membership of the state Church. For Wood, the Kirk could never be a properly
reformed church until its constitution was purified to include only those
who chose to be members and who submitted themselves to ecclesiastical
judicatories. This is a theme repeated throughout the polemics printed
by the English. The belief that the national church of Scotland 'hath been
a Church most gloriously reformed, and worthy to be a Pattern to all
others' only served to promulgate error in Wood's estimation.[48] Communion with the unrepentant multitudes, instead of bringing blessings to
the saints, brought punishment for blasphemy and the curse of the law.
The Kirk fostered an atmosphere in which outward trappings of holiness,

such as attending sermons, partaking of communion and singing psalms, merely covered up the wickedness of people's hearts, allowing them access to the Kirk without requiring any true reformation to take place within their lives.[49] Therefore the worship of the Kirk becomes corrupt. Finally, for Wood, the creation of the National Covenant gave final evidence of the Kirk's depravation. When the degenerate masses of Scotland foolishly engaged in a covenant with God, they obligated themselves 'under such horrible pains, to defend that which they never knew, they bound themselves over to the curse of the Law'.[50]

The final section of *The Dead-Man's Testament* is the product of the anonymous Scot who polished up the paper and delivered it to the English. In this addendum, he critiques the Kirk's synods, presbyteries and General Assemblies, claiming that there is no scriptural warrant for these meetings. He refutes the traditional scriptural defences of presbytery by arguing that the Council of Jerusalem (Acts 15) met only once, while the meeting of the elders at Ephesus (Acts 20:17) cannot be said to have convened regularly. Moreover, the Scottish practice of these meetings is to emit declarations, catechisms and restrictions on private worship which interfere in the freedom of Christians to gather and worship God when they please. Establishing limitations on how frequently Christians can gather and in what composition they may meet is unbiblical. It is wrong, claims the author, to force Christians to wait a week 'to hear those Preach, of whom they expected most for Edification, although their Parish-Priest had been an idiot, void of the Saving knowledge of God'. In conclusion, the work accuses the Presbyterian assemblies of being 'Popish-like' if they believe themselves to be 'the Inheritance and Church of God, by way of eminency and speciall propriety'.[51] These criticisms closely mirror the arguments put forward against Presbyterianism in England and New England during the 1640s. Independents in England accepted that Acts 15 and 20 provide examples of multiple congregations meeting together to discuss extraordinarily difficult issues, but refused to accept them as warranting a hierarchal structure. As a result, such occasional meetings were voluntary and only consultative in matters of doctrine, but not juridical. In New England such synods, although only occasional, were considered more binding upon those attending and were employed to deal with difficult issues like the Antinomian controversy in the Massachusetts Bay colony.[52] However, due to the censorship implemented by the General Assembly in the late 1640s these debates were new for Scots.

All the errors listed by Wood stem from a common source, the misinterpretation of correct church composition. *A Dead-Man's Testament* follows *The Branch of the Lord* in appealing for purer church membership and echoes *A Word of Advertisement* in criticising the corruption of the covenant and Presbyterian hierarchy. Consequently it should be seen as consistent with and an addition to the Commonwealth's continuing propaganda campaign against the Kirk. However, the work's use of a Scottish voice, like *A Word of Advertisement*, set it apart from previous critiques of the Kirk written by Englishmen and gave it greater polemical influence. Coupled with its voice-from-beyond-the-grave approach it was by far the most contentious item printed by the English propaganda machine during the Interregnum. The lasting impact of this work throughout the decade is demonstrated by the allusion to it in the title of James Durham's posthumously published book, *A Dying Man's Testament to the Church of Scotland*, published in 1659.[53]

Shortly thereafter, early in January 1652, the third 'Scottish' work came off the Leith-based press and was entitled *To the Very Honorable the Representative of the Common-Vvealth*.[54] The broadsheet is a petition and extremely rare. Only one surviving copy of the work is known.[55] Like *A Dead-Man's Testament*, Timothy Wilkes, lieutenant-governor of Leith, granted permission for the paper to be published on 2 January 1652. Addressed to Cromwell, it is an appeal from Scots willing to embrace the Commonwealth's actions as 'the designe of the advancement of CHRIST'S KINGDOM, and the just Freedom and Liberty of the People'. Although no names are given, the authors were almost certainly responsible for a previous paper to the English entitled *Overtures to the Right Honorable Commonwealth* (no longer extant) which consisted of fifteen overtures, as well as papers submitted to various Resolutioner and Protestor meetings across the central belt.[56] The authors claim to have favoured toleration for a long time but to have been suppressed by Scotland's Malignant and Presbyterian parties. As a result, they praise the present endeavours of the English in advancing religious toleration as 'the Lord's doing, and it is marvailous in our eyes' before making four supplications to Cromwell. First, that the people of Scotland should enjoy the same freedoms and liberties as their English neighbours and that this should be facilitated by a union of the two nations. Second, that godly men be appointed to govern, rather than individuals who would tyrannise over them, because they would delight to follow individuals who live implicitly by faith. Third, that God's people be given 'all due Christian freedom' to worship as their consciences dictate without fear of tyrannical suppression. Fourth, that worldly greatness not be the deciding factor in the selection of governors. These four requests established that a portion of Scotland's society, no matter how small, was not only willing to comply with English rule but actually saw this as a sort of exodus out of Scotland's Presbyterian Egypt. The English anxiously capitalised on this supplication by making it known publicly and using it as propaganda.

The publication of this work, like that of *A Word of Advertisement* and *A Dead-Man's Testament*, intended to advertise to the people of Scotland that religious opinion in the country was not uniform, even among their compatriots, and that significant religious change was on the way. That these works were published by the English army shows they were in line with the Commonwealth's agenda for Scotland. The polemical war against the Kirk continued to intensify, and the regime gladly used Scottish works in its arsenal. Although Nicoll complained in November 1651 that 'religion' (the Kirk) was 'slighted and condemned' under the new regime, poisoned by errors and heresies, things were to get much worse for the Kirk in the following months.[57]

Settled Government and Overt Attacks on the Kirk

On 15 January the parliament's Commissioners for Settling and Managing the Affairs of Scotland arrived in Dalkeith, taking up residence in Dalkeith Palace.[58] Five days later they 'discharged the printing of diurnalls at Leith, or else where';[59] an order, according to the editor of the news journal, directed at *Mercurius Scoticus*.[60] This official act censuring what was essentially their own printing press shows that a marked change in governing style was taking place, a centralisation of government. Rather than a whole-sale stoppage of printing journals in Leith, *Mercurius Scoticus* would be replaced by London-based newsbooks that shared more implicitly in a symbiotic relationship with the Interregnum government. Two months after the silencing of *Mercurius Scoticus*, the London-based *A Diurnal of Some Passages and Occurrences* began to be reprinted at Leith on 15 March 1652.[61] In June 1653 *Mercurius Politicus* also began to be reprinted in Leith.[62] These papers maintained a pro-government slant in return for inside information, which allowed them to be the first to provide breaking news. As a result, both the newsbook and the government profited from this mutually beneficial arrangement.[63] Because of the rapid transfer from the printing of one journal to another, the censure of *Mercurius Scoticus* had little impact on the printer, probably Christopher Higgins by this time, for he continued to print journals; however now they were simply reprints of the government-approved London editions. This ensured that the same news would be distributed in Edinburgh as in London, Bristol or Dublin, much to the chagrin of Robert Baillie, who lamented in 1654 that 'what the world abroad is doing we know no more than the London diurnal tells us'.[64] Under the commissioners, new laws and structured government replaced the impromptu martial law of the parliament's army. On 12 February the commissioners announced the parliament's plan for establishing their rule in Scotland.[65] Two days later they gave their own more detailed description as to how they planned on settling matters.[66] As discussed in chapter 2, this entailed the imposition of tolera-tion for anyone worshipping in 'A Gospel Way'.[67] Whether independently gathered congregations formed or not, the English regime had accomplished what it desired: the Presbyterian tyranny had been broken, and the Presbyterians' ability to impose their church government on England or interfere in English politics was unequivocally diminished.

Two triumphalist sermons formerly preached before parliament in the autumn of 1651 made their way to the press of Evan Tyler in the early part of 1652 as part of a celebration of the Commonwealth's victory not just over Scotland, but more specifically over the presbytery. These sermons stand out as unusual, for while it was common for sermons preached before parliament to be printed in England, they were rarely reprinted in Scotland.[68] In fact, these appear to be the only two reprinted in Scotland during the Interregnum. John Owen preached his sermon to parliament on 24 October 1651, a day set aside for solemn thanksgiving for the defeat of the Scots army at Worcester.[69] He heralded the victory at Worcester as one over 'those who would have been our Oppressors in Scotland', who had prepared a new antichrist to replace Prelacy, 'a heavie yoke, a beast that had it grown to perfection, would have had horns and hoofs,' and whose maintenance thereof was the great interest of the Scots.[70] In Owen's estimation, Scotland had been the instigator of the troubles between the two countries, because it had attempted to impose its tyran- nical anti-Christian form of church government upon England. Hence he urged the people of England to celebrate their victory at Worcester, as it was their duty 'to rejoyce when Babylon is destroyed with violence and fury'.[71] If the Scots had had their way, a national church would have been set up over all of Britain and none would have been able to live peaceably unless they were subjects of that Kirk. Victory at Worcester showed God's 'Providential alterations' to the Kirk's unholy plans. For their lusting and deceitful intentions in matters pertaining to religion, God crushed the Scots like a 'Cockatrice in the shell'.[72]

A second sermon of thanksgiving preached by Peter Sterry also found its way to the printing press at Leith. Equally uninhibited in its criticism of the Kirk, Sterry preached *England's Deliverance from the Northern Presbytery* to parliament on 5 November 1651 (the anniversary of the gunpowder plot).[73] He made a corollary between England's salvation from the popish 'Gun-powder-Treason' and the victory over the Scots at Worcester explaining that both were divine acts of deliverance from antichrist.[74] His epistle of dedication for the printed sermon professes his intention for the work to be a warning to his Christian brethren about the hidden dangers of the presbytery: 'For this I have desired in my Preaching, in my Prayers, to work with GOD, even for the opening of the eyes of men to see, that the same spirit which lay in the polluted Bed of Papacy, may meet them in the perfumed Bed of Presbytery.'[75] Based on Jeremiah 16:14–15, Sterry focused on God's promises to deliver His people 'out of Egypt "out of the NORTH".'[76] His selective restructuring of Jeremiah 16:15 in order to emphasise the 'North' as representative of Scotland continues throughout the piece.

According to Sterry, the godly in England face two 'capital enemies' in the forms of Papacy and Presbyterianism, both of which share similar anti-Christian traits. Both maintain an unhealthy devotion to forms, which tends to assume 'a Spiritual and Civil power to it self' and causes Scripture to become the letter of the law, robbing it of its spiritually nurturing power and leaving it 'but a breathlesse Carkass, or a Dead Letter'.[77] The diminution of Scripture's power and value is evident in both churches. While the Roman Church prohibits the use of the Scriptures in the vernacular, the Kirk is little better, since it prohibits the interpretation of Scripture 'which the Holy Spirit brings forth to every man in his own spirit'.[78] Furthermore, both Rome and Scotland's Kirk are greatly guilty of Pharisaic suppression of those who exhibit spiritual enthusiasm or who seem to act contrary to their interpretation of the Gospel. 'Both the Papists and the Scots Presbyterians,' he posits, 'are like fishermen in the River Thames who set up their baskets to catch "Lampries" who swim against the current.'[79] In addition, they interject in the politics of the temporal world, crossing over from the spiritual to the civil. Sterry compares the Papal bull against Queen Elizabeth, which gave England to the king of Spain for Elizabeth's apostasy, with Scotland's attempt to return England to the Stuart monarchy.[80]

Not satisfied with merely painting the presbytery with the same brush as Rome, Sterry intensifies his argument, alleging that the Kirk's actions are more destructive and more dangerous to true faith than those of Rome, because the Kirk dresses itself in the Reformation. Something that is partially reformed, or pretends to be, but underneath remains corrupted, is far more insidious than something that is wholly and visibly corrupt: an argument the Presbyterians had used against Episcopalians a decade earlier. That Presbyterians had corrupt intentions became evident through their open scheming against England. While the gunpowder plot (fomented by Catholics) intended to remove England's government, the Scots intended to subvert England's government, religion and people, and all by an 'Army made up of Highlanders, who never knew Christianity or Civility'.[81] The vile nature of the Scots' conniving overshadowed the papists', in that while Catholics secretly planned and implemented the gunpowder plot, the Scots formulated and hatched their scheme very publicly in the forum of the national Church, making the entire Church of Scotland complicit in this treachery. Although God had delivered England from popery and Prelacy, Sterry heralded the victory at Worcester, which 'saved us from the Black plots, and Bloudy powers of the NORTHERN PRESBYTERY … hath excelled them all'.[82]

The republication of these English sermons preached before parliament serve as evidence for two important suppositions. First, many in England viewed the 'defeat' of the Scottish presbytery as the vanquishing of an old enemy and its overthrow a principal objective of the war. Second, these sermons were deemed to carry a valuable message for the people of Scotland, namely, that the undermining of their Kirk had been ordained by God and they should be thankful that for a third time they too had been freed from the yoke of the beast (Roman Catholicism, Episcopacy and now Presbytery). Yet, despite the proud declarations of victory over the Kirk in the sermons of Owen and Sterry, the Presbyterian Kirk persisted as the greatest threat to the Commonwealth's stability. In April 1652 *Mercurius Politicus* reported:

> It is the onely Thorn that is left in the Paw of the English Lyon; take it out or else it will fester and gangrene. I fear it is a Thorn in the side too, for they say, they have friends still in England. Beleeve it, all your other Enemies are tame beasts to the high Presbyter, and yet with the winding and turning of a Religious pretence, and an artificial zeal against Heresie, he will, like a tame Snake (if not warily avoided) get into your bosome.[83]

For this reason propaganda against the Kirk continued to be produced. Unless an alternative to the Presbyterian Kirk could be established, the Church of Scotland would continue to oppose the Commonwealth. That same spring the *Weekly Intelligencer* heralded the success of the regime's campaign against the Kirk.

> The Parliament of England, and their Commissioners in Scotland are doing what they can for the advancement of the Gospel with authoritie to carry on that great work, which will adde much unto their glory, and stop the mouthes of all their Adversaries. And it is worth your observation, that many of the godly partie in Scotland that had heretofore hard thoughts of our Church Government, begin now to be more satisfied and to comply with us.[84]

The establishment of toleration and the increasing stability of the regime in Scotland gave the English the foundation to produce their most audacious and open attack against Presbyterianism. Rather than works by Englishmen advocating Independency, or tracts of nameless Scottish origin simply criticising the Kirk, the regime now prepared an all-out attack on the presbytery to be produced in an easily distributed package. Shortly after the arrival of the Commissioners for Settling the Affairs of Scotland (and their chaplains) and their subsequent imposition of toleration, Evan Tyler's shop printed an expanded edition of Nicholas Lockyer's sermon entitled *A Litle Stone Out of the Mountain*.[85]

Lockyer, an Independent chaplain with the English forces, took full advantage of his time in Scotland for promoting his beloved Independency. While he is best remembered for his brazen printed attack on Presbyterianism, a report from April 1652 places Lockyer in 'the north', probably in the vicinity of Aberdeen, helping to establish Independent congregations at the request of some Scots.[86] The significance of his impact in Scotland is testified by lingering Presbyterian disdain for him. Five years after he left the country his memory still evoked an emotional response from Robert Baillie, who in 1658 referred to him as 'that asse Lockier'.[87]

According to the print historian James Chalmers, the plan of the parliament's commissioners was to first establish toleration, then to turn their efforts to openly attacking the Kirk in print.[88] That the publication of *A Litle Stone* represented the will of the regime and not just the author Nicholas Lockyer is verified by the work's epistle of dedication, signed by Joseph Caryl, John Oxenbridge and Cuthbert Sydenham, the three chaplains to the parliament's newly arrived commissioners. Their dedication sets the tone of the regime's continued attack on Presbyterianism: calling for recognition of Scotland's defeats at Preston, Dunbar, Hamilton, Inverkeithing and Worcester as God's judgement against the nation's covenants and the Kirk.[89] They identify the mixed constitution of the Kirk as the primary cause of this punishment and argue the urgent need to restore the church in Scotland to a proper composition. Since the truly godly are inevitably 'lost and drowned' among the degenerate masses in a state church, they argue that the only way forward is separation from the Kirk and gathering Independent congregations.[90]

Lockyer's own preface explains it to be an appeal for the wellbeing of the elect in Scotland, who 'are in an ill vessell, which cannot possible live, in such stormes as now beat upon it, from Heaven and from the Saints, and therefore I could wish that all the godly were out'.[91] His intention is twofold. First he defends the validity of independently gathered congregations against the aspersions of Presbyterian detractors, and second, he asserts the fundamental flaws of the Kirk. Lockyer dismisses Presbyterian accusations that Congregational churches are breeding grounds of 'many monsters' and 'heresies' as slanderous libels. He singles out Thomas Edwards' *Gangraena* and Samuel Rutherford's *A Survey of the Spiritual Antichrist* as particularly defamatory and untenable attacks on Independency. Rutherford wrote in 1648 that he knew of no pure Independents in England, claiming all those gathered under that banner of Independency held some other 'unsound and corrupt tenets' in addition.[92] Lockyer retorted:

> It makes me tremble to read this expression … surely there be many Independents in England, that this good man is a stranger to, and how he should then dare to speak so of them all as he does, is fearfull, If Christians can allow themselves this kinde of latitude, to gloss upon their Brethrens words and persons, I know not how any man shall so speak, write, or live as not to be printed and staged to all the World for an Heretick.[93]

According to Lockyer, such unfair judgements were partially to blame for the present plight of Scotland. In contrast to the picture of a polluted Kirk painted by the commissioner's chaplains in their dedication, Lockyer expresses the approval that God would shower down upon Scotland if the ministers of the Kirk would recognise their error in damning the Independents and take back their sharp words 'of which their pens, pulpits, and papers are full'.[94] Hence, according to Lockyer, Scotland's guilt in the eyes of God did not rest wholly upon attempts to make England Presbyterian, or on the impurity of the Kirk, but also for its defamation of noncon-formist Christians in England. From a defence of Independency in the face of Presbyterian criticism, Lockyer proceeded to his own attack on the Presbytery.

For Lockyer, the Kirk has three primary flaws: first, an improper constitution; second, a tyrannical rule by elders; and third, an idolatrous devotion to presbytery. He chose Acts 15:3 as the Scripture on which to base his sermon: 'They were sent on their way by the church and travelled through Phoenicia and Samaria, telling the full story of the conversion of the Gentiles, and causing great rejoicing amongst all the Christians.'[95] From this very brief Scripture he asserts that the proper constitution and opera-tion of the church can be deduced: 'The complexion of the visible Church under the Gospel, is said here to be conversion, the constituting matter, converted ones.'[96] Since the Church is expressed as being comprised only of converts, he questions how Presbyterians can criticise Independents for loosing themselves from corrupt mixed churches and gathering together people who show the signs of being truly converted. He cites Galatians 1:22 as giving full warrant for gathering properly constituted congregations out of corrupt ones, just as the first Christian churches gathered out of 'that ... Church of the Jewes'.[97] To explain the proper constitution of the Church, he uses the story of Simon Magus, just as James Brown did in his dispute with James Guthrie.[98] Although Simon convinced the Apostles that he was truly a member of the body through a public confession and an apparent outward conversion, when it became evident he was 'one not in Christ' the church shunned him as a hypocrite.[99] From this the Church must recognise its commission to admit only those who show the signs of election, and if anyone admitted to fellowship should prove to be a reprobate they must be removed. Likewise, if the church becomes corrupted by unrepentant multi-tudes, then the elect should separate themselves and reconstitute into a new congregation just as early Christians broke away from synagogues. For Lockyer the Scottish Kirk urgently required the truly godly to withdraw since 'the bad wil cast out the good, sooner then they wil condescend to cast out themselves'. In fact, Lockyer perceives the Kirk's depravity as so complete that he brands it 'not a man but a carcasse'.[100] Unless the Kirk give birth to something new, it was beyond resuscitation.

Lockyer's second complaint regarding the presbytery is the diminished role of the Christian in the functioning of a congregation. For Lockyer, all believers should be participants in the Church, by which he means actively taking part in its government. Just as Catholicism and Episco-pacy are 'usurpers and Lords over the flock of Christ' because they make Christians spectators and remove from them the power given to them as believers, the Presbyterian Kirk also deprives 'the people of God of their best Liberties'.[101] Before the 'Council' of Laodicea in the mid-fourth century, Lockyer alleges, the church was democratic.[102] After this, however, representatives began to be selected to rule over the Church, and the role of elders became that of rulers. He argues that elders should not have absolute power over the congregation since 'the spirit of discerning ... is not confined as a peculiar to the Presbytery, or Eldership of the Church'[103] and especially since the power of the keys 'to bind are given to the whole church, which is constituted of converted believers'.[104] For this reason, the elders of a church have no greater claim to the power of the keys than any other believers within the church. The keys were given to Peter not as an Apostle or an elder, but as a believer.[105] Since all believers are given a share of that power and because all share in the spirit of discernment, the Church must operate in an 'Organicall' way.[106] Lockyer uses the example of the body to explain this. Some members are eyes, while others are hands or feet, but all must work in unity if the body is to function effectively. He would disagree with anyone who argued that this model implies elders alone serve as the part of the body which dictates the function of the congregational body.

The Biblical model of eldership, explains Lockyer, means that elders should be elected by the congregation and aid in the governing of the church. 'So long as they go right' they are 'to be honoured and followed; but if otherwise, to be admonished, and if impenitent, to be rejected'.[107] While they may have a special designation, elders are not to be raised up or set over a congregation.[108] Since no elder has complete power over a congregation and since they must operate as a part of the body, Lockyer contends that there can be no eldership in which elders are appointed over congregations of which they are not themselves members. This carries over into an argument against presbyteries quite conventional in relation to the Presbyterian–Independent dispute of the 1640s and similar to the arguments in *A Dead-Man's Testament* against the use of Acts 15 and 20 to establish the legitimacy of Presbyterian hierarchy.[109] Citing Acts 20:28, Lockyer establishes the limitations of eldership, excluding any warrant for rule external of the congregational elders' charge to: 'keep guard over yourselves and over all the flock [not flocks] of which the Holy Spirit has given you charge, as shepherds of the church of the Lord'.[110] As in Cotton, Norton and others, foreign elderships, or visiting elders, may provide counsel, but they do not have any authoritative jurisdiction.[111] An elder's jurisdiction reaches only as far as his pastoral power.[112] To support this assertion he cites 1 Peter 5:2, 'look after the flock of God whose shepherds you are; do it, not under compulsion, but willingly'.[113] Every congregation is fully self-sufficient, because it is complete and 'hath sufficiencie within it self, to exercise all the ordinances of Christ; to ordain, to excommunicate' without the intervention of 'foreign' elders.[114] Preaching, he claims, is held in higher regard by the Apostle than binding and loosing, therefore if Christ trusts churches to preach (a greater thing) then surely he trusts them bind or loose (a lesser thing).

Finally, he strikes at the people's deep devotion to the Kirk, suggesting that extreme devotion to the presbytery polluted that form of church government by making it an obstructive idol, hindering the worship of God, impeding any other Christian forms and fomenting intolerance towards nonconformists. Presbytery had become an idol in Scotland. This is not an allegation found only in Lockyer. An English journal of December 1651 equates the Scots' admiration for Presbyterianism with the devotion of Ephesus for the goddess Diana, likening the production of the covenants and the promotion of presbytery with the making of 'silver schrynes for Diana'.[115] For Lockyer and others of his persuasion, the Kirk had stepped out of one kind of idolatry at the Reformation to tread in another. He urged the godly in Scotland to heed the words of 2 Cor. 6:17 and 'Come away and leave them, separate yourselves, says the Lord; touch nothing unclean. Then I will accept you.' This final accusation hit at the signing of the National Covenant and the Solemn League and Covenant, which placed the preservation of the presbytery at the forefront of Scottish national politics. Throughout this work Lockyer slyly moved his attack from the mixed multitude of the Kirk to the tyrannical nature of its organisation.

While these arguments were not radically new in relation to the Presbyterian–Independent debate in England during the 1640s, it must be remembered they had never before been broached with the Scottish public. The General Assembly had banned all books tending towards Independency or separation in 1647, the year before the publication of Norton's *Responsio*, Cotton's *The Way of the Congregational Churches Cleared*, Allin and Shepard's *Defence* and Hooker's *Survey of the Summe of Church Discipline* in England.[116] Hence this was all radically new to most Scots. Although delegates of the Church of Scotland were integrally involved in the debate over ecclesiastical government in England, as far as the population of Scotland were concerned it was an external debate taking place abroad. With regard to the intricacies of the debate, they were completely unaware. As a result, Lockyer's work brought the debate to the Scottish populace for the first time.

Although Lockyer attacked the composition, structure and even the nation's devotion to the Kirk, probably the most important aspect of this work is its brevity. The work comprised 138 pages bound into a small pocket-sized volume.[117] It is an excellent piece of propaganda because its economy makes the work easily digestible. Following in the example of the regime's earlier pieces of propaganda against the Kirk, the work adheres to the tradition of religious polemical pamphlets in England: directed to the general public and for that reason kept concise. By keeping the work short and to the point the author increased the likelihood of the general public taking the time to read it.

Softening Regulation and Presbyterian Response

The Commonwealth's continuous attacks upon the Kirk began to take
their toll in 1652. In the latter part of the year, the English newsbook
Mercurius Britannicus reported the clergy preaching vehemently against
the intervention of the English into Scottish affairs, complaining that they
had removed first the bonds between the king and his people, then between
'the Magistrate and the people' and now finally between 'the Minister and
the people'.[118] Yet the imposition of toleration and the attack of Lockyer
did not mark an end for the Kirk, only an end to its silence. Significantly,
the replacement of the Commonwealth's initial martial rule in Scotland
by political commissioners also marked the end of stringent control of
Scotland's presses. Despite its initial show of power in censuring *Mercurius Scoticus*, civilian government took a more lax approach to the press.
Gradually, the apathy towards the control of printing characteristic of
Interregnum England began to creep into Scotland. The Kirk began to
create printed works of its own, beyond those of the bickering Protester–
Resolutioner conflict, intended to defend Presbyterianism and thwart the
threat of Sectarianism.

In 1652 two of Edinburgh's great printing presses sprang back into
action: Gideon Lithgow and The Heirs of George Anderson. Within this
atmosphere of lightened censorship, James Guthrie produced a treatise
on the role of elders in the church.[119] Although not explicitly billed as a
response to Lockyer, the subject and its publication so soon after *A Litle
Stone* suggests that it was a motivating factor for the Protester. Paramount
among his motivations for producing the work, he cited vindication of
'the Doctrine of our Church concerning these Church-Officers, that the
mouths of such who speak evil may be stopped, and others who stumble
may be satisfied'.[120] Echoing Lockyer's criticism of elders as rulers and his
claim that they were an invention of man, Guthrie set out to establish the
divine origins of the office of ruling elders.[121] He explained their specific
warrant as being distinctive from ministers, doctors and preaching or
teaching elders.[122] Guthrie asserted that the earliest foundations for the
office of ruling elders originated in the Jewish church, and then turned to
evidence in the Fathers, citing Ambrose, Tertullian, Basil and Augustine to
support the early origins of this office in the Christian church.[123] The work
described the proper calling of elders, their election and their authority to
rule over the church. He supported the rule of elders in individual congregations but, in direct opposition to Lockyer, also in presbyteries, synods
and general assemblies, and taking it a step beyond to all 'diverse Nations
professing the Faith of Jesus Christ'.[124] 'In all Assemblies of the Church,
Ruling Elders being therto rightly called, have power to sit, write, debate,
vote, and conclude in all matters that are handled therein, Acts 15:2 and
6:22–3,' claimed Guthrie.[125]

The importance of this work rests not in its defence of eldership, but what it reveals about elements within the Kirk rapidly responding to overt English polemics against their Presbyterian Church structure. According to Wariston, the tract provided an important reply to those who criticised the ability of the pure minority in the Kirk to purge the degenerate masses, a criticism found in Lockyer's *Litle Stone* and elsewhere. Guthrie maintained that even in a congregation where none can be found who are godly enough to serve as elders, the book of discipline provides that out of two or three congregations the presbytery may choose elders to rule over the whole 'and so debar from the table the ignorant and scandalous', but 'not to cast the whole multitude out of church fellowship'.[126] What is more, his ability to get this work printed in Scotland in 1652 illustrates the loosening of England's initially very tight control of Scotland's presses. Its speed in publication may have been greatly aided by it being a defence and definition of the proper role of elders rather than an overtly anti-English or anti-Independent rant.

Nonetheless, Lockyer's work continued to be a thorn in the side of the Kirk. The Resolutioners appointed James Wood to produce a response to the work, but he was extremely slow in doing so. Baillie wrote to him on 14 February 1653 and accused him of lethargy: 'Will yow let Lockier triumph whole yeares? O laziness, laziness!'[127] Not until 1654, two years after the publication of *A Litle Stone*, did Wood's response to Lockyer make its way into print. Judging by the magnitude of the work it seems unlikely that laziness is what slowed the author down. *A Litle Stone Pretended to be Out of the Mountain* is a bulky response to Lockyer's little book, in which every point made by the English chaplain is exhaustively refuted. Including the two appendices added against the Independents in Aberdeen, who 'it seemeth they have been in a manner his proselytes', the book comprises 386 pages.[128] The sheer volume of the work meant that while Wariston took the time to read it, most ordinary Scots probably did not.[129]

Wood claims that he does not charge Independents with perverse intentions, as he highly respects Hooker, Cotton and others, but argues they have been so 'dazzled' by the idea of establishing a pure, visible church they risked destroying the foundations of all Reformed churches.[130] For this reason he set upon the task of refuting every point made by Lockyer *ad nauseam*. To begin, he criticises the Englishman's attempt to found an ecclesiology upon such a short piece of Scripture (Acts 15:3), especially if Lockyer interprets the text to mean the Apostles only drew the converted.[131] 'The preaching of the Gospel,' argues Wood, 'being a draw net ... catches good fishes and bad together, and the outward Kingdom of God, as a field wherein are tares and wheat growing together.'[132] How can a church be filled with only those truly converted? Lockyer says that very spiritual men can discern. Who are these very spiritual men? Are they the leaders?

Would that not be against the way of Congregationalists to have leaders deciding who can come in and who cannot?

For Wood, the Independents teeter precariously on the brink of heresy. If they claim that they are able to discern who is truly elect and some of their members prove to be regenerate, then they profess Arminianism, because they claim that humans 'may have the practice and power of godlinesse, and afterward let it go'.[133] If they reject this, then they must set standards of morality for whom they will admit, which tends towards Donatism.[134] The other option is the one practised by the Presbyterians, which is to admit the impossibility of knowing whether someone is actually elect, but to allow entrance into the church upon an outward profession. Wood found a further error in Lockyer's teaching that elders may not rule without consent of the congregation, claiming it to be nothing more than the doctrine of the Levellers.[135] However, for Wood the true tragedy of Lockyer's attack was not the spreading of error, but rather like Lockyer's own expression, malicious reproaches aimed at fellow Christians.

> Ah Mr. Lockier! my soul is sorrowfull and heavy to think, a man, professing Christianity, a Minister of the Gospel, standing to speak in the Lords sight, and in his Name, should have uttered such a horrid accusation and bitter invective against many whom Jesus Christ hath interest in, and will owne at the last day.[136]

Unfortunately Wood's work proved too robust to be a practical response that the average member of the Kirk would have time or energy to read. Yet by the time of its publication the common people of Scotland were not the only Scots who needed persuading. By 1652–3 a number of Scots ministers were being drawn like 'little stones out of the mountain' into Independency, which will be discussed in the following chapter.

The Protectorate and the Abatement of Anti-Presbyterian Works

The establishment of the Protectorate significantly changed how the government of England functioned, as recent scholarship is demonstrating. As Protector, Cromwell not only implemented policy, he dictated it, much like the royals who preceded him, as the figurehead of English government. As Patrick Little has argued, 'beneath the formal governmental structures, the Protector wielded enormous power'. As a result, the achievements and failures of the Protectorate must in large part 'be attributed to Cromwell personally ... in parliament, religious reform and everyday government'.[137] The inception of the Protectorate marked a significant change in the religious policy of the English government, especially towards the Kirk. As Protector, Cromwell espoused his own vision of the Christian republic as being dependent not merely on mutual toleration amongst Christians but unity between them. This had been his desire for years, declaring in 1648: 'I profess to thee I desire it in my heart, I have prayed for it, I have waited for the day to see union and right understanding between the godly people (Scots, English, Jews, Gentiles, Presbyterians, Independents, Anabaptists, and all).'[138] For this reason, when Cromwell entered Scotland in July 1650 he did not wish to dash the Presbyterian Kirk into pieces, which he could have done in 1648 but chose not to. Instead he desired to 'make all Christians of one heart' and institute a Christian Commonwealth in which all of God's people could worship as the Spirit led them.[139] This does not preclude an anti-Kirk motivation for invading Scotland. Rather, he sought to break the Kirk's intolerant stranglehold on Scottish religion in order to clear the way for building unity and solidarity between all Christian groups. Cromwell reiterated this desire in a speech made in September 1656, plainly declaring his desire 'that there might be union in all transactions relating to our affaires at home as well as abroad, and a tenderness that those either of Presbyterian, Independent, or Anabaptist forme, might not tread upon the heeles or prejudice one another'.[140] This freedom for Christians to practice as the Spirit led also allowed them to voice their opinions in matters of religion. His regard for the freedom of the Christian is best summarised in a statement often attributed to him: 'I had rather that Mahometanism were permitted amongst us, than that one of God's children should be persecuted.'[141] Only in cases of overtly seditious or blatantly heretical works did the regime enforce censorship. The inception of the Protectorate opened the presses to religious dialogue and marked the end of anti-Presbyterian papers being produced by the regime in Scotland. Even the number of Protester–Resolutioner works dwindled during Cromwell's reign as Protector as he desired a Kirk free from division, tolerant of diversity and allowing the freedom of the individual's conscience.

In March 1654, Cromwell sent for John Livingston, Patrick Gillespie and John Menzies to come to London, and in May for Robert Blair, Robert Douglas and James Guthrie as well, in order that a solution to the problems in the Kirk might be reached. However, a balanced agreement could not be established because Blair, Douglas and Guthrie refused to comply with his summons.[142] Instead, Patrick Gillespie and John Menzies pushed through 'Gillespie's Charter', giving the power to plant new ministers to the Protesters and Aberdeen Independents, compounding Resolutioner anxieties.[143] Monck's return to Scotland in the spring of 1654 ensured that a moderate approach towards Presbyterians would continue. He did not share his predecessor's deep antipathy towards the Kirk. His sympathy for Presbyterianism was reflected at the end of the Interregnum, when he expressed his desire for a settled state church in England 'Presbyterian but not rigid'.[144] Under his oversight overtly anti-Presbyterian policies abated.

Lord Broghill, president of the Scottish council between September 1655 and August 1656, also made significant attempts to resolve the issues which continued to divide the Protesters and Resolutioners. Although Julia Buckroyd argues that his attempts represent a significant break from Cromwell's policies, they do not break from Cromwell's intentions.[145] Among Broghill's endeavours, he requested Cromwell to command a conference of equal numbers of Protesters and Resolutioners in order that they might come to a compromise in the manner of filling empty charges.[146] While this and all other attempts ultimately failed to resolve the divisions within the Kirk, Broghill's strategy did entice both the Protesters and Resolutioners to plead their cases before Cromwell.[147] Broghill's efforts stemmed from the vision of Cromwell, shared by others of a moderate disposition within the regime, that unity among Christians must provide the foundation for the secure future of Britain. They were also indicative of a paradigmatic shift during the Protectorate away from 'sectarian organisation' and theology towards voluntary unity in religious co-existence. Cromwell desired unity within the Presbyterian party in Scotland just as he wished for Christian unity among the various factions in England. His wish for Presbyterians and Independents to come together began to bear fruit in England in the growth of voluntary associations of moderates from both parties, a pattern reflected to some degree in Scotland as well.[148]

The opening of channels for religious dialogue, however, also had its drawbacks for the Protector as seditious elements began to vent their displeasure. Tension between Baptists sympathetic to the Fifth Monarchists and Cromwell's government continued to grow in 1653 over the question of whether Cromwell should take on the role of Protector.[149] Cromwell's acceptance of the Protectorate on 16 December 1653 sent shock waves through the army. Many of those who had fought in the civil wars did so in opposition to monarchical government and accordingly viewed Cromwell's acceptance of the Protectorate as the re-imposition of what they had spilt blood to overturn. Just a month after Cromwell's inauguration as Lord Protector, Wariston refers to Cromwell as being 'at great straits by the opposition of the Anabaptists'.[150] With this backlash from radical Republicans and millenarians, the Kirk gradually ceased to be viewed as the greatest threat to the stability of the Interregnum regime. The government's propaganda turned from the Kirk to producing adequate defences for the newly established form of government. According to a contemporary English journal, the regime reprinted John Goodwin's *Synkretismos* in Leith in 1654 as an appeal to accept the change in government.[151] Goodwin wrote, 'whatsoever power be, they are ordained by Him [God]'.[152] A month later the press also reprinted Marchamont Nedham's defence of the Protectorate in Leith.[153] The target of the English propaganda changed from the Presbytery, which opposed the regime's tolerant stance on religion, to the religiously radical who challenged the authority and legality of a Protectoral government.

The growing vocalism of radicals may have led to a second reason that the publication of anti-Presbyterian tracts abated. When Cromwell appointed his first Protectoral parliament he intended it to pursue legislation ensuring religious liberties for all. Instead, spearheaded by London Presbyterians, parliament focused primarily on stamping out heresy. Others followed in this reaction against the sects openly speaking seditiously against the government, including the London Stationers' Company, which still owned Evan Tyler's press in Edinburgh. While Cromwell's regime ceased attacking the Kirk in the hopes of courting religious unity and as a result stability, the owners of Scotland's primary press took a very different approach, but one that had a similar affect on Presbyterians in Scotland. The Stationers' Company took the stance that stability depended upon orthodoxy over and above religious exuberance and so sided with the sentiments of London's Presbyterians and the Protectoral parliament.[154] As a result it opened its presses in Scotland to attack heresy, particularly the Quakers, who promoted personal liberty over social stability and encouraged the printing of works advocating orthodox theology.

While the diversity of the papers printed continued to increase, at no point could printing in Scotland be described as a free-for-all. At the end of March 1655, Cromwell gave 'his Highness Councell in Scotland' the power: 'to erect and make use of and comand any Presse or Presses there for printing and publishing any Proclamacons, Declaracons, Orders, Bookes or other matters wch they shall think fitt for the publique Service and to prohibit the use thereof by any other persons, or in any Cases where they shall see cause'.[155] About this time James Brown began to print again in Aberdeen, with the bulk of his work being the republication of government proclamations. Further evidence that the Presbyterians ceased to be perceived as the primary threat is evidenced by the council in Scotland permitting Rutherford's *The Covenant of Life Opened* to be printed in Edinburgh in 1655.[156]

Scotland's presses continued to print Protester and Resolutioner works, although they were few in number until after Cromwell's death. However sectarians produced tracts aimed at other religious groups recently introduced into Scotland. Between 1655 and 1657 Edinburgh's presses produced a series of anti-Quaker tracts composed by English authors.[157] These works, along with the regime's treatment of members of the sect, elicited Quaker responses and apologetics.[158] The relaxation of the press after Cromwell became Protector even saw the publication of a tract in Leith that some historians have billed as a Catholic apologetic.[159] *Love the Precious Ointment, That Flowes Down from the Head Christ Jesus*, with all of its references to the 'Catholick' church is not, however, a Roman Catholic apologetic. It is a Quaker work pleading for love, patience and toleration between Christians, in terms similar to Cromwell's own ideas.[160]

Cromwell enthusiastically supported this aspect of Quaker doctrine, as evidenced by his great respect for George Fox.[161] Although religious tolerance may have been expanding in practice, Roman Catholicism did not benefit. In fact, in 1657 parliament produced a new act for rooting out Catholicism, which James Brown printed in Aberdeen.[162] Despite the presbytery of Jedburgh's complaint of 'sinfull Literyes', Scotland's presses remained largely free of contentious religious texts between 1655 and the Protector's death in September 1658, except for those few published against Catholics who, according to several reports, increased in number in northern Scotland.[163] Contemporary Catholic correspondence reported conversions on the islands of Canna, Eigg, Barra, Islay and South Uist to number into the thousands.[164] In fact the council in Scotland became so concerned over the presence of Jesuit priests in 1656 that they declared the death penalty should be imposed on any Catholic priest found in the country.[165] The presses picked up steam again when the Protester–Resolutioner controversy re-erupted in 1658. After Cromwell's death, the uncertainty of what would follow saw several works published in which particular views were defended and held up in the hopes they would be tolerated in the event of governmental changes.

As has been shown, the greatest control over the publication of religious works occurred between the initial arrival of the English in Edinburgh and the imposition of the Protectorate. Clear evidence supporting an English agenda against the Kirk survives in the polemics published during this period. The texts produced serve to show that the English did not attack Presbyterianism simply because the Kirk opposed their occupation and incorporation of Scotland into one Commonwealth with England. Instead the regime perceived covenanted Presbyterianism to be intolerant and therefore by its very nature fundamentally opposed to certain basic beliefs integral in the intellectual underpinning of England's Commonwealth. The Kirk had been viewed over the previous decade as, next to the monarchy, the single greatest threat to England's burgeoning desire for religious freedom and toleration. However, the degree to which different members of England's Republican government viewed the danger posed by Scotland's presbytery significantly shaped their opinions of the lengths necessary to neutralise the threat. The gradually increasing crescendo of ferocity in the polemics, before their sudden quelling under the Protectorate, gives an indication of the spectrum of opposition to Presbyterianism that existed in the regime. In an interesting contrast, predominantly Presbyterian English communities prohibited works by Independent authors during the Interregnum.[166] Therefore the struggle between religious and ideological groups transcended the Scots–English conflict.

The Commonwealth's polemical efforts against the Kirk began as passive questioning of Presbyterianism and prompts for further Reformation before swelling into more subversive texts of apparently Scottish origin. The propaganda reached its height under the Commissioners for Settling the Affairs of Scotland in 1652 with the production of openly anti-Presbyterian tracts, before withering away under the Protectorate. The forms of polemic that Cromwell encouraged during his time in Scotland from 1650 to 1651 did not intend to topple Presbyterianism to the degree that the Episcopal Church had been pulled down in England. His desire, which expressed itself during the Protectorate, was a softening of the Kirk into what Monck hoped for after the Restoration, a 'Presbyterianism government not rigid'.[167] Cromwell did not wish the Kirk to be torn down, but for it to be allowed to continue unhindered, in a tolerant manner, alongside other forms of Christian practice. Essentially, opposition to the Kirk stemmed from a long struggle in England against enforced 'formality'.[168]

However, Cromwell possessed a more moderate religious mindset than many of his fellow Republicans who sat in parliament or served in the army. The arrival of the Commissioners for Settling the Affairs of Scotland in 1652 initiated a more caustic approach to addressing the problem that the Kirk posed for the Commonwealth's plans. Fervently Independent chaplains were sent to accompany parliament's commissioners; men as equally intolerant of the presbytery as the Kirk was of them. Their venomous attacks against the Kirk led the Inverness-shire minister James Fraser to complain of the 'factious Independents ... direct opposition' to and persecution of Presbyterians.[169] The tenacious attack against the Kirk produced by Lockyer and anxiously encouraged by the commissioners' chaplains, did little to soften the opinions of the vast majority of Scottish Presbyterians towards toleration. For this reason, the polemics against the Kirk stopped when Cromwell became Protector. Cromwell desired Christian unity and harmony, not division. Although initially he fostered dissension within the Kirk as a means of dividing and conquering his enemy, after toleration had been successfully imposed and Independent congregations had room to develop, he set about the task of trying to heal the Protester–Resolutioner split. Cromwell's attempts at undermining the Kirk were for the purpose of diminishing its intolerance, thus enabling him to build a more stable foundation on which to construct his longed-for Christian republic.

4 'Neirer the patterne of the word'

A Season of Indigenous Scottish Independency[1]

Thes 207. As there seldom ariseth any turbulent Opinion or party in the Church, but by the occasion of some neglect of Truth or Duty, which by their extremities God calleth to reform.

It is a special part of our wisdom to know what is our Health by our Diseases, and to learn Truth from the erroneous, and Duty from them that swerve into extreams ... I could say the like of other Parties that have lately risen up. One sort runneth to them, and another part raileth at them; but he is the wise man that knoweth how to receive from them so much as is good, and leave the rest; could we duly improve them, we might have cause to thank God (though not them) that ever he permitted such occasions of our Reformation.[2]

Richard Baxter, 1659

Triumphalist Presbyterian histories of the nineteenth century have done much to obscure modern perceptions of the religious struggle in Scotland during the seventeenth century, especially in relation to the 1650s. In placing too much emphasis on the Protester–Resolutioner conflict, traditional historiography has diminished recognition of the degree to which Presbyterianism and its covenanted status came under scrutiny. This is particularly true among Protesters, who experienced sharp internal divisions over interpretations of how Commonwealth policy reflected their own desires for a purer Kirk and to what degree the two were compatible. This chapter focuses on groups who either separated themselves from the Kirk or were separated from the Kirk by ecclesiastical censure but continued to function as Independent gatherings in Scotland during the Interregnum. In general, there are four different circumstances addressed in this chapter: first, ministers who were deposed by the Kirk but continued in their ministries with the support of their congregations; second, individuals who voiced support for the Commonwealth and advocated the gathering of Independent congregations; third, Scots who actually formed their own Independent congregations; fourth and finally, Gillespie's faction of Protesters for whom the distinction between rigid Presbyterianism and Independency blurred. These occurrences demonstrate that the Commonwealth's religious aims in Scotland were not in vain, as an underlying distrust of Presbyterianism had already been established through the Kirk's actions in the previous decade.

Some of the earliest evidence of separation from the Kirk during the Interregnum occurred among a small and predominantly enigmatic group of ministers in Orkney. Few Orcadian records survive from the early years of the Interregnum due to the lack of a functioning presbytery in Orkney from July 1650 until mid-1654. On 10 June 1650 the General Assembly deposed all but two of Orkney's ministers for subscribing a declaration in support of the invasion of Scotland by the marquis of Montrose.[3] In total, between nine and twelve ministers were deposed in Orkney and another seven in Caithness.[4] In an attempt to alleviate the clerical vacuum created in Orkney, the commissioners of the General Assembly sent John Harper, David Kennedy and James Wallet (all expectants) north in January 1651.[5] However, even with these individuals helping to serve in the 'vacant' Orkney parishes a significant problem remained. While they could preach, they were not ordained and so could not participate as constituent members in the reconstitution of the presbytery. This lack of a presbytery in Orkney meant four years of relaxed discipline in the islands and provided those individuals sent to fill vacant charges with little disciplinary leverage.

After labouring in Orkney for three years without ordination, Kennedy along with John Gibson travelled to Edinburgh for induction into vacant charges. The presbytery of Edinburgh ordained and admitted them to the charges of Birsay-Harray and Holm (respectively) on 10 May 1654, citing the lack of a constituted presbytery in Orkney and the recent shortage of meetings in Caithness (due to the presence of Cromwellian troops who garrisoned Helmsdale, Dunbeath, Dochmaluag Castle, Girnigoe/Sinclair Castle, Anderwick Tower, Canisbay and Thurso at various times) as the warrant for their intervention.[6] Yet more interesting for the present study is the primary reason cited by the presbytery for ordaining the two men, because 'deposed and excommunicat ministers have begunne to excercise the ministry there, [and] like so to continue unless some actuall ministers be admitted and sent hither'. Although the parish charges had supposedly been 'vacant' for four years, at least some of the ministers deposed in 1649–50 continued their ministries despite the censures against them. One of these ministers was Gordon Graham, who 'intruded' in his parish of Sandwick and Stromness until his reinstatement on 28 July 1658, meaning he potentially served in his old charge for eight years after his deposition.[7] Crucially, this situation could only have occurred with the support of his congregation, which denotes the parish operating in a proto-Congregational model in direct opposition to the General Assembly. More importantly, Graham was not alone in ignoring the judgement passed by the Kirk. Other ministers seem to have continued to work in their old charges as well. William Watson (Hoy and Graemesay), George Johnston (Orphir),

John Balvaird (Rousay and Egilshay) and David Watson (Westray) were all deposed in 1650 but apparently remained active in their parishes until being restored in either 1658 or 1659.

The difficulty of deciphering the situation in Orkney during the Interregnum is further compounded by the 1660 pre-Restoration deposing of the minister of Stronsay for being a fully fledged Independent of the English variety. Patrick Waterstone, one of the two Orkney ministers who had avoided being deposed in 1650 by not signing the declaration in support of Montrose, reportedly separated himself 'from the whole Church of Scotland, and judicatorie thereof, by ane uncontrollable Libertie to erect himself into ane Congregational Church'.[8] When Waterstone actually separated from the Kirk is uncertain, because he may have had an Independent church for some time protected from Presbyterian interference by the February 1652 English imposition of religious toleration. That he favoured Independency before the end of the Interregnum is indicated by his subscription to a petition requesting religious toleration submitted to the Commonwealth parliament in the summer of 1659.[9] Although Stronsay is an island some miles east of Kirkwall and the Orkney mainland, English troops were active throughout Orkney and garrisoned both Kirkwall and Noltland Castle on Westray. One English report declared that the Commonwealth's influence exerted from Orkney 'extend[s] to above 150 miles', possibly referring to control of Shetland as well.[10] Stronsay's geographical isolation probably served as a greater buffer from the presbytery (after it was re-established in 1654) than from the influence of the English. The fact that Waterstone was deposed in March 1660, only four months after the English army had withdrawn from Orkney, might suggest that the presbytery could only move against the minister after the English had withdrawn, thus leaving open the possibility he had maintained a Congregational church for some time.

It would be overstating the case to claim that all those ministers who carried on their work after being deposed in 1650 were acting as Independents in the English sense of the term, as Waterstone clearly did. However they were proceeding in direct opposition to an act of the General Assembly. Perhaps they were encouraged to reinstate themselves in their parish ministries by the English soldiers who began to garrison Orkney early in 1652. The language of the presbytery of Edinburgh's declaration certainly suggests that these ministers did not continue in their charges immediately after being deposed, but resumed after some space of time. English encouragement probably played an important role in Waterstone's separation as it certainly did elsewhere in Scotland. Needless to say, whether the deposed ministers acted under English influence or not, they represent a larger change in Scotland. The degree of unity under a national presbytery expressed in the National Covenant of 1638 began to show cracks by 1648. The synod of Moray noted that William Watson, minister of Duthil, replied to a 1646 order from the General Assembly to preach against the sects in England by declaring: 'How can we speak against Sects seing we are the most abominable sect in all the world because of our government.'[11]

Importantly, remote Orkney is not the only place in Scotland where ministers continued to tend to their congregations despite being deposed or even excommunicated. In January 1650 George Muschet, minister of Dunning, and John Graham, minister of Auchterarder, were similarly deposed for 'malignancy'.[12] Yet despite the censures against them, both men continued in their ministries and 're-invested themselves' to their churches and stipends. On 8 June 1652, representatives from the synod of Perth served notices for the ministers to appear before the synod convening in the Kirk of Dunning on the following morning. The events that transpired have been immortalised in *A Fight at Dunin in Scotland, Between the Scots Women and the Presbyterian Kirkmen*, which, although sometimes described as a satirical work, reports true events, albeit in the interest of English propaganda.[13]

According to the surviving account, when the messenger from the synod arrived to deliver the summons to John Graham, the minister was not home. Instead the messenger relayed the order to Graham's wife. That night she and approximately 120 other women, and some men dressed in women's clothes, according to the Kirk's account, met in the woods near Aberuthven and armed themselves with wooden clubs and bagpipes. Before dawn they marched to Dunning and took possession of the kirkyard. When an infuriated minister of the synod attempted to enter the Kirk, 'those Amazons' beat him 'for his paines'. A full-scale riot ensued. Members of the synod were driven from the village, losing a dozen of their horses and several of their hats in the mayhem. The English version of the story singles out Alexander Rollock, minister in Perth, claiming that he lost his hat, cloak and horse in his flight from Dunning. After running a mile from the village he threw himself down before an English soldier and on bended knee begged him for protection from the fearsome women. This version goes on to relay that the synod re-gathered under the protection of Lord Freeland near Forgandenny and condemned the entire lot of the fairer sex to be 'wicked'.[14] English journals spun this event in relation to the revolt against Episcopacy in 1638, supposedly started by Jenny Geddes' reaction to the prayer book: 'the Kirkmen look upon [this] as a very ominous disaster, that the women, who began with the Bishops in the years 1638. 1639. should now likewise begin with them'.[15] In October the synod planted Andrew Rollo into the 'vacant' charge of Dunning despite Muschet's continuing ministry. The situation remained unchanged until the synod reinstated Muschet in April 1660. Thus even in southern Perthshire examples survive of ministers continuing in their duties with the support of their congregations in opposition to church judicatories, even by means of armed or mob violence.

The deposition of ministers for opposition to the prevailing party within the Kirk represents an important aspect of the events both in Orkney and in Perthshire. In his study of depositions under the covenanters between 1638 and 1651, David Stevenson explains that only 10 per cent of the 236 depositions during the period were due wholly to scandalous behaviour.[16] The remaining 90 per cent 'were depositions of those who opposed, or failed to support enthusiastically enough, the predominant faction in the Kirk'.[17] Unsurprisingly the peak years for depositions were 1639 – the year after the signing of the National Covenant – and the years following Scotland's failed engagement with the king (1648). In the three years between the Engagement and the defeat of the Scots at Worcester the Kirk deposed 105 ministers, most for holding the wrong political views. Neutrality towards the Engagement was enough, according to Stevenson, to be labelled an enemy of the Kirk by the radical covenanting party (Kirk party) which, with the aid of Cromwell's army, seized control of Scotland's government in the Whiggamore Raid of 1648.[18] The policy verged on hypocrisy and members of the Kirk party recognised it just as clearly as their opponents. At the same time that the Kirk was defending the Covenant, supporting the king and advocating a national presbytery in England, it was purging Presbyterian ministers at home. In describing the divergent experiences of representing the Kirk in the Westminster Assembly and the Kirk party within the General Assembly, George Gillespie relayed to John Livingstone, 'he was hardly a moneth [in London] before he was in danger to turn malignant, and hardly again a month in Scotland, but he was in danger to turn a sectary'.[19]

The inquisitorial proceedings fuelled by the radical party of the Kirk were not limited to individual ministers. Presbyteries that neglected to produce condemnations against the Engagement came under scrutiny and were visited by special commissions of visitation made up of the 'most zealous brethren of Edinburgh, Lothian and Merse'. The Presbyteries of Dun, Chirnside, Ross, Sutherland, Shetland and of course Orkney and Caithness all received visits from these commissions. Such factious party politics did little to quell concerns over Scotland's adherence to the covenants, especially after the defeats of their covenanted army at Dunbar and Worcester. In this way the harsh politics, infighting and unjust purging of godly ministers within the Kirk fostered dissatisfaction and resentment towards centralised ecclesiastical government, thus paving the way for Independency to be introduced into Scotland.

The Fertile Soil of Discontent

With the arrival of the English army late in the summer of 1650 a massive influx of alternative religious ideas was introduced into Scotland for the first time. For many Scots this must have been quite a confusing set of circumstances, being exposed to ideas and sects that they had never heard of and more varieties of Protestantism than they ever knew existed. For others it probably represented an exciting revelation. Looking back on the closing months of 1650 Nicoll commented that

> the names of Protestant and Papist wer not now in use ... in place theairof rais up the name of Covenanteris, Anti-Covenanteris, Croce-Covernanteris, Puritanes, Babarteres, Roun-heidis, Auld-hornes, New-hornes, Croce-Pet[it] ioneris, Brownistes, Separatistes, Malignantis, Sectareis, Royalists, Quakeris, Anabaptistes.[20]

Partly due to the influx of these new ideas, partly as a reaction to the devastating defeat of Scotland's 'Covenanted' army at Dunbar and, more significantly, as a reaction to the factionalism experienced within the Kirk over the previous decade, a more overt anti-Presbyterian sentiment and scepticism towards the covenants began to swell among Scotland's populace. As a result, newly introduced alternatives to the presbytery did not fall on infertile or untilled soil. Division within the Kirk and harsh party persecutions created fissures in the Presbyterian disposition of Scotland, like small crevices in a monolithic granite crag, where sectarian seeds found just enough soil to grow. As these new religious ideas took root they forced the fractures ever wider, further eroding the uniformity of the Kirk and securing themselves more space to mature. As early as 1 January 1651 Nicoll commented on growing fears that some ministers of the Kirk were beginning to favour the 'Cromwellites'.[21] In April the Kirk generally acknowledged the gravity of the situation in a declaration for nationwide fasting and humiliation when they instructed prayer 'for those who have fallen into the wayes or errors of the enemie'.[22] Ferment and fear grew throughout the summer of 1651, but with Cromwell's army still south of the Firth of Forth some hope of mounting successful military resistance to their army and heresies persisted. However, the defeat of Scotland's forces at Worcester on 3 September 1651 dealt the Kirk a significant blow. The Presbyterian factions that had already begun to develop in Scotland became increasingly polarised with the result of further ostracising those in the middle.

The Resolutioners interpreted the defeat as the result of overly stringent purging of their forces at the battle of Dunbar, which meant that both Dunbar and Worcester had been fought with remnant armies rather than with the full strength of the nation. Protesters interpreted the defeat as judgement against taking up the Malignant cause of the king and thus a betrayal of religious commitments made within the covenants. These are the two contemporary interpretations of events put forward in most accounts of Scottish history. However, some voiced a third interpretation and reaction to the defeat of Scotland's covenanted cause. This third explanation argued that the Kirk unjustifiably interfered in politics under the guise of the covenants, especially in their prompting of Scotland's involvement in the English civil wars, leading the nation astray and resulting in its present circumstances.

A paper termed the 'Declaration and vindication of the poor opprest Commons of Scotland' denounced involvement in English affairs, but singled out the greatest atrocity as the manner in which the poor people of Scotland had been oppressed by their own gentry and clergy. 'We humblie declare that we can find no records in Scripture, Ecclesiastick Historie, nor the historie of no nation under heaven can shoe that ever yr hes beene a people so opprest, bornen downe, and trampled over as we these many years past by our fellow subjects.'[23] The paper identifies the oppressors as the opportunists and fanatics who took the aims of the covenant to an extreme under the rule of the Radical Kirk party which came into power under the aid of the English army in 1648. The poor suffered greatly, argued the author/s, but particularly between the Kirk party's declaration in favour of Charles II and the Scots final defeat at Worcester. Under Covenanter governments large tariffs were placed on foodstuffs in order to provide for an army to fight first against the king and then against England's parliament.[24] Yet when the English invaded Scotland in 1650 these same radical elements in positions of authority carried out 'ridiculous' purging of the army before Dunbar, which they termed a 'Divilish dark plot' and betrayal of the kingdom of Scotland, leading to the 'most disgraceful' defeat in the history of Christendom. And despite the travesty that unfolded, those responsible for the demise of Scotland continued in their narrow way.

The work, praised by Thomas Urquhart, singles out the Kirk party (many of whom became Protesters) for 'lying in their bastard hatching uncleaness' by continuing to believe they were the only godly party in Scotland and planting as many of their own into vacant charges as possible.[25] The mistreatment of the poor and devout people of Scotland by fellow Scots led the authors to declare that the poor class of the nation would gladly live peaceably under English rule on two conditions: first, nothing be put upon Scotland that would 'molest consciences' or 'imply perjury'; and second, no Scots, or at least none of those involved in the government of the Kirk party, be given positions of trust in the new government. This sentiment illustrates the utter despondency felt by some Scots towards the fruits of Scotland's labours carried out in the name of the covenants. The author/s of this work verbalised what James Paterson explained in his history of Ayr and Wigton, namely that some Scots were 'happy' to be controlled by a power other than the radical factions under whom Scotland had suffered so greatly in the 1640s.[26] When the paper began its circulation is uncertain, but by 28 January 1652 it had been printed.[27] More importantly, however, this was not the only paper produced regarding this point. Nor did this represent the only dissent expressed towards the Kirk.

At a Protester meeting held in Edinburgh in early October 1651, the full breadth of the religious milieu beginning to form in Scotland came into view for the first time.[28] Never had a religious conference in Scotland had such a radically disjointed range of religious perspectives. Numerous sectarian doctrines were put forward in the congress, which lasted between sixteen and eighteen days.[29] Most of the dissenting ideas came from elders who advocated an end to the national presbytery, the lawfulness of lay preaching by any 'haiffing the Spirite to preach', a denunciation of sabbatarianism, and the rejection of paedo-baptism in favour of believer's baptism.[30] Others brought the covenants into question in varying degrees. John Livingston, minister of Ancrum, declared from the pulpit of St Giles' that covenants were not equal to Scripture and Scotland 'too much' idolised them.[31] John Menzies, professor of divinity at Marischal College and minister of Greyfriars (Aberdeen), and Alexander Jaffray, former provost of Aberdeen, went a step further.[32] They questioned whether the covenants were even legal.

Alexander Jaffray, one of the emissaries who travelled to Breda in 1650 to negotiate the return of Charles II, was taken prisoner at the battle of Dunbar and remained in the custody of the English for 'five or six' months.[33] During this internment he spent a great deal of time in frequent conversations with John Owen, Lieutenant-General Fleetwood and Oliver Cromwell himself.[34] These dialogues set Jaffray's mind into motion, prompting him to mull over the present circumstances, 'the clear evidences of the Lord's controversy with the family and person of our king' and the apparent providential dispensation of God's judgement against Scotland. Upon his release early in 1651 Jaffray returned home to Aberdeen 'in the end of February or March' still pondering these questions. Although he initially tried to suppress his doubts, fearing that openly expressing them would lead to suffering, especially if the 'King's party should prevail' (Scotland continued to hold out against Cromwell's forces), Jaffray could not curb his doubts.[35] Instead he entered into discourse with John Menzies (professor of divinity at Marischal College and minister of Greyfriars church, Aberdeen)[36], John Row (minister of Aberdeen's third charge and instructor of Hebrew at Marischal College)[37], William Muir (elder in the Kirk, professor of mathematics and principal of Marischal College)[38] and the layman Andrew Birnie (regent in Marischal College)[39] over his uncertainties. So sincere was his desire to discuss his ideas candidly with those pious men that he even allowed them to peruse his personal journal so that they could see the progression of his thoughts.[40] To Jaffray's relief he found that these men were burdened with the same questions, and they found in each other kindred spirits.

During the summer of 1651 Jaffray composed a summary of his thoughts and sent them to 'some good men in the south', but failing to receive a satisfactory answer he travelled, along with John Menzies, William Muir and Alexander Skene, to the previously mentioned Protester conference.[41] On the evening of 6 October Jaffray and Menzies met privately with Lord Archibald Johnston of Wariston, James Guthrie and Patrick Livingstone, leading members of the Protester party. Despite several hours of discourse the conference did little to appease the concerns of either Menzies or Jaffray, so the following day Jaffray submitted a paper 'containing my thoughts of the causes of the Lord's controversy with the land' to the Protester assembly.[42]

Jaffray's paper no longer survives, but entries in his diary provide a good account of how he perceived the existing state of affairs. For Jaffray, 'the dreadful appearance of God against us at Dunbar', after so many public appeals to Him, represented not a judgement against the propriety of Scotland's adherence to the covenants, as many of his contemporaries argued, but rather a judgement against the covenants themselves. He argued that Scotland had fallen in love with Presbyterianism as 'the only way of Jesus Christ'. Consequently, the maintenance and expansion of the presbytery had been the primary intention of the covenants. And so Scotland's great guilt laid in pridefully attempting to impose its chosen form of church government upon others and holding it up as the sole form of Christian church government. 'Without doing Presbyterians any wrong,' he states, 'it is not the only way of Christ, as they would have it, and as in the covenant all sworn to it.[43]

Jaffray's paper caused a great stir in the Protester meeting and prompted a private conference with John Carstairs, Samuel Rutherford, Patrick Livingstone and James Guthrie, the leading figures of the Protester party. They spent all morning of 9 October debating in Wariston's chamber, but neither side conceded any ground.[44] The men from Aberdeen, however, did agree to take no further action before additional meetings could be arranged. Significantly, the influential role of Jaffray's paper in the unfolding of events within the Protester party has been overlooked. Only after Jaffray submitted his paper to the conference and met for a second time with Protester leaders did Wariston turn his attention to the production of his *Causes of the Lords Wrath Against Scotland*, which represents his attempt to enumerate the sins responsible for Scotland's culpability in order to shift the blame away from Jaffray's arguments against the covenants and Presbyterianism.[45]

The debate sparked by Jaffray's paper at the Protester meeting in October 1651 raises the question of why so much dissent appeared so quickly in the Kirk. Additionally, why did it surface in the Protester party? The answer lies in the nature of that party. While the Resolutioners interpreted the covenants as treading a balance between the preservation of Presbyterianism and the maintenance of Scotland's traditional political structures and monarchy, the Protesters were much more religiously radical, willing to flirt with abandoning political structures and even support for the monarchy if it would provide a purer Kirk.[46] They had pinned all their hopes upon their covenanted status and been the primary instigators for purging the army before the battle of Dunbar. They had advocated 'For the Covenant' as the battle cry at Dunbar. Consequently, the annihilation of Scotland's army, patterned after the army of 'Gideon', left many devastated and questioning how to interpret God's providence. While some Protesters chose to interpret their defeat as an indication of additional hidden sins requiring repentance, others, like Menzies, Jaffray and their fellows in Aberdeen, made their queries deeper. The Protesters by nature were simply the more religiously radical group in the Kirk. It was easier for religious radicals to shift from one extreme to another than it was for moderates to become radical.

Moreover, the Protesters represented the portion of the Kirk who generally desired a more experiential form of Christianity, demonstrated in their exuberant multi-day communion celebrations.[47] They were overwhelmingly the individuals described by Louise Yeoman who adhered to Presbyterianism in the previous decades because it protected 'the inner world from being smoored by exposure to a lifeless time-serving episcopal ministry, and ceremonies'.[48] They shared the New England Independents' high esteem for conversion experiences, which explains the popularity of Thomas Shepard's writings in Scotland throughout the 1640s despite the crackdown on 'Independent' works.[49] For this reason, individuals devoted to Presbyterianism because of the high value it placed on the personal religious experience were perhaps more susceptible to interpreting the defeats at Dunbar and Worcester as divine judgements for particular faults, than the generally more pragmatic Resolutioners. The Protester emphasis on personal conversion and vibrant personal religious experience gave them a natural affinity for the Independent concept of congregations including only those likely to be elect. Perhaps some came to view gathered congregations as the next logical step from the conventicles that formed under Episcopacy in the 1620s and '30s.[50] Certainly even those Protesters who rejected separation from the Kirk, like Andrew Cant, envied how Independency maintained the purity of the sacraments.[51] If 'conversion' and a 'new birth' represented an integral aspect of the desired experience of the Covenanters, as Yeoman suggests, then the arrival of Independency which advocated the inclusion of only those converted through an intense spiritual experience, may have been perceived by the more radical and experiential Covenanters (which the Protesters certainly were) as the arrival of a purer manifestation of a covenanted religious experience.[52] Another indication of the desire for intense personal religious experiences that the Protesters shared with Independents is exhibited in the Protesters' experimentation with personal covenants during the Interregnum.[53]

Scottish Sectarians

Disputes over the Kirk and the covenants did not reach their apex in the October Protester meeting. Jaffray's submission initiated a series of papers handed in to various meetings across the country. The first was a 'twelve-headed' paper given to the Protester meeting at Edinburgh in mid-November 1651 and also probably to the commissioners of the General Assembly in the same month.[54] Although the paper itself no longer survives, James Balfour has preserved an outline.[55] The paper challenges 1) Scotland's adherence to both the covenants and 2) monarchy; 3) coercing the most ignorant in the land to adhere to the covenants; 4) the passionate and bitter invectives against the godly in England; 5) espousing of the Malignant cause; 6) pollution of the Kirk's ordinances by inclusion of the 'vilest' men; 7) the idolising of men; 8) refusing the treaty offered by the English parliament; 9) promotion of the presbytery as the 'vtermost attainable perfectione of reformatione'; 10) 'the smothering of light and withdrawing from duties'; 11) the neglect and oppression of Scotland's poor; and finally 12) attempting to carry on the Reformation with scandalous and unsuitable people in places of trust. Little is recorded of the response that the paper elicited from fellow Scots, but approving English journals referred to it as 'By ane Godly Scott' or 'by a godly brother'.[56]

When the Protesters reconvened in Edinburgh in late December they received another paper of 'fifteen overtures' entitled 'Overtures to the Right Honorable Commonwealth of England' submitted by a group of Scots.[57] By now the Protesters termed them 'malignants', describing them as 'some few who formerly were accounted pious and gracious men, that were of this mind, their judgments being now corrupted by sectarian principles'.[58] Accusations of Malignancy, however, were utterly unfounded. Instead, the authors of these overtures represent converts to the English concepts of religious freedom and toleration, and thus increasingly sceptical of the covenants and Presbyterianism. Or perhaps it might be more correct to say that due to an increasing scepticism towards the covenants and Presbyterianism, these 'Scottish Sectarians' embraced English notions of religious freedom and toleration. Unfortunately, the only known copy of the overtures is now lost, but before the document disappeared W.I. Hoy preserved their substance.[59] His account can in turn be partially verified by William Row's fragmentary preservation.[60] According to Hoy, the fifteen overtures request

> that only the 'certain' Godly in Scotland[61] are to be entrusted with power although the uncertain are to be considered as brethren, that malignants and noblemen are to be cast out of power and the former brought to trial, and also have their land sequestered, that minor posts not be used as merchandise but given to the English or faithful Scots, that Scots law be replaced by English law, that actions against the present government be punished, that liberty of

conscience be granted in religion, blasphemies and heresies be curbed, the mouths of ministers be stopped who preach seditious doctrine, gathered churches conform to the primitive apostolic pattern, and that the Power of the Presbytery be abolished that 'the name of a national church may perish under heaven in Brittaine'.[62]

Nothing about these requests is 'malignant'; a common slander used to discredit opponents and usually referring to interest in temporal issues over and above right religion. On the contrary, the overtures themselves denounce Malignants while perfectly reflecting the religiously motivated aims of the Commonwealth expressed in the *Declaration of the Army, now in Scotland* written at Musselburgh on 1 August 1650, and the Terms of Union produced a few months later by parliament. The 'Scottish Sectaries'[63] who produced this paper embodied the success that the Commonwealth hoped to attain in their conquest of Scotland. Needless to say, these overtures found little favour among the majority in the Protester meeting. Although the authors who submitted the paper attended the meeting, the overriding opposition to their position caused them to withdraw after only one day of discussions.

It is unfortunate that while we can glean from the overtures what the authors stood for, we lack any certainty as to who they were. W.I. Hoy in his exploratory study of the period suggests that the Aberdeen Independents and the Scottish Sectarians were a homogenous group by claiming the Aberdeen ministers suspended by the 1652 Resolutioner General Assembly were the 'Scottish Sectarians'.[64] However, what was happening in Scotland in 1651 and 1652 cannot be identified as a cohesive movement. Instead, different individuals and groups in different parts of the country were working through their own queries. What they had in common was a general distrust of the Kirk's actions during the 1640s, and a sensitivity and receptiveness to the religious and political messages of the English. For instance, Jaffray and Menzies worked within the context of a localised Aberdeen movement focused on the proper composition of individual Christian congregations and the legality of the covenant. The Scottish Sectarians who composed these (and subsequent) overtures were probably located in the south of the country. While they shared some ideas, in late 1651 the Scottish Sectarians were quick to promote political union with England, the gathering of Independent congregations, and the dissolution of the national presbytery at a time when the Aberdeen Independents had not yet even settled on separation for themselves. Additionally, when the Aberdeen Independents finally did write in May 1652 suggesting they might separate, they made no mention of any of the previous Scottish Sectarian declarations. More importantly, neither did Wariston in either of his two replies to Aberdeen. Wariston, being in the inner circle of the Protester movement, would have had intimate knowledge of both the Aberdeen Independents and the 'Scottish Sectarians' who attended the Protester meeting in December. Had any of those who signed the Aberdeen letter of 24 May 1652 been involved with the composition of the Scottish Sectarian overtures he would have known. Wariston's silence in this regard suggests no involvement of the would-be Aberdeen Independents in the production of the 'Overtures'.[65]

In general the Aberdeen Independents and the Scottish Sectarians can be distinguished in two ways. The Aberdeen Independents focused primarily on the shortcomings of the national church in terms of its impact on the purity of local congregations and the sinful effect of propagating Presbyterianism under the guise of the covenants. While they may have become involved in politics, as Jaffray later did, it was not until after they had settled their religious queries: the health of the church being their primary interest, particularly at the local level. Many Scottish Sectarians also embraced Independency but were initially concerned with replacing the oppressive political structures in Scotland and securing their own participation in the functioning of Commonwealth government. Though Scotland's ventures in the name of the covenants prompted both groups to look for change (and they moved increasingly towards the same goals), they started in different places. These two different positions correspond to two distinctive reasons why Scots may have embraced Independency. First, either as a rejection of the coercive power of the national church, which dominated the consciences of its members; or second, for more ecclesiologically based reasons, such as desiring purer congregations and ordinances. While the two are not mutually exclusive, neither are they inherently linked.

While the ringleaders of the Aberdeen Independents can be identified through historical accounts and their subscription to declarations, the Scottish Sectarians are significantly more enigmatic. The anonymous author of *A Word of Advertisement* and the author of the 'twelve-headed' paper can probably be numbered among the Scottish Sectarians; beyond that it is difficult to identify particular individuals without making sweeping assumptions. So it may prove to be of greater use to identify individuals sympathetic to their 'sectarian' sentiment. Some likely candidates are John Swinton (younger) of that ilk, Sir James MacDowall of Garthland, Colonel William Lockhart of Lee, Sir Walter Dundas (laird of Dundas and governor of Edinburgh Castle), William Dundas (younger brother of the laird of Duddingston),[66] John Ho[o]me ('servitor' to Dundas of Dundas), Major Andrew Abernethie, Lieutenant Robert Andrew, Captain Holburne, Lieutenant William Govan, Major William Johnston, Colonel Gilbert Ker, Colonel Archibald Strachan, and the three brothers Sir James Hope of Hopeton, Sir John Hope of Craighall and Sir Alexander Hope.[67]

William Clarke described Swinton, John Hope and James Hope as the men who came 'nearest to our [the Commonwealth's] principles' in March 1652.[68] Swinton, John Hope and Lockhart served as judges and members of Commonwealth parliaments under the English and might in some degree owe their allegiance to personal religious changes. Swinton voted against levying troops to oppose Cromwell's invasion in 1650 and eventually became a Quaker; Lockhart formed a gathered congregation in his home in May 1652; Hope is reported to have encouraged John Owen to return to Scotland and preach in 1653.[69] When Hope died in 1654, Nicoll noted that his opinions were viewed as erroneous by many contemporaries, as he thought poorly of the ministers of the Kirk and perceived God to be doing a great work through the English.[70]

MacDowall of Garthland, who also served in Commonwealth parliaments, signed a petition in 1659 requesting a permanent religious toleration be imposed in Scotland and that all previous Scottish legislation opposing toleration or preventing religious diversity be abolished.[71] Johnston, Home and Ker were all dealt with either by the Committee of Estates or the commissioners of the General Assembly for favouring the Independents or surrendering their posts in order to join with the English in 1650 as Swinton, William Dundas, Abernethie, Govan and Strachan purportedly did.[72] On 24 March 1651, William Dundas, Walter Dundas, Colonel Archibald Strachan, Swinton, John Home, Major Johnston and Major Abernethie 'with divers others' were all summoned to appear before the Committee of Estates for complying with the 'sectaries'.[73] In April 1651 the commissioners of the General Assembly reissued summons for Swinton, William Dundas, Lieutenant Andrew, and Lieutenant Govan for their compliance with the 'Sectarian Army now infesting' Scotland.[74] The commissioners ordered the excommunication of Swinton, William Dundas and Major Abernethie on 24 May 1651 for their compliance with the 'sectaries', while Walter Dundas only received a further summons.[75] According to William Row, Major Abernethie had 'always spoke favourably of Independency and against Presbyterian government' and the commissioners claimed him to be partially responsible for the surrender of Edinburgh Castle.[76] Major William Johnston supposedly had 'gone into that blasphemous armie of Sectaries' and remained among them in Edinburgh, where he spoke 'familiarlie' with their officers and generally complied with them.[77] Strachan commanded a regiment in the army of the Western Association, but following personal correspondence with Cromwell became disenchanted with the Malignancy of Scotland's cause and joined the English in December 1650.[78] The Kirk suspected he also played some part in convincing Dundas to surrender Edinburgh Castle.[79] Accordingly, on 12 January 1651 the Kirk excommunicated Strachan and 'deliuered [him] to the deivuell' for being too sympathetic towards the 'sectarians'.[80] Gilbert Ker also served as an officer in the Western Association before surrendering to the English in December 1650. Captain Holburne was called before the king and parliament in December 1650 for suspected 'underhande dealling' with Cromwell's informants.[81] By

William Dundas' own account, his disenchantment with Presbyterianism
began before the Interregnum and he may have even been under threat
of excommunication before 1650.[82] Certainly he attempted to obtain
some banned books, labelled 'Sectary Books' by the Kirk, from a London
merchant sometime between the General Assembly's ban in 1647 and the
arrival of the English army.[83]

Another possible candidate to fit the Scottish Sectarian mould is John
Mein, accused of treason and sentenced to death for giving information
to the English in 1650.[84] Mein is of particular interest, and should be
included in this list of individuals, because in the 1620s his father faced
the wrath of both civil and ecclesiastical authorities for promoting and
holding religious conventicles, which he and his contemporaries called
'congregations'.[85] The elder Mein also served on the Kirk party's commissions for purging between 1648 and 1650.[86] So there is some reason
to believe the younger Mein's sympathy for the English may have been
motivated by religious dissent towards the Kirk, making him another
strong candidate.

While none of these men can be proven to have had any association with
the previously mentioned documents, they all displayed sympathy with
the English religious agenda, a characteristic of the Scottish Sectarians.
Wariston accused Swinton in August 1651 of 'comending the Sectaries to
the skyes'.[87] Others like Sir John Chiesly admitted later in the decade to
be tired of Presbyterianism but probably did not adhere strongly enough
to this opinion in 1651 to be considered a potential author.[88] These few
examples of only prominent individuals demonstrates a significant number
of potential candidates for the authorship of the supplications for union
and toleration. Thus the lack of names attached to the overtures does not
diminish their value as a testament to the changing political and religious
climate in Scotland.

The Protester meeting responded to the 'Overtures to the Right
Honourable Commonwealth' by drafting its own letter to Cromwell, but
disagreements over the appropriate tenor delayed its completion until 2
January 1652. The letter denounced the great variety of errors that the
English presence introduced: the intervention in Kirk matters; silencing
ministers who preached about political matters; public preaching by
soldiers; disruption of Kirk services; printing of anti-Presbyterian tracts;
gathering of Independent congregations; subordination of the church to
the state 'in the things of Christ'; as well as the duplicitous nature of the
conquest of Scotland by their fellow covenant takers.[89] Additionally, it
urged the preservation of the Presbytery. The Protesters submitted a copy
of the letter to General Lambert, the acting commander-in-chief of the
army in Scotland, but he refused to grant a pass to the young messenger
instructed to deliver it to Cromwell and reportedly answered the letter
with the foreboding comment, 'Soon may your fears fall upon you'.[90]

Copies of the letter reached English journals, which ridiculed calls for the preservation of the presbytery and mocked the 'suffering' of those who 'goe aboute to be persecutters'.[91]

The same day that the Protesters finished their letter, the English regime printed 'a declaration with some overtures' by the Scottish Sectarians as a broadsheet entitled *To the Very Honorable the Representative of the Common-Vvealth*.[92] The paper constitutes a rare testament to the aims and objectives of the Scottish Sectarians. Having recognised that their discussions with the Protesters made little progress, they had retired and set about producing a second supplication to the Commonwealth, including a declaration of their purpose in doing so. Upon receiving the paper the English printed it under the authority of the lieutenant-governor of Leith, Timothy Wilkes. He called the authors 'diverse Good People of Scotland' and deemed it 'very essentiall to the welfare of the Godly and honest Party in Scotland, and of great advantage to the carrying on the great Work of God in the world'. The authors' intentions in making their appeal to the English government were, they claimed, to save the godly in Scotland who risked being crushed 'by the Ocean-like inundations of Malignant [secular] and Presbyterian Confluences'. Four requests are made, and they differ little from those in the previous supplication. First, that Scotland and England be made into one equal commonwealth in which citizens of both nations may share the same liberties and privileges. Second, that godly governors be chosen who show great integrity, live implicitly by faith and will not tyrannise over those they are appointed to govern. Third, that God's people be given 'all due Christian freedom' to practise their faith without threat of cruelty or coercion. Finally, those who are selected to rule should be chosen not for their worldly status but for their piety and integrity.

While there is no doubt of the Scottishness of the authors, there is some evidence of a particular English influence. The authors suggest 'the poor, foolish, and contemned things of this World, are suitablest to our Lords designe: By the mouth and strength of such, he perfecteth his praise: It is *the little stone out of the mountain without hands*.' The phrase 'little stone out of the mountain', taken from Daniel 2:34, is the title of a sermon preached in Edinburgh by Nicholas Lockyer in 1651 (and printed in 1652).[93] Lockyer worked feverishly in Scotland to promote the gathering of congregations. The message of this English advocate of Independency fits well with the desires of those Scots growing increasingly weary of the covenants and the Presbyterian Kirk they underpinned. Within weeks of this paper's publication Whitelocke noted the printing of the 'vindication of the poor oppressed commons of Scotland' on 28 January.[94] Increasingly, those dissatisfied with Kirk and Covenant found a voice.

Separation

By the close of 1651 dissent began to move from the pages of written and printed papers into the sphere of physical action. Nicoll lamented the bleak state of ecclesiastical affairs at the close of 1651.

> Divisiounes, distractiounes, and hart birninges among all soirtis of pepill, both Kirk and Stait; Many of the ministrie fomentaris of divisioun, dealing too rigidlie with sum, and too favorablie with utheris, seiking out rather the pepillis schame than thair syn; quhairon followit manifold errouris and hereseis, sum ministeris refuisand to baptize infantes, utheris taking upon thame to marry men privilie haiffing twa wyfes on lyff.[95]

Reports of gathered churches began in the closing months of 1651. On 16 December 1651 *Mercurius Scoticus* conveyed the situation in the vicinity of Linlithgow, where a Mr Baugh[96] gathered a 'Proselized Congregation' of 'people suitable to his owne minde'.[97] In this account he cleverly foiled a parish minister's attempt to end his ministry: when the minister of the Kirk cut the rope to the church bell he simply tied the two pieces of rope back together and summoned his flock. In early January, news from the Highlands described 'a very precious people who seeke the face of God in Sutherland and divers other parts beyond Invernesse ... [who] will rather leave their owne Ministers and come to private houses where our officers and souldiers meete together'.[98] Three months later Lilburne reported that 'the Lord is pleas'd to open the eyes of many to draw them out of their old formes [Presbyterianism] into a neerer communion with those that truly feare God amongst us, and divers are become Members of [gathered] Churches, and many more would if meanes were not wanting amongst them'.[99] And again a few days later, 'there is an increase of good people who daily some way or other are sweetned towardes us, and become more united in their affections and judgements, only there wants some meanes to lead many into a clearer light that are waiting for it; and I could with this were nott soe much neglected by the State as it is'.[100]

The first significant break from the Kirk was reported in March 1652, one month after the English regime officially imposed toleration in Scotland on any who would worship in 'a gospel way'. Nicoll states a 'malignant and independant party in the North' separated from the Kirk because they found that 'bloody' and 'barbarous' events always accompanied Scotland's Presbyterian government.[101] While he includes the entire text of their declaration of separation, Nicoll neglects to include the names of those who signed it, and hence has forced his readers to speculate about its authorship. Although it has long been assumed this declaration refers to the Aberdeen Independents, this assumption is incorrect since they did not publicly profess their affinity to Independency until 24 May 1652 and did not officially separate until October. The clue to answering something about who these separatists were lies in the presbytery book of Strathbogie.[102]

In June 1652 William Gordon of Dumbennan stood before the presbytery of Strathbogie under threat of censure for 'false, lying, scandalous reproaches against the Kirk of Scotland'.[103] Rather than succumbing to threats of an ecclesiastical reprimand, Gordon responded by submitting a declaration of separation to the presbytery matching Nicoll's almost *verbatim*. The similarity between the declarations is so close it suggests they come from a common source. That is to say, Gordon either had direct contact with the authors of the first declaration or shared contact with the same source. The Aberdeen Independents seem an unlikely source for this declaration, for they were not yet ready to declare separation for themselves. However, the presbytery of Strathbogie did receive a letter and some 'public papers' from John Row on 28 April, probably including a paper questioning Presbyterianism that he had submitted to the synod of Aberdeen five days earlier.[104] Therefore it is not beyond the realm of possibility that a dialogue relating to separation took place between the group moving towards Independency in Aberdeen and some in Strathbogie more eager to separate from the Kirk.[105] Evidence in the presbytery of Strathbogie's records suggests that they perceived Independency as a local threat by March 1652. George Meldrum (possibly the 1651 graduate of Marischal College who became a prominent minister after the Restoration) spoke to the presbytery about the danger posed by Independency and offered a defence of Presbyterian ecclesiastical government.[106] Pleased with his work, the presbytery provided him funds to continue his studies.

The threat of Independency noted by the presbytery corresponds with the arrival of a significant English military presence in the area, whose 'great numbers ... remaining in their boundes' disrupted ecclesiastical business.[107] Soldiers garrisoned Rothiemay Castle at the northern end of Strathbogie and Kildrummy Castle just to the south, as well as a number of other locations in the north-east. Perhaps one of these garrisons served as the source for the declaration of separation; or perhaps, as Hoy suggests, it came from Nicholas Lockyer, who travelled widely throughout the country promoting separation. Lockyer definitely visited the north-east of Scotland in the spring of 1652 at the invitation of some Scots who wished him to oversee the gathering of Independent churches.[108] Perhaps the subscribers of Nicoll's declaration, who separated in March, are the same individuals who requested Lockyer's help. If this is the case, they may have composed the declaration with Lockyer's help. Or possibly Lockyer provided the document for them. A prepared statement for use by rural Scots represented a legitimate enterprise, since research into the literacy of rural parishes in the 1630s has deduced that less than 20 per cent of the population could read.[109] Whatever the precise circumstances, Gordon had some association with the authors of the declaration in Nicoll's journal and here is a case of separation in north-eastern

Scotland completely outside the presbytery of Aberdeen and separate from the famous Aberdeen Independents. Approximately a year after William Gordon's declaration, Sir Robert Gordon of Gordonstoun and his family, 'the most considerable part of the parish', 'defected' from the kirk at Ogston in April 1653. Two months later his son-in-law, David Barclay of Ury (father of the famous Quaker Robert Barclay of Ury who later served as governor to the Scots–Quaker colony in East New Jersey), publicly rejected the doctrine and discipline of the Kirk, declaring it to be a false church.[110] By October Gordonstoun had begun building a new church at Kinnedar.[111] What became of the gathering there is uncertain, but Gordon died in 1656. It is interesting to note that the north-east of Scotland, and Strathbogie in particular, was again a hotspot for separation when Congregationalism rekindled in the nineteenth century.[112]

Whatever the precise circumstances, Gordon had some association with the authors of the declaration in Nicoll's journal, and here is a case of separation in north-eastern Scotland completely outside the presbytery of Aberdeen and separate from the famous Aberdeen Independents who separated five months later. Evidence for other separations in the north-east around this time also exist. Andrew Ballenden, at the prompting of English soldiers, entered the vacant parish charge of Drumoak. There he worked 'upon the independent and congregaionall course' for several months before appearing before the presbytery of Aberdeen to recant in October.[113] Drumoak may have been one of the 'severall Kirks about Aberdeen' who had reportedly fallen off and deserted the presbytery, according to the London-based news journal, *Mercurius Politicus*, in March 1652.[114]

Aberdeenshire and Strathbogie were not the sole bastions of success for the English message of separation. Nicoll reported in May 1652, without any geographical specification, laymen taking upon themselves the role of the ministry without a 'lauchfull calling' and preaching, performing weddings and baptisms, and publicly debating their new doctrines.[115] The Kirk excommunicated Alexander Cornwell, minister of Muiravonside near Linlithgow, in 1652 for privately performing marriages, some of which were reportedly polygamous, and for baptising 'old people'.[116] In Edinburgh, the Scotsman Colonel William Lockhart of Lee, who served the Commonwealth as a judge and later as a diplomat to France after marrying Cromwell's niece, opened his home on 29 May 1652 for a gathered congregation to meet.[117] Lockhart had served during the Engagement in 1648 and been taken prisoner by the English. During his internment he spent time in Hull, where he conversed regularly with the governor, the politically and religiously radical Robert Overton, and in Newcastle, where his fellow Scots accused him of being too friendly with the Particular Baptist Paul Hobson.[118] 'Lockhart might have been released for money, but,' wrote Sir James Turner, 'whether it was to save that, or to enjoy the too acceptable company of Paul Hobson that he remained in Newcastle, he knows best.' Yet Turner was sufficiently certain of Lockhart's allegiances to brand him a 'great Independent'.[119] Robert Baillie reported in a letter dated 8 July that a group separated from the Kirk in Fenwick despite tearful sermons against schism preached by the parish minister, William Guthrie.[120] Evidence of a more general support for 'sectarian' or Independent religion within the burgh of Glasgow is evidenced in reports that, following a great fire in the city on 15 June 1652, ministers throughout the municipality preached it to have been God's judgement 'for compliance with the sectaries'.[121] Most famously, the General Assembly of 1652 censured Thomas Charteris, the minister of Stenhouse, for refusing to baptise infants.[122] These events, along with others doubtlessly lost forever, led English journals to report in November 1652 that many Scots were coming out of the divided Kirk into 'the Congregational way' and prompted the minister of Kilwinning, James Fergusson, to preach several sermons against toleration, error, separation and Independency.[123]

The momentum of Independency carried on into 1653 when a 'Congregational' church gathered in the vicinity of Kirkintilloch and Lenzie, with the Englishman John Beverley settled into the charge at the calling of twenty-seven people, thus forcing the Presbyterian minister to preach 'in the fields, or in a barne' without a stipend.[124] The Commissioners for Visiting Universities in Scotland planted Francis Craw, a Scots Protester with Independent leanings, into the charge of Chirnside in September.[125] In August 1654 Wariston relayed a report from James Guthrie indicating that a congregation of Scots and English soldiers were meeting together in Stirling.[126] That same year, two English Independents, John Collins and John Stalham, were sent to minister in Scotland.[127] Stalham served in Edinburgh for a year before returning to England probably sometime after March 1655.[128] John Collins, educated at Harvard,[129] remained in Scotland until 1659, being called to a new Independent church in Leith in 1658 which, although Congregational, rejected paedo-baptism.[130] Yet careful reading of the few surviving sources indicates that Stalham, Collins and Beverley were not the first English ministers to serve civilian congregations rather than as chaplains to the army.

In July 1652 three English Independents were sent to Scotland in response to a request from the Commissioners of Scotland for some ministers to be placed in English garrisons and other convenient places.[131] Besides the two ministers sent as chaplains (James Brown and Thomas Twisse),[132] Samuel Mather, Thomas Brag and Sidrach Simpson were given £500 to travel to Scotland.[133] Whether Simpson travelled or not is uncertain; if he did, his stay in Scotland was very short. Mather and Brag definitely did make the journey. Brag stayed in Scotland until September 1653, being latterly at Stirling, where he was described as serving as a 'minister' rather than a chaplain. Perhaps he ministered to the congregation of English soldiers and Scottish civilians mentioned by Guthrie. When Brag left Scotland, another Englishman, Samuel Bryan, replaced him as 'minister at Stirling'.[134] Samuel Mather, eldest son of Richard Mather and graduate of Harvard (MA, 1643), resided in Leith, where he reputedly ministered to a church until November 1654, when he was called to Ireland.[135] Robert Dalliel, sometime minister of Swanton Morley, Norfolk, also received £200 pounds to relocate and serve as a minister of the Gospel in Scotland in March 1655.[136] Yet despite these several glimpses of ministers and congregational gathering in Scotland during the middle years of the Interregnum, the Scot Thomas Charteris remains the only minister whose career as an Independent in Scotland can be properly charted.

After a brief stint at Stenhouse (near Hamilton), where Baillie claims he abandoned 'his poor charge', Charteris was called as minister to an Independent congregation gathered under English encouragement at Kilbride (East Kilbride).[137] There the gathered congregation, for which Charteris received 'the best stipend in the west' of £1,200 a year, consisted of only twenty to thirty members of a parish comprising over 2,000 people. Charteris took the manse, glebe and church for his own use, leaving the bulk of the parish to build a new manse for a replacement Presbyterian minister and provide a stipend out of their own pockets. Reasons for further grievances against the minister come from reports that Charteris subsidised his massive stipend through horse breeding and trading. Not surprisingly, Baillie and subsequent Kirk historians, as well as Quaker historians, construed the demise of Charteris as divine judgement.[138] One Saturday evening in June 1656, while stroking a horse as it grazed in the kirkyard, Charteris received a powerful kick in the chest and died from the injury early the next morning. While Craufurd, as a later Kirk historian, inherited contempt for Interregnum separatists, Baillie's dislike for Charteris was altogether more personal. Baillie had been awarded the stipend of Kilbride in January 1651 for his work at the University of Glasgow.[139] No doubt it perturbed him when the stipend ended up in the pocket of Charteris, a separatist, rather than in his own.

The growth of Independency did not go unnoticed by the Kirk, but Baillie noted the difficulty of dealing with 'schismatics' in mid-1652. Besides the support that Independents enjoyed from the English regime, internal divisions within the Kirk prevented the General Assembly from effectively moving against them. In a letter outlining the problem, Baillie cited Thomas Charteris as a prime example of how a lone schismatic, who could have been easily censured in earlier years, managed to continue.[140] Yet the problem extended beyond censuring Independents already active in Scottish parishes, because new ones continued to enter kirks. A month after Beverley's induction into the charge at Lenzie, the commissioners of the General Assembly considered the 'inorderly way of intrusion of young men to the ministry in congregations without consent of Presbyteries'.[141] Two days later they passed an act prohibiting 'disorderly and violent intruders' into vacant charges and ordered presbyteries to deal in an ecclesiastical way with all 'disorders, usurpations, and incroachments upon the liberties of the Kirk and the consciences of the people'.[142] Ostensibly powerless after the imposition of toleration in the previous year, this declaration had much more bark than bite. Its only real influence was that it probably confirmed the English decision to disperse the General Assembly when in met in July, and to prevent it from convening again during the Interregnum.

While the existence of Independently gathered congregations can be confirmed in Aberdeen, Edinburgh, Kirkintilloch/Lenzie, Fenwick, Stonehouse, East Kilbride, Perth, Linlithgow and possibly Birse, Durris, Kinkellar, Strathbogie and elsewhere, it is regrettable that few details of these groups other than merely their presence can be ascertained. This is, however, a problem for historians of gathered congregations throughout Britain for this period, as few records for Independent churches in England survive either. In Scotland the lack of source material is largely due to two factors. First, Independent gatherings formed completely separately from local Kirk congregations and beyond the corrective reach of their kirk sessions, so they are not mentioned in their records. When, as happened at Kilbride, gathered churches displaced Kirk congregations, the Presbyterians were forced into 'the field'. No longer a bastion imposing social conformity, Kirk congregations necessarily became introverted in some aspects of their discipline. In at least one case, the records of the kirk session appear to have completely ignored the separation, despite Baillie's adamant claim that some separated from William Guthrie's Fenwick congregation.[143] Second, because they flourished under the protection of the widely dispersed English garrisons, Independents had alternative communities to turn to for support.[144] For this reason, re-evaluation of the Independents of Aberdeen, the group for whom the greatest number of records survive, is necessary and beneficial to understanding of the development of Independency in its wider Scottish context.

The Aberdeen Independents

After Jaffray and Menzies' meeting with their Protester counterparts in Edinburgh in October 1651, stirrings of separation in Aberdeen remained relatively quiet until late in the following spring. On 23 April John Row submitted a paper to the synod of Aberdeen requesting that each presbytery and every minister in those presbyteries carefully review the acts of the General Assembly and 'other thingis ordered by our reformerris' in consideration of several points. What are the moral qualifications required of ministers, elders and deacons? What level of public penitence is required before reinstating sinful members? What is required from believers before ministers dispense the sacrament of baptism and communion? What are the qualifications required for an individual to be considered a constituent member of a visible church?[145]

The submission of Row's paper raises the question of what prompted action in Aberdeen after Jaffray and his fellows had been dormant for the better part of six months. The impetus probably stemmed from several sources, but one factor in particular seems to have been of paramount importance. The commissioners of the English parliament granted toleration and protection in February 1652 for groups wishing to gather in a 'gospel way' outwith the Church of Scotland.[146] In January the Kirk had moved against individuals in and around Aberdeen who verbally criticised presbytery and the covenants, including Sir Alexander Irving of Drum, and husband and wife Paul Colinson and Marjorie Inglis, for 'defection from the trew protestant reformed religion, according to the Covenant'.[147] Fear of censures may have kept many on the cusp of division quiet, but the imposition of toleration and the steps taken to enforce it took the sting out of the Kirk's bite, enabling anyone who harboured Independent sympathies, or even displeasure towards the Kirk, to take action. In March the *Weekly Intelligencer* reported that 'the Parliament of England, and their Commissioners in Scotland are doing what they can for the advancement of the Gospel with authoritie to carry on that great work … many of the godly partie in Scotland that had heretofore hard thoughts of our Church Government, begin now to be more satisfied and to comply with us'.[148] The separation of others near Aberdeen in early April perhaps hastened the actions of Row and his counterparts.[149] Moreover, contemporary reports that 'two eminent' ministers had joined gathered churches may have piqued Row's interest in surveying his peers to see if any others were tempted to separate.[150] In any case, none of those involved with Jaffray, Menzies and Row were yet prepared for actual separation in the spring of 1652.

After 'eight or nine' weeks of conferences between Jaffray's faction and the 'most learned ministers in Aberdeen', they composed a famous letter voicing support for the 'Congregational way' on 24 May 1652 and sent it to the Protesters in Edinburgh. In his journal Jaffray asserted the purity of their intention.

> Some Christians in Aberdeen, men and women, having for a long time been convinced of these things, (long before ever a thought of them was with me,) found themselves obliged to endeavour to have the ordinances administered in a more pure way, than there was any hope ever to attain to have them in the national way. But before we would conclude to do any thing of this, it was thought necessary, first to impart our purpose to some Christian friends, and to be willing to hear what they could object against our resolution.[151]

Written as a sincere letter to beloved fellow Christians, it is both a declaration of their judgement and a plea for correction if their opinions are

mistaken. It raised questions with regard to two fundamental character-
istics of the Kirk: its constitution or inclusion of members; and its form
of government. Much along the lines of the paper submitted by Jaffray in
October 1651, the authors declared that their questions arose from 'the
Lord's dispensations toward the land' and begged for providential interpretation of Scotland's demise at Dunbar and Worcester.[152]

For the Aberdeen Independents, the blame for Scotland's present state
lay with a fundamental error in the ecclesiology of the national church.
From the Reformation the Kirk had started with a fundamentally wrong
assumption. Rather than include the masses and then weed out the clearly
degenerate, the Church of Christ should start by gathering together true
believers:

> To us it seems, for aught we can search in the word, that none should be
> admitted as constituent members of a visible church, but such as with a profes-
> sion of the Truth join such a blameless and gospel-like behaviour, as they may
> be esteemed, in a rational judgment of charity, believers, and their children.
> Such were the churches founded by the apostles, which ought to be patterns for
> us, as appears by the titles given to them, 'saints, sanctified, justified, purchased
> by the blood of Christ,' &c.[153]

New Testament labels used to describe the Church, such as 'saints', 'sanctified' and 'justified', were interpreted by the Kirk, like most other Reformed
churches, to mean the invisible elect among the visible church. Jaffray and
his fellows opposed this interpretation, stating: 'We cannot acquiesce to
that common answer, that these expressions are to be understood of the
better part.'[154] Instead, the Church should be comprised only of those
who show signs of true sanctification, by means of a sincere profession
of faith accompanied by outward signs of grace. This resounded with the
sentiments of English propaganda advocated by English radicals like the
Baptist James Brown and the Independent Nicholas Lockyer. 'It is certain,
our churches were not constituted according to this rule,' they wrote. '[Y]
ea, alas! few of our precious men will acknowledge it to be a rule.'[155]

For Jaffray, Menzies, Row, Muir and Birnie, the signatories of the
letter, this mixed multitude in the church resulted in the corruption of
the sacraments, 'which we know not how to partake of, without sin, in
our multitude'.[156] Citing 2 Cor 6:14–17, they argued that by partaking
of the Eucharist with profane individuals they sinfully affirmed them
as members of Christ's body. The problem was clear: the church was
overrun with 'heathenish idolators' and something needed to be done.
The difficult question they faced was how they could remove the degenerate masses and restore the Church of Scotland to its right relationship
with God. After struggling with the issue for months, they resolved that
only separation from the Kirk, although far from their original intentions, could rectify the situation. Too much corruption had been allowed
in the Kirk for far too long, and now no alternatives remained by which

the sinful mixture in the church could be resolved. Following closely the rationale and language of Lockyer, they argued that it was impossible for the minority to purge the more numerous 'sour leaven'.[157]

Through their evaluation of the problem facing the Kirk and the best means of responding to it, they came to view the Presbyterian system of church government as being fundamentally to blame for creating the pollution. And equally, they identified the culpability of the covenants for ensuring that the problem would continue. The authors professed to initially have trodden warily in light of their conclusions regarding both Kirk and covenants, recognising they too had sworn to uphold them, but they asked which is the greater sin: having too hastily agreed to the covenants and then realising the fault and correcting it, or continuing to support a perverted church under the guise of impious covenanted obligation? They concluded that there could be no way forward within the Presbyterianism of the Church of Scotland before declaring 'so far as we can see the congregational way comes nearer to the pattern of the word than our classical form'.[158] Yet rather than this being the apex of their argument, this statement served as their starting point.

Besides inherently fostering corruption, Jaffray and his fellows explained that Presbyterianism also stripped Christians of the powers of jurisdiction and censure given to them by Christ, and subjected them to presbyteries, synods and assemblies. Reiterating arguments used by Independents in the 1640s and recycled by Lockyer, they argued that 'the people had no small influence in matters of discipline' in the early church, but Presbyterianism swallowed up these rights.[159] For the authors, congregations were not only the base component bodies of the church, but whole and complete 'churches' endowed with all necessary powers of jurisdiction and censure. So besides taking away ecclesiastical powers from individual congregations, the presbytery also removed their right of democratic self-rule, or made it only superficial, with the real power being reserved for Presbyteries, synods and general assemblies.

All in all, the authors seem to have been greatly influenced by English propaganda published in Scotland in the previous year. Following quite closely the arguments put forward in Lockyer's *A Litle Stone*, the declaration from Aberdeen worked through the same progression of thoughts. First, Scotland's repeated defeats at the hands of the English are all signs of God's judgement against the sins of the nation.[160] Second, the source of Scotland's sin is the ill state of its church and the idolatrous nature of Presbyterianism.[161] Third, the problem cannot be solved by purging.[162] Fourth, new, pure congregations need to be gathered out of the old corrupt churches.[163] Fifth and finally, properly gathered congregations, being whole and complete, must govern themselves. External rule over congregations is both 'an invention of man' and a corruption of the original democratic nature of the early church.[164] Further evidence from a later letter by Row indicates that the authors, who were certainly influenced in their interpretation of current events by contemporary English propaganda, may have relied more heavily on Lockyer and his fellow propagandists for their understanding of Independency than might initially be thought.

Despite claims by Wariston that Aberdeen had Thomas Hooker's *Survey of the Summe of Church Discipline* (1648) and Cotton's *The Way of Congregational Churches Cleared* (1647) as foundational works for their espousal of Independency,[165] Row stated three days after signing the letter of 24 May that he had not read either of the works, nor had he ever seen them.[166] Perhaps the works were in the libraries of one of Aberdeen's universities, but not necessarily. As mentioned earlier, the 1647 General Assembly of the Kirk passed an act prohibiting works promoting Independency or Separation. The Kirk cracked down so stringently, according to William Dundas, that ministers intercepted the mail of suspect persons and confiscated parcels. As a result, 'a Box with about Three Pound Sterling worth of Books' sent to Dundas by a London merchant aboard a ship destined for Prestonpans never made it to its intended recipient. John Oswald, minister of Prestonpans, seemed to have anticipated the shipment and confiscated the books as soon as they arrived.[167] With such strict censorship in place, Aberdeen's colleges may have been prevented from acquiring the works, in which case Lockyer and the other Englishmen in Scotland with Cromwell's army likely served as the primary source for their burgeoning Independent thinking. Therefore it should not be surprising that many of the responses elicited by the declaration accused the authors of falling under the spell of Nicholas Lockyer.

An excellent insight into the thinking behind one individual's adherence to the declaration has been preserved in the personal letter of John Row, mentioned above, written to his 'deare brother'.[168] It conveys his personal thoughts and serves to underline the sincerity of all the signatories. In the letter Row pleads with his brother, 'I cannot think bot you are affected with our sinfull mixtures'.[169] He expresses his perception of the overwhelming corruption in the Kirk, claiming less than one in one hundred Scots to be fit for communion. While conceding that some congregations might have twenty people free from ignorance and scandal, many have none.[170] From this, Row deduces a bare profession must not be enough to warrant membership in the visible church. Referring to the Kirk's *Directory for Church Government*, he argues that since members of the visible church are called visible saints, the Kirk has an obligation to separate 'the precious from the vile'.[171] Purging would be 'sweit', but it is impossible because the majority of the General Assembly, synods and presbyteries are 'corrupt'.[172] As a result, Row and his fellows found it necessary to seek a middle way between the 'Papists ... in on extreame' and the Brownists and separatists on the other. Although the 'old rules' of the Kirk empower congregations to use the power of the keys granted to them by Christ to censure and excommunicate, they are prevented from using them. Elderships, synods, presbyteries and assemblies usurp the power of congregations to act.[173] 'Strange,' he explains,

> ane adulterie fals out in Aberdene, and yet we may not excommunicat him, bot ane extrinsicall and a superior judicatorie must doe it, yea, doe it all; Christ hath given excommunicatione to the Church quhere the offence is done, yet not one of those how able soever darre excommunicat, yet that eldershipe and breithren can know the cace better nor an Ecumenick Synod.[174]

It would be wiser, in Row's estimation, to remit all censure to congregations since they have a better knowledge of their own business and possess all necessary power to carry out the action. As for the covenants, although intended to further reformation, if they prove to inhibit it in any way then they must be subject to re-evaluation; especially since so much of what transpired since the original signing of the National Covenant in 1638 opposed true Reformation. He further urges his brother not to interpret his thoughts as meaning that there is no 'Church in Scotland', but rather that faults within the Kirk desperately needed to be attended to. Finally, he assertes his position to be the way in which 'the Lord's word hath swayed my mind'. Though Row fully expects persecution, excommunication and loss of livelihood, he hopes his 'brother' will comfort Row's mother, telling her not to believe false reports.[175] In addition, he asks for a genuine reply to his thoughts. Row's personal account demonstrates the sincerity of the authors in writing the 24 May letter. He and his colleagues did not wish to destroy the Kirk but to help it attain the degree of Reformation intended by their predecessors.

The letter from Aberdeen of 24 May 1652 initiated a massive flurry of correspondence. According to Jaffray they received 'large letters from many good men, both south and west', and Wariston affirms that several individuals wrote to dissuade them.[176] David Dickson and Alexander Brodie of Brodie both sent letters, neither of which survive.[177] Samuel Rutherford also wrote, warning the would-be Independents to take account of the great danger others would be subjected to through their separation.[178] A change to 'another Gospel-way' would exclude all non-believers, preventing those who most needed the Gospel from hearing it preached and leaving them 'to the Lions and wild beasts of the Forest, even to Jesuits, Seminary Priests, and other seducers'. These would be great dangers at any time, but especially so when Commonwealth legislation stripped the magistrates of any power to force attendance to the Kirk where the Gospel was preached.[179] Rutherford made two requests in this brief letter: first, that all involved should observe a day of Humiliation in order to seek the God's judgement; second, that a conference be held at the earliest convenience 'before you fix Judgment and Practice on any untroden Path'.[180]

John Nevay, minister at Newmilns and nephew of Andrew Cant, and some other Protesting ministers in the Presbyteries of Ayr and Irvine also wrote 'against the hazard of Independency':

> We have heard to ye afflicting of our spirits that some of you ... are inclining to that which is called the congregationall way, and that some others are lyk to goe a greater lenth. We know not what truly may be in the report, and from o[u]r souls ... wish there were none at all. Yet have conceave it our duty to acquaint yow with what we heare of yow ... That yea in ye zeal and pane of God, may carefull watch and guard against the snares of the tyme, the wyles of the devill and may keep your garments undefiled ... A dividing way evin from the precious and godly in the land, both ministry and professors; as we judg is not to be allowed of God: so wee are persuaded it will both weaken ... if not utterly impossibilitate the so much desyred and longed for reformation.[181]

Yet Wariston was the first to respond to the Aberdeen letter. He wrote his first letter on 9 June 1652 and composed a second letter early in September. These two letters, totalling about 40,000 words, survive in Wodrow's collection in the National Library of Scotland and are an invaluable addition to what is known about the situation in Aberdeen.[182] Wariston began writing to Aberdeen before he ever saw their 24 May letter. After Lockhart gathered a congregation in his home in Edinburgh, Wariston began to 'look over thes things which was now most lyk to trouble the Churche of Scotland', namely separation and the growing threat of Independency.[183] At the behest of Andrew Cant, minister of Aberdeen and Jaffray's father-in-law, Wariston began to draft a letter to Jaffray, Menzies and those who had questioned the Kirk in the Protester conferences in October 1651. After completing about half of it, he received the letter of 24 May from Aberdeen, accompanied by a personal letter from Jaffray, which has not been preserved.[184]

Like Rutherford's later letter, Wariston's intended to persuade the would-be separatist to take no action until formal meetings could be arranged to discuss the validity of separation with those of a different mind. He asserted that even the most rigid grounds for separation held by the Brownists would not allow for separation without first seeking counsel with those from whom they were separating. Thus any separation without prior consultation with their Protester brethren would be a 'new practice' against those established by Independents in England and New England, and even the Brownists.[185] He also warned of the dangers of moving too quickly, alleging that Thomas Charteris regretted separating from the Kirk without first seeking proper counsel. This appeal to be methodical led Wariston to inquire by whose doctrine separation would take place. Would it be the Independents of England or New England, or would it be under the tenets of the Amsterdam separatists or those of the Brownists?[186] Wariston showed a broad knowledge of writers for and against separation, citing John Cotton, Thomas Hooker, John Norton,

Giles Firmin, Thomas Brightman, Francis Johnston, John Ball, Daniel Cawdrey and others, including 'several old books betuix the Brounests and aunsuerers to them' that had 'providentially' come to his hands out of David Calderwood's library.[187] Although Wariston claimed to have 'borrowed' the bulk of the literature, he likely possessed a wide array of sectarian books since, according to William Dundas, when the minister of Prestonpans confiscated his shipment of books they ended up in Wariston's possession.[188] In fact, Wariston probably received a large number of banned books, as the General Assembly had appointed him in 1638 to judge which books were acceptable and which were not.[189] Hence, Wariston dictated the General Assembly's 'Index' of religious texts. In addition to having access to many Independent works, he also showed familiarity with recently published books. His citation of Firmin's work, published only a few months earlier, indicates both an influx of English works by 1652 as well as Wariston's up-to-date knowledge of the relevant sources. Although he claimed to be unfamiliar with the hypotheses and concepts that underpinned the tenets of Independency in England and New England (which is unlikely, considering he represented Scotland in the Westminster Assembly), he certainly demonstrated an excellent awareness of the sources and identified persecution under Episcopacy as their primary motivation and justification.[190] In this light, he inquired, what case did those in Aberdeen have for separation? Had they suffered persecution as the Independents of England or those who fled to New England under the oppression of Episcopacy?

In addition to questions over their grounds of separation, Wariston also inquired by what means they intended to constitute new congregations. Would they require everyone in their new congregations to be truly elect? If so, did this not imply that all members shared an equal state of grace?[191] He questioned the validity of such a premise for gathering congregations, pointing out rather facetiously that even Saul as a persecutor did not distinguish between those who made an outward profession and those who showed 'positive evidences of holynes'.[192] God's election cannot be known; therefore this new model of the church would be based on guesswork. Even Cotton, Wariston pointed out, agreed that it was better to error on the side of charity. Historically a confession of faith had always been sufficient for admission into the church and enough, at least initially, to be called 'holy'. As a result, there would always be some hypocrites in the church, which is clearly made evident throughout the New Testament.[193] Since positive evidences had never been the foundation for inclusion in the visible church, separation from a church based on a lack of external evidence of election, such as exemplary holy living, would be hypocritical.[194] If anything, such a separation would only serve to weaken Christ's church further. Separation, Wariston explained, was like divorce, which 'causes a wife to cease being a wife'.[195] Withdrawal of the elect from the Kirk would cause the Church of Scotland to cease being a church. Hence, those who separated ran the great risk of committing a sin that damaged both those separating and the church they separated from, since diminishing the church 'diminishes Christ's kingdom' and rendered any further purging of the scandalous virtually impossible.[196] Instead of rashly rushing to separate, which would divide the Kirk, Wariston urged them to fulfil their covenanted responsibility and purge the scandalous, as the Kirk teaches, thus healing the church of her ailments and making her stronger.[197] Beyond Scotland, Wariston argued of pan-European repercussions to full-blown schism within the Kirk. Esteemed by Reformed churches throughout Europe, a rejection of the Church of Scotland threatened to appear to be a rejection of all Reformed churches, potentially weakening the Protestant cause across the continent. Do not bury the Kirk that 'begot and buire us' without further conference, he pleaded, as she 'deserves at leist a more honorable buriall from hir avne tho these should compt hir but a name that she leaveth and is deid'.[198] This request for further counsel represented the fundamental intention of this letter. Urging his audience to ponder the queries put forward to would-be separatists by Giles Firmin in his recently published *Separation Examined*,[199] he expressed his belief that reconciliation could yet be achieved: 'there is no differenc betwixt Presbyteriall and Congregationall men for ought evir I could read albeit therbe anent the admission of members in ye constituting of a church but we are in ye cais of repairing an old hous and not of building a new one from the foundation.'[200] It may be to Giles Firmin that Wariston owed, if not this argument, at least this terminology.[201] After showing the letter to David Dickson and other ministers of Edinburgh, and receiving their approval, he sent the document along with a recent a recent tract by Rutherford 'anent the visible church' on 9 June.[202]

Wariston's parcel arrived in an Aberdeen where tensions ran high. Andrew Cant preached against Menzies and Row, and vice versa, to the detriment of their congregations.[203] Rent by dissension, the synod of Aberdeen convened on 30 June to discuss Row's April appeal for ministers and kirk sessions to reflect upon the composition and requirements of membership within the Kirk. Those present unanimously approved the constitution and government of the Church of Scotland, except for John Row, John Menzies and John Seaton. The three dissenting ministers submitted their own paper, explaining they had 'for a considerable space of time' sought the mind of God before finally coming to the conclusions that there were no scriptural grounds 'for our classicall subordination' and 'o[u]r sinfull mixtures, and promiscuouse administration of ordinances, without due distinction betuixt the precious and thie vile' was no less than sinful.[204] The synod declared their conclusions 'contrary to the Word of God to the covenants and to the judgement of the General Assembly'. Row, Menzies and Seaton were suspended, referred to the Resolutioner commission of the General Assembly, prohibited from meeting either publicly or privately, and forbidden from taking part in any activities tending towards separation or subversive to Presbyterian government.

Despite increasing strain in Aberdeen, the letters of Rutherford, Wariston and others had their desired effect. No further steps toward separation would occur until further discussions. 'After seeking God in this,' wrote Jaffray, 'we could not see how we could refuse this their offer of conference, as a means by which the Lord might further make known his mind to us.'[205] Jaffray and Menzies again travelled to Edinburgh, where they met for two half-day conferences on the mornings of 19 and 22 July with Cant, Rutherford, James Guthrie, Patrick Gillespie and John Carstairs in Wariston's chambers. They discussed the constitution of the church, pollution of ordinances, and how communion might be administered in a more pure manner than the 'national way', but came no closer to resolving their issues.[206] Both the Protesters and the Aberdeen contingent conversed very calmly, except for Andrew Cant, who stormed out of the meeting. The conferences ended with Jaffray and Menzies even more confirmed in their thoughts and the Protesters 'having exonerated themselves very freely and lovingly'.[207] Still conscious of the gravity of their actions, the Aberdeen contingent agreed to host further discussions, this time in Aberdeen, with Rutherford, Guthrie, Gillespie and John Carstairs. Wariston and his colleagues were limited in their time. The Resolutioner General Assembly was preparing to meet in Edinburgh, and they intended to prepare 'Remonstrances' against the meeting. However, Wariston's concern for the situation in Aberdeen was so great that upon completing his papers against the Resolutioner meeting, he produced a 'postscript to my letter upon that poynt that the ordinances ar not polluted to us who useth al means to prevent known wicked men's winning to them'.[208] Meanwhile, the Resolutioner-controlled General Assembly convened on 20 July 1652.[209] On 21 July they suspended four ministers, two from Aberdeen (Row and Menzies) and one from Old Aberdeen (John Seaton), as well as Thomas Charteris, who had already officially separated from the Kirk.[210] For Row, Menzies and Seaton the censure had little sting as it came from the Resolutioner party, with whom those favouring Independency in Aberdeen held little or no hope of reconciliation.[211] However, for the Resolutioners, this advocacy of separation by ministers who had once been Protesters fuelled their already deep-rooted distrust of that camp.

On 6 September 1652 Wariston sent a second letter to Aberdeen. Sources relating to the doctrinal formation of the Aberdeen Independents are sparse. Hence, this second letter, coming on the heels of extended discourse with Jaffray and Menzies, is an extremely important document, providing enhanced insight into the progression of their thinking beyond the initial inclinations expressed in their letter of 24 May. The work focuses primarily on the necessary requirements to be called a visible saint and the relating expectation of church constitution, and runs to nearly 26,000 words. This focus signifies the importance that these issues continued to have, and the length reflects Wariston's respect for the gravity of the situation. For Wariston, the desire to name only those with apparently discernible evidence of real inward sanctification as visible saints is far too narrow and results in two interrelated errors. First, the Aberdeen group err in assuming that real inner sanctification is required for membership in the visible church. On the contrary, he argues, there are seven means by which an individual can be called a visible saint and hence accepted as members of the visible church: 1) inward grace evident through holiness, 2) an outward calling, 3) covenants or covenanted profession, 4) being born to professing parents, 5) through baptism, 6) professed subjection to the Gospel, or 7) confirmation by the better part of the congregation.[212] Second, as a result of this misunderstanding of membership requirements, they err in interpreting the proper composition of churches, making it much too narrow and excluding too many. Following Guthrie's argument against Brown, but to a conclusion about the visible church rather than the invisible church, Wariston cites the principle cause of this misunderstanding as an improper interpretation of universial terms; in Scripture 'all' need not mean 'every', and 'none' does not necessarily mean 'absolutely no-one', as Ranters and Arminians interpreted the terms.[213]

Instead, the church is obliged to accept all who sincerely profess faith, and it possesses no warrant to judge the validity of professions, unless there is blatant scandal or sinful behaviour in the individual's life. Drawing on Richard Baxter, Wariston contends: first, a serious confession of faith is a 'probable sign of trew faith'; second, the church is bound to judge such professors as likely to be true believers; third, the church is thus obliged to accept them into membership; fourth, this profession is 'an infallible evidence of sincere faith'; and fifth, the church has no warrant to judge if the individual's faith is sincere or not, except in the case of gross scandal.[214] Although this might leave the church open to charlatans, the church's obligation is to err on the side of inclusion and 'charity'. Wariston maintains that from the earliest days of the church, hypocrites had infiltrated it, going as far as to state that all the churches described in both the Old and New Testaments were comprised predominantly of reprobates. All visible churches are 'heterogeneous mixes', and even in the best-constituted churches mentioned in Scripture, of the many called only a few are chosen.[215] This mixture must be tolerated because the standard requirement for membership in the church, as demonstrated in Acts 11:26, is merely a 'dogmatic faith' or a sincere profession of orthodox faith;[216] a truth, he argues, accepted even in the churches of New England, where they admit that congregations will be mixed.[217] Requiring evidence of sanctification before admission to membership is fallacious. The great difference between the Independents and the Kirk, in his estimation, rests on whether a serious profession of faith is enough for church member-ship.[218] The great error being purported in Aberdeen is the requirement of positive evidences, in addition to a confession of faith, in order for real sainthood to be attributed and membership to be extended.[219] This strict interpretation of membership lacks charity and risks excluding sincere believers, something even Cotton and Hooker would deny.[220] It is better, safer and more Christian to error on the side of charity: 'We should do in Gods ordinances all *ex fide*; as well as *cum charitate*.'[221] Where is charity in separating from the Kirk? Where is charity in casting out or rejecting confessing believers? Exclusion of those confessing belief, without evidence of scandal or hypocrisy, has never been the way of Christ's church.

At this point, unlike later generations, Wariston could accurately claim schism to be foreign to the Church of Scotland.[222] The Kirk had long rejected separation as a viable means for dealing with corruption, even when the question of mixed communions represented a burning issue under Episcopacy.[223] 'And so 20 yeirs agoe non of the godly in Scotland scrupled to goe to pure communions, though persons knowinlie prophane come to the same.'[224] He claims the New England divines Cotton, Cobbet and Norton all supported this point.[225] In Scotland, the temptation to separate from impure members within congregations had histori-cally been rejected for three reasons. First, separation runs a great risk of being sinful because it judges others when Christians are called to esteem others as 'better than ourselves' and so is to the detriment of weaker Christians.[226] Second, separation is not progressive in terms of Reformation, but actually prevents the reform by removing the neces-sary tools: it is the 'unchurching [of] the whole' and weakens the chance of purging within the body that remains.[227] Third, the Kirk is endowed in the *Book of Discipline* with the tools to remove corruption through purging rather than separation. Hence purging should always be the first reaction. Responding directly to the challenge put forward in Lockyer's *A Litle Stone*, that purging the degenerate masses by the pure minority is impossible, Wariston refers to James Guthrie's *Treatise on Ruling Elders* published in February, declaring the Presbyterian Church of Scotland to be prepared for such a situation.[228] In the event that suitable elders cannot be found in a congregation, the presbytery may choose elders from two or three other congregations to rule over them all. In this way, righteous elders may purge congregations of hypocritical members and cultivate the church until it is able to appoint elders from within.[229] Therefore the problem of mixture in the Kirk is not a flaw in the Presbyterian system of church government, but the failure or neglect of many within the church to fulfil their obligations of maintaining purity of membership. Wariston challenges the would-be separatists to try purging in the manner of the Kirk first, which is their covenanted duty, before abandoning the Church of Scotland.[230] Wariston's letter concludes with an appeal for the

Aberdonians to be patient for a bit longer, urging them to ponder his arguments, to carefully read Rutherford's tract that he had sent in June and, most importantly, to try to deal with the 'leaven' in their congregations by purging, and not by 'deserting the camp'.[231]

One final document pertaining to this ongoing discourse between Aberdeen and their Protester companions in the south must be addressed. Lying almost completely forgotten, there is a manuscript housed in New College library identified in the catalogue simply as an 'Unidentified Scottish MS on Congregationalism and Church Government … 165?'.[232] Although the history of the document is mysterious, it is now possible to put the work into its original context, identify an approximate date for its production and, importantly, identify its author. In fact, it may be that this document is the tract 'anent the visible church' written by Samuel Rutherford and sent by Wariston to Aberdeen. Previously, the importance of this document's link to Aberdeen has been misunderstood, just as Rutherford's letter to Aberdeen was not fully recognised until John Coffey rightly identified it as addressed to the Aberdeen Independents.[233] Key to understanding its context is recognising that the tract's link to Aberdeen is much greater than simply the reference to the 'Brethren in Aberdeen' in its closing lines. The framework of the document actually builds around excerpts from the letter of 24 May. The author systematically quotes directly from the letter of 24 May, and then refutes the Aberdonians' assertions. The overall premise of the tract is the same as Wariston's, arguing that separation from a rightly Reformed Kirk is wrong and lamenting that a completely new pattern of separation is being constructed in Aberdeen: 'we are sorry in your first stepps yow are involved in a deeper pitt of separatione then all the single Independants in old and new England.' The author justifies his claims through copious citations of Hooker, Cotton and other New England Independents.[234]

With regard to the authorship, two pieces of evidence point towards Samuel Rutherford. First, Wariston's letters state that Rutherford produced a paper in response to contemporary questions over the constitution of the visible church. This gives chronological evidence of Rutherford producing a tract around this time that is as yet unaccounted for. The challenge to this theory is the short period between the arrival of the Aberdeen letter sent on or around 24 May and Wariston sending his letter on 9 June. If Rutherford composed the tract, he did so in little more than a week. Yet the speed of the tract's production may be suggested in the lack of wide-ranging citation. In the following year Rutherford wrote a similar tract on the obligation of magistrates to oppose heresy, which bears striking similarities to the New College document both in penmanship and format, utilising a wide range of continental and Latin authors.[235] While time may have limited the author's ability to employ a wide variety of sources to refute the Aberdeen Independents, Rutherford's mastery of Cotton and Hooker would have enabled him to produce an adequate response within the allotted time.[236] Moreover, since Rutherford was actually in Edinburgh when the Aberdeen letter arrived he could have immediately begun working on a response. It is possible that Rutherford may have been among the number of Protesters who looked over Wariston's letter before he sent it. Second, the work uses several turns of phrase nearly identical to Rutherford's letter to Aberdeen, in which he argues that excluding good people from churches leaves them vulnerable to 'lions and wild beasts of the forest, even Jesuits, seminary-priests, and other seducers ... For the magistrate hath no power to compel them to hear the Gospel, nor have ye any church-power over them, as ye teach'.[237] The New College manuscript asserts: 'The magistrate cannot compel them to hear the gospell, nor ar they under any pastorall care of yours, nor have yow any calling of Christ as lawfull pastors, doctors, or elders, to feed them, must they not then be left to seminary preists, Jesuits, Arminians, Socinians, Antinomians, antiscripturists, [libertines] ever to prey upon.'[238] There are additional similarities, such as repeated references to 'golden candlesticks', taken from Revelations 1–2, that feature in both of the documents, as well as in Rutherford's later *The Covenant of Life Opened* and *A Survey of the Survey*.[239] Such vivid imagery, which runs throughout Rutherford's works, sets the work apart from the writings of Guthrie, Wariston and the other Protesters of their persuasion. The manuscript's repeated references to Cotton and Hooker may further justify Rutherford's authorship, or at least that the author had been involved in the debate against Independency from the 1640s, and more specifically within the Westminster Assembly.

Scotland's representatives at the Westminster Assembly witnessed the flurry of New England texts produced by English Independents in 1648 to justify English Independency. As a result, Rutherford and his fellow representatives from Scotland identified New England as the ideological bastion for the practice of English Independency. While Wariston's continuing interest in censorship probably encouraged him to read the latest sources, such as Firmin and Baxter, which he cites in his epistle, the author of the manuscript rebutted the Aberdeen Independents almost solely from the texts issued four years earlier as the classic defences of Independency.[240] Rutherford was less interested in more recent voices in the discourse. For him, New England's arguments were the intellectual foundation of all British Independency. A decade after their publication, he continued to write against them as the basition of congregational ideology. Rutherford had the New England sources at his fingertips, but more importantly they were well embedded in his mind. These factors all lead me to ascribe this work to Samuel Rutherford and to place the work in the series of discourse instigated by the Aberdeen letter advocating separation.[241] The importance of this work is not in any original arguments against Independency, but in

Rutherford's perception that the unfolding events in Aberdeen merited an immediate written condemnation. This tract, along with the letters written by Rutherford, Wariston, David Dickson, Alexander Brodie of Brodie, and Nevay and his fellow Protesting ministers of Ayr and Irvine, demonstrate the gravity of the situation as far as the Protesters were concerned. Separation from the Kirk loomed as a real and immediate threat that could not go unchallenged.

By mid-August, English commentators had already reported a complete separation in Aberdeen, but they did so prematurely.[242] Shortly after Wariston's second letter, Rutherford, James Guthrie, Patrick Gillespie and John Carstairs arrived in Aberdeen for what would be their penultimate discussions.[243] To their great disappointment they found upon arriving that John Menzies, Aberdeen's 'ringleader', was sick, as was the elder and principal of Marischal College, William Muir.[244] The emissaries stayed in Aberdeen for 'seven or eight days' and met frequently with two ministers (probably Row and Seaton), some of the college's regents (surely Birnie was among this number) and Jaffray.[245] Menzies' absence led William Row to conclude that little could be resolved without his presence, but in truth Jaffray's diary attests to their minds being already made up.[246] His account portrays these meetings as the last hurdle before they could separate in good conscience. The Protesters, on the other hand, left feeling that the impending separation would only open the door for further heretical doctrines, lamenting 'there were some also there that were against infant baptism, and were in danger to be tainted with other errors'.[247]

Within a matter of weeks, the synod of Aberdeen reported the official separation of Row, Menzies and Seaton from the Kirk 'to independencie'.[248] This report on 21 October 1652 puts the secession from the Church of Scotland a full year after Jaffray's paper to the Protester assembly in Edinburgh and five months after the letter declaring their judgement in favour of Independency over the Presbyterianism of the Kirk. Although their opponents still probably perceived their separation as rash, the Aberdonians had been patient and given their Protester counterparts every opportunity to dissuade them. Even after their official separation, they seemed to move slowly. The synod appointed four ministers to meet with them. Whether or not the Aberdeen Independents met David Lindsey, William Douglas, William Strachan and Robert Keith is uncertain, but the seceders did wait several more weeks before consummating their new gathering.

In November 1652 the Aberdeen Independents gathered in Greyfriars' kirk (the chapel of Marischal College and Menzies' church) for their first 'public' partaking of the 'ordinance of the Lords Supper'.[249] Their contemporary Robert Pittilloch probably referred to this event when he wrote: 'a very considerable number of Ministers, Magistrates, and the vulgar sort of people, separated from the promiscuous constitution of a National Church, associated themselves together, and in the presence of the mixt multitude did break bread together, as a seal of their resolution never to return to the errour of the multitude any more'.[250] Despite the attentiveness of his work, Hoy ends the story in Aberdeen without noting this gathered communion. For him the appointment of John Row as principal of King's College the following year marked the height of indigenous Independency in Aberdeen. G.D. Henderson reports further events in Aberdeen with regard to Menzies, Row, Jaffray and Seaton, but he too stops short of expressing the overall importance of the movement. According to Henderson, 'the Independents held a Communion service together in the Greyfriars' Kirk at Marischal College, but thereafter abandoned the idea of forming a separate Church'. He suggests that although they did not die out immediately, as there were reports from the following year that 'Separatists, Anabaptists, Independents and others of that manner, the growth of which goes on apace within the bounds', it was not long before they gave up their cause.[251] This claim probably rests on two statements. First, Row's *Life of Blair* contends that 'they strove to erect separate gathered and independent congregations, but could not effectuate it'.[252] Second, Pittilloch states 'in a short space hereafter, the zeal of their Patrons became cold, and they not onely found want of freedom and protection from those of whom they expected it'.[253] But these claims may rest on the understated nature of the gatherings more than on any evidence of failure. The truth is, despite evidence being in short supply, the Independent movement in Aberdeen did not fade away following the gathered communion. If anything the Independency movement swelled. Over the next year Menzies and Cant duelled sermons in the pulpit. Cant would preach presbytery to be *jure divino* in the morning and Menzies would denounce it in the afternoon.[254] They vehemently vied for the adherents of the congregation, most of whom remained with Cant, but Menzies' sway was strong. Among the communicants of his gathered church were Cant's daughter and her husband, Alexander Jaffray. Although the movement may never have reached grand numbers, it did make significant gains, particularly in Aberdeen's universities, where Baillie claimed in 1654 'almost all in both colledges, from Remonstrators, had avowedlie gone over to Independencie and Separation'.[255]

In England, Independent gatherings formed in two ways: either in the gathering of an entirely new Independent congregation operating separately from the local parish, or as a gathering of individuals from within the parish in order to administer the sacraments to only those most likely to be elect. The minister of the St Stephen's Coleman Street parish church in London, John Goodwin, stopped administering sacraments within his church in 1644.[256] Instead, he administered the sacraments only to godly individuals gathered from within the parish and beyond who met regularly in either the church or his home. While Goodwin continued to preach to the parish church, the gathered community to whom he provided the sacraments formed into 'an artificial, extended kin group, both secular and spiritual in nature' that transformed from a purely religious grouping to 'a nexus of social, political and spiritual bonds'.[257] This may be what happened in Old Aberdeen. The kirk session of Old Machar's in Old Aberdeen complained that their minister, John Seaton, refused to administer the sacraments in February 1654. Their frustration drove them to hand over the church's cloths, communion cups and kirk session book to William Douglas, professor of divinity at King's College, in April.[258]

If this was the pattern in Old Aberdeen, an alternative pattern may have been employed in new Aberdeen, where the chapel of the college did not serve as a parish church. An example of using a college chapel to form an extra-parochial congregation in England can be drawn from one of the key proponents of Independency who inspired them. While John Owen served as dean of Christ church, Oxford, he purportedly formed a Congregational church in the chapel of Christ Church (not a parish church).[259] This scenario is strikingly similar to the Aberdeen Independents, who had close ties to the university and whose only recorded meeting took place in the chapel of Marischal College. The group in Aberdeen could have continued to meet in Greyfriars' as long as they had the support of the university, as it did not become a parish church until 1828.[260] With the principal, the professor of divinity/chaplain and at least one regent involved in the gathering, this seems probable and sheds new light on Baillie's comment that nearly everyone in Aberdeen's colleges embraced Independency.[261] In fact, it seems logical that if the bulk of Marischal staff supported a gathered congregation, the college's chapel would be a reasonable place to meet. Yet even if Greyfriars' had not been available, it would not have prevented them from gathering. Another English example exhibits a collegiate-based congregation gathering without the use of any church building. At Magdalen College, Oxford, Thomas Goodwin, the president of the college, ministered to a Congregational church meeting in his home.[262] Such gatherings rooted in academic communities outwith parishes offered havens where, as Jaffray described the yearnings among his fellows in Aberdeen, the ordinances could be administered 'in a more pure way ... than the nationall church'.[263] As with the community at Magdalen College, no records of membership survive for the Aberdeen gathering.[264] However, it may be inferred from entries in Jaffray's diary that two women named Jane Ramsay and Elsinet Smith were involved, at least for a time.[265]

In contrast to reports by William Row and Robert Pittilloch of Independency failing, numerous English reports in the closing months of 1652 indicate 'gathered churches' progressively building steam in Scotland.[266] One journal stated: 'The Gathered Churches in Scotland go on so successfully, that many who derided them, begin to admire them, and love them.'[267] Another claimed 'hundreds forsake the old tyrannical Presbytery, and cleave to our party'.[268] In February 1653 several English journals carried happy news from Aberdeen: 'The honest party at Aberdeen are now withdrawing from under the rigourous yoak of their Kirk sway, and are, some of them, very cordial and clear to the interest of England.'[269] Yet the swelling success of Independency did not mean that the Kirk ceased to oppose separation where it was able. The departure of Andrew Ballenden of Drumoak from the Kirk, at the prompting of the English soldiers in local garrisons, caused the synod of Aberdeen to summons him in October 1652. Ballenden appeared and duly repented of his error. Despite his willing recantation the synod decided to make him an example, requiring him to sign a declaration professing his error and vowing to leave Scotland, never to return under pain of excommunication.[270] Whether the synod actually intended this sentence to be carried out is uncertain. Whether it even could be carried out is equally uncertain, as travel restrictions put into place by the English army required a government-issued pass. In any case, the synod sent a clear message. It was taking a strong stance against separatists wherever it could.

The following April a quite different series of events transpired. After missing several presbytery meetings, the synod of Aberdeen ordered a trial of the life, doctrine and conversation of John Forbes, minister of Kincardine O'Neil, in response to reports that he had grown dissatisfied with Presbyterianism, or at least its present form in the Kirk.[271] Although no further mention of Forbes occurs in the synod records, Pitilloch asserts he separated from the Kirk and held a gathered congregation in Kincardine. Despite the presbytery's attempt to censure Forbes, he quietly withdrew from the Kirk. Although he remained under threat of excommunication until his death in late 1657 or early 1658, Forbes never conformed.[272] These two examples indicate the limitations of the Kirk's ability to censure separatists. They could only effectively move against those who recanted and submitted themselves to the authority of presbyteries or synods. Essentially, submission to censure had to be voluntary. Had Andrew Ballenden not given way to a guilty conscience, or if he had simply dismissed the synod's threat of excommunication, he could have continued his gathered ministry just as Forbes purportedly did. These events in the vicinity of Aberdeen demonstrate how toleration functioned in Scotland.

Although Presbyterians might attempt to levy ecclesiastical pressure against dissenters, adherents to Independency found support in various quarters, especially in Aberdeen. The English army represented the first source of support. Their presence prevented violent persecution, called 'Club Law' by the Quakers. Anyone favouring Independency had the support of the local English troops, who came to the aid of Alexander

Irving of Drum in his stand against the presbytery of Aberdeen and likewise probably offered protection to Forbes. Besides the support of the English regime, the Independency movement in Aberdeen had created its own safe haven. Even in the early days of Jaffray's questioning of the covenant and Presbytery, he approached individuals in places of influence within his alma mater, Marischal College. Significantly, the first individuals gathered together all had ties to the college. William Muir served as principal, John Menzies as professor of divinity and minister to the college's chapel, John Row as an instructor of Hebrew and Andrew Birnie as regent. This gave them significant influence within Marischal College, but by March 1653 their influence extended over both of Aberdeen's colleges.

Early in 1653, the newly formed Commissioners for Visiting Universities replaced the principals of Edinburgh, Glasgow and Aberdeen universities. They appointed Robert Leighton principal of Edinburgh in February and Patrick Gillespie, who had already showed signs of compliance with the English, principal of Glasgow – much to the chagrin of Robert Baillie and several other ministers of Glasgow who opposed his appointment.[273] The reason for Leighton's appointment is uncertain but probably stemmed from his moderate disposition. Contemporaries considered him a sincere individual who actively sought peace and the unification of the two parties in the Kirk. As principal he urged Edinburgh's students to avoid 'that itch for polemical and controversial theology which is so prevalent and infectious', and he seems instead to have taught a more moderate, but orthodox, Reformed theology than either the Protester or Resotioners.[274] As Crawford Gribben puts it, in an age when the three traditions of 'Edinburgh Ramism, Westminster orthodoxy and Crowmellian toleration' predominated, Leighton managed to maintain an 'ambivalence' in selecting which Reformed tradition to 'enforce'.[275] Gillespie, on the other hand, received his appointment through having proven himself loyal to the English regime, as had the college's new rector, George Lockhart of Lee – William's brother – who had joined 'heartily enough' with the English.[276] According to his critic, Robert Baillie, Gillespie and his appointments to the college faculty were all 'for their common masters sake the English'.[277] From the English perspective, the appointments of both Leighton and Gillespie served to advance Commonwealth policies. Leighton represented a moderate and amenable voice in Edinburgh, where Protesters and Resolutioners so frequently bickered, while Patrick Gillespie represented the faction of the Kirk which dominated the west of Scotland and proved more loyal to the English than either Wariston or Guthrie would ever be.

In Aberdeen, where both colleges actually functioned as a single university during the Interregnum,[278] the English appointed John Row principal and Gilbert Rule, who also favoured Independency, as sub-principal.[279] Their appointments solidified what had already become apparent in

Aberdeen. Independency now officially dominated both of the burgh's colleges. Coupled with the induction of Gillespie in Glasgow, it meant that parties not only amenable to, but actually compliant with, Commonwealth religious policies dominated two of Scotland's four universities. Moreover, from as early as Row's appointment in March 1653 the Aberdeen Independents worked closely with Gillespie's party of Protesters.[280] While Rutherford, Wariston, Guthrie and other leading Protesters distanced themselves from the Aberdeen Independents, Gillespie's faction worked hand in hand with them. When Gillespie sought to appoint a new regent to Glasgow University he called for a young man from Aberdeen, Andrew Burnet, for whom Gillespie received testimonies from 'all the apostates in the Colledge of Aberdeen'.[281] This incensed Baillie, but he found Gillespie's refusal to oblige Burnet to subscribe to the covenant even more irksome.

At a time when a significant fissure began forming within the Protester party over how to respond to English rule, links between the English regime and those showing support for the Commonwealth solidified. Wariston, Guthrie, Rutherford and the majority of Protesters in the East strongly opposed any supplication to the English or acceptance of their interference in matters of Scottish religion. Gillespie, on the other hand, and a growing body of Protesters in the west showed themselves more than willing to bow to English authority.[282] While preaching in an Edinburgh pulpit in October 1654 Gillespie even publicly prayed for the health and preservation of the Protector, and for God 'to bless all his proceidings'![283] By the latter part of 1656 both Patrick Gillespie and John Livingstone openly fraternised with the English regime, preaching in 'the English church to their Councell and Judges', going home in the private coach of Lord Broghill (president to the council in Scotland), preaching to the judges in Glasgow and entertaining them at home.[284]

Gillespie's Protesters and Disciplinary Minded Independents

In 1653 the English regime began to shower favour upon those showing an inclination towards their religious policies. During this year the English Congregationalist John Beverley entered the charge at Lenzie, a parish within the presbytery of Glasgow.[285] Holfelder suggests that the passive acceptance of the appointment by Gillespie's party demonstrates their tacit acceptance of the regime's involvement in religious matters and the founding of a mutual agreement to support the appointment of Independents in some vacant charges, if the English would enter Protesters (of Gillespie's party) in others.[286] However, this interpretation of events interpolates too much Presbyterian sentiment and underestimates the proactive role of Gillespie's faction in entering Independents into vacant charges. Rather than a passive acceptance of English dominance, Gillespie's faction actually exhibited a significant change of tack.[287] In fact, Gillespie's faction of Protesters had just as much to do with Beverley's placement as the

English did, since they reportedly ordained him to the charge.[288] Two years later they planted another Englishman, named William Muircroft, in Cathcart.[289] Baillie complained of this collusion in July 1654.

> When a very few of the Remonstrants and Independent party will call a man, he gets the Kirk and the stipend; but whom the Presbytery, and well near the whole congregation, calls and admits, he must preach in the fields, or in a barn, without stipend. So a sectary is planted in Kilbride, another in Lenzie [or Kirkintilloch], and this guyse will grow rise to the wrack of many a soul.[290]

However, Beverley differed from many of the other English ministers who served in Scotland during the first two years of the Cromwellian occupation. In 1659 he published *Unio Reformantium*, which called for unity between Presbyterians and Congregationalists, based upon a shared heritage as Reformed Churches and strengthened by the strict concepts of discipline shared by the New England Congregationalists and Protesters, as contrasted to the 'unlimitted' toleration permitted in England.[291] In the same work he praised James Guthrie and declared that the greatest number of godly ministers in Scotland were Protesters rather than 'loose' Resolutioners.[292] This is an interesting laud, considering that Guthrie cared little for Beverley or any of the Independent ministers serving in Scotland. Patrick Gillespie, however, shared Beverley's desire for strict discipline within congregations. He believed this could never become the norm in Scotland so long as the Resolutioners predominanted, so Gillespie cast in his lot with English Independents, who advocated strict discipline rather than toleration. In many ways it mirrored attempts by Independents and Presbyterians in England to establish unity between 1652 and 1655.[293] To borrow a quote from the English context, it seems as though Gillespie's party and strict disciplinarian Independents, like Beverley and John Stalham,[294] recognised that 'Presbytery, and Independency [are] not two religions: but one religion to a godly, honest heart; it is only a little ruffling of the fringe'.[295] Holfelder approached the state of the situation when he wrote: 'While the majority of Protesters still clung to the theory of a comprehensive national church comprised of both the elect and reprobate, in practice they had moved towards a much more exclusive position – one which was not at all dissimilar to the Independency of the separatists.'[296] In fact Gillespie's party had accepted many aspects of the English message of Independency without actually separating from the Kirk. The mutual respect between Gillespie's Protesters and these disciplinarily rigid Independents illustrate the formation of a new loosely knit religious party in Scotland. This cooperation indicates that Gillespie's party had probably given up national Presbyterianism as a viable model through which the purity of particular congregations could be maintained – giving a measure of credence to David Stevenson's claim that some Protesters were willing, 'at least temporarily', to abandon 'the claim that

Scotland was bound by the Solemn League and Covenant to impose her religion on England'.[297] Certainly a number of Gillespie's contemporaries accused him of deserting Presbyterianism and observed divisions among the Protesters. James Burn, the bailie of Glasgow, alleged that Gillespie 'did disclaim' the Covenant, while Baillie accurately identified the difference between the Guthrie–Rutherford–Wariston party of Protesters and those Protesters complying with, or falling into, the errors of the English.[298]

Although Baillie accused Gillespie of defending widespread toleration, his accusations were probably unfounded. When Thomas Charteris took charge of an Independent church in 1652 and came under accusations of Anabaptism, Gillespie, John Carstairs and Francis Aird prevented the synod of Glasgow from censuring him. Gillespie's Protesters defended him as a 'godly man' in the face of Baillie's protest to the contrary.[299] Rather than implying that Gillespie tolerated Baptists, it more probably suggests that Charteris, like the Aberdeen Independents, had qualms about the necessary standards for parents admitting an infant for baptism.[300] Certainly Stalham, who had proven himself to be no friend to Baptists,[301] regarded Charteris as highly as Gillespie did when he described Charteris as 'a precious' minister of the Gospel.[302] Disciplinarily rigid Independents like Beverley and Stalham, who came together with Gillespie's group, were not interested in extensive toleration. They adhered to strict Calvinist doctrine, including limited election, and strongly opposed what they perceived to be heresy, as is demonstrated by Stalham's work against the Quakers written while ministering to a gathered congregation in Edinburgh.

In contrast, the Protesting party of Guthrie, Rutherford and Wariston consistently opposed both separation from the Kirk and compliance with the English. On 17 March 1653, they wrote a letter entitled 'Declaration of Exhortation to the Separatists in Aberdeen'. Despite being addressed to the straying brethren in Aberdeen, it was equally addressed to 'all others within the land who being members of this Kirk have already declined or do anie way incline to the wayes of Separation'. Once again, the main body of Protesters cited the primary tempation for separating from the Kirk as the laxed admission standards to communion. Although they understood this criticism, they warned of the danger of being prematurely lured into innovation. It is easier, they argued, to see flaws in Presbyterianism when one has had a long acquaintance with it than it is to see the errors of Congregationalism 'while it is but new to them and doe but see litle or no thing at first of the evill'. Despite deep affection for those who had separated in Aberdeen and their great efforts to find a compromise, the majority of Protesters (led by Wariston, Guthrie and Rutherford) would not accept or tolerate separation from the Kirk, especially since the Resolutioners accused them of acting out their own separation.[303]

The Resolutioners were equally concerned with the events unfolding in Aberdeen. Gillespie's collusion with English Independents, his appointment as principal of the University of Glasgow by the English regime, and his ties with the Aberdeen Independents, all gave the Resolutioners reasons for growing increasingly sceptical of the Protester faction and fearful of the growing threat of Independency, especially its ascendancy in Aberdeen's colleges. In 1653, the commissioners of the General Assembly instructed the Resolutioner William Douglas, professor of divinity at King's College, to keep tabs on Independent and Baptist activities in Aberdeen, record how it was being dealt with and report his findings.[304] In 1654 the Resolutioners' own rebuttal of the Aberdeen Independents appeared in print in the form of two appendices in Wood's *A Little Stone Pretended to be Out of the Mountain*. Begun as a reply to Lockyer's *Litle Stone*, the events of 1652 in Aberdeen prompted Wood to refocus his work and broaden its scope.

Wood's first appendix makes two primary points. First, he warns the Aberdeen Independents that they are bound to arrive at loggerheads with one another as they begin to deliberate the intricacies of their new broadly defined doctrines. In particular, he mentions their growing debate over the requirements for paedo-baptism, and predicts the escalation of the discussion from the requirements made of parents in order for children to be baptised into the gathered church to whether baptism makes children complete members of the church.[305] Although there are no records detailing the particulars of the question in Aberdeen, the issue naturally arose in other communities facing a similar experience. A decade later, Congregational churches in New England struggled to come to terms with the implications of their gathered-ecclesiological identities and requirements for membership. The question in New England centred on second- and third-generation members of gathered churches. They debated whether the child of a baptised adult who professed faith and lived piously but who had no personal conversion experience could be baptised and, if so, whether such a child could partake of communion or have a voice in congregational decision making. The Massachusetts synod of 1662 decided that infants of a confessing but conversionless parent could be baptised, but they should be barred from access to communion or having a voice in governing the church until they could demonstrate a conversion experience of their own. This became known as the 'Half-Way Covenant' and established a two-tiered status of church membership.[306] Although the debate in Aberdeen probably had not reached this complex definition of baptism and membership by the mid-1650s, the implications of paedo-baptism within a gathered church would inevitably have arisen and are indicative of the difficulty in reaching a consensus when defining the boundaries of a new community (or an old one, for that matter). These difficult questions relating to baptism and membership probably account for many of the accusations of 'Anabaptism' against Scots Independents. Rather than 're-baptising' adherents, they more likely refused baptism to children that the Kirk would have deemed as coming from fit parents. This issue would have been particularly problematic for individuals like Charteris, who turned a parish kirk into a gathered congregation, thus leaving the local inhabitants wanting for services traditionally provided by the parish minister. Second, Wood argues that by separating from a properly reformed church the Aberdeen Independents repeated the errors of the Donatists and Novatians. Both Augustine and Cyprian clearly spelled out the heretical nature of separation from a true church on the grounds of corruption, and Wood declares that only through wilful ignorance to the warnings of the Church fathers could the replication of such basic errors be explained.[307]

In his second appendix Wood inquires why none of those involved vented affection towards Congregationalism before the Scots' defeats at Dunbar and Worcester, and states, as did Wariston in his letter, that their silence represented calculated deceit. Even more disturbing, while they had held conferences with the Protesters, who shared their strict views in relation to dealing with the king, they made no attempt to discuss their imminent defection with the Resolutioners, who made up the more numerous party in the Kirk and who controlled the General Assembly. This indicates that the spirit leading them to separate was not of God but rather one of dissension.[308] The rest of the appendix focuses on the fallacies held by the newly gathered Congregationalists of there being no ecclesiastical authority over that of the individual congregation and of members of the congregation having equal authority with elders. Wood argues that Presbyteries, or an equivalent, had from the earliest church been responsible for overseeing congregations.[309]

Institutional Support for Independency

Despite the opposition of the Resolutioners and the majority of Protesters, the Aberdeen Independents continued to flourish. Perhaps the greatest boon for them came in March 1654, when in the interest of religious unity Cromwell summoned Patrick Gillespie, John Livingston and John Menzies to London upon Gillespie's prompting.[310] Cromwell's invitation owed much to a belief within the English regime that the Protesters were the most likely party in the Kirk to cooperate: a reputation based almost completely on Gillespie's willingness to comply with the English, which had won over Colonel Robert Lilburne (commander-in-chief of the forces in Scotland from December 1652 until April 1654) and possibly the successful cooperation between the Aberdeen Independents and Gillespie's party.[311] Livingstone tried to decline the invitation on the grounds of ill health; however when Lilburne informed him that he would either go voluntarily or as a prisoner he willingly travelled to London.[312] Gillespie and Menzies, in contrast, jumped at the chance, but due to ill health Menzies went some time later than Gillespie. After meeting with the Protester and Independent representatives, Cromwell summoned Robert Blair, Robert Douglas and James Guthrie in May.[313] All three made excuses and refused to attend.[314] Douglas did so most gracefully. He wrote to Lord Broghill, with whom he shared old acquaintances, begging him to relay his apologies to the Lord Protector and explaining his unwillingness to be the sole representative of the Resolutioners position 'in matters of so great importance'.[315] Blair's and Douglas' refusal to participate would prove to have disastrous consequences for the Resolutioners.

Gillespie and Menzies took full advantage of their audience with the Protector, assisting in the production of an ordinance which came to be known as 'Gillespie's Charter'.[316] Passed on 8 August 1654, the ordinance represented the Scottish version of the scheme instituted in England the same year to try new ministers before entering them into charges or state stipends. For Resolutioners like Robert Baillie the ordinance represented their worst fears come true: that the Kirk 'shall be cast under such a Committee as now guides all ecclesiasticall affaires in England ... the most whereof are Anabaptists and Independents'.[317] The ordinance divided Scotland into five regions and gave the power of authorising and planting ministers to designated individuals.[318] Furthermore, it restricted the Commissioners for Visiting Universities to filling vacant charges only with individuals certified by a quorum of any four or more (at least two being ministers) designated triers. According to Frances Dow, Gillespie's participation is evidenced in the fifty-seven Scots chosen to be triers, the vast majority being either Protesters or full-blown Independents.[319] While Gillespie's faction dominated the west, in the vast region defined as north of Angus, which included present-day Aberdeenshire, Banffshire, Morayshire, Inverness-shire, Ross and Cromarty, Sutherland, Caithness, Orkney and Shetland, a quorum could be substantiated by Row, Menzies, Jaffray and Muir.[320] The more rigid Protesters of the Guthrie–Rutherford–Wariston variety did not miss this fact. They wrote to Cromwell and General Monck complaining about the fact that such a vast area of Scotland could be controlled by four avowed Independents.[321] Contemporaries complained that 'Independents, enemies of the Church of Scotland, are admitted on it' and 'deposed men' are given power to 'govern the admission of other ministers'.[322]

Gillespie's Charter also established the duty of parliament's commissioners to provide out of the public funds 'a competent maintenance, for such ministers who have Gathered Congregations in Scotland' and likewise to ensure the availability of stipends for 'godly ministers ... free to labour ... in the way of the church of Scotland'.[323] Neither the Resolutioners, largely excluded from positions of trying candidates, nor the rigid Protesters were willing to concede to such an invasive English encroachment into Scottish religion. The combination of giving Independents so much influence over a vast region of Scotland coupled with Gillespie's hand in the work drove an even greater wedge between the factions within the Protester party and further convinced the Resolutioners that none of them could be trusted. Synods across the country produced declarations against the work.[324] Despite the great power that the ordinance appeared to give for settling charges, several 'Congregationall Ministers who have been instruments of much good in Scotland' felt it necessary to inquire of Cromwell, via Monck, how the ordinance would affect them and how it should 'incurrage them to goe on in that good worke which they have begun'.[325] No names are attached to the letter, but Thomas Charteris (East Kilbride), John Beverley (Lenzie), John Collins (Edinburgh) and John Stalham (Edinburgh) were all in Scotland serving as ministers to gathered congregations rather than as military chaplains. Samuel Mather (Leith) and Samuel Bryan (Stirling), also in Scotland at the time, may very well have been in the same situation. In short, the authors feared that the ordinance undermined their roles by giving control back to factions within the Kirk. Barely a week later, Cromwell reassured them that competent stipends would continue for ministers of gathered churches no matter what the triers had to say.[326] As a result, previously established gathered congregations found themselves exempt from the ordinance.

Despite the major boost that the ordinance seemed to give to Independents and Gillespie's Protesters, the charter ultimately flopped. Many of those nominated refused to fulfil their role as triers, essentially nullifying the act.[327] For this reason, the charter, although reaffirmed by Broghill in September 1655 as the official policy of the English regime and remaining so until July 1656, has been hailed by historians as a dead letter.[328] The following year several of the 'triers' appointed in the charter sent a letter to the council in Scotland explaining why they refused to take up their position.[329] They listed as one of their reasons, among others, that the inclusion of Independents 'unchurch … all the constitute congregations in Scotland' and argued this to be an integral aspect of the ordinance: 'absolutlie ordained to be sett on foot and established'.[330]

Despite the overall failure of charter, there is some evidence that in the region 'be-north Angus', Independents put the ordinance to good use. Sometime between 1653 and 1656, John Seaton entered the first charge of Old St Machar's. Seaton had served as the minister of the second charge since 1650, but when he declared for Independency in 1652 the congregation refused to hear him preach.[331] He managed to remain in the second charge, but when William Strachan, minister of the first charge, died in 1653 the congregation and the synod refused him the vacant first charge.[332] However, by January 1656 Seaton had been planted in the first charge.[333] How and when this occurred is uncertain, but it is likely the appointment took place sometime between 1654 and 1656, when Gillespie's charter remained in effect, facilitated by a Jaffray–Menzies–Row–Muir quorum.[334] Additionally, ministers of Moray and Ross, also in the region labelled 'north of Angus', complained to Resolutioner brethren in the south of Hugh Anderson's entry into the charge of Cromarty.[335] They called Anderson, a 1651 graduate of King's College, former regent of King's College and son-in-law of John Row, 'a man of suspectit principles' because of his 'education' and his links to 'them of the separatione way'. According to Anderson's critics, 'his actings since his entrie speak too much of his inclinatione that way and of his aversness from the Approvin government of our national church'. Interestingly, in light of Gillespie's charter, they also identified his friends and supporters in acquiring the charge of Cromarty as being John Row and Patrick Gillespie, and complained of commissioners who, under the 'present power', sought to visit presbyteries and plant ministers in a way traditionally reserved for the presbyteries themselves. In January 1657 Baillie still identified the charter as a major factor in Scottish ecclesiastical politics, and wrote to James Sharp in London urging him to labour 'to get abolished that very unjust commission visiting Universities ... which M. P. G[illespie] did attain, that no Independent should violently take a the church and stipend of any parish, as was done in Kilbryde and Leinzie, and much less that such should take up our Universities, as they have done Aberdeene, etc.'[336]

The power to plant and remove ministers was not the only incentive given by Cromwell to compliant ministers. When Menzies and Gillespie returned from London in August 1654, they secured not only the legislative support of the English regime but also financial support for their respective universities.[337] 'An Ordinance for the better Support of the Universities in Scotland and the Encouragement of Publick Preachers', the official name of 'Gillespie's Charter', granted lands and rents to the universities of Glasgow and Aberdeen, while making no mention of Edinburgh or St Andrews.[338] The act transferred all lands formerly belonging to the bishop of Galloway to the University of Glasgow and those having belonged to the bishop of Aberdeen to the University of Aberdeen, with two thirds going to King's College and one third to Marischal. The Aberdeen colleges also received fishing rights on the rivers Dee and Don as well as the North Sea. In addition, two hundred merks were to be given annually to both universities.[339] This generosity demonstrated Cromwell's willingness to heap benefits upon sympathetic and loyal individuals and institutions. Over time, Gillespie's critics took notice of the great many gifts that the Protector bestowed on the principal of Glasgow University.[340]

In later years the universities benefited from additional gifts. In 1657 the government granted the University of Glasgow permission to print Bibles in any language and to produce all necessary academic books, a privilege not given to any other university in Scotland.[341] With the money given to the university in Gillespie's Charter and subsequent money granted by the municipal government, Gillespie funded substantial building work at the university, which even Baillie, his perpetual critic, could not refrain from reservedly praising.[342] However, it was the University of Aberdeen that continued to receive the most frequent favours. In 1658 Cromwell granted a charter to the University of Aberdeen, serving to reaffirm the provisions promised under Gillespie's charter and further accentuating the privileged status of the university.[343] That same year Row set about extending King's College by adding a square tower on the northwest corner of the quadrangle, housing amenities such as a fully fitted billiards room. Among those contributing to the building project were a host of Englishmen. In total, donations from English soldiers equalled about £500, £120 of which came personally from General Monck. Other Englishmen contributed, including William Clarke (Monck's secretary), Colonel Thomas Fitch and Major John Hill, all of whom gave at least £20.[344] The generosity of the English soldiers, no doubt coupled with the desire to further endear themselves to the Protector, led to the college naming the new building 'Cromwell's Tower'. The successful fundraising at King's College encouraged a similar project to begin the following year at Marischal, with plans for building a 'Public School' in the grounds of college. Oxford, Cambridge and Eton each contributed to the project. Cambridge gave approximately 40 merks, and Oxford just over £53. The most generous donor was found in the Aberdeen Independents' old friend and mentor, Nicholas Lockyer. Having recently been appointed provost of Eton in January of that year, he and John Oxenbridge, a fellow at Eton and another former Independent chaplain with the army in Scotland, gave £185 for the building project at Marischal, which had essentially become the seedbed of Independency in Scotland.[345] Thus relations between Lockyer and the Aberdeen Independents continued long after Lockyer left Scotland. Obviously such generosity did little to scupper accusations that Menzies, Row and crew were proselytes of Lockyer. Baillie did not fail to recognise the reason for Aberdeen's preferential treatment. They were under the dominance of Independents, who used Scotland's universities 'for the corrupting of our youth'.[346] It is also interesting to note that among the students of divinity at Marischal College during this time was James Fraser of Brea (MA 1658), and it may have been his studies under the tutelage of Menzies and Row that laid the foundations for his later unique theological position.[347]

The Twilight of Seventeenth-Century Scottish Independency

Despite the fact that Hoy and Henderson seem to indicate the high point in the Independency movement in Scotland was the gathered communion in Aberdeen in November 1652, or the months immediately following, and Wariston claimed that the death of Charteris in June 1656 marked the demise of the only two 'gathered congregations in Scotland', the overall evidence suggests that the movement continued for much of the 1650s.[348]

In December 1656, Baillie again protested that the Aberdeen Independents not only continued to thrive but continued to collude with Gillespie's party of Protesters. He called them 'our northern separatists … with whom we must joyne in silence'.[349] At that time controversy swirled over the parish charge of Eccles, where a Protester minister had been planted but could not settle due to opposition. Baillie feared that with the support of the English regime and the Commissioners for Visiting Universities a Protester would be placed in the charge or, even worse, that John Livingstone might bring 'a professed Independent' from 'Aberdeen's nest'.[350] A month later, Baillie continued to rail against the Independent congregations formed earlier in the decade at Lenzie and East Kilbride, and their usurpation of Scotland's universities 'as they have done in Aberdeen'.[351] Baillie's comments imply that Gillespie's faction still favoured some of the Independents and possessed the power to plant them, as the report of Hugh Anderson's entry into the far-off charge of Cromarty seems to imply.[352] With regards to the balance of power in Glasgow in October 1657, Nicoll wrote: 'matteris in Kirk Session were totalie gydit by him (Gillespie), and none elected elders or deacons but by his approbation and accordance … he gydit and governit in that town'.[353] Additional support for the ongoing success of the movement is reported in that year when Jaffray, then a resident in Edinburgh, explained that only geographical separation prevented him from having those 'with whom formerly [he] walked in fellowship at Aberdeen' baptise his newborn son.[354] As late as 1658 a new Independent congregation formed in Leith under the English minister John Collins.[355] Nonetheless, by that year the movement was in overall decline. A significant blow for the Aberdeen Independents came in November 1657 when John Seaton, minister at Old St Machar's, left Scotland to take charge of a gathered church at Felton-bridge, Northumberland.[356] Why he left is uncertain, but by the end of 1658 the Aberdeen Independents seem to have completely disappeared.

What happened to bring about the end of the Aberdeen Independents, and what became of other gathered churches? Several factors probably contributed to the demise of the movement in Aberdeen. First of all, from about midsummer 1652 Alexander Jaffray's consistent involvement with the group ceased. Soon after the submission of the 24 May letter, Cromwell appointed him director of the Scottish chancery. He accepted the post in June, and apart from the eight months he spent in London serving as a member of the Commonwealth parliament from July 1653 to February 1654, Jaffray spent six months during 'the Session' in Edinburgh, and the other six months of the year in Aberdeen.[357] Being absent for half the year would have made his involvement increasingly marginal. In November 1656 Jaffray moved his family to Edinburgh, initially settling in Newbattle, where his father-in-law Andrew Cant had served as minister (1639–41), before relocating to Abbey Hill.[358] This series of events marked the removal of a major stabilising influence from the Aberdeen Independents, which must have been greatly missed, given the remaining strong personalities of Menzies and Row. More than that, Jaffray's absence marked the removal of the *primum mobile*, as his father-in-law, Andrew Cant, termed him.[359] In Cant's estimation, Jaffray remained the major 'stumbling block' in Aberdeen in January 1656, so his complete absence from November affected the Aberdeen Independents significantly.[360]

Importantly, Jaffray underwent a metamorphosis of his own, which is highlighted by a short entry in his journal. Thomas Jaffray, his son, was born in Edinburgh in 1657. Several children were born into the family during the Interregnum, but previously Alexander had been either in Edinburgh – with the family continuing to live in Aberdeen – or in London when his children were born.[361] Now, however, the family resided in Edinburgh, where he was neither a member of a gathered church nor any better inclined towards Presbyterianism. Being geographically separated from those with whom he 'formerly walked in fellowship at Aberdeen', he resolved to find a Kirk minister who would perform the sacrament in a private manner and allow him to declare publicly that the baptism served only as an induction into the 'universal or catholic church' rather than a particular national church, as well as voice his objection to national churches. After meeting Jaffray and discussing his objections and stipulations, John Sinclair, minister of Ormiston, agreed to perform the sacrament on these terms.[362] However, when Sinclair arrived at Jaffray's Newbattle home on 12 May 1657, he rescinded his offer to allow Jaffray to voice his objections publicly to national churches on the grounds that the presbytery of Edinburgh would be none too pleased with his baptising the child of a sworn schismatic, especially after acquiescing to such terms. Instead Sinclair suggested, for both their sakes, that someone else present the child for baptism. Not wanting to cause problems for the minister who had already gone out of his way to help him, Jaffray allowed Robert Porteous, a bailie of Newbattle, to present the child for baptism.

If Jaffray still persisted in his aversion to the national church, why did he have his child baptised by a Kirk minister? Jaffray desired to 'give an evidence to the godly men of the Presbyterian way, of my willingness to live peaceably and in love with them, partaking with them in all duties, so far as I may do it without sin; though in the matter of their constitution and form of government I differ from them'.[363] Essentially the position Jaffray held, which Cromwell had advocated, was not that Presbyterianism was essentially bad, but that it was rather overbearing on people's consciences and in its national structure was incompatible with the existence of congregations in their purest possible form. He did not hold the belief that the presbytery could not be allowed to continue, just that it could not continue to dominate the consciences of others. Having been converted to the Cromwellian concept of Christian unity, Jaffray desired 'all such as fear him [God], may "walk in love", as becomes the children of one Father' and thus sought to do as much as possible to engage with fellow Christians without sinning against his conscience.[364] The following year (1658) he allowed his wife to present their newborn twins for baptism within a Kirk 'under certain limitations', and contemplated taking communion with those who 'most purely' administered it.[365] Explaining his position, he wrote:

> I ever thought it, and still think it my duty, so far as I may without sin, to go along with any of the Lord's people: – while [or until] the Lord clear up our darkness, we must bear one another, or [we shall be likely to] devour each other. And I am confident, it is our duty, not only to bear with one another, wherein we may without sin, but to walk together. Only special care should be had in this case, that, (in that peremptory and peevish disposition of *the most part of the godly in this land*, who can be satisfied with no less, than to have all men conform to *them* and be of *their* judgement,) – I say, especial care should be had, that, by our *conforming* to such, we do not *confirm* them in their sinful mistakes; and therefore, upon all occasions that are convenient, would testimony be given against their errors.[366]

Although Jaffray and the Aberdeen Independents originally fell under the influence of Lockyer, who advocated strict separation, even isolation, from ungodly 'leven', some of them gradually drifted towards a position similar to Beverley's and evidenced by Gillespie in his dealings with the English. Ideologically they remained Independents and believed that they must continue to witness against the Presbyterian error of demanding conformity (what Davis calls 'formality')[367] on their unbending terms, but in pursuit of unity they attempted to engage with the 'purer' sort both within the national church and without. Gillespie's own faction were, in some ways, closer to Independency than they were to even their fellow Guthrie–Rutherford–Wariston Protesters because they likewise gave up on the national model of the presbytery espoused in the covenants and the requirement to impose it on others. Essentially, they took a step towards the model of congregational government exhibited in New England.

Jaffray was not alone in coming to a sort of *via media* between isolationist separation and embracing the absolutist position of the national Kirk. An ambiguity in distinctions between the position of the Independents and some of the Protesters began to take shape. Besides the compliance shown to Independents by Gillespie's Protesters, in 1655 Menzies demonstrated compliance with the more rigid Guthrie–Rutherford–Wariston Protesters. The separation by his former Protesting brethren for the sake of purer administration of ordinances greatly disturbed Andrew Cant. He desired purer ordinances as well, but he could not bring himself to separate from the Kirk. In 1653 he came up with a scheme for restricting communion to individuals willing to submit themselves for public trial.[368] This sparked a major controversy in Aberdeen. The Resolutioners perceived Cant as dangerously flirting with an ecclesiology all too similar to the Aberdeen Independents'. The Resolutioner majority in the synod accused any who might adopt this policy as acting out a 'practical separation' from the congregation and the Kirk.[369] Moreover, they called the proponents of the scheme 'innovators, practicall separatists, schesmaticks, mackers of divisioune ... backsliders from the guid old way' and 'pharisaical'.[370] Yet acting on a suggestion made by Guthrie that John Menzies might be convinced from proceeding any further in that 'neu way' of Independency, Cant sought Menzies' backing for his controversial plan. Guthrie warned Cant not to get drawn into the errors of the Aberdeen Independents, but suggested 'in vhat else he may condescend to gaining of him (Menzies) I vish he suld doe'.[371] So Cant pitched his proposal to the Independent. By January 1656 he convinced Menzies to 'go along with' the plan, which closely resembled the practice of the London Independent John Goodwin, who preached to the whole of his parish but only administered the sacraments to those of the gathered whom he deemed acceptable. However, by January 1656 communion limited to those publicly tried had already occurred twice, so Menzies' support was not to effectuate limited communions, but merely for support against the swelling pressure in both the presbytery and synod of Aberdeen.

From Cant's perspective this scheme must have seemed like a compromise between Menzies' actual separation and their shared desire for purer ordinances; or, perhaps, it was an attempt to bring the Aberdeen Independents back into the Protester fold. In either case, Cant worried about the precariousness of Menzies' support, fearing that he might simply opt for that 'new congregation' 'sealed' by the communion of November 1652.[372] Cant urged Wariston to write to Menzies and encourage him to continue his support for the new communion format. During the summer of 1655, Brodie noted that Menzies sat in the presbytery meetings to consult, but that he could take no part in decision making, which may indicate that his attendance was related to his professorship in the university and not his religious affiliation.[373] So how did Menzies help Cant? Perhaps Menzies' influence can be seen in May 1656, when the Resolutioner majority in the synod of Aberdeen attempted to quash Cant's scheme. Just after Cant arrived at a meeting of the synod to which he had been summoned, English soldiers intervened. An officer representing the garrison commander (probably Michael Richardson at the time)[374] entered the meeting and ordered the synod to cease interfering in Cant's business.[375] Menzies' sway with the English, exhibited in his role in the production of Gillespie's Charter, could easily account for this military intervention. The collusion between Cant and Menzies should not, however, be interpreted as an end of Independency in Aberdeen. In fact, a contemporary Catholic report denotes three parties in Aberdeen: one headed by Cant, another by Menzies and a third party of 'Independents'.[376] While the controversy played out, Cant persisted in identifying both Row and Jaffray as Independents. Cant actually asked Wariston to write 'scharplie' to Row 'reproving him for what he hath done, and desiring him, yea, conjuring him to do no more' and to Jaffray, as the separatists' primary instigator, urging him to stop encouraging the congregation.[377] So the Aberdeen Independents continued. Moreover, the assistance Menzies provided to Cant does not necessarily mean that he stopped being an Independent. Menzies' support for Cant represents his willingness to support a venture advancing a degree of reform that he and his fellows had sought but had been unable to effectuate earlier in the decade without schism. Menzies remained separated from the church until about June 1658, when he returned to the Protester fold, which only served to further muddle the distinction between Independents and Protesters.[378]

As far as the Resolutioners were concerned, such collusion only reaffirmed their belief that none of the Protesters was a Presbyterian. As Holfelder put it, the Protesters had separated into 'some form of erastian, neo-Independency'.[379] G.D. Donaldson, David Stevenson and John Coffey have all recognised the contradictory position of the Protesters.[380] According to Coffey, although Rutherford never separated from the church he could no longer tolerate the degeneration of the Kirk brought about through its mixed-multitude membership. As a result, 'one of the greatest seventeenth-century defenders of divine-right Presbyterianism finished his days as a rebel against the church polity he had sought so hard to establish'.[381] As the decade progressed, Rutherford and other Protesters found themselves irresistibly drifting away from an emphasis on national presbytery towards discipline within congregations, although Guthrie and Rutherford would never have admitted as much. Donaldson, drawing on Baillie, suggests evidence of this shift in the Protesters' rigid restrictions to communion in Glasgow and Aberdeen, which tended 'towards something like a "gathered congregation".'[382] However, the best indication of the extent to which the distinctions between Independency and the Protesters' Presbyterianism had blurred is evidenced by a report from the Quaker Francis Howgill. According to Howgill, when he arrived in Scotland in 1657 he found large numbers of English soldiers attending Kirk services presided over by Scottish ministers, despite those ministers being the 'false Prophets ... and incendiaries' who had embroiled 'all the poor people of this Nation in blood to fight for their imagined calfe Presbitery'.[383] After the dissolution of the 1653 General Assembly, the Kirk's national assembly did not meet again for the remainder of the Interregnum, while synod and presbyteries were intermittently barred from convening.[384] Writing in 1659, James Guthrie declared that these measures had in a 'great measure overthrown' the government and discipline of the Kirk.[385] This vacuum of Presbyterian power reduced the practice of discipline in the Kirk to something not all that different from Independency. Discipline predominantly had to be congregationally based, and depended on the offender subjecting him or herself to the authority of the congregation.[386] As one Scottish critic put it, 'the general and lawfull assemblies of this church ar wholly taken away the provinciall synods and even presbyteries and kirk sessions seim to be whooly taken away because as non of thes are expressly acknowledged: so it wold appear that all the lawes concerning ye same ar annulled an made voyd'.[387] For moderate Independents within the army, a disempowered Presbyterian Kirk free of general assemblies was less officious than the radicalism of Quakers, Baptists and Fifth Monarchists. The compliance between Gillespie's Protesters, Aberdeen Independents and the disciplinarily strict English Independents blurred the clear patterns of Independency provided by Lockyer and Owen. As a result, many English soldiers happily found the Calvinist doctrine that they craved consistently voiced from Scottish pulpits without the Presbyterian baggage they had risked so much to usurp. So at least for some English soldiers, the distinction between their Independent congregations back home and a Presbyterian Kirk devoid of 'tyrannical' general assemblies, presbyteries and synods – as the editor of Wood's *A Dead-Man's Testament* termed them – began to diminish.[388]

By 1658 the vast majority of Scots who had stepped out of the Kirk to embrace Independency ended up following one of three paths. Some, like Jaffray, who as late as the spring of 1657 differed little from the Kirk theologically except in his interpretation of the role and function of external ecclesiastical government over a congregation, took a more tempered view of the Kirk and tried to coexist with it but could not in good conscience restore his membership. This would have been the same for some of his counterparts in Aberdeen. After the dust of their separation had settled, the overwhelming majority of Aberdeen Independents were still thoroughly Calvinist and Reformed in their theology. Though initially unified in their agreement that gathered congregations were a better alternative to Presbyterian mass inclusion, the Cromwellian ideal of toleration tempered their position. They attempted to maintain fraternal links and foster unity with various Christian groups, but chose not to ally themselves with any particular gathering. Jaffray remained, as one slightly biased late eighteenth-century source put it, 'in private for some years, a solitary mourner not joining with any profession in religion' until after the Restoration.[389] But in truth, Jaffray remained an 'Independent' without a congregation until well after the Restoration, as did William Dundas, whose chronologically deficient account of his own experience explains that he too eventually joined the Quakers, but probably not until after 1666.[390]

Some others, however, did not remain as neutral as Jaffray and Dundas did during the latter years of the Interregnum. For some, the introduction of Independency into Scotland set them onto a new trajectory of rapid religious progression over a relatively short period of time. According to Baillie's reports, several members of Thomas Charteris' Independent congregation in East Kilbride, including the Hamilton family, 'turned quakers' before the minister's unfortunate demise in 1656.[391] There is also evidence to believe this affected the gathered church at Lenzie, where at least one dispute with local Quakers occurred.[392] Some other members of Charteris' congregation reportedly became Baptists.[393] So, in the span of less than four years a number of Scots became convinced of Independency, joined Charteris' congregation and then subsequently turned Quaker or Baptist. For these individuals, their progression might best be interpreted in light of Jonathon Scott's suggestion that sectarianism within the England of the 1650s represented not 'a series of *movements* but ... a succession of *moments*'.[394] Hence, for some Scots, Independency served as an initial starting point in a progression towards other more radical positions. Margaret Anderson represents an example of this progression in Aberdeen. The wife of an Aberdeen bailie, Anderson was a member of the Aberdeen Independents before her baptism at the hands of a Baptist soldier before the end of the Interregnum. By the time of her death in 1663, Anderson had joined the Quakers.[395]

The rest of the Aberdeen Independents who, like John Menzies and probably Andrew Birnie, maintained orthodox Reformed theology throughout, found themselves gradually drifting back into the Presbyterian Kirk, since they only differed on principles of ecclesiology.[396] This was a step closer to Gillespie's position than Jaffray was willing to go, but Menzies and others eventually came to view their position on ecclesiastical government as differing from the Kirk's more in degree than in kind. For this reason, it is likely that many of the Aberdeen Independents swallowed their pride and returned to the Kirk, a process which may have been hastened by the re-eruption of the Protester–Resolutioner debate following the death of Cromwell. However, according to Jaffray's testimony, those formerly belonging to the Aberdeen Independents continued to be viewed by the main body of Protesters as, along with Gillespie's faction, proto-Independents after their return to the Kirk. As a result, hostile exchanges between Cant and Menzies continued after the latter rejoined the Kirk.[397] The reunion also seems to have left some of the former Independents, 'that handful who fear him in Aberdeen' as Jaffray referred to them, excluded from the ordinances served in Aberdeen's churches. Jaffray had hoped that the appointment of James Durham – who along with Robert Blair had avoided joining either faction in the Protester–Resolutioner dispute – to one of Aberdeen's vacant charges would facilitate reconciliation in Aberdeen and allow the former Independents access to the sacraments. The presbytery unanimously called Durham in December 1657, but he died the following summer before he could make the move to Aberdeen.[398] Jaffray lamented his death and prayed that God would 'point out some other way, whereby the work of the gospel and the ordinances, in purity may be administered there'.[399] The implication is that Row no longer ministered to a gathered congregation. What course he took is uncertain. The ecclesiastical records of Aberdeen make no further mention of him until after the Restoration, when he attempted to ingratiate himself with the king by writing an anti-Cromwellian poem.[400] It did little to help him. Refusing to conform to an Episcopalian settlement, he was removed from his principalship.

Thus it would seem that the disappearance of Scottish Independent congregations by the end of the Interregnum owed much to renewed pressure to rejoin the Kirk, the development of a party within the Kirk sympathetic to the aims of the Independents and a trajectory towards more radical positions. Just as Baillie, Rutherford and the English Presbyterian Thomas Edwards had warned before the English army arrived in Scotland, Independency proved to be a springboard into other 'errors' rather than a static ending point for those questioning the Presbyterian Kirk. By 1654 a plethora of options were available to Scots malcontented with the Presbyterian Kirk. Moreover, a fluid religious marketplace developed in which denominational drifting was both permitted and protected. For any individuals who actually remained inclined to Independency until the Restoration, their freedom to keep gathered congregations disappeared. The incoming tide of Prelacy and uniformity swept away toleration just as the 'ocean-like ... confluences' of Presbyterianism and Malignancy described by the Scottish Sectarians in their appeal to the English government in January 1652.[401] The Restoration served to drive Independents only mildly displeased with the presbytery towards the Covenanters, because even those with qualms about a national Presbyterian Kirk viewed it as the better alternative to Episcopacy. Others like Jaffray and Dundas who could not reconcile themselves to the Kirk were driven into more radical forms of dissent. In 1662, repulsed by both the Covenanters and Episcopacy, Jaffray and several others in Aberdeen embraced Quakerism and established a long-lasting tradition in the burgh, which in subsequent decades extended to New Jersey and beyond.[402] This preservation of Quaker ideologies and their Scottish exportation to the New World two decades after the Restoration, serve as a testament to the long-lasting impact of the religious policies introduced by the English during the Interregnum and the emphasis on separation and gathered churches.

The English advocacy of toleration and Congregationalism did not find success in Scotland purely of its own accord. The Kirk's increasingly extreme interpretation of the covenants and its harsh dealing with ministers who did not follow the party line during the 1640s had already begun eroding the unity of the Kirk before a shot was fired at Dunbar. Defeats at Dunbar and Worcester, after lofty promises by radical Presbyterians that their covenanted army would prevail, simply served to reinforce doubts. Disappointment, disillusionment and infighting within the Kirk tilled the soil of discontent and frustration that provided fertile ground for the religious seeds sown by the English during the Interregnum. For this reason, the preaching of Independency and toleration of Protestant variations struck a chord with many Scots who had either suffered under the persecution of the Kirk or had become disenchanted with the apparently empty promises of divine blessing in return for a covenanted nation willing to expand the influence of Presbyterianism by military means. While the Kirk did not experience excessively widespread separation, there is evidence that a wide range of Scots viewed, at least for a time, the English concepts of Congregationalism and toleration 'as nearer the patterne of the Gospel' and chose them over their own rigid and sometimes harsh covenanted Presbytery. All of this was supported by an intriguing trilateral relationship between the English regime, Gillespie's party of Protesters and Scottish Independents.

5   The 'Lamb's War' in Scotland

The Rise of the Quakers and the Fall of the Baptists[1]

Oliver Cromwell's initial foray into Scotland in the summer of 1650 relied heavily upon England's various radical Protestant groups within the army. However, the relationship between Cromwell and these groups changed after his ascendancy to power in December 1653. The military regime of the Commonwealth gradually shifted to a civilian government under a Protector, leaving many who had risked life and limb to fear that the monarchy they had fought to bring down had been reimposed under a different name. This chapter will focus on how the changing relationship between Baptists, Quakers and the government thwarted early successes in introducing sectarian religious forms into Scotland, and demonstrate how their remarkable change of circumstances during the course of the Interregnum in Scotland eventually encouraged them to act together in an unprecedented ecumenism, if only for a very brief time.

During the 1650s the Baptists and Quakers had a complex and entangled relationship with one another. T.L. Underwood's work *Primitivism, Radicalism and the Lamb's War* wonderfully lays out their similarities and differences, and most importantly the things that linked them together.[2] In relation to the Presbyterians of the Kirk and the moderate Independents promoting religious toleration within the Commonwealth/Protectorate, Baptists and Quakers sought to realise and experience a 'primitive' Christianity much more fully than either the moderate Independents or the Presbyterians.[3] The Baptists, through rigid membership requirements, initiation via believer's baptism and stringent discipline, sought to imitate the early church as it is described in the New Testament; while the Quakers, through the direct guidance of the Inner Light, believed that they actually experienced the Apostolic Church directly. For the Quakers, neither the early church nor Christ's death and resurrection were temporally distant. They believed that both persisted as a perpetual part of their immediate religious experience. 'Thus the Christ whom Baptists thought of as preaching, crucified, buried, resurrected, and ascended into heaven some sixteen hundred years before,' explains Underwood, 'became for Quakers the Christ within them, who spoke and was crucified, buried, resurrected, and ascended – all within.'[4]

Similar desires for a more immediate experience of the primitive church brought them together while at the same time driving a wedge between them. For Quakers, the Baptists' imitation of the New Testament church failed to fully claim the power of Christ, the Church or the Holy Spirit because they believed 'to have the immediate experience that the earliest Christians had … required the internalization and spiritualization they practiced'.[5] In other words, proper forms do not equate with real experience. Equally, the Baptists were wary of Quaker claims that seemed to minimise the historical death and resurrection of Christ while overestimating the religious freedom manifested through the Holy Spirit. This led to conflict between them, because both groups recognised the basic desire driving the other but could not condone the conclusions of the other. Quakers believed that Baptists stopped short of fully realising the nature of the Church, while Baptists perceived that Quakers took things much too far.

Yet despite the apparently perpetual conflict between these groups, both mainstream Puritan and Presbyterian circles perceived them as being at the same radical end of the Christian church because of their shared desire to experience more fully the primitive church, which manifests itself particularly in their soteriological and sacramental doctrines.[6] Thus when the two groups arrived in Scotland en masse during the Interregnum, the Kirk perceived them as two heads of the same heretical hydra.[7] The differences between them were merely of degree: Baptists were slightly more radical than the Brownists, and Seekers were the most radical of them all.[8]

Because mainstream Puritans and Presbyterians linked these two groups together as radicals, they became increasingly entangled in each other's business, as well as with other radical groups like the Fifth Monarchists. Any aspersion or negative public opinion vented against any one of these groups had the knock-on effect of casting a shadow on all the groups perceived as being part of the extreme or radical end of the religious spectrum. As the government of the Commonwealth became increasingly civilian (especially after the inception of the Protectorate), and a status quo pattern of religious and political settlement became evident, the discontent publicly vented by the Fifth Monarchists served to draw increased attention to the politically dissident nature of other religious groups holding radical ecclesiologies. Pressure on Quakers increased as they challenged social hierarchies and refused to remove their hats to social superiors, despite the desire of George Fox and other leading Quakers that the Friends avoid any involvement in political intrigue.

A second dimension brought Quakers and Baptists into regular contact. They often vied for the same proselytes. In fact, a dynamic struggle existed within the army in Scotland between various sectarian groups vying to win over soldiers to a particular sect. The Baptist Miles Sindercombe had, according to C.H. Firth, joined the army solely for the purpose of promulgating his doctrines within the army in Scotland.[9] These endeavours were not limited to either the Baptists or to gaining the adherence of those yet uncommitted to a particular sect. Indeed, the Quakers often targeted Baptist meetings as good places to find proselytes.[10] As is often the case with groups who have more in common than they would like to admit, a strong antipathy existed between them, which Underwood charts through the polemical publications that the two groups produced against each other in England. In Scotland, the Quakers and Baptists shared very much the same relationship as they did in England. Both groups contended for the same potential new members and bitterly opposed each other's errors, as George Fox found out when angry Baptists confronted him during visits to Leith and Perth in 1657.[11] It was those Baptists, declared Fox, who were 'the ground and cause of our banishment out of this place'.[12]

Despite these aspects which linked them, the two factions had different introductions into Scotland and became integrated into Scottish culture in different ways. The Baptists entered into Scottish society closely bound to the English regime in power after victory at Dunbar. The close relationship between the newly forming Baptist congregations and the governmental regime both ensured support for Baptist success in the early years of the Interregnum and eventually loomed large in their downfall. Quakers, on the other hand, entered Scotland predominantly as a civilian movement. While this presented its own challenges in terms of gaining a foothold in Scotland, it served to provide them with a distinctly different base of support and ensured from the beginning that they were not reliant upon governmental protection or support.

Baptists and the Army

Baptist ideas did not enter Scotland for the first time during the Interregnum. Reports in 1642 state that the Laird of Tulliefruskie (possibly a Gordon) came under the influence of Baptist doctrines before being quickly censured by the Kirk.[13] In 1647, the Kirk excommunicated a Scotswoman named Christian Blyth, who subsequently fled to England to escape continued persecution.[14] On previous occasions the Kirk had moved quickly to suppress what it perceived as a grotesque error and the source of all other heresies. However, the Kirk's situation under Cromwell's regime differed greatly from the decade before. The English victory at Dunbar ushered in a decade of religious toleration in which thousands of religiously radical Englishmen occupied the country and ventured into virtually every corner of Scotland. It did not take long before the evangelical efforts of the Baptists began to visibly bear fruit.

By 1652 Baptist gatherings began to form across Scotland. The most famous of these met alternately in Edinburgh and Leith before permanently settling in the port town. Local tradition holds that the building in which they met can still be seen above the old citadel's gate on Dock Street, but in fact that structure is a later addition.[15] In 1652 Baptist gatherings met in Perth (St Johnston), Cupar and possibly at or near Dundee. There were also probably meetings in Ayr, Aberdeen and Inverness, locations where Baptist churches definitely met later in the decade.[16] There may have been no Baptist congregation in Stirling in 1652, but there certainly was in 1653 when the aggressive and confrontational Baptist chaplain of Colonel Fairfax's regiment, James Brown, arrived in the town. The gathering seems to have continued to meet in Stirling for the rest of the decade, as Monck reported in 1659 that some individuals in the town promoted the Anabaptist cause while seeking to put down the local ministry.[17] Brown may also have had links with Baptists in the regiments garrisoned at Falkland and Perth, who he visited in January 1654 as part 'of that dutie which is incumbent on me in reference to them'.[18] The Baptist historian David Douglas, and subsequently James Scott, have alleged that Baptists were so prevalent in the army and so widely dispersed throughout the forces that Baptist groups gathered and met in most of the garrisons and citadels throughout the country.[19] A claim not beyond the realm of possibility, as the contemporary historian James Heath (1629–64) put it, the army that invaded and occupied Scotland 'swarmed' with Baptists.[20] Certainly Baptists reached remote places. Evidence suggests that during the Interregnum Baptists groups were spread from the Borders to Caithness, and possibly beyond.

A significant amount of information about Baptists in Scotland has been fortuitously preserved in the records of the Baptist churches in Hexham, Northumberland and Fenstanton, Cambridgeshire. Among these documents is a letter from an English Baptist named Edward Limburgh, who found himself in Jedburgh in October 1652.[21] Despite complaints of the country's spiritual deadness and his lamentations over lack of fellowship, it is unlikely that Limburgh was as spiritually isolated as his letter seems to suggest. What brought Limburgh to Scotland is somewhat uncertain. Frances Dow suggests he was a missionary, which is a legitimate claim as Baptists in Scotland actively evangelised, but it is equally likely that he was simply an enlisted soldier in a regiment quartered at Jedburgh.[22] In either case, Limburgh perceived his sojourn into Scotland as providential.[23] His complaints of the spiritual destitution of his new surroundings came fresh upon his arrival to Jedburgh and seem to stem largely from being geographically removed from the Baptist church at Hexham that had baptised him into their fellowship only one month earlier.[24] It is therefore probable he missed the spiritual euphoria experienced as a newly baptised member of a gathered congregation rather than there being a complete lack of fellowship in his new surroundings. Since this is Limburgh's only surviving letter we do not know what became of him, but as he settled into his quarters he may have come to find other English soldiers in the same situation.

Another source supporting the existence of Baptist communities in remote or rural parts of Scotland indicates the existence of a gathering in Helmsdale (Sutherland), where Colonel William Packer's regiment garrisoned the castle in 1656. Although Packer, himself a fervent Baptist, was in the south of England in 1656 he sent a letter to the regiment encouraging the soldiers to stand strong in their religious convictions. The work does not survive, but according to the Quaker Jonas Dell, Packer espoused the General Baptists' doctrines of baptism by immersion, the prevalence of free will and the possibility of falling from grace, while warning them not to fall into the errors of the Quakers.[25] This account tantalisingly brings to memory reports from January 1652 that 'a very precious people' in Sutherland and 'diverse parts beyond Inverness' left their Kirks in order to attend meetings of officers and soldiers gathered in private homes.[26]

Scots began to take serious notice of the Baptist presence among them as early as October 1651, when compatriots in a Protester meeting held in Edinburgh famously put forward some Baptist ideologies.[27] The following May, Nicoll reported that Alexander Cornwell and Thomas Charteris were carrying on some strange practices and maintaining 'Anabaptist' principles.[28] In September 1652, not being fully aware of the situation in Aberdeen, Lamont falsely reported that John Row and John Menzies had become Anabaptists and utterly refused to baptise infants.[29] Other rumours about Row's family were in circulation about this time. In his letter of 27 May 1652, Row felt it necessary to deny that his wife had been baptised by Baptists near Dundee.[30] Baptist principles came closer to home for the Fife-based diarist John Lamont in October 1652, when the General Baptist James Brown arrived in Cupar as chaplain to Colonel Fairfax's regiment. Brown's ministry in Cupar was anything but quiet. Well-known for his penchant to seek public debates, the inhabitants of Cupar witnessed the hitherto completely foreign practice of rebaptism when Brown dipped several soldiers 'over heads and ears' in the River Eden.[31]

Despite the relatively few recorded accounts of baptisms, these were not isolated events. According to Lamont, throughout March 1653 a significant number of rebaptisms occurred in the Water of Leith.[32] In April, public baptisms by immersion took place three times a week in the tributary. On Mondays, Wednesdays and Fridays people were baptised at Bonnington Mill, with as many as fifteen people receiving the ordinance in a single day, sometimes with several hundred onlookers. According to Nicoll, unlike Lamont's report of English soldiers being baptised, in Leith it appears that many Scots of both sexes and various social ranks received the sacrament.[33] The only individual immersed in the Water of Leith known by name is Lady Craigie-Wallace, described by Lamont as a Scotswoman from the west of Scotland, probably in the immediate vicinity of Ayr.[34] Although reports of baptisms from other parts of the country are lacking, it is not improbable that around the many garrisons spread throughout the country similar incidents could have taken place, especially around the large citadels of Perth, Ayr and Inverness. At least one baptism took place in Aberdeen, where Baptists maintained a significant presence.[35] Others may have occurred in Dundee, where rumours of Row's wife being baptised 'above Dundie' might suggest that baptisms took place in Dighty Water.[36] It is far from beyond the realm of possibility that individuals were 'dipped' in the Tay, the Dee or the Don, the River Ness or perhaps in Lady Craigie's Well in Ayr; in the case of Ayr, there is supplemental evidence in the kirk session records, where an accusation is recorded of a parishioner being 'rebaptised and diped in the Ladie Craigies Well'. In this instance the kirk session vindicated the accused and 'processed' the libeller.[37] Yet the account suggests that the well of Craigie-Wallace, baptised in Leith the previous year, may have become a recognised centre of Baptist activity. Certainly by 1653 the growth of the Baptists in Scotland represented a serious source of concern, leading to rumours and accusations running rife. Looking back on 1653, Nicoll declared that 'this yeir Anabaptistes daylie increst in this natioun, quhair nevir nane wes befoir, at leist durst not avow themeselffis: bot now many maid oppin professioun thairof, and avowit the same'.[38] According to another credible source, the growth of the sect in Scotland so heightened fears among Protesters that they produced a paper in March 1653 denouncing the 'new Scots Dippers'.[39]

The hastening success of the Baptists in the country during 1653 was by no means coincidental. From December 1652 until April 1654, Colonel Robert Lilburne, brother of the politically volatile John Lilburne, served as commander-in-chief of the forces in Scotland. An ardent Baptist, Lilburne did all he could to promote their cause in Scotland.[40] While officially following the Commonwealth's policy of promoting religious toleration and the gathering of independent congregations, he actively sought to bolster the Baptist presence in Scotland.[41] In the spring of 1653 a Baptist minister recently ordained in Hexham arrived in Dalkeith. His name was Edmund Hickeringill (or Hickhorngill) and he had been sent by the Baptist congregation in Hexham to take up a chaplaincy in Scotland. Soon after his arrival a former Baptist chaplain turned officer convinced Hickeringill of the limitations put upon ministry through chaplaincy, and persuaded him that a secular military commission would provide him with greater freedom for evangelistic outreach.[42] The suggestion that a military commission as opposed to a chaplaincy might provide greater freedom for missionary work is a telling claim that demonstrates the wide-ranging freedom English soldiers had to promote their own religious views within the bounds of their military duties.

Before Hickeringill could make his wishes known, Lilburne, who hosted the English Baptist in his own quarters (Dalkeith Palace), appointed him as a chaplain to his own regiment.[43] The appointment lasted only a short time, but while serving as chaplain to Lilburne's regiment Hickeringill was given freedom to be involved in the Baptist church that met alternately in Edinburgh and Leith. The members of that congregation, including Major Abraham Holmes (later implicated in Overton's plot) and more significantly the Fifth Monarchist Major-General Thomas Harrison, implored the newly arrived English Baptist to join their congregation.[44] However, Hickeringill's chaplaincy was short-lived. Fulfilling his promise to give Hickeringill the first open commission that might come available, Lilburne made him a lieutenant in Colonel Daniel's regiment in Perth. Clearly Lilburne felt that keeping a Baptist in his army as a soldier, although not as desirous as filling the vacancy of a chaplain in his regiment, better served his overall purposes than letting him return to England.

Links between Hexham and the Baptists in Scotland, particularly Lilburne, were very good. The few surviving letters in the Hexham records dated between March and September 1653 record at least two members of the Hexham congregation joining the Edinburgh/Leith church.[45] Besides lay connections, the church in Hexham also strove to provide ministers for their brethren in Scotland, whose congregations they termed 'sister churches'. Although the first emissary proved to be a failure, Lilburne continued to enlist the help of the Hexham congregation in providing Baptists for service in Scotland. Shortly before receiving his secular commission, Hickeringill wrote to relay a message from Lilburne to the church in Hexham:

> I am desired by Col. Lilburne to propose to you, that bro. Tillam, Bro. Anderton, Bro. Stackhouse, or any other fitly qualified brother amongst you, will bestow his talents in the condition of a chaplain to a regiment, about which place there are divers honest Scotch people that long to be gathered into the same gospel order with us, but they want a faithful pastor.[46]

The letter is important for two reasons. First, it demonstrates Lilburne's personal desire for the promotion of the Baptist movement in Scotland; second, it expresses his conviction that Scots beyond Edinburgh and Leith desired to join Baptist churches.

Hexham responded by sending Thomas Stackhouse. Initially visiting as a messenger, he soon accepted an invitation from Lilburne to serve as minister to the Edinburgh/Leith congregation and returned to Scotland. It is an impressive feat that the church at Hexham, only established in mid-1652, sent two men as Baptist ministers within a year of their formation.[47] Hickeringill and Stackhouse are both examples of the missionary fervour of the English Baptists. Baptised together on 25 August 1652, they both travelled to Scotland within a year to spread Baptist doctrines.[48] This may not have been the only congregation with whom Lilburne had correspondence, as it is only through the fortuitous preservation of these letters by the church at Hexham that we know of this important relationship. That no such correspondence exists in the official letter book preserved in the Clarke manuscripts demonstrates the strictly personal nature of Lilburne's desire to promote the Baptist movement in Scotland.[49] There may also be some reason to believe that the churches in Scotland were involved with Baptist Association meetings taking place in England, as a member of the church at Leith travelled to Fenstanton in Oxfordshire very close to the time of a meeting of the Abingdon Association in 1656.[50]

Another English Baptist, Captain John Gardiner, also made inroads with the Scots. Gardiner had himself served as a chaplain for at least two years in Scotland before giving up the post in preference to a commission as a captain. He convinced Hickeringill against serving as a chaplain. Like the Independent Lockyer, Gardiner actively promoted his own particular sect, serving as an avid missionary of Baptist doctrines throughout his stay in Scotland. According to Baillie, Gardiner travelled widely in the spring of 1652, actively 're-baptising'. From the tenor of the letter, this may have been in Fife, although soon thereafter Gardiner garrisoned Dunottar Castle, which the English captured in May.[51] Gardiner also baptised Margaret Anderson, wife of the Aberdeen bailie John Scot, presumably in Aberdeen.[52]

James Brown represents a fourth prominent Baptist working in Scotland whose career as a chaplain has already been discussed, but it is important to keep in mind his active ministry from late in the summer of 1652 through to 1654.[53] During this time he served at Cupar, Stirling and Burntisland, where he baptised soldiers (and certainly anyone else he could proselytise) and disputed with the local clergy, declaring against double predestination and the magistrate's right to interfere in religious matters. The Baptist church with which he was involved in Cupar in 1652–3 continued to meet in the years after he left. According to a report from the Fife minister William Row, dated 30 July 1656, some Scots had 'laitlie' been rebaptised in Cupar.[54] Four Scotswomen who joined the Baptists in Fife can be listed by name: Elspet, Isobel and Christian Miller, and Isobel Webster.[55] All four women faced the censures of the Kirk, but only Christian's excommunication is recorded in the presbytery records in July 1658.[56] As late as February 1659 the synod of Fife still endeavoured to reprimand Isobel Webster and her husband William Thomson, an Englishman, who had been wed by Brown in 1653. Both Webster and Thomson were eventually persuaded under increasing pressure from the local community to repent of their 'errore and defection to Anabaptisme' and coerced into taking their four-year-old child to be baptised in the parish Kirk.[57]

Other prominent figures involved with the Baptist congregations in Scotland included the Particular Baptist Major Abraham Holmes and, much more importantly, the Fifth Monarchist Major-General Thomas

Harrison, who both participated in the congregation in Leith. What is important to note about these central characters is that they were all part of the military structure. In fact, the eminent Baptist historian W.T. Whitley rather overzealously declared that 'every commander in Scotland, and the Commander-in-Chief (speaking of Lilburne, not his replacement Monck) was a Baptist at one time'.[58] Certainly, Scots joined the Baptists, as the examples of Lady Craigie-Wallace, Margaret Anderson, Isobel Webster and the Miller sisters indicate. However, during the Interregnum the infrastructure of Baptist churches in Scotland consisted of English soldiers: the leading members were English officers and troops, and the ministers were predominantly military chaplains. As in Ireland, the relationship between the Baptists and the army must be viewed as a significant reason for early success.[59] In contrast to the Scottish Independency that developed in Aberdeen, Baptist churches in Scotland were at best English-dominated congregations containing some Scots converts. Besides reports that Charteris and Cornwell may have adopted some 'Anabaptist' practices, there is no evidence to suggest that any Baptist churches gathered under Scots ministers. In fact, the dominance of the English in leadership of Baptist churches is suggested in the republication of William Kiffin's confession by the Edinburgh/Leith congregation.[60] A short letter describing the congregation's intentions in reproducing the Confession of Faith prefaced the work printed in March 1653. Most telling in the brief introduction, which explains that the church met alternately between Edinburgh and Leith, is that at least two of the four signatories were English soldiers.[61] The reliance of this sect on the English military establishment ensured that the Kirk could do little to oppose it, but equally left it vulnerable as the Protector's attitude towards the Baptists began to change.

Apprehensions among moderates began to surface in the latter part of 1652, a full year before Cromwell became Protector. In October, John Owen preached against the radical sects in parliament. He distanced the Independents from any sects tending towards agitation or civil unrest, denouncing such views as intolerable.[62] 'There is nothing more opposite to the spirit of the Gospell,' spoke Owen, 'then to suppose that Jesus Christ will take to himselfe a kingdome by the carnall sword and bow of the sonnes of men.'[63] Oliver Cromwell's acceptance of the Protectorate on 16 December 1653 outraged many Baptists, Fifth Monarchists and others who perceived his assumption of the title of Lord Protector as contrary to the principles they believed the Commonwealth to have been established upon. One Edinburgh diarist, perhaps reflecting the popular opinion of his community, singled out the 'Anabaptists' as the most outspoken in their dissent.[64] Thurloe likewise reported, 'it is beleived, wee shall have very much troble from the Anabaptists'.[65] Increasingly, Baptists came to be viewed as inherently linked with Fifth Monarchists, and as a result many within Cromwell's government believed that the Baptists could never be satisfied with a civilian government. Despite James Fraser's lament over the variety of sects 'tollerated or winked at' by the English government, tensions began to build between those who desired further radical changes and the moderate Independents in power within Cromwell's regime.[66]

Swelling discontent towards the Protectorate government among religiously radical groups, coupled with rumours of plots against the Protector, prompted the regime to keep a watchful eye on those groups with a high proportion of dissenters.[67] This in turn led to the more radical sects feeling increasingly alienated from the moderate Independents who dominated the government. Some Baptists perceived the growing distrust that the Protector held for their sect and attempted to sweeten his disposition towards them, while others continued to smoulder with discontent.[68] In Scotland, where things were already volatile in the wake of Glencairn's Rising, spies and informants watched dissidents especially closely. Radical opposition to the Protectorate could not be tolerated within the army, since military unrest threatened the stability of English rule in Scotland and, as a result, the safety of England itself.

Throughout 1653 the security of Scotland escalated as an issue for concern. Lilburne did his best to contain the royalist rising led by the earl of Glencairn, but proved progressively less successful.[69] He attributed the mounting air of rebellion to the clergy of the Kirk, a lack of law and order in the Highlands, and a persistent fear of Charles II invading Scotland with an army of foreign mercenaries.[70] The proportionately high ratio of the Baptist sect among the soldiers in Scotland, a group in which some members openly opposed the Protectorate and whose growth had been actively facilitated by the efforts of the commander-in-chief of the forces there, served to heighten fears in London that a discontented army in Scotland might represent a serious threat to the Commonwealth. Hence a change of leadership was imminent. For several months the regime had intended to send General Monck to Scotland to relieve Lilburne as commander-in-chief of the forces. However, the war with the Dutch lingered on and prevented Monck from reaching Dalkeith until 22 April 1654.[71] Not only did the arrival of Monck signal the end of preferential treatment for the Baptists within the army in Scotland, but, weary of all radicalism, he watched the Baptists with great care. In fact, it has been suggested that Monck's original appointment as commander-in-chief of the forces in Scotland when Cromwell marched south after the Scots in 1651 was because of his conservatism.[72] Certainly, when he returned in 1654, many of his contemporaries believed that he 'went to Scotland to keep the Anabaptist party quiet'.[73]

During 1654, distrust of Baptists steadily increased throughout the three nations. Early in the year Thurloe received reports of Baptist discontent in Wales.[74] Several reports also came from Ireland in March and April illustrating a general sense of unrest and identifying the Baptists as the root of the problem.[75] By October it was widely believed the Baptists were on the brink of an armed revolt.[76] In April unfolding events in Scotland gave Cromwell and Monck reason to fear that a similar threat existed in Scotland. In April 1654, Colonel Matthew Alured, formerly garrisoned in the citadel at Ayr (a Baptist hotbed) and in the previous year commander of all the forces of the west of Scotland, was sent to Ireland to recruit troops to garrison the citadel at Inverlochy. Within weeks of his arrival in Ireland, Alured became implicated in subversive activities.[77] Cromwell wrote to General Fleetwood on 16 May, explaining 'I am sufficiently satisfied of the evill intentions of colonel Alured ... tendinge to the makeinge up a just suspicion ... I doe thinke fit to revoake colonel Alured from that ymployment.'[78] Cromwell relieved Alured of his command and ordered him to report to London. Fleetwood sent two trusted officers, Lieutenant-Colonel Finch and Major Reade, to accompany Alured's recruits to Scotland in order to keep an eye on them and 'to discover what is working in Scotland'.[79]

Upon arriving in London, Alured met with some disaffected Baptists and Levellers in and around the capital, which did little to put Cromwell's mind at ease.[80] In September he signed a petition along with Colonel John Okey and Colonel Thomas Saunders, both of whom had served with him in Scotland, against Cromwell's usurpation of power, rule without an elected parliament and control of a standing army; declaring all these things to be against 'those Fundamental Rights and Freedomes of the Commonwealth, that were the first Subject of this great Contest'.[81] Before the petition could be distributed, troops raided Alured's residence and confiscated the document. Alured was arrested, cashiered and imprisoned. Okey and Saunders avoided incarceration but lost their commands, while the Leveller John Wildman, who has been identified as the actual author of the work, published it under the title *The Humble Petition of Several Colonels of the Army*.[82] Distributed with another seditious tract entitled *Some Mementois for the Officers*, several copies of the petition were confiscated on their way to Scotland, while some further copies were later found in circulation in Scotland.[83] This series of events did more than just cast a shadow over Alured and those individuals associated with him in London, they also heightened suspicions of Baptists in Scotland, particularly soldiers in Ayr, where he had been garrisoned since March 1652. The regime believed that they posed a real threat to the Protector and the established government of England.

In the meantime Cromwell's regime attempted to satisfy religious radicals venting displeasure towards the Protectorate. Cromwell courted the various religious groups, meeting with them to discuss the settlement of religious toleration. In mid-December it became clear that religious toleration would continue for all Protestants who lived peaceably, steered clear of gross heresy and refrained from disrupting the public peace.[84]

This reassertion that a broad religious toleration would continue did little to quell Cromwell's detractors, many of whom as millenarians desired a particular ideal of godly government that they believed to be unattainable under the Protector.[85] In December, the Scot Robert Blair noted that Anabaptists openly showed contempt towards the Protector, and it became a generally acknowledged fact that a strand within the Baptist and the Fifth Monarchy movement viewed Cromwell as the prime obstruction to their goal: the physical implementation of Christ's kingdom on earth.[86]

About a month after the arrest of Alured and his accomplices in London, a new plot slowly came to light in Scotland.[87] The intrigue, which took several months to unravel, came to light by the discovery of a letter distributed to various regiments throughout Scotland. At the beginning of December 1654, a group of Baptists with Fifth Monarchy leanings met in a private home in Aberdeen and produced a letter alleging that the 'many vowes, declarations and solemne appeals to the most high, and … the price of all that blood, and treasure' expended during the civil wars risked being profaned by the establishment of the Protectorate. The implications for all those who shed blood or made promises to God in order to establish a godly Commonwealth were grave. They stood precariously in the face of God's divine wrath if they idly accepted the change of government.[88] According to Daniel Davis, one of the messengers instructed to deliver the letters, copies were intended for Major Henry Dorney (deemed by Baillie to be a 'sectarian preacher', possibly in Glasgow), Captain Thomas Spilman (who may have been in Perth, but in that month was sent to England), Captain Earley in Stirling and Ensign Snow in Glasgow. Another was sent to Captain Parkinson, whom Samuel Oates decribed as being 'so farre northward'.[89] In total, letters were sent to twelve or fourteen regiments. Davis' letters, however, were never delivered. Upon hearing that a second messenger (John Greene) had been apprehended and imprisoned for distributing seditious papers, Davis burned the copies entrusted to him.[90]

The letter itself lacked an overtly seditious message; that is to say it did not openly advocate mutiny or incitement to rebellion. Instead it laid out the immorality of supporting the Protectorate without voicing concerns over the justice of such an extreme change of government devoid of the people's consent. In view of the imminent danger brought about by the abandonment of 'the good old cause', the authors invited representatives from the various regiments in Scotland to meet and discuss the matter at the Green Dragon Pub in the Canongate of Edinburgh on 1 January 1655. Despite the generally moderate tone of the letter, two aspects in particular prompted further investigation by Monck and Timothy Wilkes, the deputy governor of Leith. First, the letter questioned the authority of the Protector and advocated meeting secretly to discuss an active response. Second, the distribution of the letter to individuals throughout the country suggested a network of discontent. In less than a week a number of arrests were made and details of a wider plot began to be revealed.[91] Through subsequent investigation it became apparent that the primary participants in the production and distribution of the letter held similar Baptist sentiments and also that there were a number of other seditious works in circulation.

Those investigating laid much of the blame on Major-General Robert Overton who, despite having no part in the production of any of the subversive documents, clearly had knowledge of the meeting in Aberdeen and the ensuing distribution of the letter. As a result the event came to be known as 'Overton's Plot'. His failure to report the details of such a questionable and potentially seditious meeting made him a prime accomplice in Monck's eyes. As a result Timothy Wilkes, who oversaw the early stages of the inquiry, ordered Overton's papers to be searched. In his personal case were discovered some lines of anti-Cromwellian verse written in Overton's own hand.[92] The authorities took Overton into custody and sent him to London for trial. Cromwell perceived Overton's involvement as particularly seditious as he had personally promised the Protector, before returning from Hull to his commission in Scotland in 1654, to refrain from anything resembling insubordination and vowed to quit his commission if he felt disaffected towards the government for any reason.[93]

Overton's involvement remains a bit of a mystery. In 1659, when questioned about Overton's imprisonment for over four years without charges ever being filed against him, Judge Advocate Henry Whalley, who had carried out the investigation in Dalkeith, testified before parliament that he had found a second letter among Overton's papers. 'I found one letter sealed with silk and silver ribbon,' explained Whalley. 'It had no hand to it. The contents were that there was an intent to murder the Protector and Lord Lambert and six others. I was sorry to find it.'[94] While Overton may not have hatched a plot, he at least harboured knowledge of it. His great crime was his failure to disclose this information to Monck, an error for which he paid a great price. Overton's high profile as a Major-General, his connection to the plot and the belief among his contemporaries that he was an 'Anabaptist' all heaped additional pressure on the Baptists in Scotland.[95]

In the course of the investigation, several other Baptists came to be implicated. The inquisitors identified Captain John Hedworth as the author of the original Aberdeen letter. Several other officers and the Baptist chaplain Samuel Oates signed the document.[96] Major John Bramston, a known Baptist, was found to have been integrally involved in the ideological formulation of the plot, and seems to have had more of a hand in the seditious nature of the meeting in Aberdeen than had Overton. Bramston testified he had no desire to attend the proposed meeting in Edinburgh, but claimed Overton urged him to do so. If true, this claim could only have been because Bramston did not deem the Edinburgh meeting sufficiently radical for himself, as he aggressively opposed the Protector. Bramston also confessed to penning a second letter referred to as 'An Epistle to the Churche atte the Glassehouse' as well as a tract entitled 'Reasons why those who did signe ye late addresse to the Lord Protector are not to bee communicated within the ordinances of God'. In addition, he admitted to possessing a tract against fellowship with Baptists who accepted the Protectorate, produced by the English Particular Baptist Paul Hobson.[97] Any reference to Bramston's second letter must be conjecture, as no copy survives. However, the short title given indicates that the Particular Baptist congregation meeting in the Glass House, Broad Street, London were the intended recipients.[98] These may have been among the papers that Monck reported as being printed in Scotland at the end of 1654.[99]

The wide array of radical papers of Baptist origin in circulation in Scotland, coupled with the discovery of suspect letters intended for Baptists gatherings in England, gave authorities further reason to fear a wider Baptist conspiracy. Soon thereafter the regime rounded up several Baptists and Fifth Monarchists in England and Ireland, including Major-General Thomas Harrison and John Wildman, for suspected involvement in a series of 'Anabaptist plots' aimed at overthrowing the Protector.[100] In Scotland, John Nicoll explained the events as part of a wider plot carried out by 'Anabaptists', intending not to undermine the state but the 'Protestant churches' in Scotland, England and Ireland.[101] As a result, a host of senior officers of Baptist persuasion were arrested and subsequently cashiered from the army in the Scotland.[102] Not all of those implicated received punishment. Major Abraham Holmes of Monck's regiment, for instance, retained his commission probably because he forwarded the copy of the letter that he had received to Monck.[103] Yet Baptists generally portrayed events as a campaign of persecution against the Baptists: 'seeking the perfection of Liberty', they found themselves cast out of the army and 'brow beat[en]' in a manner 'inconsistent with Christianity'.[104]

As details gradually came to light, the general, popular account held that a core of 3,000 troops, under the command of Overton, intended to seize Monck and remove him from his commission in Scotland. These soldiers then intended to march into England and rendezvous with several thousand additional troops raised by Haselrig and waiting for them in Newcastle. From there, the army would march south against Cromwell.[105] The investigation in Scotland continued into March under Judge Advocate Whalley, who repaired to Dalkeith to take charge of the inquiry. He made no link between the meeting at Aberdeen and any particular larger plot, but he concluded that the letter produced in Aberdeen on 18 December tended 'to sedition, mutiny, and devisions in the armey'.[106] For the Baptist movement in Scotland, links to a seditious plot proved to be a heavy blow that put them at odds with both the English government and the Scots.

The Baptists in Scotland replied in two ways. First, the Baptist congregations in Leith, Edinburgh and Perth (St Johnston) produced 'The Humble Address of the Baptized Churches, consisting of Officers, Soldiers and others walking together in Gospel Order' sent to the Protector and printed for a wider audience in an attempt 'to cleare our innocency from those … aspersions we are Charged with … Wee [desire to be] noe more under suspition of guilt (in this matter) of our Society'.[107] In doing this they admitted that the bulk of the plotters were in fact Baptists, but argued that they were of a different disposition and disowned them: 'Though our bretheren … [we] … beare our testimonies against such as great sinners and as Enemies to the publick peace and welfare of the Nation.'[108] In stark contrast, some of the Baptists who opposed the Protectorate took a second and quite a different view of events. The eighteen points in Bramston's paper against communion with Baptists who supported the Protectorate transparently expressed his Fifth Monarchy tendencies and equated any degree of acceptance of Cromwell as Protector as a denial of the first principle of all Christians and the Baptists in particular – to have no other king but Jesus. In other words, to embrace Cromwell's new government meant accepting guilt for all the blood shed in the civil wars.[109] A growing chasm opened between moderate Baptists, who embraced the Cromwellian ideal of mutual religious toleration, and the more millennial Fifth Monarchist variety, who were absorbed in what they perceived to be an eschatological struggle to establish God's kingdom in the British Isles and eventually throughout the whole world.

This latter type were the Baptists that the regime feared and who Monck cashiered from the army in the early months of 1655. However, all Baptists were affected by the negative aspersions and rumours being spread about them. By 22 February all of the signatories of the Aberdeen letter had been cashiered from the army.[110] Cromwell's spymasters carefully watched Baptists and regularly reported on their activities and disposition.[111] Their meetings continued to gather, but support for their missionary endeavours in Scotland stopped. Samuel Oates would prove to be the last Baptist chaplain employed in Scotland.[112] Although the government sent other chaplains to serve both regiments and civilians in Scotland, they were of the Independent variety. No one affiliated with potentially radical or seditious sects gained employment in Scotland. The relationship between the Baptists and the army became increasingly strained. In Ireland, Henry Cromwell's chaplains actively preached against the Baptists in 1655.[113] Although their congregations in Scotland continued to meet, they became increasingly insular. Their days of actively proselytising Scots were over, yet Scotland's Baptist communities maintained their involvement in wider Baptist networks. A second edition of Daniel King's *A Way to Sion Sought*, printed in Edinburgh in 1656, showed their awareness of the current issues being disputed in Baptist circles stretching throughout Britain and

Ireland. This edition includes a postscript dedicated to the raging debate among Baptists as to whether the laying on of hands should be required for admittance of new members. The postscript appears nowhere other than in this Edinburgh edition. While this demonstrates a continuing interest in wider Baptist discourses, their expansion and influence within the government of Scotland had greatly diminished. The removal of the most influential officers of their persuasion left an officer class overtly suspicious of the remaining Baptists in their ranks, forcing the sect's members to do their best to keep a low profile and avoid drawing any more attention to themselves than necessary.

The implication of Baptist involvement in Overton's Plot also detrimentally affected their relationship with the Scottish population. Presbyterian opponents took full advantage, spinning out their own versions of what had transpired, with the nefarious nature of the plot growing increasingly extreme. One report from Edinburgh alleged that an armed band of 'Anabaptists' meant to rendezvous at Newhaven and, after entering Edinburgh on horseback over the frozen Nor' Loch, to massacre all inhabitants of Edinburgh before burning the captial to the ground.[114] Despite the complete absence of truth in these rumours – reminiscent of Münster a century before – they fuelled fears among the Scottish populace. For those already holding distrustful inclinations towards the Baptists, the revelation that the government in England could not trust them only served to exacerbate fears among Scots. Rumours of the 'bloody' nature of the plot even circulated among English soldiers.[115] As a result, the involvement of Scots civilians with the Leith congregation dwindled. In November 1655, a letter sent to Baptist brethren in England noted the decline of civilian membership and relayed the information that the congregation comprised mostly soldiers.[116] By 1657, according to Robert Blair, the Baptists were more feared in Scotland than was Cromwell.[117] Their association with the plot in late 1654 set them on a downward trajectory in Scotland.

Quakers and the Scottish Populace

'Overton's Plot' rekindled awareness of the radical nature of English religion among the Scots in the spring of 1655, which in turn drew attention to the significant growth in Quaker numbers over the previous twelve months. According to Nicoll, Quakers attracted both English and Scots, men and women, and drew 'many' away from the Kirk. In addition, they interrupted sermons in several of the capital's churches.[118] Nicoll was not alone in noting the swell of religious radicalism in Scotland in 1655. 'The swarming of errours,' wrote Brodie in August, were 'mor then at ani tym.'[119] Although present in Scotland during the early years of the Interregnum, prior to their growth spurt in 1654 the Quakers had been relatively quiet, partly due to their predominantly civilian composition and evasion of political involvement. Both features set them in sharp contrast to the Baptists.

Consensus among historians traditionally locates the first Scottish Quaker meeting in the west of Lanarkshire, near Glassford, where John Hart of Glassford and Alexander Hamilton of Drumbowy, along with Hamilton's wife and sister, began to meet regularly in 1653.[120] Soon other meetings formed at Garthshore and Bedcow (straddling Luggie water near Kirkintilloch and Lenzie). According to G.B. Burnet, author of the seminal work on Quaker history in Scotland, these meetings met for an entire year before any English Quakers knew of them or had contact with them.[121] However, while Scottish Friends may have developed in relative isolation from groups in England, it is extremely unlikely that they did so without any contact with English Friends.

Some answers as to how these Scots-based meetings of Friends formed can be gleaned from closer analysis of some of the key figures involved in the west of Scotland. Alexander Hamilton and his family are known to have been members of the gathered church formed by Charteris at Kilbride. Their formation of a Quaker meeting did not sit well with Charteris, who threatened them with excommunication in 1656. Only two weeks before the deadline set for the Hamiltons to denounce their error, Charteris met his fateful end. Thus Baillie and subsequent Presbyterian historians were not alone in viewing the demise of Charteris as an act of divine providence.[122] As members of a gathered congregation it is likely that the Hamiltons had closer contact with the English soldiers stationed in that part of the country than did their fellow compatriots, having already embraced a religion their Presbyterian neighbours would have deemed 'English'. Perhaps this is how they met Quaker soldiers and came to be convinced. Hamilton and his family certainly do not represent the only Scots drawn into Independency before moving to a more radical position.[123] Whether John Hart attended Charteris' congregation is uncertain, but Wariston claims that a total of eleven members from Charteris' congregations became Quakers before his death in 1656.[124] Another possible means of exposure, once again via the English army, may have been their shared vocation. Hart, Hamilton and a fellow proselyte named Hew Wood all laboured as agricultural workers. Baillie notes that 'sundry in Clydesdale, of the most zealous Remonstrant yeoman' – meaning perhaps farmers or servants – were among the first converts.[125] Perhaps through provisioning English garrisons situated in close proximity, such as at Strathaven (Avondale Castle), Hamilton, Douglas or Kilmarnock, they met Quakers.[126] The arrival of the army early in the 1650s and their longstanding local presence in that part of Scotland makes them prime suspects for the introduction of Quakerism, as J. Torrance has argued.[127]

Despite the later universal acceptance that the group in Glassford represented the first Scottish Quakers, the near-contemporary Scots antiquarian Robert Mylne (*c*.1643–1747) seems to indiciate an earlier proselyte. Mylne, who correctly identified the 1654 tract *Love the Precious Ointment* as a Quaker rather than Roman Catholic document, also claimed Thomas Wood, author of *A Dead-Man's Testament*, to have been a Quaker.[128] There is no other evidence either to support or challenge Mylne's claim that Wood, who died in 1651, was in fact a Quaker.[129] However, the presence of English soldiers in Leith from September 1650 provided ample opportunity for the convincing of local people. Even if Wood died two months before the publication of his tract, he would have lived for a full year in an English-occupied Leith. The great difficulty is determining the influence of Quakers in the army as early as July 1650.

One important question is how early the term 'Quaker' can be used. The 'society of Friends' began in 1647 with the gathering of Seekers by George Fox in the north of England. Not until 1650 did the name 'Quaker' concretely refer to the Friends. Moreover, it might be argued that the movement did not really take root as a national movement until Fox established a base at Swarthmore Hall in the latter half of 1652. Yet for the purposes of this chapter the impact of Quakerism in Scotland must be assigned prior to the close of 1650, because that is when John Nicoll first took notice of the movement in the country.[130] Consequently, if Nicoll reports Quakers in Scotland in late 1650, it is not beyond the realm of possibility that Wood could indeed have been influenced by Friends within the army. A second report, from November 1652, might also suggest a Quaker presence in Scotland prior to the Glassford gathering. The English journal *Faithful Scout* reports some 'Shakers' being brought before the English judges because 'there actions are such as doth much trouble the godly people, not onely Presbyterians, but such as are for the Congregational way, they do loath and detest such blasphemous and vilde practices'.[131] Nothing could be proven against them in this trial, and no other information about their identities is given. Whether these 'Shakers' were actually Quakers – since their title may not have yet been known in rural Scotland – is uncertain, but notice of such enthusiastic activity is important. It is probable that Quakers arrived with the army and found converts from a very early date. Quakers certainly had a special relationship to the English, as Scottish Quakers writing to the parliament in 1659 claimed responsiblity for saving the lives of numerous English soldiers during the Interregnum.[132]

Besides the Friends' meetings formed among Scots in the west in 1653, another began the same year in the home of the Colonel William Osborne; 'one of our first apostates to [the] English' in 1651, according to Robert Baillie. Later, he became an open leader of the Quakers in the streets of the capital.[133] From 1653 until he moved to the west in 1657, a Quaker meeting met in his Edinburgh home.[134] Richard Rae, an Edinburgh shoemaker, also preached Quakerism in his native land, while other Scottish meetings formed in Lesmahagow, Douglas, Lenzie and Ford, all in the west.[135] Although Lanarkshire, the vicinity of Kirkintilloch and Edinburgh were hotspots, Scots elsewhere became convinced. Alexander Brodie notes in his journal that William Gordon, Laird of Lunan (Angus), had embraced Quaker doctrines by 1656. This report is intriguing, as Redcastle, a possible Cromwellian garrison in the later half of the decade, is less than a kilometre from Lunan. Brodie also reports that Christian Russell, a woman from Elgin, embraced Quaker doctrines in 1656.[136]

From 1654 the sect experienced a significant boon, with the arrival of a flood of English Quaker missionaries. At least fifty visited Scotland between 1654 and 1657, twenty in 1655 alone.[137] They travelled widely, reaching both Orkney and Shetland. Two Quakers even visited Lochaber in December 1657.[138] They intended to visit the garrison at Dunstaffnage Castle, but the bitter winter weather prevented it. Instead they stayed in the town of Lochaber (present-day Fort William) for several days, proclaiming the truth to the residents of the town. Contemporary reports note that new Quaker missionaries arrived in the region weekly.[139] Some finance for their endeavours came from the funds of Swarthmore. In 1654, James Graham in Edinburgh received ten shillings to purchase books. The following year, Swarthmore allocated over £25 for various Friends travelling to Scotland; a great deal considering a Friend travelling to New England only received £2.[140] Francis Howgill reports encountering a young Scots Quaker in Oxford, sometime between 1654 and 1656, who was preparing to return home to proclaim the truth.[141] These missionaries preached the inner light to both English and Scots, civilians and soldiers. Monck wrote to John Thurloe in February 1658 of 'what labour and pains those Quakers take to get proselytes'.[142] The significant influence of these missionaries came in increasing the radical nature of Quakerism in Scotland.

The new missionaries interrupted services of both the Kirk and the gathered churches. They preached in or outside parish churches and took advantage of public gatherings such as markets, horse races and even executions as opportunities to spread the truth. Very few reports of Scottish Quakers instigating public disturbances exist before 1656. Even Quakers in the English regiments tended to keep quite a low profile prior to the arrival of missionaries. In Inverness, for instance, only with the arrival of the often-troublesome nineteen-year-old John Hall in 1657 did any Quaker venture to interrupt a service in the 'steeplehouse'. Hall chose to intrude upon a Baptist church.[143]

This increase in both the number of Quakers and their radicalism did not go unnoticed. Within the year they faced excommunication for their heresy. Interestingly, the first threat of excommunication of a Quaker in Scotland did not come from the Presbyterian Kirk, but rather from Thomas Charteris, who had himself only recently been settled in the gathered church at East Kilbride. Quakers represented a very real threat not only to Presbyterian ministers, but also to Independent and Baptist gatherings. From the Quaker perspective, all of these groups represented fields ripe for the picking. It was in fact the gathered churches in Aberdeen, represented by John Row, John Seaton and a student of the university named Alexander Gordon, who complained to the garrison commander about John Hall, an English Quaker missionary, interrupting Seaton's sermon in Old St Machar's in March 1657. This incident is interesting, because it pitted not only English Quaker against Scots Independents, but also English Quaker against fellow Englishman. After ridiculing Seaton in the pulpit, Hall turned his attention to the university, calling it 'a cage of unclean birds'. When an Englishman named Proctor intervened, the English soldier lodging Hall, Cornet Ward, threatened Proctor with imprisonment in the guardhouse. [144]

Such disturbances meant many in the English regime found the growth of Quakers as disturbing as the Kirk did. The English Independent John Stalham, preaching in Edinburgh with a stipend from the Council of State, published his *Contradictions of the Quakers* in March 1655 as a response to the interruption of both Kirk services and those of English gathered congregations.[145] Fed up with their shenanigans, Stalham set out to expose their many errors in print. In preparation he read as many Quaker tracts as he could get his hands on and gathered accounts of their behaviour and doctrines from other ministers, including the 'precious Gospel Minster' of Kilbride, Thomas Charteris.[146] In total, Edinburgh presses produced three anti-Quaker works in 1655 – none of which, interestingly, were written by Scots.[147] Recognition of the Quakers' potentially dangerous opposition to mainstream Protestant religion became increasingly apparent to the establishment, both Scots and English.

By 1656 pressure against Quakers was increasing throughout the British sphere of influence, with the regime in Ireland proclaiming Quakers to be their greatest enemy and the government of Massachusetts banning them from the colony.[148] Scotland represents no exception to this trend. The first case of Quaker persecution in Scotland took place in June, when the Scotsman William Stockdale and the Englishman John Bowron were 'shamefully' driven by a large group from the town of Strathaven.[149] This sort of mob violence is what Quakers referred to as 'Club Law' and tended to occur in places without English garrisons, at the prompting of the local Presbyterian clergy.[150] A month after the incident in Strathaven the bailiff of Hamilton, at the behest of the town's minister, imprisoned two Scots Quakers, Alexander Hamilton and John Hart.[151] In October, Stockdale, John Gill and several of the Friends from the Glassford meeting were again violently driven out of Strathaven. On this occasion the Quaker chronicler stressed that blood was shed.[152] No clear reason is given for the sudden appearance of violent persecution against a meeting which had been gathering there for three years. The most likely factors responsible for the change were the removal of the garrison from Avondale Castle in the village of Strathaven and the imposition of new legal acts and judicial positions.

Late in 1655 General Monck faced continued pressure to cut the cost of occupying Scotland, despite his profession to 'have already quitted as many guarrisons as possibly wee may with safety'.[153] Avondale Castle in Strathaven may have been one of those garrisons recently abandoned. Certainly by 1656 it ceases to appear upon garrison lists.[154] Its reduction did little to endanger the stability of English control in the region, since garrisons at Lanark, Kilmarnock, Hamilton and Douglas remained. It did however change things for the Quakers who met at nearby Heads (a hamlet of Strathaven), by leaving the village as an island free from any immediate English presence almost equidistant from the four remaining garrisons in the region. The removal of the garrison significantly affected how Quakers could be treated. While two violent attacks on Friends in Strathaven occurred in the summer and autumn of 1656, in the garrison town of Hamilton Quakers preaching in the street experienced incarceration but not physical abuse. A later English Quaker missionary also attested to the intervention of English soldiers, who even if unsympathetic to the Quaker movement would prevent gratuitious public violence. When Stephen Crisp visited Dalkeith in 1659, he reported that only the intercession of the soldiers garrisoned there kept Presbyterians from killing him.[155] Unlike Baptist gatherings with their close ties to the English army, Scottish Quakers formed among locals outwith the vicinity of garrisons. Since convinced Friends considered each other equals they did not need externally supplied clergy or leadership and thus could establish themselves in a way that Baptists could not. Freedom from unnecessary bonds to English garrisons made them upwardly mobile, but it also made them far more vulnerable to persecution.

Two new acts of legislation served as a second important factor permitting the increase of persecution against Quakers. In September 1656 parliament passed An Act Against Vagrants in an effort to crack down on individuals travelling without passes. 'Itinerant Quakers,' wrote Burnet, 'who for the time being had no fixed abode and no "occupation" except the unpopular and "suspect" one of spreading their doctrines, thus fell very easily within the meaning and scope of the Act'.[156] For Scots uneasy over the arrival of roving Quaker missionaries, this act provided a guise for the legal persecution of unwanted visitors. It is likely that this legislation served to justify actions taken against Quakers in the parish of Lanark in October 1656. Under the anti-vagrancy law William Muir of Rowallan, a local justice of the peace, took Stockdale, Hamilton, Hart, Andrew Brown and George Wilson into custody at Kilmaurs in February 1657.[157] In the following year, the JP for Rutherglen likewise ordered the English Quaker Richard Pinder to be imprisoned and subsequently passed from constable to constable until returned to England.[158] Visiting and local Friends alike faced the same treatment within his jurisdiction, although Scottish Quakers did not face deportation.

The act against vagrants followed on from and acted in cooperation with the Protectorate's definition of the parameters of toleration. On 15 December 1654 the government declared that no one would be challenged in their liberty of conscience or prosecuted (save Papists and Prelates) so long as they refrained from preaching gross heresy or 'doe any overt or publique act' to disturb the public peace.[159] Significantly, this definition of toleration negatively affected both the Ranters and Quakers, who were prone to public displays and enthusiastic public proselytising. Under these provisos, local Quakers could be persecuted in their own hometowns if local ministers or townspeople complained of their behaviour as disorderly. Those commissioned with maintaining law and order found themselves entrusted with great power under their own discernment as to what constituted an act of public disorder. It also gave significant power to the auditors, for in eliciting a riotous response the Quaker might be deemed a disturber of the peace. However, the real significance of this policy came to the fore with the establishment of justices of the peace in Scotland.

As part of their pattern for maintaining order in Scotland, the English revitalised the office of JP in February 1656.[160] Coupled with the act against vagrancy and the prerogative to discern what constituted disturbing the peace, JPs considerably dictated how religious radicals would be treated in their jurisdictions. William Mitchell of Douglas, for instance, was brought before the JPs in Hamilton at the behest of the local clergy for an 'unlawful' Quaker marriage. The court offered him the choice of paying a fine of twenty shillings or receiving twenty lashes. Refusing both options he instead received twenty-nine days of imprisonment. The Scots clergy, unsatisfied with this punishment, received an order from another JP, Gavin Hamilton of Raploch, for Mitchell to be turned over to a captain enlisting soldiers to fight in France. Mitchell found himself 'violently' removed from the tolbooth in Hamilton and transferred to the tolbooth in the Canongate of Edinburgh. Only the intervention of George Monck prevented him from becoming an indentured soldier in the French army.[161] Hence JPs had immense power to deal with religious dissidents, but the affection of these individuals towards Quakers varied widely. So while the earl of Nithsdale and John Swinton of Swinton, between them the JPs for Berwickshire, Dumfriesshire and Haddington, and Colonel Ashfield in Glasgow were sympathetic to the Friends, others, particularly James Stewart of Castlemilke (acting in Hamilton), William Lawrie of Blackwood and Gavin Hamilton of Raploch (both acting in Lanark) were not.[162] The incident of William Mitchell also demonstrates how the system could be abused by the Quakers' opponents. If the sentence handed out by a JP was not deemed harsh enough, a more rigid judge might be sought to provide a different verdict.

In the spring of 1657, sensing that threats of excommunication were doing little to deter Quakers, the synod of Glasgow made concerted efforts to discourage them by intensifying labours to ostracise them socially. They declared that anyone found to be a Quaker would face immediate excommunication, and at the end of May the presbytery of Lanark excommunicated seven Friends.[163] In addition, the synod declared that any member of the local communities trading with, entertaining or lodging any Quaker risked censure.[164] The days when the English army would automatically intervene for those suffering for conscience's sake had passed. Monck's warrant of 2 December 1651 prohibiting magistrates to 'seize upon, meddle with, or any ways molest the persons or estates of any excommunicated person, or ... *to desist from dealing or trading with the said excommunicated persons*, without order from the commonwealth of England or their commissioners' no longer represented the policy of the English.[165] Subsequent to the synod's order, Quakers were stoned or beaten, while those housing them in Newmilns (Ayrshire), Strathaven, Lesmahagow, Kirkintilloch, East Kilbride and Glassford were arrested under the orders of JPs sympathetic to the Presbyterians.[166] Other JPs, however, used their position of influence to protect Quakers. George Fox reported, also in 1657, that the governor of Glasgow, Colonel Richard Ashfield, 'being a justice of peace' prevented Presbyterian persecution of the Quakers within his jurisdiction.[167] Ashfield's generosity included granting passes for two English Quaker missionaries to travel through Fife and on to Inverness at their leisure, something that greatly displeased the governor of Perth, Colonel Daniels (also a JP).[168]

Despite the potential protection provided by a tolerant JP, the Presbyterian persecution against Friends gathered pace through 1657, bolstered by the English army's own persecution of Quakers within their ranks. Appeals from a handful of officers across the country prompted widespread purging. Lieutenant-Colonel Miles Mann in Inverness and Colonel Daniels in Perth complained of the 'sottish stupid generation of Quakers' and asked Monck to take actions to 'prevente these blasphemous hereticks from corrupting the soldyery'.[169] Heeding these requests, Monck asked for Cromwell's permission to take drastic action in the face of a growing Quaker problem.[170] Sedition, like the subversive plotting exhibited by some Baptists in 1654, did not represent the paramount reason for Monck's request. Instead, concern over the rapid spread of Quaker doctrines and the Friends' refusal to recognise social protocol – such as removing one's hat or saluting an officer – justified their removal. Major Richardson, the governor of Aberdeen, wrote to Monck: 'I think it not their principle to fight nor to own authority longer than it may serve their own ends.'[171] Mann reaffirmed this threat: 'theire principalls are spreading soe they are much prejudiciall to the decipline of the army'.[172] As Barry Reay suggests, these traits were unfavourable to military discipline.[173] However, incidents in March involving the hot-headed Quaker John Hall in Aberdeen and his ensuing visit to Inverness no doubt served to affirm Monck's decision.[174] He wrote to Cromwell, stating 'truly I think they are very dangerous people should they increase in your army'.[175] The first discharges took place before Cromwell even replied to Monck's request. On 13 March the army cashiered Richard Popplewell after nearly eight years service.[176]

When Cromwell's reply arrived on 22 April, the Protector confirmed the course of action already begun by Monck.[177] His compliance probably resulted from multiple reports during the spring that another Fifth Monarchist plot was afoot, in which 'its sayd the Anabaptists and Quakers were chiefly active in the conspiracy'.[178] During the months of March, April and May, and then again in October, November and December, the army cashiered soldiers in Scotland simply for being Quakers.[179] In total, approximately forty soldiers were removed from nine of the seventeen regiments in the country.[180] Importantly, though, these were not recent recruits to the army. All had served at least seven years, several since the beginning of the civil wars.[181] Despite their long history of faithful service they came to be viewed as a potentially dangerous liability, outweighing the value of their service.

Although some Quaker soldiers gave up their commissions before being formally cashiered, their mistreatment did not go unnoticed by the wider community of Friends. Francis Howgill, a Quaker missionary in Scotland during the purging, wrote an open letter to the commanders of the army in Scotland in July urging them to reflect upon the previous years of fighting, remember God's deliverances and consider how they could in turn persecute the people of God who had risked their lives in the common cause. How unjust to persecute those who had taken part in the blessings bestowed by God. And why had they come to be removed? Because, according to Howgill, the commanders of the army sought to have themselves 'worshipped with caps & knees, and in language, such as all the holy men of God never owned nor knew ... [you] have forgotten the rock from whence you were hewn', and 'because they [Quakers] cannot submit to your wills, nor give that to man which belongs to God'.[182] But such pleas did little to change the policy of the government.

After December, the removal of Quakers from the army in Scotland ceased. Some soldiers and their wives continued to be convinced in the closing months of 1657. Ashfield, known to Monck in March 1657 as one who 'favour[ed]' the Quakers but who was not convinced until at least the very end of December, avoided losing his commission despite hosting a Friends' meeting in his home. Similarly, George Fox convinced Captain Samuel Poole, his wife and several officers during a visit to Burntisland.[183] So there continued to be some individuals interested in providing protection for Scottish Quakers, as Burnyeat attested in his journal when describing the protection he received from soldiers in the south-west of the country in 1658.[184] But the purge of soldiers in 1657 did mean two things. First, a significant warning had been given to the Quakers in the army, causing the movement to become even more civilian-based. Second, the removal of the Quakers meant that the dominant radical group left in the army (for the next year at least) were the Baptists, who strongly opposed Quaker doctrines. Protection for Quakers from English soldiers from March 1657 can only be described as simply hit or miss. Some soldiers, like Ashfield, assured protection for Quakers, while others, like the Baptists that Fox encountered in Perth, drove them from town.

At least fifteen English Quakers visited Scotland as missionaries in 1657, the most notable being George Fox, who entered the country on 10 September 1657. Despite all the troubles facing Quakers, he maintained major drawing power. Soon after crossing the border into Scotland the innkeeper where his party lodged relayed an invitation from the local earl to visit his home. No specifics are given, but it is generally accepted this was the Catholic earl of Nithsdale, whose seat was Caerlaverock castle.[185] He apparently had some affinity towards Quakerism, for he expressed to Fox and his fellow travellers that were it not for a funeral he had to attend he would have liked to accompany them on their trip.[186] From the Borders, Fox and his entourage continued north to visit established Quaker meeting houses in Douglas, Heads, Badcow (Bedcow), Garthshore, Glasgow, Leith, Edinburgh, Linlithgow, Perth and probably Dundee. They also visited the house of William Osborne, who guided Fox and his party through Scotland. His house, according to Burnet, was located near the Campsie Fells, a conclusion he possibly derived from the fact that it was the minister of Balfron who finally excommunicated Osborne from the Kirk.[187]

During Fox's stay with Osborne, an important and often overlooked event took place. Under the literary supervision of Fox and his English travelling companions, the Scots compiled *The Doctrins and Principles of the Priests of Scotland*.[188] Astonishingly, historians have overlooked the significance of the work's Scottish authorship. George Weare, listed as the author on the London-printed title page, was in fact George Weir of Lesmahagow, who along with his mother (Katherine Hamilton) and two sisters (Katherine and Janet Weir) suffered for their faith at the hands of the presbytery of Lanark.[189] Some of Weir's altercations with the clergy of Lanarkshire are given in the work, as are some of the experiences of other Scots Quakers such as John Hart (joint founder of the meeting at Glassford), Andrew Brown (Glassford), John Lowcock (Glassford) and William Mitchell (Douglas).[190] At least three of the authors attributed to the work are definitely Scottish Quakers, while the other three are too enigmatic to say for certain. The work is written with a clear 'us' and 'them' distinction in which the authors denounce the violence and doctrines preached by the Kirk's clergy. However, rather than being an indication of foreign authorship, it is an indication of the authors' deep-seated sense of being Quakers as opposed to the national Presbyterian church that censured, beat and imprisoned them. Throughout the work these Scots Quakers name and shame the ministers in the local churches of Strathaven, Lesmahagow, Glassford, Glasgow, Dalserf, Bothwell, Lenzie, Edinburgh and East Kilbride who opposed them physically and theologically.[191] They denounce the 'Club Law' advocated by the ministers and declare the antichristian nature of such abuse. 'Ye may see Christ and the Apostles taught another doctrine,' they wrote, '*Love your enemies*, and thou teachest to stone them, contrary to Christ and his Apostles, we doe conclude it [persecution] to be the doctrine of the Devill.'[192] And again, 'Allase for you ye poor silly Priests, and mad Presbyterians! Is this your work to set people to stone, and cry up club Law, and Law to chop off their heads? is this the way to convert them? ye should goe to convert them, instruct them, convince them, love them, heap coals of fire upon.'[193] Thus the difference between the authors and the ministers they malign is not one of national identity but religious identity. For this reason the appeal of Scottish Quakers to their fellow Scots for dialogue rather than persecution is a moving testament to the degree of religious change that took root in Interregnum Scotland.

The Doctrins and Principles of the Priests of Scotland also gives an indication of the particularly intense opposition of the Scottish clergy to the doctrine of the Inner Light, the primacy of continuing revelation beyond the Scriptures, and the Quaker rejections of physical baptism, predestination and the doctrine of limited atonement. In many ways the acceptance of Quaker doctrines by Scots represented a complete rejection of the dogmatic principles of the Kirk: a revolt against the harsh Calvinism dominating the religious conscience of Scotland, as well as the actions of both Kirk and state since the signing of the National Covenant in 1638. This is why the Scottish clergy responded so vehemently to Quakers. While Independents erred in the proper form of church government, Particular Baptists additionally misunderstood the importance of paedo-baptism and General Baptists carried both of those errors, plus completely misunderstanding the doctrines of predestination, election and atonement, the Quakers threw most of these concepts out the window. They rejected physical sacraments, the concepts of predestination and limited atonement, and not only any form of national church organisation, but eldership within particular congregations. Any one of these errors would have been intolerable, but the combination of them all caused the Presbyterian clergy to view Quakers as the antithesis of the church, a sort of anti-church. This accounts for Presbyterian anger towards Scots convinced by

Quakerism and the vehemency which provoked the minister of Lenzie to inform one Scottish Quaker 'that if the Lawes were right they would chop of[f] all the Quakers heads'.[194] Yet despite the avid opposition to the movement by the established Church of Scotland and the removal of Quakers from the army, the Friends continued to win converts.

Through the missionary endeavours of Fox, Howgill, Alexander Parker and others, several Scots were convinced in 1657. Among them were such prominent individuals as Lady Margaret Hamilton (possibly the daughter of the duke of Hamilton), John Swinton of that Ilk, Sir Gideon Scott of Highchester, Walter Scott of Raeburn, Charles Ormiston (brother of Gideon Scott), Anthony Haig of Bemersyde and his brother William.[195] Through the closing years of the Interregnum, English and Scottish Friends fostered close relations. For example, the English Quaker and brewer Edward Billing served as a cornet in the army until discharged in October 1657 for being a Quaker.[196] Later, when serving as part-proprietor of the East New Jersey colony, Billing and his partners looked to appoint a governor for the colony in 1679. Looking to old ties in Scotland, they chose the Scots Quaker Robert Barclay for the position.[197]

Sectarian Unity in the Closing Years of the Interregnum

In the space of five years, religious radicals shifted from being the bedrock of the army and a Commonwealth dream to being perceived as the single greatest threat to its continuance. Moreover, a significant change had taken place within the government. Increasingly moderate Independents joined Cromwell in the inner circle of the government, further pushing the radical ecclesiology and eschatological vision once so integral to the successful formation of a Christian Commonwealth to the fringe.[198] Exacerbated by ill health and concern over their continual penchant for plotting, Oliver Cromwell sent orders dated 10 June 1658 to the commissioners in Scotland, instructing them to 'See that no Baptist holds any office of trust, nor practices law, nor keeps a school'.[199] Though an English source reported Baptists to be the 'major party' in Leith, this public denouncement from the Protector put them into a state of shock.[200] 'They neither rejoice with those that rejoice, nor morne with those that morne,' explained Timothy Langley, 'as to the present: but they still looke like a commonweale of there owne.'[201] Henceforth, Cromwell's spymasters kept an exceptionally close watch on both the Baptists and the Quakers in Scotland, providing him, and subsequently Thurloe, with frequent updates as to their disposition.[202] Not surprisingly, the impact on Baptists was greater than the removal of Quakers from the army. Some evidence regarding the nature of Quaker meetings is provided in Langley's reports on the sect in Edinburgh and Leith. At the end of 1657, separate meetings of Friends existed in both places. The Leith meeting comprised mostly women who met daily in a hired room. Among their number Langley postulated that 'they have got a small parcell of Scotts into their crew', about a dozen, but 'they have great hopes of gaining a lady in Edinburgh'. With regard to the wider Quaker movement in Scotland, he explained that they were gaining 'many' proselytes in the west of Scotland.[203]

Fears about Baptists persisted. The discovery early in September 1657 of a pocket-sized Baptist tract in Leith led many to believe they were preparing to hatch a new plot.[204] Langley soon after reported them to be in a 'mousing posture'.[205] Reports of Cromwell's death gave them only brief optimism, and by November melancholy consumed them and they complained of having been outwitted. An indication of the depths to which the sect had fallen may be indicated by the formation of an Independent church in Leith in the beginning of November. Although they shared the Baptists' rejection of paedo-baptism, they refused to have anything to do with the Baptists who were meeting in Leith or the wider fellowship. The drastic shift in policy towards Baptists led to nothing short of a kind of persecution, though not to the degree that J. Scott's exaggerated claims suggest.[206] Cromwell's orders did not implement a wholesale removal of Baptists from the army in the manner of Quaker cashiering. There are no records in Monck's order book for particular officers or troopers being removed from their posts, but this does not diminish the significance of what took place. To some degree, the action taken against Baptists in 1658 represented a more significant persecution than that which the Quakers had experienced, because this time around the victims were predominantly civilians and represented the fruition of a long, gradual reaction against radicalism. However, in the final year of the Interregnum several important events marked the lasting and important impact of the introduction of Protestant diversity to Scotland. The proceedings against the Baptists did not go unnoticed, and in the following year a Scots advocate branded the betrayal of the Baptists and the failure of the Protector to assure toleration as a 'hammer of persecution'.

Robert Pittilloch was admitted to the public office of advocate in the year 1651.[207] Early in the Interregnum he showed little interest in religious liberties, even publishing a tract condemning a printed Baptist sermon by Salomon Saffrey (comptroller for the English regime in Edinburgh) in 1652.[208] However, over the next few years Pittilloch made a significant swing towards the religious and political views of the Commonwealth. By early 1659 Monck was lauding his many years of service to the Commonwealth.

> March 11, 1658/9. – Certificate, that the bearer, Mr. Robert Pittiloch, Advocate, hath for severall yeares past expressed much affection to the interest of the English in Scotland, and was in the beginning of November 1654 appointed Sollicitor for his Highnesse the Lord Protector and Commonwealth: In which office hee continued till the 11th of February 1656, att which time he was appointed by his Highnesse' Councill in Scotland to serve as Advocate to the

State, in which hee served till June 1659. And during the said imployments (as well as before) hee behaved himself faithfullie, honestlie, and diligentlie, and exercised the same with much ability and advantage to his Highnesse' interest.[209]

From his loyal service to the Protectorate, Pittilloch earned a voice of credibility and in 1659 he used his voice to appeal the plight of those who embraced patterns of Christianity introduced during the Inter-regnum under what he described as a failed toleration. For Pittilloch, the Protectorate betrayed proselytes in two ways. First, the English government failed in its duty to maintain the religious toleration promised to the Scottish people. Second, he claimed the existence of a Presbyterian plot to oppress and persecute anyone opposed to a strong Presbyterian national Kirk, which Cromwell's acquiescence helped to facilitate.

To elaborate Pittilloch's first point: three times, he argued, the people of Scotland were promised the freedom to practise Protestant religion as they wished. Initially, this occurred in the signing of the Solemn League and Covenant. The English parliament had obliged itself 'to take what is done to another as done to themselves, in the prosecution of the true ends of the Covenant'.[210] While the Kirk viewed this as a pledge to Presbyterian church government, parliament had interpreted it as preservation of Reformed religion within acceptable parameters. The next promise came in the army's declaration at Musselburgh on 1 August 1650, in which they declared 'where ever the lot of Gods inheritance shall appear to be found in Scotland, we shall think it our duty to the utmost hazard of our lives, to preserve the same' and 'though ye be scattered, the Lord will in his due time bring you together, and bind you up as his jewels, and make you one with those that fear the Lord amongst us'. Though this declaration came from the army rather than the parliament itself, it represented nothing short of a promise from Englishmen to provide religious liberty. Finally, the commissioners of the parliament promised as one of the fundamental principles of their rule in Scotland in February 1652 to 'protect and incourage such as walk soberly and christianly, albeit serving God in a different way from the Presbyterian and National Church'.[211] Despite three separate pledges to extend the religious toleration enjoyed in England to the people of Scotland, the government had utterly failed to do so. In fact, this failure was so complete that the government permitted and even carried out the persecution of English and Scots Christians adhering to English models of Protestant religion.

For Pittilloch, the primary driving force behind the persecution of Quakers and Baptists in Scotland was the Presbyterian Church of Scotland. Despite being stripped of all authority to judge men's consciences early in the rule of the Commonwealth, gradually Presbyterians regained their power. In arguments that echo sixteenth-century Anabaptists' claims that the rise of Constantine initiated the downfall of the Christian church,

Pittilloch pinpointed the change of religious policy towards the Kirk to the 'raising' of Cromwell to the Protectorate. Through a series of policy changes seeking to ingratiate the fractured elements within the Kirk, Cromwell gave them increasing influence in ecclesiastic and judicial matters in Scotland. Initially Gillespie's Charter (August 1654) provided a quorum of four Scots certifiers within each of the five regions the power to certify ministerial candidates, thus qualifying them to receive stipends from the state. Although in the region 'be-north of Angus' several Independents were made triers, overwhelmingly the rest of those chosen were (in Pittilloch's estimation) rigid Presbyterians. Despite the evidence examined in chapter 4 for the compliance of Gillespie's Protesters with disciplinarily strict Independents, they certainly showed no toleration to Baptists, Quakers or any other group failing to meet their strict standards of Calvinist doctrine. Although the ordinance actually had little impact, Pittilloch claimed that the Presbyterians made use of this 'Episcopal Dignity ... for establishing their own Creatures in the Ministry'.[212] But even the power to plant ministers did not satisfy them, for they wished to be able to depose them as well. The establishment of the Commissioners for Visiting Universities in June 1652 prevented the deposition of ministers by any authority other than their own.[213] Yet by August 1656 the government had completely relinquished control in religious matters at a grassroots level.

Under a deal brokered by Lord Broghill, the president of the Scottish council, who greatly favoured the Resolutioner majority with whom he had longstanding personal ties and religious sympathies, the English agreed to turn the power of certifying candidates for ministry to the Resolutioners in return for an implicit promise that the ministers would live peaceably, refrain from subversive activities and stop praying for the king.[214] This gave the Presbyterians complete power to plant and remove ministers. The settlement marked a radical shift of policy in Scotland. Broghill had little concern for the advancement of sects. Rather, he pursued a policy intended to ensure that the majority in Scotland would leave peaceably and that moderate religion would prevail. Completely unsympathetic to the rigid Protesters of Wariston, Guthrie and Rutherford's party, Broghill called them 'Fifth-monarchist-presbyterians' because of their unwillingness to recognise any authority other than their own.[215] Broghill's chosen settlement and the failure of Gillespie's Charter affirm that Gillespie's party, who were willing to accept English rule and to work alongside disciplinarily strict Independents, were too small to broker a deal settling Scotland's religious divisions on the national rather than regional level. This settlement, which represented a major departure from the policy earlier in the decade of supporting the growth of sects, demonstrated Cromwell's willingness to compromise on his dream settlement of a mutually tolerant Christian Commonwealth in order to guarantee more immediate stability in Scotland.

For Pittilloch the restoration of Presbyterians to a position of power left gathered churches vulnerable and undermined all earlier efforts to establish them. No matter what Presbyterian emissaries in London might claim to the Protector and parliament, Scotland did not universally desire the restoration of Presbyterian domination. He marked it a great error for anyone in England to believe that all Scots were Presbyterians who desired a national church.[216] To justify his claim he gave the names of several ministers of the Kirk who had separated either into Independency or who had become Baptists, including the familiar names of Thomas Charteris, John Seaton, John Row and John Menzies. In addition he also listed several individuals for whom Pittilloch's account is the only explicit record of their separation, noting that John Mercer (Row's son-in-law, Kinkellar) and John Young (Birse) 'verbally converted to make progress with such as were separated', and that William Youngstone (Durris) and John Forbes (Kincardine O'Neill) sided with the Baptists.[217] While their separation may indicate the success of Commonwealth policies in propagating alternatives to the national Kirk, these ministers' subsequent suffering marked its failure. Pittilloch claimed that Seaton's withdrawal to England was one of flight, and alleged that both Youngstone and Forbes 'died of grief', as did John Row's wife.[218] However, these were not the sum of the government's failure in protecting converts. Even more shameful, under the Protector's order of 10 June 1658 several Scots lost their government posts simply for being Baptists. The government might not have been able to protect the consciences of defected clergy, but they certainly could have refrained from firing Scots solely on the basis of religious affiliation, especially when the government had advocated proselytism away from the Kirk earlier in the Interregnum. Claud Hamilton represented one such casualty. Originally he worked in Edinburgh as a commissary, but after being transferred to Stirling he eventually lost his employment altogether.[219] Similarly, William Dundas (supervisor to the government's messengers), Archibald Weir (sheriff or keeper of records), Alexander Dick of Haddington (clerk to the peace) and James Lindsay (collector) were all removed form their posts.[220] Others reportedly had to leave the country due to the persecution they faced.[221] Only Robert Gordon (clerk to the exchequer and subsequently presenter of signatories) escaped dismissal, as being 'related to a person of Power greater than himself' he merely found himself demoted to a position of less importance. After these removals, parliament needed to replace them and had little knowledge of the capable candidates.[222] The Resolutioners took advantage of the privileged status granted them in 1656 and provided a list of viable candidates void of sectarians and Protesters. Pittilloch identified this as another instance of the English government acquiescing to the Kirk to the detriment of those who had bravely accepted the religious ideals which formed the bedrock of the Commonwealth. For Pittilloch, this represented the ultimate example of England's failure to uphold the promises made to the 'godly' in Scotland.

Importantly, Pittilloch does not stand as the only Scot to publish against the persecution of those promised toleration. In 1659 several Quakers, particularly in the west of Scotland, produced a declaration of their sufferings through excommuncation at the hands of Kirk ministers, under which interdict they were removed from their homes, shunned by their communities and prevented from employment and commerce with their neighbours out of 'slavish fear' of 'Landlords' hostile to Quakers.[223] Although an important document, it is far less unique than Pittilloch's: Quaker meetings throughout Britain and Ireland produced similar papers. The document demonstrates how integrally connected the Scottish meetings of Friends were with their English brethren, and the ascendancy of Quaker identity over and above nationality. Yet more importantly, Scotland's Quakers not only joined with their fellow Quakers, but in the face of persecution they demonstrated closer ties with other sects in Scotland than sects in England did at any time during the Interregnum.

On 7 May 1659 the Rump parliament reassembled for the first time since being dissolved by Cromwell in April 1653, nullifying all proceedings of Union during the interlude, including the Ordinance of Union passed in April 1654.[224] As a result, establishing terms for a permanent Act of Union became a priority for the continued stability of the Commonwealth, rekindling the debate over the terms of the settlement. In the early days of the newly reformed parliament, Wariston, the only Scot appointed to the Council of State, spoke against the inclusion of a declaration of religious toleration in any Act of Union.[225] His words caused a great stir, and by Wariston's own admission his speeches against toleration became a topic of discussion throughout London. The premise of his argument alleged that 'few or none' in Scotland supported toleration and its exclusion from an Act of Union would bolster favour among Scotland's Presbyterians.[226] Some other Scots, of a different judgement to Wariston, heard his speeches and implored the supporters of toleration in Scotland to produce a supplication to the parliament requesting its inclusion in any legislation for union. Swinton and Garthland, MPs for Scotland, may have been among this number, as in May they had advocated union on the terms set down in 1651 and 1652, which included religious toleration.[227]

In July 1659, some persons 'well affected' to the English Commonwealth 'in the vicinity of Edinburgh' produced a petition. They lobbied for the permanent establishment of the religious toleration introduced into Scotland in February 1652, and requested the abolition of all previous Scottish legislation opposed to toleration. Although promised in 1652, toleration clearly had not prevailed. Various groups had suffered during the previous two years simply for their religious persuasions. The petitioners sought the religious liberty enjoyed in England to be extended northwards once and for all.

> We desire heartily to bless God on your behalf, and to own you in the prosecu-tion of that glorious Work so long contended for against *Usurped Tyrrany* in the middest of us ... It is therefore our humble Desire, for ourselves, and several others in this Nation, That you will take care to provide for our just Liberties; that we may share in those Gospel Priviledges that the truly Godly in England contend for, and expect to be secured in by you: And that any Laws or Acts of Parliament of this Nation contrary hereunto may be abolished; either by some Proviso to that effect to be inserted in the Act of Union, or by some other more expedient way, as you shall think fit.[228]

C.H. Firth attributed the supplication to 'gathered churches', by which he meant the Independents.[229] However, Scots contemporaries were quick to point out that its subscription included more than just Independents. Robert Blair noted that the document served as a unifying point for multiple sectarian groups who had over the decade fallen out with each other, suffered persecution and now come together to plead for rightful toleration.[230] One Edinburgh diarist argued for a primarily Baptist author-ship, while Baillie and William Douglas noted that Quakers made up the bulk of signatories.[231] The truth is that the petition served as a rallying point for all of the sectarian groups in Scotland.

Despite Robert Blair's assertion that 'few Scots of any note' signed the petition, the signatures provide fascinating insight into a shared endeavour by Scots Quakers, Independents and Baptists in a petition pleading for mutual toleration. Essentially, these individuals resolved to overlook their differences, understanding that successfully securing toleration meant all for one, or none for all. Through analysis of the signatures given to the petition, an indication of the religious diversity of the signatories can be given for the first time. Among the more than 200 signatures given to the petition are the names of Archibald Weir, James Lindsey and William Dundas of Dundas, all of whom *The Hammer of Persecution* identified as having been removed from government posts in 1658 for their Baptist sympathies, as well as Robert Gordon, who was demoted for Indepen-dency.[232] The former Protester Thomas Ireland, James MacDowall of Garthland and 'Peter Inglish' (probably the part-time propagandist for the English living in Leith, author of *The Survey of Policy* (1653)) also signed.[233] So did William Dundas (brother of the laird of Duddingston), Lieutenant William Govan and Andrew Abernethie, who the Kirk excom-municated for joining the English in 1650/1 and who reputedly favoured Independency.[234] Other signatories included John Home (servitor to Dundas of that Ilk) accused of joining the English in 1651 but not excom-municated for it, and Henry Hope, a Scot who served as treasurer for the High Court of Justice.[235] Patrick Waterstone, the Orcadian minister who officially gathered an Independent church on the island of Stronsay sometime before 1660, also appears as a subscriber.[236]

Among the Quakers who signed the petition are a significant number from meetings in the west of Scotland, such as Robert Tod, Andrew Gray, John Lococke, William Mitchell, John Hart, Andrew Hamilton, Andrew Brown, Thomas Jack, Alexander Hamilton, Gabriel Hood, John Hutcheson, William Gray and John Mitchell, all mentioned in the earliest recorded history of Quakers in the west of Scotland.[237] Additionally, several other individuals from the west of Scotland described in the 1659 London edition of *Doctrins and Principles* as having been excommunicated from the Kirk for being Quakers also subscribed the petition: Robert Smallie, James Finley, James Cook, William Hamilton, Robert Gray, Thomas Craige, John Robbins, Robert Hamilton, John Hamilton, John Torrance, Alexander Hart and Gavin Hart.[238] All of these individuals signed the earlier Quaker petition to parliament. That the Kirk excommunicated them suggests that they were one-time members of the Church of Scotland, that is to say, they were Scottish. Prominent Quakers from other parts of the country also signed, including William Osborne, Anthony Haig of Bemersyde, Andrew Robison [Robeson] and Richard Rae, the latter two being in Edinburgh.[239] Another Scottish signatory, William Welch, the clerk to the Admiralty, may also have been a Quaker (his wife Sarah certainly was).[240]

Though the petition claimed to be from Edinburgh and its immediate vicinity, subscribers evidently came from a much wider area, as Patrick Waterstone's signature demonstrates. Although Pittilloch's claim that 'thousands in Scotland separated from the National Church' is probably exaggerated, this supplication exhibits a significant number of Scots continuing to pursue the ideals of toleration to the end of the decade.[241] But importantly, the numbers here only represent the male portion of Scots separated from the Kirk. Lady Gordon is the only female subscriber to the paper. Taking other women into account, the numbers would swell drastically. The spymaster Timothy Langley reported in late 1658 that Quakerism in Edinburgh was particularly strong among women, and the trend among Baptist adherents (at least in Fife) indicates a high proportion of female proselytes.[242] Moreover, women account for seventeen of the forty-two signatures on the Quaker petition produced earlier in the summer. While the petition cannot provide an accurate estimate of how many people considered themselves members of a sectarian party, its significance lies in what it shows about Scots of previously factious inter-relationships, unwilling to conform to the national Kirk, speaking in a united voice to request 'Gospel Priviledges' for all Protestant sects.

On 27 July 1659 Colonel Ralph Cobbet and two unnamed Scots presented the petition to parliament, much to the lament of Wariston, who was saddened to report that over 200 Scots had signed it.[243] William Row suggests that William Dundas and Robert Gordon delivered the petition, noting their presence in London serving as 'the devil's agents, for toleration', although Garthland was in London as well.[244] Parliament responded positively to the petition and expressed appreciation, but its submission compounded the debate over union, prolonging it so much that the issue remained unresolved when parliament dissolved on 13 October.[245] Although relieved by the failure to complete an Act of Union that included toleration, Presbyterians found their joy muted by fears about what the positive reaction of parliament might 'provoke' from the sectarian petitioners.[246]

News of the petition sent shockwaves through the Kirk. Some feared that the Lord would imminently withdraw from Scotland and that religious errors might burst forth in even greater abundance.[247] Opinions differed within Presbyterian circles over an appropriate response. Both the synods of Fife and Galloway wrote declarations against the petition, while the presbytery of Kirkcudbright declared on 17 August 1659 that the petition

> tends to the overturning of the wholl work of reformation of religion amongst us both in doctrine worship government and disciplin and to the abolishing of all wholesome laws and acts of parliament made for the securing of these precious interests ... [we] Doe declair the said petition to be a dreadfull violation and breach of the oath of god lye upon us both with nationall covenant and the solemne league and covenant ... and lykwayes to be a most malicious design ... so to open a wyder gap to the plottering of all error and heresie of sin and iniquity and of all manner of confusion upon this poor kirk and nation.[248]

Other presbyteries debated whether the best course of action would be to reply against the petition or altogether ignore it. Andrew Hay of Craignethan advocated that presbyteries voice their utter opposition to toleration as incompatible with the Presbyterian government of the Kirk. Robert Baillie, despite being a rigid opponent to sectarianism, contrarily urged the presbytery of Glasgow to make no response on account of two dangers: first, if only the aspect of toleration was disputed, it would serve as a tacit acceptance of other aspects of uniting the two countries; second, there was the great difficulty involved in striking a balance between condemning toleration in light of the covenants and avoiding making enemies among the Independents and Anabaptists among the 'Chief Statesman' in the parliament. Erring either way could be costly to the Presbyterian cause in the long run.[249]

The presbytery of Edinburgh, along the lines of Baillie's advice, took its time and produced a declaration against the petition in July, printing it in October.[250] It directed the brunt of its attack against the Quakers, or those acting 'under the pretence of a *new light*', declaring it disingenuous to label the petition as being prescribed by those in the vicinity of Edinburgh when the signatures represented individuals spread across the country.[251] What surprised the presbytery most was the collusion of several sects, including ones which had previously professed themselves 'opposite to the way of the Quakers'.[252] As far as the presbytery was concerned, the petition could be presented in no other way than an 'endeavour to pluck up the hedge planted by God about His Vineyard, and to open a door to the atheisticall and profane under pretence of new lights'.[253] But not all Scots agreed with this interpretation.

Before the end of 1659 a Scot, possibly residing in London but a native of Edinburgh, defended the sincerity of the petitioners' pious request in *Some Sober Animadversions*.[254] The author argued that the petition merely requested what had already been promised in 1652, and asserted the necessity of removing Scottish legislation opposing toleration.[255] In contrast to the Presbyterian accusations of 'breaking down hedges', the author framed the petition as a request for continuity. The petition requested nothing new, only assurance that Scots would experience exactly the same Gospel privileges 'enjoyed' by the English.[256] In response to accusations of schism from Christ's body (the Kirk), the author inquired whether it was not the responsibility of the godly to distance themselves from 'grossly mixed communions' in light of the biblical imperative, 'Come out of her, my people' (Rev. 18:4).[257] He then turned the question on its head: if toleration tended to 'overturn the Kirk', then was not the Kirk the problem rather than toleration? Independents, Baptists and Quakers all professed in the petition to have no qualms about allowing toleration.[258] Presbyterian aversion to toleration and inability to function alongside it might suggest that Presbyterianism was incompatible and unwarrantable within the framework of a Christian Commonwealth.

While proponents of toleration in Scotland found bold voices in 1659, their desire for mutual toleration found no resonance within the wider political environment of the Commonwealth. The request by Scotland's Baptists, Quakers and Independents stood in stark contrast to the events transpiring in England during the closing months of 1659, which threatened the continuation of the Commonwealth and overshadowed disputes about toleration in Scotland.[259] By December 1659 it looked as though England might experience a third civil war. Monck's forces in Scotland sided with the Rump parliament and represented the moderate interests of the Commonwealth. The army in England, led by Major-General John Lambert, carried the support of the religiously radical elements within the nation. Richard Baxter described Monck's stand against Lambert as a struggle against the 'usurpation of the fanaticks (Anabaptists, Seekers, &c.)', as support for both sides polarised religious grounds.[260] In the face of seditious letters sent to undermine Monck's control over the army in Scotland, a second purge of Baptists, this time solely within the army, took place in October. In total about 140 officers found themselves discharged or imprisoned in Edinburgh or Tantallon castles, or else they deserted by the beginning of December.[261] In Ayr alone thirty soldiers were discharged, all described as 'Capt. Spencer's people ... of that church', that is, Baptists.[262] Even long-time supporters of Monck, like Abraham Holmes, deserted their posts in Scotland, establishing allegiance on grounds of religious persuasion. Holmes left Scotland and secured Carlisle for Lambert as conflict between the two armies began to look inevitable.[263] On 31 December the army discovered a series of printed papers of Baptist origin denouncing Monck's position that were circulating in Leith, prompting a search for hidden presses in the port town and further action against the sect.[264] A third purge of the sect served as the terminal blow for the Baptists in Scotland. By the beginning of 1660 the removal of all Baptist soldiers marked the complete dismantling of the Baptist infrastructure in Scotland.

Interpreting Divergent Experiences

After the Restoration, Scottish Episcopalians, Presbyterians and the secular authorities alike singled out Baptists and Quakers as being particularly necessary to suppress, because they represented the ideologies that underpinned the Commonwealth throughout the Interregnum. In 1661 the Scottish parliament produced an act against all meetings of Baptists or Quakers, quashing the promises of toleration extended to them under the Commonwealth.[265] Despite being targets of the same legislation and policies of persecution, Baptists and Quakers experienced drastically different fortunes at the end of the Interregnum and into the Restoration in Scotland. This section will attempt to explain why these two groups, whose similarities were discussed at the beginning of this chapter, fared so differently in the face of Presbyterian and Episcopalian opposition.

Baptists disappeared almost immediately after the Interregnum, and may have vanished even before then. Their failure to maintain the success they experienced during the early years of the Interregnum rested primarily on their poor strategy of integrating into Scottish society. From the arrival of the movement, their infrastructure depended heavily upon the English army for ministers and support. When that relationship, which seemed to be under constant pressure, became strained in 1655 (Overton's Plot), frayed in 1658 with Cromwell's orders to remove Baptists from places of trust, and severed in 1659 with the wholesale cashiering and imprisonment of all Baptists in the army, the sect found itself in no fit state to carry on. Its last gasps in seventeenth-century Scotland are not recorded, but once Monck marched south it could not have lasted long. Those Baptists not discharged or imprisoned fled to England, meaning that the army remaining in Scotland held no sympathies for Baptists. In such an inhospitable setting, even those Scots Baptists who nobly held out in Fife earlier in the year could not have continued. Without local garrisons for support, and facing censures from the Kirk that included bans on trading with 'sectarians', Baptists would very quickly have found themselves isolated both socially and financially, as the Quakers had complained in their appeal to parliament in 1659. In short, the Baptists' over-dependency on the English regime meant that they never established themselves autonomously from the army.

In relation to the Scots, Baptists failed to overcome their affiliation with the infamous 'Anabaptists' of the continent. Before the movement even arrived in Scotland, Baillie and others had ideologically linked them to what had happened at Münster more than a century before.[266] They never adequately dealt with the continued correlation between themselves and the 'Anabaptists' by either embracing the label and making it their own, or effectively rejecting it. Instead they meekly accepted it with only mild reservations, as is evidenced in their declaration of faith in 1653, where Baptist meetings sheepishly referred to themselves as the gathered churches of Christ 'commonly (though unjustly) called Anabaptists'. Rather than distancing themselves from such negative correlations, they actually reaffirmed those stereotypes by becoming embroiled in multiple failed conspiracies. As a result, Baptists actually confirmed the negative images portrayed by Baillie in 1647 and gave rise to new myths of violence and slaughter.

With regard to the Quakers, claims by James Torrance and G.B. Burnet that the movement in Scotland represented an overall failure are misleading and myopic. Though the Quakers never achieved the numerical success in Scotland that they did in England, nonetheless they attained something remarkable and worthy of note. They represent the only religious group introduced into Scotland during the Interregnum to survive uninterrupted to the present day. This is an astounding feat, especially in relation to the increasing persecution faced during the 1660s in which they actually spread over the country and numerically increased. Their growth over the Restoration period owes much to seeds planted by other sectarian activity in Scotland during the Interregnum. In Aberdeen, for instance, Alexander Jaffray (a former Independent) and Margaret Anderson (a former Baptist) became convinced early in the 1660s. William Dundas, likewise, joined the Quakers during the Restoration years after a stint of Interregnum Independency.

So why were the Quakers the only sect to survive beyond the Interregnum, especially when Independency was so close doctrinally to the Kirk? The survival of Quakerism in Scotland rests predominantly on three points. First, theologically the Quakers offered a distinct alternative to the Kirk. The close doctrinal similarity between the Independents and the Kirk actually served as a primary reason why Independency failed in Scotland, the only significant difference between them being the Independents' emphasis on changing from a top-down national structure of ecclesiastical government to the basic powers of church government being retained in individual congregations. In short, Independency simply differed too little to warrant holding out, especially in the face of Restoration Episcopacy. Baptists offered a different doctrine of Baptism and sometimes Arminian theology, but those who took strides in this direction often found it easy to take additional steps towards the Friends. Quakers were, in terms of seventeenth-century Protestantism, the opposite end of the spectrum to the Kirk's hard Calvinist theology. They represented something completely 'other'. In contrast to the Kirk's strict doctrine of double predestination, Fox and the Scottish Friends preached free grace revealed through the Inner Light in All, and the death and resurrection of Christ as 'a propitiation for the sins of the whole world'.[267] This did not represent the universal atonement of later Quakers, but was an evangelical message for all humanity to cleave to Christ and to a salvation not dependent on cold election but on hope that through embracing the Inner Light (Christ) and believing its continuing revelation the faithful will find the salvation that God intends for them. Whereas the Kirk preached unconfirmable election shrouded in doubt and manifested in countless testimonies, which Fox simply interpreted as 'the greatest part of men were ordained for hell', the Quakers offered hopeful action. 'Therefore all people believe in the light as Christ commands,' proclaimed Fox, 'and own the grace of God your free teacher: and it will bring you your salvation for it is sufficient.'[268] Set against a Kirk which could bar members from the sacraments, the Quakers internalised them. As a result they offered a more immediate experience of Christ, free from obstruction or censure by temporal ecclesiastical courts, and provided a stronger sense of the priesthood of all believers than that offered through the Kirk's stringent control or the Episcopacy that followed. This no doubt appealed to some. Quakers offered a distinct alternative in a culture dominated by a strict hierarchical church that maintained orthodoxy by censure and reprimand: freedom and empowerment to actively take control of one's personal and spiritual life free from any clerical mediation. In fact, the Quakers were so distinct from the theological thinking of the Kirk that no Church of Scotland minister even bothered to publish against them.

A second key factor contributing to Friends' success through the Interregnum and beyond rested in their shared self-identity. As Kate Peters notes, Quakers took ownership of the label 'Quaker'. Although intended to be slanderous, they made it a 'banner of unity'.[269] This provided distinct borders for the movement, allowing it to formulate a solidified identity that other sectarian groups, like the Ranters, never attained. Whereas Baptists could not shake off the negative associations of their continental predecessors and eventually had to accept an unwanted nomenclature, the Quakers' ability to take an aspersion and through their propaganda embrace it as a positive identity allowed them to take ownership of their title and assert their distinctiveness.

Third and finally, Quakers were the best-prepared sect to survive through the Interregnum and flourish after the Restoration because in

Scotland, as in England, they were born and bred in turmoil. Scottish Quakers never enjoyed close links with the establishment, nor had they ever really experienced wide-ranging protection from the government. Despite the Protector's great admiration for Fox, in distant Scotland the military regime viewed Quakers as a nuisance and liability.[270] Unlike Baptists and Independents, who offered new communities of support under the protection of either the government or Baptist soldiers during the Interregnum, the Quakers rarely found any institutional support and consistently faced the threat of Presbyterian-motivated 'Club Law'. As a result, the Quakers had long experience of being persecuted and persevering. From 1650 until 1687, the decision to join the Quakers included an inherent acceptance of possible persecution and social exclusion in Scotland. Yet for those Scots who became convinced, persecution did little to inhibit the joy of pursuing the truth. As the Scottish Quaker Andrew Robeson put it: 'Who shall turn it backwards? Tho breirs, & thorns may now spring up, their comes a day of burning.'[271] The open recognition of possible persecution provided the Quakers with a strength and resilience unmatched among the religious groups taking root in Cromwellian Scotland. Far from being a failure, the Quaker movement in Scotland overcame great odds and opposition to establish a distinct religious movement that survives uninterrupted for over 350 years. In fact, in the years immediately following the Interregnum, Friends felt a sense of triumph, interpreting the reimposition of Episcopacy as God allowing a temporary triumph of the Beast in order to punish the sins of their Presbyterian persecutors. 'Hath he not washt away thy laite oppressors as with a flood? And was it not because they provocked him with anger?' 'Altho the Lord suffers a floode of prophanity (Episcopacy) to wash down a Fabricke of false worship in hiposcrisie that was idolatrously weavd in the land,' wrote Robeson in 1662, eventually God would remove all anti-Christian forms, allowing the Quakers and all tolerant Christians to thrive.[272]

Unfortunately for the Baptists, they fell into the caricature given to them by their enemies. Through their involvement in radical dissent, manifested in political intrigues, they ostracised themselves from the government that had relied upon them so heavily during its campaigns against the king and the Kirk. When the favour of English government turned against them, they were left with no friends in times of trouble. Lacking the grit that the had Quakers developed through years of opposition, the Baptists quickly folded under Presbyterian opposition once the army had forsaken them. It would be sixty years before any Baptists would again make headway among the Scots. By that time, the Quakers represented an established group in Scotland, both in Lanarkshire and Aberdeenshire, and had made forays into the New World.

Conclusion

The question may be asked: What impact did the introduction of sectarian religion during the Interregnum have upon Scotland? If any, was it lasting? While the Quakers represent the only religious group introduced during the Interregnum to survive beyond the Restoration period, the relationship between the people of Scotland and alternative forms of Protestantism to the presbytery is a crucially important subject. The religious controversy within Interregnum Scotland between the Kirk and sects has largely been overshadowed by the subsequent struggle between Episcopacy and Presbyterianism in the 1660s and 1670s. Successive historians of the Kirk have looked back over the seventeenth century as a time when it twice triumphed over Episcopacy and the doctrines of the Kirk dominated those of the Independents in the Westminster Assembly of Divines. However, in practical terms, the price paid for the advancement of the Presbyterian cause weighed heavily upon the people of Scotland. It embroiled them in two English civil wars and led to England's invasion of Scotland in 1650. The human cost was enormous. Just in Scotland's defeats at Dunbar and Worcester (3 September 1650 and 1651 respectively) approximately 20,000 Scotsmen were taken prisoner, many of whom died in captivity or were shipped as indentured servants to the colonies, most of them never returning home.[1]

Far from being a decade in which the only questions relating to presbytery and the covenants were regarding how to best propagate them, Scotland's devotion to the Kirk, covenants and king all came under intense scrutiny during the Interregnum. This intense re-evaluation was exacerbated by the polemic dialogue carried on by the English army and the Kirk before the battle of Dunbar. Both sides asserted that the righteousness of their actions over the previous decade and the divine sanction of their chosen forms of church government would be vindicated by the outcome their conflict.[2] In an age when providential dispensationalism prevailed, this greatly raised the religious stakes for both England and Scotland. The decimation of Scotland's army in such an emphatic manner at Dunbar, after boasting so many advantages, prompted men like Alexander Jaffray,

Thomas Wood and Colonel Archibald Strachan to begin asking whether defeat should be viewed as a divine judgement against the ideologies to which Scotland had pinned their hopes: Kirk, covenants and presbytery. They began to entertain the possibility that the way forward might be outside a national Presbyterian Kirk.

The fact that this questioning and subsequent disillusionment corresponded with the arrival of the English army – which had not only predicted God's judgement against the Kirk, but offered a plethora of alternatives to Scotland's state church – provided a platform for English zealots within the army to preach the merits of their own preferred patterns of Protestantism. But while the more radical sects were eager to trample down the Kirk and to proselytise Scotland to their own doctrinal factions, they were out of touch with what Cromwell and his fellow moderate Independents desired. Cromwell's desire, which became increasingly clear after he became Lord Protector, was not for everyone to accept a uniform pattern of church government, liturgy and practice, because he was an anti-formalist.[3] He was not even seeking a simple toleration for all Protestants. What he truly longed for, as Blair Worden has identified, was unity among all Christians.[4]

The policy of the Commonwealth, after an initial period of producing anti-Presbyterian works intended to undermine the dominance of the Kirk, sought to build bridges with the godly in Scotland rather than to remove all traces of Presbyterianism from the country. Cromwell did not oppose the general premise of a Presbyterian establishment, only an intolerant presbytery that lorded over the consciences of others. From the perspective of an English regime pursuing religious unity, a national presbytery represented rigid 'formality' understood to be incompatible with Christian liberties.[5] The evidence from the Interregnum suggests an English policy of tolerating the Kirk so long as it did not attempt to oppress the consciences of those who chose 'another gospel way'. That is why the official policy of the English regime did not promote one particular sect over another. For Cromwell, this represented the most difficult aspect of dealing with the radicals in his army, as they tended to persecute each other and persisted in being the greatest obstacle for him to overcome in establishing the Christian Commonwealth that he longed for. 'Is it ingenuous to ask for liberty, and not to give it?', and: 'Where shall we find men of a universal spirit? Everyone desires to have liberty, but none will give it.'[6]

This official policy, that is promoting toleration and the gathering of congregations, shines a light on Major John Cloberry's unwillingness to facilitate a second dispute between James Brown and James Guthrie. Their first encounter had not, in Cloberry's view, contributed to Christian unity. It also explains why Robert Lilburne, being an avid Baptist, distributed sermons by John Owen that advocated the gathering of the godly out of a dead church. Under the Protectorate, the differences between Independents and Presbyterians, from the regime's perspective, were minimised. After the conquest of Scotland and the subjugation of their ideological opponents, the Protector and Lord Broghill (during his stay in Scotland from September 1655 to August 1656) made great efforts to bring the fractured Kirk together and to bring it into a positive co-existent relationship with the government. Certainly, Gillespie's faction of Protesters demonstrated that with a degree of compromise Presbyterians could not only co-exist but thrive under the Commonwealth's religious policy, that is, if they could see past their desires for pan-national conformity. The collusion between Gillespie and the English Independent John Beverley illustrates that a moderate position could be reached, in which some Presbyterians and Independents found contentment, with the focus shifting from the structure of a single national church government to a shared desire for strict discipline within individual congregations. As demonstrated in chapter 4, seeking unity between Presbyterians and Independents on these grounds was not unique to Scotland.[7] In this way, a small group of individuals on both sides found common ground in Interregnum Scotland that could not be agreed to in the Westminster Assembly. Of course this compromise was not acceptable to the majority of the more stringent sort on either side, but it represented a hopeful start. It was along these lines that Broghill's hopes ran when he wrote to Cromwell in February 1656 of plans to ease both Protesters and Resolutioners into union under the Protectorate, and boasted of the benefits that the Protector could reap among English Presbyterians if this could be done.[8]

The Protector, whose personal sway in national policy has been emphasised in recent scholarship,[9] made great efforts to reach a compromise between Presbyterians and the Independents because he desired unity and toleration amongst the godly, and he generally numbered both groups among the godly. In appointing committees to certify ministers, he 'endeavoured to settle a way for approbation of men of piety and fitness for the work, and the business committed to persons both of the presbyterian and independent judgment, men of as known ability and integrity, as, I suppose, any the nation hath'.[10] Thus with the inception of the Protectorate the government's policy of energetically promoting Independency in Scotland shifted to finding common ground. The aim was to find unity among the godly, with some kind of equilibrium between Independents and Presbyterians, and hopefully radical sects as well. The underlying premise remained the toleration of the rights of the congregation through the softening of the Kirk's rigid hierarchy, minimising the Kirk's ability to work from the top down by the dissolution of the General Assembly and the prevention of presbyteries and synods meeting when tensions ran high.[11] It seems that many of Cromwell's troops accepted this policy as well, since the Quaker Francis Howgill scolded the multitude of English soldiers attending Kirk services in 1657 for countenancing the Priests and Teachers of this Nation, and upholding the same worship, which some of you in years past would have been ashamed of, and are not you going to learn of them, and to be taught by them, who before Dunbar, Prophecyed all your destruction, and your totall overthrow, and delivered you up to Satan as Hereticks: and so were ... incendaries to imbroyl all the poor people of this Nation in blood to fight for their imagined calfe Presbitery; and are they now become your Teachers?[12]

That the distinction between Independency and the rigid Presbyterianism of the Kirk seems to have blurred for some English soldiers is a further example of the successful fruition of Cromwell's policy. But this should not be viewed as such a difficult step for English troopers of an Independent leaning since the aspect of Presbyterianism that they so hated, the intolerant ecclesiastical government, had largely been removed through the abolition of the General Assembly and the disenfranchising of synods and presbyteries by English intervention. In the absence of a domineering ecclesiastical government, English troops of the Independent variety, with all their deep-seated fears of the inherent corruption of state churches, could in good conscience attend Kirk services to hear the Calvinist preaching that so many of them loved. Although the rift between the Resolutioners and Protesters did not mend under the Protectorate, Menzies' return to the Kirk and Gillespie's compliance with English Independents demonstrate that Cromwell's desire for an amicable resolution between Presbyterians and Independents achieved some success in Scotland. A further example of the pursuit of Christian unity came in Jaffray asking the minister of Ormiston, as the minister of *a kirk* (as opposed to being a minister of *the Kirk*), to baptise his child. This is the sort of Christian co-existence that Cromwell sought: free from any struggle for power or preferment. In the example of Jaffray, it found a greater success in Scotland than it often did in England, where sects struggled so hard for supremacy over their rivals.

Ascertaining a precise number of Scots who accepted sectarian doctrines is not possible. However, it is wrong to accept James Guthrie's 1659 claim that 'scarce' one in a thousand Scots was 'infected' as evidence of minimal impact – as Hoy did – without noting Guthrie's admission that 'some hundreds' had joined with sects.[13] Guthrie gauged the health of the church by overall national adherence, and so the presence of several hundred sectarians 'being openly fallen off to Independency, some to Anabaptism, some to Quakerism' may have seemed 'inconsiderable in comparison to the Body of this Church'.[14] For this reason, Guthrie could disparage claims of success by opponents of the Kirk as unjustifiable. Yet in making such claims he failed to recognise the ecclesiological perspective of those 'sects' who by self-definition perceived themselves to be a small amount of 'wheat' collected out of the 'chaff' majority. As a result, measuring success by numerical quotas is unfair in light of their distinctly different ecclesiological definitions. While the national Kirk strove for uniformity and wholesale inclusion of Scotland's populace hedged by a national covenant with God, the radical groups, which formed during the Interregnum, believed that they would always be the righteous minority. Achievement should therefore be measured in terms of an established presence, represented by a strong voice advocating their principles. By such standards even Guthrie would admit sectarian success by the end of 1659, as they already had 'no small footing amongst us' and 'strongly' pleaded for continued toleration for all Protestants save Episcopalians.[15] Hence Guthrie argued that 'sectarians' represented a dangerous leaven in Scotland which, although proportionately small in comparison to the national church, ought to be feared for their 'growth and increase ... in Scotland'.[16]

The success of the religious revolution in Scotland during these ten years manifested itself in two ways: first, the survival of the Quakers beyond the Restoration until the present day, which Alan Macinnes calls 'the one British religious legacy of the 1650s ... within the indigenous population of Scotland';[17] second, the petition for 'Gospel Priviledges' in Scotland, presented to parliament in 1659. Putting aside the habit of measuring the success of the church by numerical membership, we may be able to appreciate the degree of change experienced by those who in the space of a decade went from supporting violent expansion of a particular ecclesiastical structure to embracing Cromwell's desire for Christian unity and toleration. The Scots who signed the petition for 'Gospel Priviledges' in 1659 (whether Baptist, Quaker or Independent) had progressed a step beyond their English counterparts, whose sectarianism brought about the downfall of the Commonwealth just a few months later.

The stand-off between Monck and Lambert in the closing months of 1659 bore witness to the narrow ambitions of two factions which had formed within the English regime. The extreme Baptists and Fifth Monarchists who dominated the army in England desired to usher in a new kingdom of Christ and could see no compromise short of a millenarian facilitation of Christ's Second Advent. Equally, the moderate Independents had abandoned the Christian confraternity fundamental to the Commonwealth ideal when they expelled those difficult-to-control elements from the army in Scotland. By excluding the radical elements so fundamental in the establishment of the Commonwealth, the moderate Independents and pragmatic Republicans signalled the imminent failure of that body politic. Religious divisions became a fundamental obstacle for the successful maintenance of the Commonwealth. Even Cromwell, 'the most tolerant man of his age', as L.F. Brown termed him, reached a limit of tolerance towards sects and died at odds with both the Quakers and the Baptists.[18] In Scotland, however, the Commonwealth ideals of religious toleration and confraternity persisted among a loosely knit circle of individuals. In signing the petition requesting the maintenance of Gospel privileges for all sects, Scottish proselytes to 'English' religions shone brighter in their principles than the missionaries who had brought the message of toleration and the politicians who had advocated it. This pursuit of mutual toleration was the 'Gospel Pattern' of co-existence between inherently divergent Christian communities that the Protector had advocated until his death.

Notes

Introduction

1 John Morrill, 'Seventeenth-Century Scotland', review of Walter Makey, *The Church and the Covenant* (1979), Frances Dow, *Cromwellian Scotland* (1979), J. Buckroyd, *Church and State in Scotland 1660–1681* (1976), in JEH, 33.2 (1982), 266–71, 268.

2 K.D. Holfelder, 'Factionalism in the Kirk during the Cromwellian Invasion and Occupation of Scotland, 1650 to 1660: The Protester–Resolutioner Controversy' (PhD Thesis, University of Edinburgh, 1998).

3 Holfelder, 8.

4 J. Beattie, *History of the Church of Scotland during the Commonwealth* (Edinburgh, 1847).

5 R.B. Knox, 'A Scottish Chapter in the History of Toleration', *Scottish Journal of Theology*, 41 (1988), 57.

6 *AGA*, 30.

7 *AGA*, 75–6.

8 *APS*, 610; *AGA*, 160; William Orme, *Memoirs of the Life ... of John Owen* (London, 1820), 487; R.B. Carter, 'The Presbyterian–Independent Controversy with Special Reference to Dr. Thomas Goodwin and the Years 1640–1660', 2 vols (PhD dissertation, University of Edinburgh, 1961), ii:10.

9 *AGA*, 160.

10 J. Scott, 'Baptists in Scotland During the Commonwealth', *RSCHS*, 3 (1929), 174–85; J. Scott, 'Baptist Witness during the Commonwealth', *History of the Baptists in Scotland*, ed., G. Yullie (Glasgow, 1926), 24–39; R.B. Hannen, 'Cupar, Fife, 1652–1659', *BQ*, 10(1940–1), 45–9; G.B. Burnet, *The Story of Quakerism in Scotland 1650–1850* (London, 1952); J. Torrance, 'The Quaker Movement in Scotland', *RSCHS*, 3 (1929), 31–42; J. Torrance, 'The Early Quakers in North-East Scotland', *Transactions of the Banffshire Field Club* (Aberdeen, 1936), 67–87.

11 G. Donaldson also briefly touched on the influence of English sects during the Interregnum: 'The Emergence of Schism in Seventeenth-Century Scotland', *Scottish Church History*, ed., G. Donaldson (Edinburgh, 1985), 204–19. However, as his contribution totals only three pages (217–19) it will not be discussed here.

12 G.D. Henderson, 'Some Early Scottish Independents', *TCHS*, 12 (1933–6), 67–79, and reprinted in G.D. Henderson, *Religious Life in Seventeenth Century Scotland* (Cambridge, 1937), 100–16.

13 W.I. Hoy, 'Entry of Sects Into Scotland: A Preliminary Study', in D. Shaw, ed., *Reformation and Revolution* (Edinburgh, 1967)

14 See note 54 on p. 222 below.

15 B. Evans, *The Early English Baptists*, 2 vols (London, 1862–4), ii:190; Hoy, 181.

16 For futher information of the Protester–Resolutioner controversy see Beattie and Holfelder's studies.

17 Abbott, *Cromwell*, i:283–8.

18 These letters have only briefly been referred to in the work of Hoy (186–7), but not

mentioned at all in Donaldson, 'Schism' or Henderson, 'Some Early Scottish Independents'.

19 Hoy, 190–7.
20 NLS, Wod.Fol.XXX(24, 26). See chapter 4.
21 EUL, La.I.368; NLS, Wod.Qu.XVII. See chapter 2.
22 NLS, Wod.Fol.XXX(27). See chapter 5.
23 NCL, MSS Box 28.5. See chapter 4.
24 David B. Barratt, *Sects, 'Cults' and Alternative Religions* (London, 1996), 16, 38.
25 J.G.G. Norman, 'The Relevance and Vitality of the Sect-Idea', *BQ*, 27 (1977–8), 248–258, 249.
26 B. Johnson, 'On Church and Sect', *American Sociological Review*, 28 (1963), 542; W. Stark, *The Sociology of Religion*, vol. 2, *Sectarian Religion* (London, 1967), 1.
27 Stark, *The Sociology of Religion*, 2.
28 Sir James Balfour, *The Historical Works of Sir James Balfour* (Edinburgh, 1824), iv:309; Alexander Peterkin, ed., *Records of the Kirk of Scotland* (Edinburgh, 1838), 640; John Nicoll, *A Diary of Public Transactions and Other Occurrences, Chiefly in Scotland, 1650–67*, ed., D. Laing (Edinburgh, 1836), 18, 19; Henderson, *RLSCS*, 104, 269.
29 *Perfect Passages* (Nov. 5–12, 1652), 567.
30 William Dundas, *A Few Words of Truth from the Spirit of Truth* (1673), 5.
31 Christopher Feake, *A Beam of Light* (London, 1659).

Chapter 1

1 *Mercurius Politicus*, July 15–22, 1652, pp. 1739–40 [E671:12]. The italics are mine.
2 J. D. Ogilvie, 'Papers from an Army Press, 1650', *Edinburgh Bibliographical Society Transactions*, 2 (1938–45), 420.
3 What David Stevenson has called 'The Kirk Party' came to power in 1648 through the Whiggamore Raid. See Stevenson, *Counter-Revolution*, 103–49; J.D. Grainger, *Cromwell Against the Scots* (East Linton, 1997), 8.
4 Evidence for the discontent among English moderates can be found in William Prynne, *Sad and Serious Political Considersations, Touching the Invasive War Against Our Presbyterian Protestant Brethren in Scotland ... Against Their Covenant, for the Great Slaughter of Those Their Brethren in Covenant* (London, 1650).
5 John Morrill, *The Nature of the English Revolution* (London, 1993), 116–17.
6 Nicoll, 17.
7 Abbott, *Cromwell*, i:268.
8 Stevenson, *Counter-Revolution*, 95–6.
9 Morrill, *The Nature of the English Revolution*, 35, 115.
10 B. Bradshaw and J. Morrill, eds, *The British Problem, c. 1534–1707* (Houndsmill, 1996), 29.
11 Stevenson, *Counter-Revolution*, 72; Morrill, *Nature of the English Rev.*, 91–117.
12 Morrill, *Nature of the English Rev.*, 68.
13 W.C. Dickinson and G. Donaldson, eds, *A Source Book of Scottish History* (London, 1954), iii:122–3. The italics are mine.
14 Letter to Robert Blair dated 19 May 1644. Baillie, *L & J*, ii:185–6.
15 *The Scottish Politike Presbyter, Slaine by an English Independent* (London, 1647).
16 Henry Marten, *The Independency of England Endeavoured to be Maintained* (1648), 4.
17 Stevenson, *Counter-Revolution*, 75.
18 26 December 1647. Clarendon MSS. 3685, 2686.
19 *RCGA*, ii:22–5, 189; COSGAC, *The humble representation of the Commission of the General Assembly to the Honourable Estates of Parliament upon their declareation lately communicate [sic] to us, Edinburgh, 28 Aprile, 1648* (London, 1648), 27; COSGAC, *A Solemn Testimony Against Toleration and the Present Proceedings of Sectaries and Their Abettors in England, in Reference to Religion and Government, with an Admonition and Exhortation to Their Brethren There, from the Commissioners of the General Assembly of the Kirk of Scotland* (Edinburgh: Evan Tyler, 1649).

20 A.I. Macinnes, *The British Revolution, 1629–1660* (Houndsmill, 2005), 194.

21 Abbott, *Cromwell*, ii:268; Whitelocke, 459.

22 Christopher Love, *A Cleare and Necessary Vindication of the Principles and Practices of me Christopher Love* (London, 1651), 49.

23 Evans, *The Early English Baptists*, ii:200–1.

24 T. B., *A Message from the Lord General Crumwel to the Communalty of the Kingdom of Scotland* (London, 1650), 4.

25 Balfour, iv:88–9, 96–7.

26 Dow, 26; *Mercurius Scoticus* (23–30 Sept., 1651), 69.

27 Walter Makey, *The Church of the Covenant, 1637–1651* (Edinburgh, 1979), 85ff; Alexandra Walsham, *Providence in Early Modern England* (Oxford, 1999), 19; Stevenson, *Counter-Revolution*, 188–90; B. Worden, 'Providence and Politics in Cromwellian England', *Past and Present*, 109 (1985), 57; William Haller, *Liberty and Reformation in the Puritan Revolution* (New York, 1967), 8.

28 Margo Todd, *The Culture of Protestantism in Early Modern Scotland* (London, 2002), 402.

29 Peter Donald, 'Archibald Johnston of Wariston and the Politics of Religion', *RSCHS*, 24 (1991), 131.

30 Jaffray, 61.

31 Walsham, *Providence in Early Modern England*, 13, 19.

32 W.S., *Presbyteries Triall* (1657), 43–4.

33 Ann Hughes, '"Popular" Presbyterianism in the 1640 and 1650s: The Cases of Thomas Edwards and Thomas Hall', in Nicholas Tyacke, ed., *England's Long Reformation: 1500–1800*, The Neale Colloquium in British History (London, 1998; 2000), 255.

34 Ann Hughes, 'Approaches to Presbyterian Print Culture' in J. Anderson and E. Sauer, eds, *Books and Readers in Early Modern England* (Philadelphia, 2002), 97–116; 110.

35 Baillie, *L & J*, ii:190; Ann Hughes, *Gaengraena and the Struggle for the English Revolution* (Oxford, 2004), see ch. 5.

36 Baillie, *L & J*, ii:193, 201–2, 215, 251, 279, 352, 416.

37 D. Stevenson, 'A Revolutionary Regime and the Press: The Scottish Covenanters and their Printers, 1638–1651', *Union, Revolution and Religion in 17th-Century Scotland*, Collected Studies Series (Aldershot, 1997), XV:321, 323, 325.

38 Hughes, 'Approaches to Presbyterian Print Culture', 111.

39 Thomas Edwards, *Gangraena* (London, 1646), 16–17.

40 Todd, *Culture of Protestantism*, 25.

41 COS, *Causes of a Publick and Solemn Humiliation* (Edinburgh: Evan Tyler, 1650); *The Impartial Scout*, July 5–12, 1650 [E777(23)].

42 *RCGA*, ii:421.

43 *A Seasonable and Necessary Warning*, 4.

44 COS, *Directions of the Generall Assembly Concerning Secret and Private Worship.* (Edinburgh: Reprinted by Evan Tyler, 1650), 4.

45 COS, *Directions*, 7–8, 9.

46 M.J. Seymour, 'Pro-Government Propaganda in Interregnum England, 1649–1660' (University of Cambridge, PhD Thesis, 1987), 11–12, 20.

47 George Chalmers, *The Life of Thomas Ruddiman* (London, 1794), 117; Ogilvie, 'Papers from an Army Press, 1650', 420.

48 Jason Peacey, *Politicians and Pamphleteers* (Aldershot, 2004), 199. John Hall was paid a stipend by the Commonwealth government to accompany Cromwell into Scotland and put his polemical tools to use. See ch. 3.

49 Abbott, *Cromwell*, iii:283.

50 1) The coronation of Charles II as king not only of Scotland but also of England and Ireland; 2) the threat that the Scots would march south on the king's behalf; and 3) the Scots' rejection of a treaty with the English (England and Wales, Parliament, *Declaration of the Parliament of England, upon the Marching of the Armie into Scotland* (London, 1650), 6–7).

51 Abbott, *Cromwell*, ii:302; *Perfect Diurnal*, August 12, 1650; *RCGA*, iii:13–15.

52 England and Wales, Army, *Declaration of the Army of England, Upon their March into Scotland* (Newcastle: S[tephen] B[ulkley], 1650). [EEB 1641–1700, 1439:33]. The work was signed in the name of Cromwell by his secretary John Rushworth.

53 Abbott, *Cromwell*, ii:288; *Several Proceedings*, 24 July 1650; *Perfect Diurnal*, 22 July 1650. Thanks to Professor John Morrill for pointing out the use of the term 'Forlorn Hope'.

54 J.Y. Akerman, ed., *Letters from Roundhead Officers Written from Scotland and Chiefly Addressed to Captain Adam Baynes* (Edinburgh, 1856), 1–2; Grainger, 18.

55 Ogilvie, 'Papers from an Army Press', 421. EEB, 1641–1700, 1439:33. Copies with Bulkley's imprint survive in Queen's University (Belfast), the British Library, Worcester College (Oxford), Newcastle Central Library and Society of Antiquaries of Newcastle-upon-Tyne.

56 *Perfect Diurnall*, 26 July 1650; *Several Proceedings*, 15 July 1650.

57 Abbott, *Cromwell*, ii: 302. Referring to *Vindication of the Declaration of the Army*.

58 P. Toon, *God's Statesman: The Life and Work of John Owen* (Exeter, 1971), 43.

59 William Orme, *Memoirs of the Life, Writings, and Religious Connexions of John Owen, D.D.* (London, 1820), 126n.

60 Laurence, 159; Toon, *God's Statesman*, 43.

61 England and Wales, Army, *A Declaration of the Army of England upon Their March Into Scotland to All That are Saints, and Partakers of the Faith of God's Elect, in Scotland* (London, 1650).

62 *Perfect Diurnall*, 15–22 July (1650), 369. [E777(30)].

63 Abbott, *Cromwell*, ii:283.

64 Abbott, *Cromwell*, ii:288.

65 Abbott, *Cromwell*, ii:284–5.

66 Abbott, *Cromwell*, ii:286.

67 Abbott, *Cromwell*, ii:285.

68 Abbott, *Cromwell*, ii:286.

69 Laurence, 71.

70 COSGAC, *A Short Reply to the Army's Declaration* (Edinburgh, 1650), 2.

71 COSGAC, *Short Reply*, 16–17.

72 COSGAC, *Short Reply*, 12.

73 Ogilvie, 'Papers from an Army Press', 422. No original copies survive, only London reprints: England and Wales, Army, *A Declaration of the Army of the Commonwealth of England, to the People of Scotland* (London, 1650).

74 Ogilvie, 'Papers from an Army Press', 423.

75 Whitelocke, iii:450.

76 Abbott, *Cromwell*, ii:296; *Perfect Diurnall*, (5–12 August 1650), 410 [E778:18].

77 Whitelocke, iii:450.

78 *Declaration of the Army ... to the People of Scotland*, 3; Abbott, *Cromwell*, ii:290; *Perfect Diurnall*, 22 July 1650; *Several Proceedings*, 24 July 1650.

79 *Declaration of the Army ... to the People of Scotland*, 6; Abbott, *Cromwell*, ii:291.

80 *Declaration of the Army ... to the People of Scotland*, 5, 7; Abbott, *Cromwell*, ii:291.

81 Abbot, *Cromwell*, ii:290.

82 Nicoll, 19.

83 *A Large Relation of the Fight at Leith Neere Edenburgh* (London, 1650), 1–4; *A Perfect Diurnall*, 16–24 Sept. 1650, 505.

84 Whitelocke, iii:450.

85 Committee of Estates, *An Answere from the Committee of Estates, To a Printed Paper Directed to the People of Scotland, and Signed in Name of L.G. Cromwel, and his Officers* (Edinburgh, 1650), 4.

86 Stevenson, *Counter-Revolution*, 131, 147, 150–3, 158–9, 165–7; Grainger, 8, 11, 13–15, 33, 36.

87 COS, *For the Under-Officers and Souldiers of the English Army, from the People of Scotland* (Edinburgh: Evan Tyler, 1650); English Army, *A Declaration of the English Army Now in Scotland*, 7–8.

88　Ian Gentles, *The New Model Army in England, Ireland and Scotland, 1645–165* (Oxford, 1992), 386; Gardiner, *C & P*, i:259–60; Abbott, *Cromwell*, ii:267–71, 286; Whitelocke, iii:460–2; Grainger, 10.

89　Abbott, *Cromwell*, ii:282.

90　Edmund Ludlow, *The Memoirs of Edmund Ludlow: The Lieutenant-General of the Horse in the Army of the Commonwealth of England, 1625–1672*, ed., C.H. Firth, 2 vols (Oxford, 1894), i:252; Daniel MacKinnon, *Origin and Services of the Coldstream Guards*, 2 vols (London, 1833), i:4.

91　Grainger, 20.

92　Oliver Cromwell, *A Letter Sent to the Generall Assembly of the Kirke of Scotland* (London, 1650), 3.

93　Cromwell, *A Letter Sent to the Generall Assembly*, 3–4; Abbott, *Cromwell*, ii:302; *RCGA*, iii:21; NLS, Wod.Fol.XXIX.(45).

94　Church of Scotland, General Assembly, *West-Kirk the 13. Day of August, 1650* (Edinburgh: Evan Tyler, 1650); *RCGA*, iii:26; NLS, Wod.Fol.XXIX.(47); Wariston, ii:xi–xii.

95　*The Lord Gen. Cromwel's Letter: With a Narrative of The Proceedings of the English Army in Scotland, and a Declaration of the General Assembly, Touching the Dis-owning their King and his Interest* (London, 1650), 7.

96　Abbott, *Cromwell*, ii:306; NLS, Wod.Fol.XXIX(46).

97　Wariston, ii:19.

98　Abbott, *Cromwell*, ii:306; *The Lord Gen. Cromwel's Letter*, 11.

99　Wariston, ii:18.

100　*To the Right Honourable the Lords and Others of the Committee of Estates, The Humble Remonstrance and Supplication of the Officers of the Army* (Edinburgh: Evan Tyler, 1650); Edward Walker, *Historical Discourses, upon Several Occasions* (London: W.B., 1705), 167–8; David Laing, ed., *Correspondence of Sir Robert Kerr, First Earl of Ancram and His Son, William, Third Earl of Lothian*, 2 vols (Edinburgh, 1875), ii:285.

101　*RCGA*, ii:461.

102　Wariston, ii:19–20.

103　Edward M. Furgol, *A Regimental History of the Covenanting Armies 1639–1651* (Edinburgh, 1990), 326–7.

104　*RCGA*, iii:9.

105　Balfour, iv:89; *RCGA*, iii:16. According to Edward Walker, between 3,000 and 4,000 of the 'best Men' were purged between 2 and 5 August (Walker, *Historical Discourses*, 165). See also Grainger, 28–9. *RCGA*, iii:16

106　Wariston, ii:19. According to David Stevenson, the removal of soldiers on August 16 was 'by far the most thorough purge of the army yet undertaken' (Stevenson, *Counter-Revolution*, 145).

107　*Mercurius Scoticus giving the world ground upon this evident truth, videlicet, that the Scottish rebels, the Presbyter, or Kirckfaction never intended that Charles the second should be their King* (Rotterdam: P.C., 1650), 10; Balfour, iv:89.

108　England and Wales, Army, *A Declaration of the English Army Now in Scotland, Especially Those among Them, That Know and Fear the Lord* (London, 1659). The work is in the British Library, but this bibliographical information is incorrect. The last page is dated Musselburgh, August 1. 1650. The incorrect dating is most likely due to its being bound with a later work. A second edition was printed: England and Wales, Army, *A Declaration of the English Army Now in Scotland, Touching the Justness & Necessity of their Present Proceeding in That Nation* (London, 1650).

109　*A Declaration of the English Army Now in Scotland*, 13–14, 16.

110　Baillie, *L & J*, ii:185–6.

111　Baillie, *L & J*, 13, 15.

112　Tai Liu, *Discord in Zion: The Puritan Divines and the Puritan Revolution 1640–1660*, International Archives of the History of Ideas: 61 (The Hague, 1973), 74–5.

113　Gottfried Seebass, 'The Importance of Apocalyptic for the History of Protestantism', *Colloquium*, 3 (1980), 24–35, 25.

114 English Army, *A Declaration of the English Army Now in Scotland*, 12.

115 *A Declaration of the English Army Now in Scotland*, 15.

116 *Cromwelliana*, 83; *The Fifth Monarchy, or Kingdom of Christ, in Opposition to the Beasts, Asserted* (London, 1659), 20.

117 Cromwell, *A Letter Sent to the Generall Assembly*, 4.

118 C.J. Guthrie's introduction to *RCGA*, iii:xxx.

119 *RCGA*, iii:22.

120 John Vicars, *A Caveat for Covenant-Contemners and Covenant-Breakers* (Edinburgh: Evan Tyler, 1650).

121 *A Perfect Diurnall*, 16–24 Sept. 1650, (E.780, II), 505; S.R. Gardiner, ed., *Letters and Papers Illustrating the Relations Between Charles the Second and Scotland in 1650* (Edinburgh, 1894), 135.

122 *Perfect Diurnall*, 22–29 July 1650, 391; *Journal of the House of Commons* (London, 1803–13), vi:483.

123 Grainger, 38–40. Grainger estimates the forces at Dunbar to have been 12,000 English and 16,000 Scots. According to Stevenson, the Scots had almost twice the number of troops as Cromwell, listing Cromwell's forces at 11,000 and the Scots' at 20,000 (Stevenson, *Counter-Revolution*, 178).

124 Abbott, *Cromwell*, ii:314.

125 Gentles, *The New Model Army*, 398.

126 Worden, 'Providence', 55–99; Walsham, *Providence in Early Modern England*, 19.

127 Worden, 'Providence', 69.

128 Worden, 'Providence', 81–2.

129 Oliver Cromwell, *A Letter from the Lord General Cromwel from Dunbar* (London, 1650), 10.

130 Worden, 'Providence', 57.

131 Gardiner, *C & P*, i:297.

132 Cromwell, *A Letter from the Lord General Cromwel from Dunbar*, 6–7, 8.

133 Oliver Cromwell, *The Lord General Cromwell His March to Sterling* (London, 1650), 6.

134 *RCGA*, ii:xi.

135 John Rushworth, *A True Relation of the Routing the Scottish Army near Dunbar, Sept. 3* (London, 9 Sept. 1650), 5; Cromwell, *A Letter from the Lord General Cromwel from Dunbar*, 8; *A Letter To the Right Honorable William Lenthall Esq. Speaker of the Parliament of England* (London, 1651), 5; *A Great Victory God Hath Vouchsafed by the Lord Generall Cromwels Forces against the Scots* (London, 1651), 4.

136 Henry Scobell, *A True Relation of the Proceedings of the English Army now in Scotland, From the Two and twentieth day of July, to the First of August* (London, 1650), 14.

137 John Canne, *Emanuel, or God with us. Werein Is Set Forth Englands Late Great Victory Over the Scots Armie, in a Battle at Dunbar, Septemb. 3. 1650* (London, 1650), 22.

138 Thomas Hutchinson, *A collection of original papers relative to the History of the colony of Massachusets-bay* (Boston, New-England, 1769), 269.

139 Thomas Carlyle, *Oliver Cromwell's Letters and Speeches*, 3rd edn (London, 1888), vii:309–10. According to Thomas Carlyle, Cromwell was probably referring to Psalm 110.

140 Gardiner, *C & P*, i:297.

141 Abbott, *Cromwell*, ii:327; Stevenson, *Counter-Revolution*, 149.

142 Nickolls, 24.

143 Robert Douglas, *Short Information* (Aberdeen: James Brown, 1651), 1.

144 Oliver Cromwell, *Several Letters and Passages Between His Excellency, the Lord General Cromwel and the Governor of Edinburgh Castle, and the Ministers there, since His Excellencies Entrance into Edinburgh* (London, 1650), 11–12.

145 Balfour, iv:102; NLS, Wod.Fol.XXIX.(48).

146 COSGAC, *The Causes of a Publick Fast and Humiliation, To be Kept with All Convenient Diligence: By All the Members of This Kirk & Kingdom of Scosland* (Aberdeen: James Brown, 1650), 9.

147 Balfour, iv:99–107; NLS, Wod.Fol.XXX.(3).
148 Patrick Gillespie, *Rulers Sins the Causes of National Judgments: Or, a Sermon Preached at the Fast, upon the 26th Day of December, 1650* (Glasgow, 1718).
149 COSGAC, *A Solemn Warning to all the Members of this Kirk, from the Commission of the Generall Assemblie with an Act for the Censuring such an Act, or comply with the Sectarian Armies* (Aberdeen: James Brown, 1651), 5.
150 COSGAC, *A Solemn Warning*, 19.
151 NLS, Wod.Fol.XXIX.(54).
152 COSGAC, *A Short Exhortation and Warning, to the Ministers, and Professours of this Kirk* (Aberdeen: James Brown, 1651), 1.
153 COSGAC, *A Short Exhortation*, 2, 3.
154 COSGAC, *A Short Exhortation*, 4, 5.
155 Maidment, *Historical Fragments*, iv:10.
156 Jaffray, 62.
157 Jaffray, 61.
158 Dow, 102.
159 Nicoll, 35.
160 Lamont, 53–4.
161 Laurence, 71; *S & P*, xx, 380.

Chapter 2

1 Robert Wodrow, Analecta, 4 vols (Glasgow, 1842–3), iii:93.
2 Preface to: James Fergusson, *A Brief Refutation of the Errors of Tolleration, Erastianism, Independency and Separation* (Edinburgh, 1692).
3 Laurence, 74.
4 Ann Hughes, 'Public Disputations, Pamphlets and Polemic, 1649–60', *History Today*, 41 (1991), 27–33; Ann Hughes, 'The Pulpit Guarded: Confrontations between Orthodox and Radicals in Revolutionary England', in Anne Laurence, W.R. Owens and Stuart Sim, eds, *John Bunyan and His England, 1628–88* (London, 1990), 31–50.
5 Nicoll, 17.
6 Hughes, 'Public Disputations', 28–9.
7 Hughes, 'The Pulpit Guarded', 35.
8 Hughes, 'The Pulpit Guarded', 38.
9 Hughes, 'Public Disputations', 30.
10 John Ley, *A Discourse of Disputations Chiefly Concerning Matters of Religion* (1656), 33–4; Hughes, 'The Pulpit Guarded', 39.
11 Hughes, 'The Pulpit Guarded', 49.
12 Dow, 14.
13 Maidment, *Historical Fragments*, 30; NLS, Wod.Qu.XXXVII, ff 21–39.
14 'Memoirs of James Burn, Baillie of the City of Glasgow', Maidment, *Historical Fragments*, 18–19.
15 *S & P*, xxxiv–liii; Dow, 64, 293n; *S & C*, 110; Thurloe, vi:472.
16 *S & C*, 116–8; R. Renwick, ed., *Extracts from the Records of the Burgh of Peebles, 1652–1714* (Glasgow, 1910), 4, 6, 7, 12, 19, 20–1, 33, 37, 45; Row, *Life of Blair*, 310; Baillie, *L & J*, iii:249–50.
17 Baillie, *L & J*, iii:249–50; James Turner, *Memoirs of His Own Life and Times, 1632–1670* (Edinburgh, 1829), 109, 112. Construction of the citadel at Leith did not begin until 1656.
18 A.I. Macinnes, *Clans, Commerce and the House of Stuart*, 112.
19 M. Laing, *The History of Scotland* (London, 1819), iii:490; G. Davies, 'The Quarters of the English Army in Scotland in 1656', *SHR*, 21 (1924), 62–7.
20 Clarke MSS 3/11: 24 June 1658; 3/3: f. 55–7.
21 *S & C*, 31.
22 *S & C*, 364; Whitelocke, iii:442.
23 D.C. MacTavish, ed., Minutes of the Synod of Argyll, 1652–1661 (Edinburgh, 1944), ii:28, 39.

24 *FES*, iv:70.
25 Reports abound of presbyteries and kirk sessions moving to discourage their parishioners, expecially women, from drinking with English soldiers. There are also numerous cases of fornication between Scotswomen and English soldiers. Other reports are less descriptive: '6ᵗʰ June (1652) – Agnes Innes and four other women to be banisched for offences with English troopers, &c.' (Cramond, *Elgin*, 278).
26 Whitelocke, iv:91.
27 *S & C*, xlii–xliii, 149–50, 279.
28 Carruthers, *Highland Note-book* (Edinburgh, 1843), 97; *S & P*, xlv–xlvi.
29 Fraser, *Chronicles*, 397, 421; *S & P*, 350, 352, 362; Thurloe, vi:136, 167.
30 Ayrshire Archives, CH2/751/3/2, 7 March 1653.
31 M. Pottinger, 'Cromwellian Soldiers in Cannesbey, 1652 to 1655', *Caithness Field Club Bulletin*, 11 (1993), 5–8.
32 Cramond, *Elgin*, 282–3.
33 *S & C*, 339–40; *Mercurius Scoticus* (Nov. 14, 1651).
34 Dow, 27.
35 *APS*, vi, ii:746.
36 *APS*, vi, ii:747; C.S. Terry, ed., *The Cromwellian Union* (Edinburgh, 1902), 99; Nicoll, 91.
37 Laurence, 72.
38 Carlyle, *Oliver Cromwell's Letters and Speeches*, iii:96; Lomas, i:360, ii:159.
39 John Owen, *The Branch of the Lord, the Beauty of Sion* (Edinburgh: Evan Tyler, 1650); Nicholas Lockyer, *A Little Stone Out of the Mountain. Church-Order Briefly Opened* (Leith: Evan Tyler, 1652).
40 Owen, *The Branch of the Lord*, 4, 27, 28, 30.
41 Owen, *The Branch of the Lord*, 30.
42 Owen, *The Branch of the Lord*, 27.
43 *ODNB* 'Mather, Samuel'; *CSPD*, 1651–2: 610.
44 Nickolls, 48; Laurence, 71–2.
45 John Owen, *The Advantage of the Kingdome of Christ, in the Shaking of the Kingdoms of the World* (Leith: Evan Tyler, 1652).
46 Lockyer, epistle dedicatory 5–6.
47 Lockyer, 62–3.
48 Lockyer, 'to the reader', 3–4.
49 Lockyer, 46–47.
50 Oliver Cromwell, *Several Letters and Passages Between His Excellency, the Lord General Cromwel and the Governor of Edinburgh Castle, and the Ministers There, Since His Excellencies Entrance Into Edinburgh* (London, 1650), 4.
51 Cromwell, *Several Letters and Passages*, 4.
52 Cromwell, *Several Letters and Passages*, 5.
53 Cromwell, *Several Letters and Passages*, 7.
54 Cromwell, *Several Letters and Passages*, 8.
55 Cromwell, *Several Letters and Passages*, 10–11.
56 James Gough, *Memoirs of the Life, Religious Experience, and Labours in the Gospel of James Gough*, 3 vols (Lindfield, 1832), iii:51–2; Hoy, 180; M.R. Brailsford, *A Quaker from Cromwell's Army: James Nayler* (London, 1927), 32–3; Burnet, *Quakerism*, 16.
57 Hoy, 180.
58 *RHCA*, 258n; Brailsford, *A Quaker from Cromwell's Army*, 34.
59 MSS CRA 1, New College, ii:422.
60 Burnet, *History of His Own Time*, 38–9; Nicoll, 68–9; Robert Wodrow, *Analecta*, iii:94; R.B. Hannen, 'Cupar, Fife, 1652–1659', *BQ*, 10 (1940–1), 45.
61 Maidment, *Historical Fragments*, 19.
62 Nicoll, 69.
63 W. Stephen, *History of the Scottish Church* (Edinburgh, 1896), 317–8n.
64 Butler, 18–20.
65 Whitelocke, iii:248, 249.

66 Nicoll, 68.

67 Nicoll, 170. The 'New Kirk', 'Little Kirk', 'East Kirk' or 'Robert Bruce's Kirk' was first partitioned off from the rest of St Giles' in 1578. In 1600, after a request from Robert Bruce that the chapel was too small, it was enlarged. In 1634 the wall was taken down, reunifying the St Giles', before the wall was re-erected between 1639 and 1642. At this point the two churches inside St Giles' were called the 'East' or 'New Kirk' and the 'Great' or 'Old Kirk'. See: J.C. Lees, *St Giles', Edinburgh: Church, College, and Cathedral* (Edinburgh, 1889), 199–206, 228; A. I. Dunlop, *The Kirks of Edinburgh 1560–1984*, vols 15 & 16 (Edinburgh, 1988), 44.

68 Nicoll, 68–69.

69 *RCME*, i:3.

70 *RCGA*, iii:241.

71 Nicoll, 94.

72 James Meikle, *The History of Alyth Parish Church* (Edinburgh, 1933), 91; Henderson, *RLSCS*, 269.

73 Cramond, *Elgin*, 280.

74 Brodie, 78.

75 NLS, Wod.Fol.XXX.(20); Nicoll, 81.

76 *APS*, vi,ii:809–10.

77 'Instructions to the Commissioners sent to Scotland' dated 4 December 1651 (*S & P*, 394).

78 England and Wales, Parliament, *Two Declarations of the Parliament of the Commonwealth of England Concerning Scotland* (London: John Field, 1652).

79 *APS*, vi,ii:809; NLS, Wod.Fol.XXX.(21); Nicoll, 83–4; Whitelocke, iii:393.

80 *APS*, vi,ii:809.

81 Dow, 38.

82 Knox, 'A Scottish Chapter', 49–74.

83 Brodie, 19.

84 Nicoll, 85; *Mercurius Politicus* (26 February–4 March 1652), 1452 [E655(23)].

85 Thomas Murray, *The Life of Samuel Rutherford* (Edinburgh, 1828), 290.

86 *S & C*, 348; *Several Proceedings in Parliament*, 22–29 January 1652; Whitelocke, iii:385, 398–403.

87 *S & C*, 328; *Several Proceedings in Parliament*, 16–23 Oct. 1651.

88 *S & C*, 350; Whitelocke, iii:385

89 *S & C*, 352–3; Whitelocke, iii:398–403.

90 *S & C*, 353.

91 Stuart, *Aberdeen*, 117, 219–20; Whitelocke, iii:386; Row, *Life of Blair*, 297.

92 'Protestation by Sir Alexander Irving of Drum against the Presbytery of Aberdeen. 1652', *The Miscellany of the Spalding Club III* (Aberdeen, 1846), 205–6.

93 Hay, *Blairs Papers*, 215–21. Walker and Irving may be related to the authorship of W.S., *Presbyteries Triall* (1657).

94 *Mercurius Politicus*, 22–29 January 1652; *S & C*, 355.

95 Dow, 58; Whitelocke, iii:429, 430.

96 NLS, Wod.Fol.XXX(28), f. 107; Whitelocke, iii:431–2.

97 *FES*, i:200, 233, 238, 474.

98 Lamont, 58–9.

99 See 'Samuel Rutherford and Thomas Sydserff, Bishop of Galloway, "Ane discussing of some arguments against cannons and ceremonies in God's worship",' in David G. Mullan, ed., *Religious Controversy in Scotland 1625–1639*, SHS, Fifth Series, vol. 11 (Edinburgh, 1998), 14–15, 82–99.

100 H.R. Trevor-Roper, 'Scotland and the Puritan Revolution', *Religion, the Reformation and Social Change* (London, 1967), 395–6.

101 Row, 26.

102 Wodrow, *Analecta*, iii:98; MSS CRA 1, New College, ii:420; John Howie, *The Scots Worthies*, 367; Balfour, iv:298; Baillie, *L & J*, iii:165–6, 168; T. McCrie and T. Thomson, *Lives of Alexander Henderson and James Guthrie*, 153–4; Maidment, *Historical Fragments*, 5:34.

103 Wariston, ii:49, 71.

104 Nickalls, *Fox*, 316.

105 *The Faithful Scout* (29 Oct.–5 Nov. 1652), 740.

106 *Several Proceedings in Parliament and other Intelligence and Affaires* (London: 21–28 October 1652.), 2520.

107 *Mercurius Brittanicus* (26 Oct.–2 Nov. 1652), 238.

108 Nicoll, 94.

109 Lamont, 53–4.

110 James Brown, *Scripture-Redemption Freed from Men's Restrictions: Being an Answer to a Book Lately Published by Mr. William Troughton* (London: J.C., 1653), title page, 12, 14, 15.

111 Since Brown's dispute with Rutherford is mentioned in his book published in 1653 (before his dispute with Guthrie in October) it must have occurred before Brown's book went to the presses earlier in that year. Lamont, 58–9; *S & C*, 53; *A Perfect Diurnall of Some Passages and Proceedings* (London: 18–25 October 1652), 2253; *A Perfect Account.* (No. 95. 20–27 Oct. 1652), 754 [E678(25)]; and *Perfect Passages.* (No. 71. 20–27 Oct. 1652), 552 [E799(23)]; NLS Wodrow.Qu.XVII, ff.194–249.

112 Brown, *Scripture-Redemption Freed from Men's Restrictions*, preface.

113 It was soldiers of this regiment that interrupted George Hamilton at Pittenweem, 22 June 1652: 'The Last Lord's day a soldier of Col. Fairfax his regiment that interrupted [a minister of the Kirk] in the Pulpit, was Committed' (*Mercurius Politicus*, 24 June–1 July 1652, p. 1703 [E669:3]).

114 R.B. Hannen, 'Cupar, Fife, 1652–1659', *BQ*, 10 (1940–1), 45.

115 Lamont, 60.

116 The records of the presbytery of Cupar reports that the three sisters were summoned to appear before the presbytery in 1656, but Hannen asserts that their baptisms took place in 1652. Hannen, 46; Kinloch, *St Andrews & Cupar*, 177.

117 Hannen, 47.

118 *A Perfect Diurnall of Some Passages and Proceedings* (London: 18–25 October 1652), 2253; *A Perfect Account* (No. 95. 20–27 Oct. 1652), 754 [E678(25)]; and *Perfect Passages* (No. 71. 20–27 Oct. 1652), 552 [E799(23)].

119 Lamont, 58–9. The protesting English soldier mentioned by name in Lamont's account was Major Butler. This was not the only occasion when Brown and Butler seem to have been at odds. Brown recorded some of the arguments which Major Butler had put forward in *Scripture-Redemption Freed* (1653), 12.

120 Lamont, 58–9

121 James Brown, *Scripture-Redemption Freed from Men's Restrictions* (1653), intro 9.

122 NLS, Wodrow.Qu.XVII, f. 194.

123 Lamont, 58–9.

124 Hannen, 46.

125 NLS, Wodrow.Qu.XVII, f. 221.

126 Dow, 61.

127 *RCGA*, iii:469.

128 Wodrow, *Analecta*, iii:98.

129 NLS, Wod.Qu.XVII, f. 194.

130 *RCME*, i:24–5

131 Hoy, 190.

132 Wodrow, *Analecta*, iii:94.

133 Special Collections of EUL, Laing MSS III.368. Two pages of the public dispute and three letters are missing from both manuscripts, but these portions do not diminish the overall consistency of the dialogue. Wodrow's copy is located in the NLS, Wodrow. Qu.XVII. folios 194–249.

134 Hughes, 'The Pulpit Guarded', 45.

135 Brown, *Scripture-Redemption Freed*, 5–8, 12, 14–15; Lamont, 58–9.

136 Wodrow.Qu.XVII, f. 194.

137 Wodrow.Qu.XVII, ff. 195–6.

138 Wodrow.Qu.XVII, f. 194

139 Wodrow.Qu.XVII, f. 194.
140 Wodrow.Qu.XVII, f. 195.
141 Wodrow.Qu.XVII, f. 199.
142 Wodrow.Qu.XVII, f. 199.
143 Wodrow.Qu.XVII, f. 199.
144 Wodrow.Qu.XVII, f. 199.
145 Wodrow.Qu.XVII, f. 199.
146 'I will give the answer for you, seing you cannot; I say the apostle speaks to the Romans as a people in covenant with God, in a church=state as beleivers and professours; but that he doth not lay the weight of giving them all things on that, but on Christ's delivering himself up to death for them', (Wodrow.Qu.XVII, f. 202).
147 Wodrow.Qu.XVII, f. 204.
148 Wodrow.Qu.XVII, f. 200.
149 Wodrow.Qu.XVII, f. 203.
150 Wodrow.Qu.XVII, f. 203.
151 Wodrow.Qu.XVII, f. 208.
152 Wodrow.Qu.XVII, f. 209.
153 Wodrow.Qu.XVII, f. 210–11.
154 Wodrow.Qu.XVII, f. 212.
155 Wodrow.Qu.XVII, f. 213.
156 Hoy, 193–4.
157 Wodrow.Qu.XVII, f. 214.
158 Wodrow.Qu.XVII, f. 219.
159 Wodrow.Qu.XVII, f. 219.
160 'In debating with any person, (Guthrie) was most calm, and not in the least passionat; and if he observed any heat or passion break forth, he would have said, "We must now give it over; for if we turn any way passionat, the true end of this present exercise is entirely lost".' Wodrow, *Analecta*, iii:94–5.
161 Wodrow.Qu.XVII, f. 218.
162 Wodrow.Qu.XVII, f. 219.
163 Wodrow.Qu.XVII, f. 220.
164 Wodrow.Qu.XVII, f. 221
165 Wodrow.Qu.XVII, f. 221.
166 Wodrow.Qu.XVII, f. 221–2.
167 Wodrow.Qu.XVII, f. 222.
168 Wodrow.Qu.XVII, f. 213. Due to an error in the numbering of the folios in the Wodrow manuscript, after folio 222 the numbering begins again with 213.
169 Wodrow.Qu.XVII, f. 213.
170 Wodrow.Qu.XVII, f. 213.
171 Brown had apparently been accused of Arminianism before, because in his work *Scripture-Redemption Freed* he states 'for my part I never read his (Arminius') works as the searcher of hearts doth know' (Brown, *Scripture-Redemption Freed*, 76).
172 Wodrow.Qu.XVII, f. 215.
173 Wodrow.Qu.XVII, f. 216.
174 Wodrow.Qu.XVII, f. 216.
175 Wodrow.Qu.XVII, f. 218.
176 Wodrow.Qu.XVII, f. 218.
177 Wodrow.Qu.XVII, f. 219.
178 Wodrow.Qu.XVII, f. 222.
179 Wodrow.Qu.XVII, f. 222–3. Italics for emphasis are my own.
180 For the tensions between factions within the Kirk in Stirling see: R. Renwick, ed., *Extracts from the Records of the Royal Burgh of Stirling, A.D. 1519–1666* (Glasgow, 1887), 220–7; *RCME*, ii:24n, 25–9, 31–3; *FES*, iv:319, 324.
181 Whitelocke, iii:442
182 J. C. Davis 'Against Formality: One Aspect of the English Revolution', *TRHS*, 6th series, 3 (1993), 265–88.
183 *RHCA*, 565.

184 B. Worden, 'Toleration and the Cromwellian Protectorate', in W.J.Sheils, ed., *Persecution and Toleration* (London, 1984), 210–11.

185 Wodrow, *Analecta*, iii:98; NCL, MSS CRA 1, ii:420; John Howie, *The Scots Worthies*, 367; Balfour, iv:298; Baillie, *L & J*, iii:165–6, 168.

Chapter 3

1 Thomas Wood, *The Dead-Man's Testament: or, A Letter Written to All the Saints of God in Scotland, Fellow-Heirs of the Blessing with Those in England* (Leith: Evan Tyler, 1651); Nicholas Lockyer, *A Litle Stone Out of the Mountain* (Leith: Evan Tyler, 1652).

2 From Wood's dedication to the Earl of Cassilis in: James Wood, *A Little Stone Pretended to be Out of the Mountain, Tried and Found to be Counterfeit* (Edinburgh: Andro Anderson, 1654), ded. 2.

3 W.M. Clyde, *The Struggle for the Freedom of the Press from Caxton to Cromwell* (London, 1934), 228–30; Jason Peacey, 'Cromwellian England: A Propaganda State?', *History*, 91(2006), 176–99, 184.

4 Nothing was printed by Gideon Lithgow or the heirs of George Anderson until 1652. In 1653 Andrew Anderson, the son of George, replaced the imprint of 'The Heirs of George Anderson'. All of these printers were based in Edinburgh, until Andrew Anderson moved to Glasgow in 1657. Tyler's last imprint in Scotland before the restoration appeared in 1653.

5 A.J. Mann, *The Scottish Book Trade 1500–1720: Print Commerce and Print Control in Early Modern Scotland* (East Linton, 2000), 146.

6 Dow, 35.

7 H.R. Trevor-Roper, 'Scotland and the Puritan Revolution', *Religion, the Reformation and Social Change* (London, 1972), 411.

8 Dow, 32.

9 *RCME*, i:3.

10 *RCME*, i:32.

11 Oliver Cromwell, *By His Excellency. Whereas it Hath Pleased God by His Gracious Providence and Goodnesse, to Put the City of Edinburgh and Towne of Leith Under My Power* ([Edinburgh], 1650).

12 Nicoll, 23.

13 Stevenson, 'A Revolutionary Regime and the Press', XV:333.

14 Stevenson, 'A Revolutionary Regime and the Press', XV:334.

15 *CSPD*, 1651:65.

16 J.C. Irons, *Leith and its Antiquities* (Edinburgh, 1897), ii:122; *S & C*, 316; *Mercurius Scoticus*, 22–30 July 1651.

17 *The King of Scotlands Negociations at Rome for Assistance Against the Common-Wealth of England, As Also Severall Letters of the Chancellour of Scotland to the King Since His Coming Into Scotland, Taken in His Cabinet at the Late Fight Neer Dunbar* (Edinburgh: Evan Tyler, 1650).

18 William Dell, *Right Reformation: Or, The Reformation of the Church af the New Testament Represented in Gospel-Light* (Edinburgh: Evan Tyler, 1650), 5–6.

19 In New England it was a different story, where Independents adhered to a strict discipline enforced by civil magistrates which rivalled Scotland's Presbytery for vigilence in stamping out heresy. See: D.F Chatfield, 'The Congregationalists of New England and its Repercussions on England and Scotland' (PhD, University of Edinburgh, 1964), 262, 265–9.

20 Dell, *Right Reformation*, 21.

21 Dell, *Right Reformation*, 9.

22 John Owen, *The Branch of the Lord* (Edinburgh: Evan Tyler, 1650). The epistle dedicatory written by John Owen was addressed to Cromwell and dated Edinburgh, November 26, 1650.

23 Owen, *The Branch of the Lord*, 30.

24 Owen, *The Branch of the Lord*, 42.

25 Dow, 27.

26 *Mercurius Politicus*, (23–30 Oct. 1651), 1161 [E644:5].

27 J. Chalmers, *An Historical Account of Printing in Scotland*, i:f. 282.

28 Chalmers, *An Historical Account*, i:f. 282.

29 I have cross-referenced those men recorded in Furgol's *A Regimental History of the Covenanting Armies* as holding the rank of lieutenant-colonel with the lists of men appointed to the Committee of Estates (*APS*, vi,ii:536ff, 631ff) and compiled a list of seventeen names: Walter Scott, William Scott, James Arnot, Sir John Brown of Fordell, Thomas Bruce, John Cockburn of Ormiston, William Dick, James Fraser of Brea, James Hackett, Hew Montgomerie, Sir Charles Erskine, Arthur Forbes, Alexander Ingliston of Ingliston, William Ker of Newtowne, Viscount Newburgh, Sir Andrew Ker and David Weymes. The most likely of these men to have composed this work are those who served on the committee in 1649 but were not readmitted in December 1650, for by this time he would most likely have begun to favour the English. Men who served in 1649 but were not readmitted in Dec. 1650 were: Walter Scott, William Scott, James Arnot, Sir John Brown, Thomas Bruce, John Cockburn, James Fraser, James Hackett, Arthur Forbes, Alexander Ingliston, William Ker and Andrew Ker. However, most of these men went on to serve the English regime in some form or another, therefore it is extremely difficult to pinpoint one individual as being the likely author.

30 This collusion refers to the Whiggamore Raid in which the radical party in the Kirk came into power.

31 *A Word of Advertisement*, 10–11.

32 *A Word of Advertisement*, 16, 17–18.

33 *A Word of Advertisement*, 14–15.

34 *A Word of Advertisement*, 16–17.

35 It should be noted that these are the three primary reasons given in: England and Wales, Parliament, *Declaration of the Parliament of England* (1650), 6–7.

36 *A Word of Advertisement*, 21–2.

37 Thomas Wood, *The Dead-Man's Testament* (Leith: Evan Tyler, 1651).

38 *RHCA*, 389.

39 Dundas, *A Few Words of Truth*, 8.

40 *RCGA*, i:47.

41 Dundas, *A Few Words of Truth*, 8. This must have occurred in about 1649, since Dundas claims Wood died two years later.

42 NLS, 1.337.

43 Burnet, *Quakerism*, 13.

44 Wood's blindness must have set in during the final two years of his life, as Dundas makes no mention of the infirmity.

45 Wood, *The Dead-Man's Testament*, 16.

46 Wood, *The Dead-Man's Testament*, 4, 5.

47 Wood, *The Dead-Man's Testament*, 6.

48 Wood, *The Dead-Man's Testament*, 8.

49 Wood, *The Dead-Man's Testament*, 10.

50 Wood, *The Dead-Man's Testament*, 11.

51 Wood, *The Dead-Man's Testament*, 15.

52 D.F. Chatfield, 'The Congregationalists of New England', 46.

53 James Durham, *A dying man's testament to the Church of Scotland, or, A treatise concerning scandal divided into four parts* (Edinburgh: Christopher Higgins, 1659). Durham argues throughout the third section that toleration has historically proven to destroy the Church and contends that magistrates have an obligation to oppose error (154–5, 190–2, 194–201, 240–8).

54 *To the Very Honorable the Representative of the Common-wealth. The Humble Petition and Remonstrance of Such in Scotland* (Leith: Evan Tyler, 1652).

55 The only known surviving copy is held in the NLS: Ry.1.1.73. It appears to be the printer's proof.

56 For a discussion of authorship see chapter 4 in this volume. Nicoll, 63; Row, *Life of*

Blair, 289; Dow, 29; Holfelder, 144.

57 Nicoll, 65.

58 Nicoll, 79.

59 Lamont, 37.

60 *S & C*, 315.

61 C. Nelson and M. Seccombe, *British Newspapers and Periodicals, 1641–1700* (New York, 1987), 56. The journal was reprinted in Leith from 15 March 1652 until 4 January 1653.

62 Printing of *Mercurius Politicus* moved to Edinburgh in 1654 and continued to be printed until 11 April 1660, when its name changed to *Mercurius Publicus* (Nelson and Seccombe, *British Newspapers and Periodicals*, 242). George Chalmers, and others, have incorrectly recorded the starting date to be October 1653 (George Chalmers, *The Life of Thomas Ruddiman* (London and Edinburgh, 1794), 117).

63 Seymour, 60, 408.

64 *L&J*, iii:256; Peacey, 'Cromwellian England', 198.

65 England and Wales, Parliament, Commissioners for Ordering and Managing Affairs in Scotland. *By the Commissioners of the Parliament of the Common-Wealth of England, for ordering and managing affairs in Scotland. The Parliament of the Common-Wealth of England, having taken the settlement of Scotland into their serious consideration* (Leith: Evan Tyler, 1651) [February, 1652].

66 England and Wales, Parliament, Commissioners for Ordering and Managing Affairs in Scotland, *By the Commissioners of the Parliament of the Common-Wealth of England, for ordering and managing affairs in Scotland. Although the Parliament of the Common-Wealth of England, in their declaration, concerning the settlement of Scotland* (Leith: Evan Tyler, 1651) [February, 1652].

67 See pp. 50–1 of this volume.

68 Seymour, 79; J.F. Wilson notes that very few sermons preached to the Long Parliament between 1649 and 1653 were actually printed (Wilson, *Pulpit in Parliament*, 274n).

69 John Owen, *The Advantage of the Kingdome of Christ* (Leith: Evan Tyler, 1652).

70 Owen, *The Advantage*, 9–10.

71 Owen, *The Advantage*, 12.

72 Owen, *The Advantage*, 10.

73 Peter Sterry, *England's Deliverance from the Northern Presbytery* (Leith: Evan Tyler, 1652).

74 Sterry, *England's Deliverance*, 13.

75 Sterry, *England's Deliverance*, 8.

76 Sterry, *England's Deliverance*, 10.

77 Sterry, *England's Deliverance*, 15–16.

78 Sterry, *England's Deliverance*, 17.

79 Sterry, *England's Deliverance*, 18.

80 Sterry, *England's Deliverance*, 19.

81 Sterry, *England's Deliverance*, 23.

82 Sterry, *England's Deliverance*, 14.

83 *Mercurius Politicus*. (April 15–22, 1652), 1551 [E660(5)].

84 *The Weekly Intelligencer of the Commonwealth*. (23–30 March 1652), 400 [E658(8)].

85 Nicholas Lockyer, *A Little Stone Out of the Mountain* (Leith: Evan Tyler, 1652). The sermon takes its title from Daniel 2:34, in which a small bit of stone is cut from a mountain 'without hands' and this grows into a mountain in its own right. Lockyer interprets this as the formation of Independent congregations out of degenerate churches. Due to the limitations of this book it would be impossible to include a complete study of how Daniel 2:34 was used in seventeenth-century scholarship, but Calvin addressed the verse in the ninth lecture of his *Commentaries on the Book of the Prophet Daniel*. Here he identifies the stone as being Christ himself, rather than the Church. The earliest use I have found in which the 'stone' is identified as the Church is in Roger Williams *The Bloudy Tenant, of Persecution* (London, 1644). For Williams the stone is the 'Christian Church, or Kingdome of Saints' and the mountain the civil

state or 'Roman Empire' (p. 89). While this is the earliest precedent I have found for this use of the verse by Independents, the phrase was subsequently used several times in works produced in Scotland: *Mercurius Politicus* (12–19 August 1652), p. 1806 [E674:6]; *To the Very Honorable the Representative of the Commonwealth* (Leith, 1652); Francis Howgill, *To All You Commanders and Officers of the Army in Scotland* (Leith, 1657), 4.

86 Baillie, *L & J*, iii:178.
87 Baillie, *L & J*, iii:401.
88 J. Chalmers, *An Historical Account of Printing in Scotland*, i:f285.
89 Lockyer, e.d. 2.
90 Lockyer, e.d. 5–6.
91 Lockyer, to the reader, 3–4.
92 Samuel Rutherford, *A Survey of the Spiritual Antichrist* (London, 1648), 250–1.
93 Lockyer, 47–51.
94 Lockyer, pre. 6.
95 Lockyer, 1.
96 Lockyer, 2.
97 Lockyer, 46–7. Gal. 1:22: 'I was still unknown by sight to the Christian congregations in Judaea' (*RSV*).
98 NLS. Wod.Qu.XVII, f. 214.
99 Lockyer, 58–60.
100 Lockyer, 131.
101 Lockyer, 75.
102 Lockyer, 82–3.
103 Lockyer, 68.
104 Lockyer, 72–3.
105 Lockyer, 64.
106 Lockyer, 88.
107 Lockyer, 65.
108 Lockyer's position advances to a degree of 'democracy' that New England Independents had shied away from. For an explanation of the divergence between England and New England Independents on this point, see: Chatfield, 'The Congregationalists of New England and its Repercussions on England and Scotland, 1641–2', 32–42, 263–72, 274–5.
109 See p. 82 of this volume.
110 Lockyer, 99.
111 Chatfield, 42.
112 Lockyer, 109.
113 Lockyer, 111.
114 Lockyer, 119.
115 Nicoll, 71–2.
116 John Norton, *Responsio ad totam quaestionum syllogen à clarissimo viro domino Guilielmo Apollonio* (Londini, 1648); John Cotton, *The way of Congregational churches cleared in two treatises* (London, 1648); John Allin and Thomas Shepard, *A defence of the answer made unto the nine questions or positions sent from New-England, against the reply thereto by that reverend servant of Christ, Mr. John Ball, entituled, A tryall of the new church-way in New-England and in old wherin* (London, 1648); Thomas Hooker, *A Survey of the Summe of Church Discipline* (London, 1648).
117 The volume measures approx. 3˝ x 1.5˝.
118 *Mercurius Britannicus*, No. 19 (23–30 Nov. 1652), 290 [E801(4)].
119 James Guthrie, *A Treatise of Ruling Elders and Deacons* (Edinburgh: n.a., 1652). While censorship began to lessen, it was not excessively loose. Guthrie's work was published without an imprint by the printer, perhaps a sign that times were tense.
120 Guthrie, *A Treatise of Ruling Elders*, 13.
121 Guthrie, *A Treatise of Ruling Elders*, 25.
122 Guthrie, *A Treatise of Ruling Elders*, 23.

123 Guthrie, *A Treatise of Ruling Elders*, 26: 2 Chron. 19:8; Jer. 29:1; Matt. 16:21–3; Acts 4:5. Presbyterians were not afraid to use Patristic sources to support their claims. They did so excessively in the struggle against Episcopacy in the 1620s and 1630s. See: David G. Mullan, ed., *Religious Controversy in Scotland, 1625–1639* (Edinburgh, 1998).
124 Guthrie, *A Treatise of Ruling Elders*, 56.
125 Guthrie, *A Treatise of Ruling Elders*, 57.
126 NLS, Wod.Fol.XXX.(26), f.96.
127 Baillie, *L & J*, iii:214. There is some indication that James Wood was the semi-official (or at least chosen) author of polemics for the Resolutioners during the Interregnum. In the same letter encouraging him to speed up his reply to Lockyer, Baillie also called on him to reply to James Guthrie's *The Nullity of the Pretended Assembly at St. Andrews* (Leith: Evan Tyler, 1652). Baillie, *L & J*, iii:213–14; Peacey, *Politicians and Pamphleteers*, 206.
128 James Wood, *A Little Stone Pretended to be Out of the Mountain, Tried and Found to be Counterfeit* (Edinburgh: Andro Anderson, 1654), ded. 9. The Aberdeen Independents will be addressed in chapter 4.
129 Wariston, ii:232–3.
130 Doctrinally, the Kirk and New England Independents differed little other than in their interpretations of proper church polity. The theology of both was highly Calvinist, Predestinarian, and Federal, and unlike the English Independents present in Scotland during the Interregnum, both abhorred toleration not only of those of different 'denominations' but also of slight variances in doctrine. Furthermore, both Scottish Presbyterians and New England Independents agreed that the magistrate had an obligation to intervene in matters of heresy and corrupt doctrine. See Chatfield, 'The Congregationalists of New England'; Willam Bartlet, *IXNOΓPAΦIA. Or a Model of the Primitive Congregational Way* (1647), 102–4; Wood, *A Little Stone Pretended*, ded. 5–7.
131 Wood, *A Little Stone Pretended*, 1.
132 Wood, *A Little Stone Pretended*, 5.
133 Wood, *A Little Stone Pretended*, 39.
134 Wood, *A Little Stone Pretended*, 37.
135 Wood, *A Little Stone Pretended*, 217, 221.
136 Wood, *A Little Stone Pretended*, 104.
137 Patrick Little, 'Putting the Protector back in the Protectorate', *BBC History*, 8.1 (2007), 12–16.
138 Worden, 'Toleration', 210–11; Abbott, *Cromwell*, i:677.
139 Worden, 'Toleration', 210–11. He is quoting *A Declaration of the Army of England upon their March into Scotland*; Abbott, *Cromwell*, i:283–9.
140 *Clarke Papers*, iii:73.
141 Firth, *Oliver Cromwell and the Rule of the Puritans in England*, 300–1. Whether this statement can actually be attributed to Cromwell is a matter of conjecture. Certainly posterity has continued to accept the link, but many scholars remain unconvinced. Geoffrey Nuttall identifies the original source of the statement as Roger Williams ('Presbyterians and Independents Some Movements for Unity 300 years ago', *JPHSE*, 10 (1952), 5).
142 NCL, MSS MYL, f. 757; Dow, 196.
143 This resolution will be addressed in chapter 4.
144 J.K. Hewison, *The Covenanters*, 2 vols (Glasgow, 1913), ii:58.
145 J. Buckroyd, 'Lord Broghill and the Scottish Church, 1655–1656', *JEH*, 27 (1976), 359–68.
146 EUL, La.I.321(5).
147 Buckroyd, 368.
148 See chapter 4 in this volume.
149 Firth, *Oliver Cromwell and the Rule of the Puritans in England*, 326–7.
150 Wariston, ii:199.
151 'Diurnal of Occurences in Scotland', *The Spottiswoode Micellany*, ed., James Maidment (Edinburgh, 1845), ii:174.

152 John Goodwin, *Synkretismos* (London: J. Macock, 1653), 4–5.

153 Maidment, 'Diurnal of Occurences in Scotland', 194; Marchamont Nedham, *A true state of the case of the Commonwealth of England, Scotland and Ireland, and the dominions thereto belonging; In reference to the late established government by a Protector and a Parliament* (London: Thomas Newcomb, 1653).

154 David L. Smith, 'Oliver Cromwell, the First Protectoral Parliament and Religious Reform', *Cromwell and the Interregnum*, Essential Readings in History (Oxford: Blackwell, 2003), 176.

155 Maclehose, *The Glasgow University Press 1638–1931*, 40; *Scots Acts, 1648–1660*, vol. vi, ii: 827.

156 Samuel Rutherford, *The Covenant of Life Opened: or, A Treatise of the Covenant of Grace* (Edinburgh: A. Anderson, 1655).

157 John Gilpin, *The Quakers Shaken, or, A Discovery of the Errours of That Sect* (Edinburgh, 1655); John Stalham, *Contradictions of the Quakers (so Called) to the Scriptures of God* (Edinburgh,1655); James Brown, *Antichrist (in Spirit) Unmasked* (Edinburgh: Christopher Higgins, 1657).

158 Jonas Dell, *Forms the Pillars of Antichrist* (London, 1656); Francis Howgill, *To All You Commanders and Officers of the Army* (Leith, 1657).

159 *Love the Precious Ointment, That Flowes Down from the Head Christ Jesus, to All His Members; and Makes Them Dwell Together in Unity* (Leith, 1654).

160 In the catalogues of most libraries which possess a copy of this work it is listed as a Catholic apologetic. Robert Mylne, however, in one of the National Library of Scotland's copies made the proper recognition of the text as a Quaker publication (NLS 1.337).

161 D.M. Butler, *George Fox in Scotland*, 21.

162 England and Wales. Parliament, *An Act for Discovering, Convicting, and Redressing of Popish Recusssants* (Aberdeen: James Brown, 1657).

163 *APS*, vi, ii: 767; William Guild, *Anti-Christ Pointed and Painted Out in His True Colours* (Aberdeen: James Brown, 1655); William Guild, *An answer to a popish pamphlet* (Aberdeen: James Brown, 1656); William Guild, *The noveltie of poperied discovered and chieflie proven by Romanists out of themselves* (Aberdeen: James Brown, 1656). For the increase of Roman Catholicism see: Baillie. *L & J*, iii:291, 304; Jaffray, 38–41; M.V. Hay, *The Blair Papers* (1929), 187–8; C. Baxter, *Synod of Fife*, 175; Row, *Life of Blair*, 327–8; Firth, *Last Years of the Protectorate*, ii:105–6; Clarke MSS, 1/12: f. 93; Brodie, 147; Whitelocke, iv:229; Stuart, *Strathbogie*; Nicoll, 178; *RCME*, i:84; Cramond, *Extracts from the Records of the Synod of Moray* (Elgin, 1906). In 1653 a Jesuit priest was tried in Edinburgh (Whitelocke, iii:3). In Oct. 1657 the Synod of Aberdeen appointed Alexander Scrogie to go to Edinburgh to inform the Council of Estate of the rapid growth of 'poperie' in the north-east of Scotland (Stuart, *Aberdeen*, 238).

164 Peter F. Anson, *Underground Catholicism in Scotland*, 57–9.

165 Thurloe, iv:700; *S & P*, 329–30; Dow, 205.

166 Carter, 'The Presbyterian–Independent Controversy', ii:10: 'I spoke with some chiefe of Bolton, whose desire to have no erroneous Authors Or that have any tincture thereof, though mixed with never so much other good matter for feare of infection; Particularly by all meanes they would Not have One Independent writer in all the number, by any meanes how excellent soever for feare of any of there falling in love with the way for the man's sake. This means I have purposely omitted many excellent authors e.g. Tho. Goodwine, Mr. Burroughs, Greenhill, Carul [Caryl], Bridge ... Shepheard. As alsoe upon the other accompt Dr. Jerem. Taylor, Hammond, Chillingworth, Baxter' (R. C. Christie, *The Old Church and School Libraries of Lancashire* (1885), p. 23, dated 5 April 1655).

167 J.K. Hewison, *The Covenanters*, 2 vols (Glasgow, 1913), ii:58.

168 Davis, 'Against Formality', 265–88.

169 Fraser, *Chronicles*, 393.

Chapter 4

1 Declaration in favour of the 'Congregational Way' composed in Aberdeen on 24 May 1652. NLS, Wod.Fol.XXX.(24), f. 83–4 and printed in Alexander Jaffray, *The Diary of Alexander Jaffray*, ed., John Barclay, 3rd edn (Aberdeen, 1856), 167–71.
2 Richard Baxter, Baxter: *A Holy Commonwealth* (Cambridge, 1994), 134.
3 Lamont, 41.
4 Nicoll, 26; *APS*, vi:569, 573; David Stevenson, 'Deposition of Ministers in the Church of Scotland, 1638–1651', *Church History*, 44 (1975), 321–35, 335.
5 *RCGA*, iii:271.
6 Craven, *History of the Church in Orkney, 1558–1662* (Kirkwall, 1897), 218.
7 J. Smith, *The Church in Orkney* (Kirkwall, 1907), 148.
8 Craven, *Orkney*, 221.
9 NLS, Wod.Fol.XXX.(27), f 106.
10 *Mercurius Politicus* (11–18 March 1652), 1470 [E656:20].
11 Cramond, *Moray*, 100.
12 *FES*, iv:258, 268.
13 A. B., *A Fight at Dunin in Scotland, Between the Scots Women and the Presbyterian Kirkmen* (Edinburgh, 1652). Also brief accounts exist in: Whitelocke, iii:432–3 and *Mercurius Politicus* (17–24 June 1652), 1682, 1686–7 [E668:13]. For a Presbyterian account, see: J. Wilson, *Dunning: Its Parochial History, with Notes, Antiquarian, Ecclesiastical, Baronial, and Miscellaneous*, 2nd edn (Crieff, 1906), 40ff.
14 *A Fight at Dunin in Scotland*, 3, 5.
15 *Mercurius Politicus*, 1687.
16 Stevenson, 'Deposition of Ministers', 321–35.
17 Stevenson, 'Deposition of Ministers', 324.
18 Stevenson, 'Deposition of Ministers', 329; Morrill, *The Nature of the English Revolution*, 115–16.
19 W.K. Tweedie, ed., *Select Biographies* (Edinburgh, 1845), i:331; Coffey, 219.
20 Nicoll, 38–9.
21 Nicoll, 48.
22 *RCGA*, iii:343.
23 NLS, Wod.Fol.XXXI.(37).
24 For an in-depth study of taxation under the Covenanters see: L.A.M. Stewart, *Urban Politics and the British Civil Wars: Edinburgh, 1617–53*, The Northern World (Leiden, 2006).
25 Sir Thomas Urquhart, *Ekskybalauron: or, The discovery of a most exquisite jewel* (London, 1653), epistle liminary.
26 J. Paterson, *History of the Counties of Ayr and Wigton*, 2 vols (Edinburgh, 1864), i:clxxxv.
27 Whitelocke, iii:387.
28 A list of some of the ministers and ruling elders present is given in: *Mercurius Politicus* (9–16 Oct. 1651), 1134 [E643:16].
29 Lamont, 35.
30 Nicoll, 61–2, 63.
31 *Mercurius Politicus*, 7 Oct. 1651, 1138.
32 Provost in 1636, '38, '41, '49, and '51 (Kennedy, *Annals of Aberdeen*, 232).
33 According to Balfour, the release of Jaffray and John Carstairs was arranged on 22 Nov. 1650, which would have made his incarceration less than three months (Balfour, iv:168).
34 John Barclay, the editor of Jaffray's journal, also thinks there is reason to believe from his developing advocacy of toleration that Jaffray came directly under the influence of William Dell, Fairfax's chaplain and major proponent of religious toleration (Jaffray, 172–3).
35 Jaffray, 58–59.
36 P.J. Anderson, ed., *Fasti Academiae Mariscallanae Aberdonensis, 1593–1860* (Aberdeen, 1898), 34–5, 51, 211.

37 Lamont, 47; Spottiswoode, *The History of the Church and State of Scotland*, app. 25.
38 Anderson, *Fasti Academiae Mariscallanae Aberdonensis*, 28, 53.
39 Anderson, *Fasti*, 36.
40 Jaffray, 59
41 Dow, 26–7
42 Wariston, ii:147; Jaffray, 60.
43 Jaffray, 61–3.
44 Jaffray, 60.
45 Wariston, ii:148–9; Sir Archibald Johnston of Wariston, *Causes of the Lords Wrath Against Scotland: Manifested in His Sad Late Dispensations; Whereunto Is Added a Paper, Particularly Holding Forth the Sins of the Ministery* (Edinburgh: by the heirs of Geo. Anderson, 1653).
46 Baillie, *L & J*, iii:175–6.
47 Burnet, *Burnet's History of His Own Time*, 41; W. Stephen, *History of the Church of Scotland* (Edinburgh, 1896), i:325–6; L.E. Schmidt, *Holy Fairs*, 2nd edn (Grand Rapids, 32–41.
48 L.A. Yeoman, 'Heart-Work: Emotion, Empowerment and Authority in Covenanting Times' (PhD, University of St Andrews, 1991), ix.
49 Yeoman, 'Heart-Work', 35. Editions of Shepard's works were printed in Edinburgh in 1645, 1647 and 1650 (see H.G. Aldis, *List of Books Printed in Scotland Before 1700* (Edinburgh, 1970)).
50 D. Stevenson, 'Conventicles in the Kirk, 1619–37', *RSCHS*, 18 (1974), 99–114.
51 See pp. 151–3 of this volume.
52 Yeoman, 'Heart-Work', 25.
53 Baillie, *L & J*, iii:276.
54 Holfelder suggests that this paper was given in to a meeting in Kilmarnock, but gives no citation supporting grounds for making this claim (Holfelder, 144; he cites: Balfour, iv:330–3; Peterkin, 645–6). The only evidence I can find is that a supplication advancing similar ideas was composed by a 'group of sectaries' who also produced *Overtures to the Right Honorable* (the 'fifteen overtures') and *To the Very Honorable the Representative of the Common-Vvealth* (Leith: Evan Tyler, 1652) sent to the 'West' (Hoy, 182n). While this does not prevent the author of the 'twelve-headed' from being numbered among the group who composed the other tracts, the 'twelve-headed' paper referred to by Holfelder has a single author according to Balfour, Peterkin and Nicoll (67). According to Balfour, from whom Peterkin drew his information, the paper was submitted to several gatherings, but he does not indicate any in particular except the Protestor meeting at Edinburgh. Nicoll additionally claims the paper by 'ane godly Scott' (certainly the 'twelve headed' paper) was also submitted to the commissioners of the General Assembly (Resolutioners) in Edinburgh. So it seems that Holfelder confused the 'twelve headed' paper written by a single anonymous author with another paper written by a group of 'Scottish Sectaries'. A discussion of possible adherents to this group is found in the following pages.
55 Balfour, iv:330–3; Peterkin, 645–6.
56 Nicoll, 67; Peterkin, 645–6; Balfour, iv:330–3.
57 Hoy, 182n.
58 Nicoll, 63; Row, *Life of Blair*, 289; Dow, 28; Holfelder, 144.
59 Hoy, 182n. Hoy claims that the text of these fifteen overtures has been preserved in Wodrow's manuscript collection now housed in the NLS. His citation form (Wod. Col., Mil. Col, LS I 6,10) is archaic and predates their transfer from the collections of the Church of Scotland to the Scottish Records Office. The document has since been lost. For this reason we are left to rely on Hoy's citation of the source.
60 Row, *Life of Blair*, 289.
61 'The "certain" godly' refers to those bearing outward signs indicative of election.
62 Hoy, 182n.
63 Both Protesters and Resolutioners referred to the authors of this work as 'sectaries' for adopting the principles of the 'sectarian army'. Hoy uses the phrase 'Sectarian Scots'.

My use of 'Scottish Sectaries' here is an attempt to maintain the label used by their contemporaries, while at the same time identifying them as Scots who have accepted English ideologies.

64 Hoy, 186–7.
65 The portion of Wariston's diary from the end of October 1651 until April 1652 has not been preserved. However, Wariston's failure to mention the papers of the Scottish Sectarians in his large response to the Aberdeen Independents is fairly conclusive that they had no common links.
66 Nicoll, 52; *RCGA*, iii:377.
67 Row, *Life of Blair*, 250–4, 269; RCGA, iii:169–70, 243; Abbott, ii:366–74; Jaffray, 58–9; Balfour, iv:238–40, 246; Laing, ed., *Correspondence of Sir Robert Kerr*, ii:325–6; NLS, Wod.Qu.XXXVII, ff 31–2; Holfelder, 95; Coffey, 221; Stevenson, *Counter-Revolution*, 195–6.
68 *Clarke Papers V*, 56.
69 Balfour, iv:79–80; Wariston, ii:169; *APS*, vi, ii:751.
70 Nicoll, 124.
71 Row, *Life of Blair*, 338.
72 Maidment, *Historical Fragments*, 5:30; Row, *Life of Blair*, 250, 270; Whitelocke, iii:255–8; Lamont, 26–7.
73 Balfour, iv:271.
74 *RCGA*, iii:377.
75 *RCGA*, iii:437–8. According the kirk session records of Elgin, Govan and Strachan were excommunicated as well by 24 August 1651 (Cramon, *Elgin*, 279).
76 Row, *Life of Blair*, 253; *RCGA*, iii:378
77 *RCGA*, iii:378.
78 Balfour, iv:267; *ODNB*, 'Strachan, Archibald'. A jotting on the back of a manuscript in the Wodrow Collection suggests it may be part of the discourse between Strachan, Gilbert Ker and Cromwell (Wod.Fol.XXXI.(39)).
79 *ODNB*, 'Strachan'.
80 Balfour, iv:240; *Some Sober Animadversions, Humbly, and In All Meekness Offered to the Consideration of All Who Truly Fear the Lord* (London, 1659), 15.
81 Balfour, iv:250.
82 Dundas, *A Few Words of Truth*, 6–8.
83 Dundas, *A Few Words of Truth*, 9.
84 Balfour, iv:297. Only a late pardon from Charles II prevented his execution (Balfour, iv:299).
85 Hoy, 179; D. Stevenson, 'Conventicles in the Kirk, 1619–37', 101–5.
86 James Bulloch, 'Conformist and Nonconformists', *Transactions of the East Lothian Antiquaries and Field Naturalists' Society*, 8 (1960), 70–84.
87 Wariston, ii:119.
88 Brodie, 189.
89 *RCME*, i:1–12; Whitelocke, iii:389; NLS, Wod.Fol.XXX.(19).
90 Row, *Life of Blair*, 291.
91 Balfour, iv:348.
92 Row, *Life of Blair*, 291; Hoy, 183n; *To the Very Honorable the Representative of the Common-Vvealth. The Humble Petition and Remonstrance of Such in Scotland* (Leith: Evan Tyler, 1652). Only one copy survives in the NLS: Ry.1.1.73, which has been reproduced on microfilm: Mf.SP.141(19).
93 See chapter 3 in this volume.
94 Whitelocke, iii:387.
95 Nicoll, 77–8.
96 Perhaps John Waugh, minster of Bo'ness from 1648 to 1670. Arrested for praying for the king in 1654 (*FES*, i:195). If this account is correct, he abandoned his parish charge at least for a period of time.
97 *S & C*, 345.
98 *S & C*, 31; Dow, 27.
99 *S & C*, 123.

100 *S & C*, 127.

101 Nicoll, 91; Hoy, 185.

102 J. Stuart, ed., *Extracts from the Presbytery Book of Strathbogie 1631–1654* (Aberdeen, 1843).

103 Stuart, *Strathbogie*, 222.

104 See pp. 121–2 of this volume.

105 Stuart, *Strathbogie*, 220.

106 Stuart, *Strathbogie* 219.

107 Cramond, *Moray*, 114.

108 Hoy, 185.

109 Todd, *The Culture of Protestantism*, 25.

110 Cramond, *Moray*, 117. This demonstrates a strand of religious dissent long before the family's adoption of Quakerism c.1666.

111 Cramond, *Moray*, 118.

112 H. Escott, *Beacons of Independency: Religion and Life in Strathbogie and Upper Garioch in the Nineteenth Century* (Huntly, 1940).

113 Stuart, *Aberdeen*, 222–3.

114 *Mercurius Politicus* (25 March–1 April 1652), 1493 [E658:13].

115 Nicoll, 94.

116 Nicoll, 94; *FES* i:222.

117 Wariston, ii:169

118 'Sir William Lockhart of Lee', *North British Review*, 36 (February–May 1862), 90–1.

119 James Turner, *Memoirs of His Own Life and Times, 1632–1670*, ed., T. Thomson (Edinburgh, 1829), 78–9; 'Sir William Lockhart of Lee', 91.

120 Baillie, *L & J*, iii:193; Donaldson, 'Schism', 217.

121 *Mercurius Politicus* (24 June–1 July 1652), 1703 [E669:3]; Whitelocke, iii:433.

122 Nicoll, 94; Row, *Life of Blair*, 297; *RCGA*, ii:530.

123 *Perfect Passages* (5–12 Nov. 1652), 571 [E799:33]; *A Perfect Diurnal* (8–15 Nov. 1652), 2290 [E799:35]; James Fergusson, *A Brief Refutation of the Errors of Tolleration, Erastianism, Independency and Separation* (Edinburgh, 1692).

124 Some records report a church in Lenzie, while others mention Kirkintilloch. They are only a mile apart, so it seems likely that they are the same congregation. *S & C*, 265; *Mercurius Politicus* (17–24 Nov.), 2875; Baillie, *L & J*, iii:202, 217, 244; 'Diurnall of Occurences in Scotland' *Spottiswoode Miscellany II*, 140; Holfelder, 182; Baillie, *L & J*, iii:244.

125 Dow, 147, 308. Deposed for immorality in 1658, he fled Scotland and served in the vicarage of Hundon, Suffolk until his removal under the Act of Uniformity (*FES*, ii:33; *Calamy Revised*, 431).

126 Wariston, ii:314.

127 *CSPD*, 1654:195, 450.

128 He was certainly back in Essex by 1657 when he wrote *The Reviler Rebuked* (London, 1657) against Richard Farnsworth's 'attempted answer' *Vindication of the Scriptures against the Scotish Contradictators*. This work by Farnsworth was written in response to Stalham's anti-Quaker tract written in Edinburgh in 1655: John Stalham, *Contradictions of the Quakers* (Edinburgh, 1655).

129 W.L. Sachse, 'The Migration of New Englanders to England', *American Historical Review*, 53 (1948), 267.

130 Thurloe, vii:527. The congregation was not a Baptist congregation.

131 C.S. Terry, ed., *The Cromwellian Union* (Edinburgh, 1902), 99; Laurence, 72; *APS*, vi,ii:747; *CSPD*, 1651–2:191; Nicoll, 91.

132 Laurence, 72, 103, 191.

133 *CSPD*, 1651–2: 610.

134 *APS*, vi,ii:750–1. Samuel Bruen is likely the Samuel Bryan who James Guthrie asked to be a referee were he to take part in another dispute with James Brown (NLS, Wod. Qu.XVII, f. 215–18).

135 Laurence, 152; *ODNB*, 'Mather, Samuel'; Sachse, 'The Migration of New Englanders to England', 267.

136 *APS*, vi,ii:897. Collins also received £200 pounds in 1655, while Beverley only received £80, probably because he received an additional stipend from the gathered congregation.
137 NCL, MSS CRA 1, ii:421.
138 Baillie, *L & J*, iii:322–3; Wariston, iii:34–5; NCL, MSS CRA 1, ii:422; Naismith, *Stonehouse*, 116. For the Quaker account of the providential nature of Charteris' death, see chapter 5.
139 Baillie, *L & J*, iii:lxiv.
140 Baillie, *L & J*, iii:187.
141 *RCGA*, iii:548.
142 *RCGA*, iii:550.
143 A.C. Jonas, 'Extracts from the Parish Records, 1644–1699', *Proceedings of the Society of Antiquaries of Scotland*, 46 (1911–12), 27–52; Baillie, *L & J*, iii:193; Donaldson, 'Schism', 217.
144 See p. xiii of this volume for a map of English garrisons.
145 Stuart, *Aberdeen*, 217
146 Nicoll, 81; *APS*, vi:ii,809.
147 Stuart, *Aberdeen*, 117.
148 *The Weekly Intelligencer of the Commonwealth*, (23–30 March 1652), 400 [E658(8)].
149 *Mercurius Politicus* (25 March–1 April 1652), 1493 [E658(13)].
150 *S & C*, xl; *Several Proceedings in Parliament* (29 April–6 May 1652).
151 Jaffray, 65.
152 Jaffray, 167; Whitelocke, iii:441–2.
153 Jaffray, 168; Wod.Fol.XXX.(24), NLS, f. 83.
154 Jaffray, 168.
155 Jaffray, 168–9.
156 Jaffray, 169.
157 Jaffray, 169; Lockyer, e.d. 5–6.
158 Jaffray, 169.
159 Jaffray, 170; Lockyer, 82–3.
160 Lockyer, e.d. 2.
161 Lockyer, preface, 6; 'to the reader,' 3–4; 126–8.
162 Lockyer, e.d. 5–6.
163 Lockyer, 46–7.
164 Lockyer, 82–3, 92–119.
165 Wod.Fol.XXX.(24), f. 85.
166 Row, *History of the Kirk*, 533.
167 Dundas, *A Few Words of Truth*, 9.
168 In addition to the printed edition of the letter in Row's *History of the Kirk* (533–5) a copy is preserved in manuscript form in EUL, La.I.314a. There has been some conjecture about to whom this letter was addressed. David Laing, the editor of Row's *History of the Kirk*, claims it was directed to one of Row's siblings (p. 534), while the Historical Manuscripts Commission *Report on the Laing Manuscripts Preserved in Edinburgh Library* (London, 1914), ii:270 identifies the recipient as Wariston.
169 Row, *History of the Kirk*, 533.
170 Row, *History of the Kirk*, 534.
171 Church of Scotland, *A Directory for Church-Government* (Edinburgh: Evan Tyler, 1647), 2, 7, 16, 17.
172 Row, *History of the Kirk*, 534.
173 Row, *History of the Kirk*, 536.
174 Row, *History of the Kirk*, 537.
175 Row, *History of the Kirk*, 538–9. Reports circulated in 1652 that Row and Menzies had become Anabaptists and that Row's wife had been 'dipped' or rebaptised (Lamont, 47; Pittiloh, *The Hammer of Persecution*, 12–3). In this letter Row explains that he is aware of the rumours but declares (as of May 1652) they are categorically untrue.
176 Jaffray, 65; Wariston, ii:179.

177 Brodie, 26; Jaffray, 176.
178 Coffey, 222; Rutherford, *Letters*, 704–7. NLS MSS. Wod.Fol.XXX.(26); Wariston, ii:179; Brodie, 22.
179 Rutherford, *Letters*, 706.
180 Rutherford, *Letters*.
181 Jaffray, 65; NLS, Wod.Qu.XXIX(63), f. 178–9. Nevay was the cousin of Jaffray's wife.
182 These letters have only briefly been referred to in the work of Hoy (186–7), but not mentioned at all in Donaldson, 'Schism', 205–19, or Henderson, *RLSCS*, 100–16.
183 Wariston, ii:169.
184 Wariston, ii:173.
185 NLS, Wod.Fol.XXX(24), f. 85. Protesters firmly believed they had not separated from the Kirk. Instead they held that the Resolutioners had stepped out of the Kirk in pursuing the Malignant aims of the king. So Rutherford is imploring Aberdeen's would-be separatists to meet with fellow Protesters again, just as they had the previous October.
186 NLS, Wod.Fol.XXX(24), f. 86; Hoy, 186.
187 Wod.Fol.XXX(24), f. 85; Wariston, ii:169. John Cotton, *The way of Congregational churches cleared in two treatises* (London, 1648); Cotton, John, *Of the holinesse of church-members* (London, 1648); Hooker, Thomas, *A Survey of the Summe of Church Discipline* (London, 1648); John Norton, *Responsio ad totam quaestionum syllogen à clarissimo viro domino Guilielmo Apollonio* (Londini, 1648); Giles Firmin, *Separation examined: or, a treatise vvherein the grounds for separation from the ministry and churches of England are weighed, and found too light* (London, 1652); Thomas Brightman, *A reuelation of the reuelation that is, the reuelation of St. Iohn opened clearely With a logicall resolution and exposition* (Amsterdam, 1615); Francis Johnson, *A treatise of the ministery of the Church of England Wherein is handled this question, whether it be to be separated from, or joyned vnto* (1595); John Ball, *Tryall of the nevv-church vvay in New-England and in old* (London, 1644); Daniel Cawdrey, *The inconsistencie of the independent way, with Scripture and it self* (London, 1651).
188 Dundas, *A Few Words of Truth*, 10.
189 *AGA*, 30.
190 Wod.Fol.XXX(24), f. 86–7.
191 Wod.Fol.XXX(24), f. 89.
192 Wod.Fol.XXX(24), f. 87.
193 Wod.Fol.XXX(24), f. 90.
194 By 'positive evidences' Wariston does not mean a personal narrative of conversion as was required in New England. In fact, the vague nature of the phrase is intentional. Wariston is emphasising the difficulty in defining exact standards for identifying the elect.
195 Wod.Fol.XXX(24), f. 87.
196 Wod.Fol.XXX(24), f. 88, 90.
197 Wod.Fol.XXX(24), f. 86, 88.
198 Wod.Fol.XXX(24), f. 91.
199 Wod.Fol.XXX(24), f. 86; Giles Firmin, *Separation Examined*, 97–9.
200 Wod.Fol.XXX(24), f. 91.
201 'You must put a difference between Churches new erecting, and these in England, which have been Churches for so long; when I raise a house from new from the ground, I may then doe as I please, but if I be mending an old house, I must doe as well as I can, repaire by degrees' (Firmin, *Separation Examined*, 82). S. Hardman Moore, 'Arguing for Peace: Giles Firmin on New England and Godly Union', *Unity and Diversity in the Church*, in R.N. Swanson, ed., *Studies in Church History*, 32 (Oxford, 1996), 257.
202 Wod.Fol.XXX.(26), f. 86, 103.
203 Wariston, ii:174–5.
204 Stuart, *Aberdeen*, 219–20. Four other ministers (Duncan Forbes, Robert Keith, William Ramsay and George Tailifer) submitted an additional paper outlining concerns over the mixture of the 'precious' and the 'vile' at the Lord's Table, but affirmed the form of the Kirk.

205 Jaffray, 65.

206 Wariston, ii:180–1; Jaffray, 65.

207 Jaffray, 65.

208 Wariston, ii:181. An incomplete copy of this paper has been preserved in the Wodrow Collection: 'A Postscript anent the third point', NLS, Wod.Fol.XXX.(23).

209 Maidment, *Historical Fragments*, 24.

210 William Row misidentified the Aberdeen ministers as Row, Menzies and Muir (Row, *Life of Blair*, 297) and others have followed suit (Dow, 60; Holfelder, 176). Muir, however, was an elder, not a minister.

211 Protesters took little heed of Resolutioner censures either. James Guthrie, Patrick Gillespie and James Simpson were all deposed by the General Assembly in 1651, but continued in their ministries (Nicoll, 158).

212 NLS, Wod.Fol.XXX.(26), f. 95, 101.

213 Wod.Fol.XXX.(26), f. 97. He lists the verses as examples of 'all' and 'every' not being used as universal absolutes: Acts 2:41–5, 50; Acts 21:5; Ezek 10:15, 18, 22, 24–5; Deut 29:11–15, 32:11–12; Joel 1:14, 2:1, 13–17; Jer. 43:4–7. Whereas Guthrie used this argument to refute James Brown's doctrine of universal atonement, Wariston uses it to counter the Aberdeen Independents' claim that the term 'all' in reference to the visible church meant that only those showing evidences of election should be constituent members of churches. In these two arguments the Protesters posit the tensions generated by holding doctrines of rigid predestination and of a covenanted state church encompassing the masses.

214 Wod.Fol.XXX.(26), f. 96; Richard Baxter, *Plain Scripture Proof of Infants Church-Membership and Baptism* (London, 1651). It appears Wariston was not quoting from Baxter directly, but summing up the arguments he found in Baxter.

215 Wod.Fol.XXX.(26), f. 96.

216 Wod.Fol.XXX.(26), f. 99.

217 Wod.Fol.XXX.(26), f. 100; D. Korbin, 'The Expansion of the Visible Church in New England: 1629–1650', *Church History*, 36 (1967), 189–209.

218 Wod.Fol.XXX.(26), f. 98.

219 Wod.Fol.XXX.(26), f. 101.

220 The argument over requirements for membership in New England came to a head in 1662 and resulted in the formulation of the 'Half-Way Covenant'. See p. 143 of this volume.

221 Wod.Fol.XXX.(26), f. 95.

222 G.W. Sprott, *The Doctrine of Schism in the Church of Scotland* (Edinburgh, 1902), 1–22.

223 G. Donaldson, 'Schism', 205–19.

224 Wod.Fol.XXX.(26), f. 95.

225 For a study on a similar debate in the New England context, see: E.F. Hirsch, 'John Cotton and Roger Williams: Their Controversy Concerning Religious Liberty', *Church History*, 10 (1941), 38–51.

226 Wod.Fol.XXX.(26), f. 95.

227 Wod.Fol.XXX.(26), f. 96.

228 Wod.Fol.XXX.(26), f. 101.

229 Wod.Fol.XXX.(26), f. 96; Guthrie, *A Treatise of Ruling Elders and Deacons*, 31.

230 Wod.Fol.XXX.(26), f. 95–6.

231 Wod.Fol.XXX.(26), f. 102–103.

232 NCL, MSS Box 28.5. The first four pages of the manuscript are missing and the brief description attached to it simply reads: 'This manuscript ... contains a discussion of the Presbyterial as compared with the Congregational system: It seems to have been written when the Westminster Assembly was sitting, or soon after, and with reference to objections made by the "Brethren in Aberdeen" as is mentioned at the close.' Notes written on the folder containing the document attest to the enigmatic provenance of the work. As a result the manuscript has quietly collected dust on the shelf – its importance unrecognised – since arriving at New College in 1909.

233 Rutherford, *Letters*, 706; Coffey, 222.

234 MSS Box 28.5, f. 17. The author cites a number of sources from New England, but particulary Cotton's *The Way Cleared* and Hooker's *Survey.*

235 EUL, La.I.69(5): 'Portion of an unfinished treatise on the Power of the Civil Magistrate in Matters of Religion.' In this work Rutherford cited a host of continental and Latin authors.

236 By this time Rutherford had written *The divine right of church-government and excommunication* (London, 1646) and portions of *A Survey of the Survey of That Summe of Church Discipline, Penned by Mr. Thomas Hooker* (London, 1658). Wariston claimed in his letter he had read multiple sections of Rutherford's *Survey of the Survey* by June 1652 (NLS, Wod.Fol.XXX(24), f. 86).

237 Rutherford, *Letters*, 706.

238 MSS Box 28.5, f. 18. A similar reference to leaving one's charge to 'Lion and beasts' can also be found in Rutherford, *A Survey of the Survey*, 36–7.

239 Samuel Rutherford, *The Covenant of Life Opened* (Edinburgh: Andrew Anderson, 1655), 79, 390–1; Rutherford, *A Survey of the Survey*, 19, 31, 55, 103–4, 178–83, 261, 385, 412–3, 452–5.

240 In 1648 English Independents published a series of works by New England divines to defend their own practices in England, some of which they had possessed for several years. The publication of these works in quick succession was an organised barrage of polemics. See: Chatfield, 77.

241 By no means can these few paragraphs incorporate an entire ideological argument for Rutherford's authorship of the manuscript. For this reason the argument must be kept brief. It is my intention to produce a fuller analysis of the evidence in a later scholarly work, but at present the purpose is simply to identify the manuscript as integrally intertwined in the Aberdeen controversy and to sketch out some preliminary reasons why I am convinced that the work is Rutherford's.

242 *Mercurius Politicus* (12–19 August 1652), 1806 [E674:6]: 'In the mean time of all these doings, there is a blessed work going on at Aberdeen, Mr. John Menis, the Professor of Divinity, Mr Samuel Row, and Mr. Jeffereyes the Provost, and many precious Christians, are joyning themselves into a Congregationall communion: They have been here waiting on the Protestators, and have had many conferences with them at my Lord Warristons about all the points of government, and have soberly and modestly put them all to it, and ar now parted to follow on their own work ... like a little stone cut out of the mountains.'

243 *Mercurius Politicus* (7–14 Oct. 1652), 1942–3 [E678:10].

244 Row, *Life of Blair*, 300–1; Jaffray, 66.

245 Maidment, 'Diurnal of Occurences in Scotland', 87.

246 Jaffray, 66.

247 Row, *Life of Blair*, 301.

248 Stuart, *Aberdeen*, 222.

249 Jaffray, 66.

250 R. Pittiloh, *The Hammer of Persecution* (London: L. Chapman, 1659), 10.

251 Henderson, RLSCS, 108; John Davidson, *Inverurie and the Earldom of the Garioch* (Edinburgh, 1878), 310.

252 Row, *Life of Blair*, 297.

253 Pittiloh, *Hammer of Persecution*, 10–11.

254 W.S., *Presbyteries Triall* (1657), 21.

255 Baillie, *L & J*, iii:242.

256 M. Tolmie, *The Triumph of the Saints* (Cambridge, 1977), 111–16.

257 Ellen S. More, 'Congregationalism and the Social Order: John Goodwin's Gathered Church, 1640–60', *JEH*, 38 (1987), 213.

258 Munro, *Old Aberdeen*, 49–50.

259 George Vernon, *A letter to a friend concerning some of Dr. Owens principles and practices* (London, 1670), 15. Richard L. Greaves suggests there is no evidence to support this claim (*ODNB*, 'John Owen'), but Peter Toon's seminal work on Owen (*God's Statesman*, 58) does not rule out the possibility, despite a lack of solid evidence.

260 FES, vi:8.

261 Baillie, *L & J*, iii:242.
262 Nuttall, *Visible Saints*, 13; *ONDB* 'Goodwin, Thomas (1600–1680)'.
263 Jaffray, 65.
264 Toon, *God's Statesman*, 58.
265 Toon, *God's Statesman*, 118.
266 *Mercurius Brittanicus* (30 Nov.–7 Dec. 1652), 277 [E801(10)].
267 *S & C*, 370; *Several Proceedings in Parliament*, (25 Nov.–2 Dec. 1652).
268 *Mercurius Brittanicus* (26 Oct.–2 Nov. 1652), 238.
269 *Mercurius Politicus* (17–24 February 1653), 2249 [E688:10]; Maidment, 'Diurnall of Occurences in Scotland', 103.
270 Stuart, *Aberdeen*, 223.
271 Stuart, *Aberdeen*, 225.
272 Pittiloh, *Hammer of Persecution*, 10–12.
273 Baillie, *L & J*, iii:237–43; Nicoll, 108.
274 'Robert Leighton' in *ODNB*; Brodie, 41.
275 Crawford Gribben, 'Robert Leighton, Edinburgh Theology and the Collapse of Presbyterian Consensus', in E. Boran and C.Gribben, eds, *Enforcing Reformation in Ireland and Scotland, 1550–1700*, St Andrews Studies in Reformation History (Aldershot, 2006), 183.
276 Baillie, *L & J*, iii:238.
277 Baillie, *L & J*, iii:241.
278 J.M. Bulloch, *A History of the University of Aberdeen, 1495–1895* (London, 1895), 120; R. S. Rait, *The Universities of Aberdeen* (Aberdeen, 1895), 152.
279 Rule, a graduate of St Andrews, retired to England in 1656 to minister at an Independent church in Alnwick, Northumberland. Ejected under the act of uniformity, he returned to Scotland. After several turbulent years, including imprisonment on the Bass Rock, he was appointed principal of the University of Edinburgh in 1690 (Bulloch, 122; A.G. Matthews, *Calamy Revised* (Oxford, 1934), 420; *ODNB*).
280 In a manuscript letter dated 4 March 1653, Patrick Gillespie mentions having recently returned from Aberdeen, which may suggest his presence at Row's appointment (NLS, Wod.Qu.XXIX.(61)). Hoy drew this same conclusion based upon Baillie (*L & J*, iii:177; Hoy, 184n).
281 Baillie, *L & J*, iii:242.
282 Holfelder, 182–4.
283 Nicoll, 162; Lee, *St. Giles', Edinburgh*, 227–8.
284 Baillie, *L & J*, iii:322.
285 *A Perfect Diurnal*, 14–21 Nov.; Baillie, *L & J*, iii:202, 217.
286 Holfelder, 182.
287 Gillespie came to front a faction of the Protester party found predominantly in the west. What separated them from the Guthrie–Rutherford–Wariston Protesters was their willingness to make concessions with the English. As early as April 1653, the English identified this third party within the Kirk (Maidment, 'Diurnall of Occurences in Scotland', 113).
288 *FES*, ii:482; Baillie, *L & J*, 314.
289 Baillie, *L & J*, iii:314; *FES*, iii:381.
290 Baillie, *L & J*, iii:244.
291 'I pray John, or rather Brother Timpson, are we for such an unlimitted Toleration? … yea, doth not New-England Practice confirme the contrary, where even Antinomianism and all other Sects and Errours are rooted out? … and we lately by Letters from New England, that the Quakers, who so madly range as wild beasts here, yet they could not get admittance there, but such as went over with such Books about them, the Books were burnt, and the persons imprisoned, till the same Ship returned to take these back again, Are we then for such a Toleration?' (John Beverley, *Unio Reformantium. Or, The Presbyterian and Independent Vindicated, from the Contradictious Way of Free-Admission* (London, 1659), 164).
292 Beverley, *Unio Reformantium*, 24.
293 For a summary of this process in England see: Geoffrey Nuttall, 'Presbyterians and

Independents Some Movements for Unity 300 years ago', *JPHSE*, 10 (1952), 4–15.

294 Stalham served an Edinburgh congregation in 1655; his similarity to Beverley's position is evidenced by his preface to *Unio Reformantium*.

295 William Cradock quoted in Nuttall 'Presbyterians and Independents', 15.

296 Holfelder, 178.

297 Stevenson, *Counter-Revolution*, 157.

298 In Burn's estimation, this meant 'they had served their turn with the Covenant, and now it was at an end, and no more obligatory' (Maidment, *Historical Fragments*, 30). Baillie, *L & J*, iii:245, 283.

299 Baillie, *L & J*, iii:322.

300 Nicoll, 94.

301 Stalham defended his congregation in England against Baptists, including the soapboiler Thomas Lambe, in a debate at Terling, Essex in January 1643 (John Stalham, *The Summe of A Conference* (London, 1644) and wrote against the Baptist Samuel Oates in 1647 (*Vindiciae Redemptionis* (London, 1647). See 'Stalham, John' in ODNB.

302 John Stalham, *Contradictions of the Quakers ... by John Stalham, Preacher of the Gospel (for the Present) at Edinburgh in Scotland* (Edinburgh, 1655), preface.

303 *RCME*, i:37–43.

304 Davidson, *Inverurie and the Earldom of the Garioch*, 310; *RCGA*, iii:549–50; Thompson, 82.

305 Wood, *A Little Stone Pretended*, 170.

306 R.G. Pope, *The Half-Way Covenant: Church Membership in Puritan New England* (Princeton, 1969).

307 Wood, *A Little Stone Pretended*, 189–91.

308 Wood, *A Little Stone Pretended*, 361–2.

309 Wood, *A Little Stone Pretended*, 378–86.

310 Row, 313; Lamont, 68; Nicoll, 127. Oliver Cromwell to Robert Lilburne, 7 March 1654: 'you did once hint to me some purpose of Master Patrick Gillespie's thoughts to come up hither in order (as I suppose) to somewhat relating to the people of God in Scotland, I have thought fit to require the coming up of Master John Levingstone, Master Patrick Gillespie and Master John Menzies' (*Clarke Papers V*, 159–60).

311 Dow, 99, 102, 196.

312 Row, *Life of Blair*, 313.

313 NCL, MSS MYL, f. 757; Douglas was a Resolutioner, Guthrie a Protester, and Blair had avoided joining with either faction attempting to bring about reconciliation within the Kirk.

314 Row, *Life of Blair*, 315.

315 Wod.Fol.XXVI(2), f. 7.

316 *APS*, vi,ii:755; Dow, 196–8; Row, *Life of Blair*, 318; Nicoll, 135.

317 Baillie, *L & J*, iii:253.

318 *APS*, vi,ii:832. 1) Lothian, Merse and Teviotdale; 2) Dumfries and Galloway; 3) Glasgow and Ayr; 4) Perth, Fife and Angus; and 5) 'be-north Angus'.

319 Dow, 197. Some of the individuals of interest assigned to be triers were: For Lothian, Merse and Teviotdale: Sir Archibald Johnston of Wariston, Sir Andrew Kerr, *Colonel Gilbert Ker, William Dundas* (see chapter 5 in this volume; Nicoll, 52); for Glasgow and Ayr: John Carstairs, John Nevay, Francis Aird, Patrick Gillespie, John Graham, John Spreul (he wrote 'I am under some temptation to join with the English' in his journal, Maidment, *Historical Fragments*, 4:9); for Perth, Fife and Angus: James Guthrie, Robert Blair, Samuel Rutherford, James Simpson (who had asked for a conference with Lockyer, Baillie, *L & J*, iii:177); 'be-north Angus': Brodie of Brodie (see chapter 5 in this volume), *John Row, John Menzies, Alexander Jaffray, William Muir*, Robert Keith, Duncan Forbes (both Keith and Forbes subscribed to the moderate declaration against the mixing of the 'precious' and the 'vile' in response to Row's 23 April 1652 paper to the Synod of Aberdeen, *Stuart*, 219–20), Andrew Cant. Individuals known to have embraced Independency or another English sect are listed in italics.

320 *APS*, vi,ii:832

321 *RCME*, i:63, 79; Row, *Life of Blair*, 318.

322 NLS, Wod.Fol.XXXI.(44), f. 122.

323 *APS*, vi,ii:832

324 Row, *Life of Blair*, 318–19.

325 *S & P*, 185.

326 *S & P*, 193; Nicoll, 267.

327 Nicoll, 158.

328 Dow, 196, 205–6. For Broghill's support of the charter: Lamont, 91; J. Buckroyd, 'Lord Broghill and the Scottish Church, 1655–1656', *JEH*, 27 (1976), 359–68.

329 EUL, La.I.321(3). No subscribers' names are included in the manuscript.

330 EUL, La.I.321(4).

331 Munro, *Old Aberdeen*, 48.

332 D. Stevenson, *St Machar's Cathedral and the Reformation* (Aberdeen, 1981), 13.

333 Munro, *Old Aberdeen*, 51.

334 Ascertaining the impact of triers in Scotland is extremely difficult as there is no Scottish equivalent to the English records held in Lambeth Palace (MSS L. 996–999, 1662).

335 Wod.Fol.XXVI(10).

336 Baillie, *L& J*, iii:335.

337 Baillie, *L & J*, iii:282.

338 It was only after further financial gifts to both Aberdeen and Glasgow that Robert Leighton, the principal of Edinburgh University, petitioned the Lord Protector and in 1658 received a £200 annual endowment (Firth, *Last Years of the Protectorate*, ii:100; *CSPD*, 1657–8, 77; *APS*, vi,ii:877).

339 *APS*, vi,ii:831; Nicoll, 165–6; Baillie, *L & J*, iii:282; *APS*, vi,ii:832.

340 Nicoll, 267.

341 *APS*, vi, ii:762; W. J. Couper, *The Origins of Glasgow Printing* (Edinburgh, 1911), 14.

342 McCoy, *Robert Baillie and the Second Scots Reformation*, 174–8; Baillie, *L & J*, iii:385. An example of the building work is still extant in the Pearce Lodge.

343 Anderson, *Fasti*, i:287–90.

344 Rait, *Universities of Aberdeen*, 241.

345 Rait, *Universities of Aberdeen*, 151, 286. Another link between Scotland and Eton came through the fellow and chaplain of Eton, Paul Hobson, who had formed friendly ties with William Lockhart.

346 Baillie, *L & J*, iii:327.

347 Anderson, *Fasti Academiae Mariscallanae Aberdonensis*, ii:222; *ODNB* 'Fraser, James, of Brea'.

348 Wariston, iii:35.

349 Baillie, *L & J*, iii:308.

350 Baillie, *L & J*, iii:327.

351 Baillie, *L & J*, iii:335.

352 Wod.Fol.XXIV(10).

353 Nicoll, 205.

354 Jaffray, 98–9.

355 Thurloe, vii:527.

356 John Row, 'Diary', *Scottish Notes and Queries* (Aberdeen, 1894), 52. According to Row's diary, Seaton was ousted by the Act of Uniformity and returned to Aberdeen with his family in March 1662.

357 Jaffray, 68–9; Nicoll, 95.

358 Jaffray, 69–70; *FES* i:332.

359 Historical Manuscripts Commission, *Report on the Laing Manuscripts*, ed., H. Paton, (London, 1914), i:298; EUL, La.I.320.

360 EUL, La.I.320.

361 Jaffray, 99.

362 The parish of Newbattle may have been vacant in the spring of 1657 (*FES*, i:333).

363 Jaffray, 99

364 Jaffray, 119.

365 Jaffray, 114, 116.

366 Jaffray, 112.

367 Davis, 'Against Formality', 265–88.

368 Stuart, *Aberdeen*, 118–20.

369 Stuart, *Aberdeen*, 128.

370 Stuart, *Aberdeen*, 132.

371 *Report on the Laing Manuscripts*, 296; EUL, La.I.319.

372 *Report on the Laing Manuscripts*, 297; EUL, La.I.320.

373 Brodie, 163.

374 *RHCA*, 554.

375 Stuart, *Aberdeen*, 232–3.

376 *Blairs Papers*, 207. This account, uniquely, links Row to Menzies' party.

377 *Report on the Laing Manuscripts*, 298; EUL, La.I.320.

378 Baillie, *L & J*, iii:364.

379 Holfelder, 250.

380 Donaldson, 'Schism', 215–18; Stevenson, *Counter-Revolution*, 228; Coffey, 219–24; Holfelder, 250.

381 Coffey, 224.

382 Donaldson, 'Schism', 217; Baillie, *L & J*, iii:220: 'they are moving to celebrate a Communion here … They will exclude such multitudes for one cause or for another that the end will be the setting up of a new refined congregation of their own adherents.'

383 Francis Howgill, *To All you Commanders and Officers of the Army of Scotland* (Leith,1657), 2–3.

384 Dow, 102–4.

385 James Guthrie, *Some Considerations Contributing Unto the Discoverie of the Dangers That Threaten Religion and the Work of the Reformation in the Church of Scotland* (Edinburgh,1660), 72.

386 *Mercurius Politicus* noted in April 1652, two months after the imposition of toleration, that the Kirk's 'Tyrranik discipline' was limited to those who would submit to it (15–22 April 1652, p. 1551 [E660:5]).

387 EUL, La.I.321.(2), f. 1.

388 Wood, *Dead Man's Testament*, 15.

389 J. Kendall and J. Tompkins, *Piety Promoted*, 8 vols, 2nd edn (London, 1789), i:79; Jaffray, 197.

390 Dundas, *A Few Words of Truth*, 18.

391 Baillie, *L & J*, iii:323; Joseph Besse, *A Collection of the Sufferings of the People Called Quakers*, 2 vols (London, 1753), ii:494–5; Henderson, *RLSCS*, 105. Wariston puts the number at eleven (Wariston, iii:35).

392 NLS, Wod.Qu.XCVIII.(6), f. 105–7.

393 Pittiloh, 10–13.

394 John Morrill, ed., *Revolution and Restoration: England in the 1650s* (London, 1992), 10.

395 John Row, 'Diary,' *Scottish Notes and Queries* (Aberdeen), 7 (1894), 70.

396 Menzies later conformed to Episcopacy at the Restoration.

397 Baillie, *L & J*, iii:356; Jaffray, 105.

398 Stuart, *Aberdeen*, 145.

399 Jaffray, 118.

400 Henderson, *RLSCS*, 111.

401 *To the Very Honorable the Representative of the Common-Vvealth. The Humble Petition and Remonstrance of Such in Scotland* (Leith: Evan Tyler, 1652).

402 Ned C. Landsman, *Scotland and its First American Colony 1683–1760* (Princeton, 1985), 103; D. Dobson, *Scottish Quakers and Early America: 1650–1700* (Baltimore, 1998).

Chapter 5

1 The quotation refers to the dynamic relationship between Baptists and Quakers in their attempts to bring about Christ's second advent (the 'Lamb's War') as explored in: T.L. Underwood, *Primitivism, Radicalism and the Lamb's War*, Oxford Studies in Historical Theology (Oxford, 1997).

2 Ernst Troeltsch, *The Social Teaching of the Christian Churches* (Chicago, 1981), 781.

3 Underwood, 6.

4 Underwood, 34.

5 Underwood, 34.

6 Underwood, 34, 120.

7 Robert Baillie, *Anabaptism, the True Fountaine of Independency, Brownisme, Antinomy, Familisme, and the Most of the Other Errours, Which for the Time Doe Trouble the Church of England, Unsealed* (London, 1647).

8 Robert Baillie, *A Dissuasive from the Errours of the Time* (London, 1646), 6.

9 *RHCA*, 134.

10 Underwood, 16; C.W. Horle, 'Quakers and Baptists 1647–1660', *BQ*, 26 (1975–6), 344–62.

11 Fox, 243, 248.

12 Fox, 248.

13 Scott (1926), 25; Henderson, *RLSCS*, 101–2; Spalding, *Memorialls of the Trubles*, ii:203; *Some Sober Animadversions*, 12.

14 *Some Sober Animadversions*, 11.

15 John Russell, *The Story of Leith* (London, 1922), 347.

16 E.B. Underhill, ed., *Records of the Churches of Christ Gathered in Fenstanton, Warboys and Hexham, 1644–1720* (London, 1854), 165n, 333; R.B. Hannen, 'Cupar, Fife, 1652–1659', 45–9; Scott (1929), 178; D. Douglas, *History of the Baptist Churches in the North of England from 1648 to 1845* (London, 1846), 37–8; Fraser, *Chronicles*, 415; *Clarke Papers*, iv: 160–1, 258; Burnet, *Quakerism*, 27.

17 *Clarke Papers*, iv: 92.

18 NLS, Wod.Qu.XVII, f. 240.

19 Douglas, *History of the Baptist Churches in the North of England*, 37; Yullie, 26; Scott (1929), 175.

20 James Heath, *A Brief Chronicle of the Late Intestine Vvar in the Three Kingdoms of England, Scotland and Ireland* (London: J.P., 1676), 273.

21 Underhill, *Records*, 301–2.

22 Dow, 61; Yullie, 30.

23 Underhill, *Records*, 301.

24 Underhill, *Records*, 302n.

25 Jonas Dell, *Forms the Pillars of Antichrist; but Christ in Spirit the True Teacher of His People; and Not Tradition* (London, 1656).

26 *S & C*, 31

27 Nicoll, 62; Douglas, 37; Scott (1929), 177.

28 Nicoll, 94.

29 Lamont, 48.

30 Row, *History of the Kirk of Scotland*, 539.

31 Lamont, 49.

32 Lamont, 54.

33 Nicoll, 106.

34 Lamont, 54.

35 John Row, 'Diary', *Scottish Notes and Queries*, 7 (1894), 70. For evidence of the Baptist presence in Aberdeen see: Burnet, *History of his Own Time*, 38; *RHCA*, 309–10; R. Pittiloh, *The Hammer of Persecution* (London: L. Chapman, 1659), 10.

36 Row, *History of the Kirk*, 539.

37 Ayrshire Archives, CH2/751/3/2, f. 290.

38 Nicoll, 106.

39 Whitelocke, iii:481. No such tract survives.

40 F.P.G. Guizot, *Memoirs of George Monk*, trans., J.S. Wortley (London,1838), 76; Douglas, *History*, 39; Scott (1926), 26; Scott (1929), 175.

41 For Lilburne's favour towards the Protesters see: Dow, 101.

42 Underhill, *Records*, 307–8, 311–13, 317–18.

43 Underhill, *Records*, 311.

44 Underhill, *Records*, 313 and n.

45 Charles Bond is mentioned in a letter dated 22 June, and Hugh Hesloppe in August (Underhill, *Records*, 328, 332).

46 Underhill, *Records*, 319.

47 Underhill, *Records*, 389.

48 Underhill, *Records*, 319.

49 Clarke MSS, 3/1.

50 Underhill, *Records*, 180–1; B.R. White, 'Organisation of the Particular Baptists, 1644–1660', *JEH*, 17 (1966), 218.

51 *L & J*, iii:177; Laurence, 128. Hoy suggests that the letter seems to imply that Gardiner was in or near St Andrews, (Hoy, 185n).

52 John Row, 'Diary', *Scottish Notes and Queries*, 7 (1894), 70. For Lockyer, see chapter 4 of this volume.

53 See chapter 2 of this volume.

54 Kinloch, *St Andrews & Cupar*, 71.

55 Hannen, 45–9; Baxter, *Synod of Fife*, 176, 180; Kinloch, *St Andrews & Cupar*, 71, 178–82.

56 Kinloch, *St Andrews & Cupar*, 182.

57 Kinloch, *St Andrews & Cupar*, 183.

58 W.T. Whitley, *A History of British Baptists* (London, 1923), 74.

59 Crawford Gribben, 'Defining the Puritans? The Baptism Debate in Cromwellian Ireland, 1654–56', *Church History*, 73 (March 2004), 88.

60 *A Confession of Faith, of Severall Congregations or Churches of Christ in London, Which are Commonly (Though Unjustly) Called Anabaptists*, fourth impression, corrected (Leith,1653).

61 Thomas Spencer, Abraham Holmes, Thomas Powell and John Brady. Spencer was a captain and Holmes a major.

62 Tai Liu, *Discord in Zion* (The Hague, 1973), 73–4, 119.

63 John Owen, *A Sermon Preached to the Parliament ... October 13, 1652* (London, 1652), 19; Liu, *Discord in Zion*, 74.

64 NLS, Wod.Qu.XXXVII, f. 35–6.

65 Thurloe, i:621.

66 Fraser, *Chronicles*, 405.

67 Row, *Life of Blair*, 313.

68 Evans, *The Early English Baptists*, ii:200–2; Thurloe, ii:150–1.

69 Dow, 79–98.

70 Dow, 105, 114.

71 Dow, 115.

72 Douglas, *History*, 39.

73 Thurloe, ii:414.

74 Thurloe, ii:64, 93.

75 Thurloe, ii:149, 163, 213, 216.

76 Thurloe, ii:641.

77 *RHCA*, 285, 464, 550.

78 Thurloe, ii:285.

79 Thurloe, ii:295.

80 Thurloe, ii:313.

81 Matthew Alured, *The Case of Colonel Matthew Alured* (London, 1659), 9–15.

82 Barbara Taft, 'The Humble Petition of Several Colonels of the Army: Causes, Character, and Results of Military Opposition to Cromwell's Protectorate', *The Huntington Library Quarterly*, 42 (1978–9), 15–41; Gardiner, *C & P*, iii:211; Liu, *Discord in Zion*, 138–9.

83 Nicoll, 145. A manuscript copy of *Some Mementois for the Officers and Shouldiers of the Army* has been preserved in the Wodrow Collection: NLS, Wod.Qu.XXIX(56).

84 Clarke MSS, 1/13: f. 120; 1/14: f. 170.

85 Liu, *Discord in Zion*, 118–43.

86 Row, *Life of Blair*, 319.

87 For a summary of 'Overton's Plot' see: Gardiner, *C & P*, 227–32. Hoy incorrectly dates the discovery of the plot as January 1656 (Hoy, 197).

88 Clarke MSS, 1/15: f. 26; Thurloe, iii:29–30; Nickolls, 132–3.

89 Baillie, *L & J*, iii:361; *RHCA*, 258, 260, 438, 440.

90 Thurloe, iii:206.

91 Thurloe, iii:45.

92 Thurloe, iii:75–6; *RHCA*, 393.

93 Gardiner, *C & P*, 227–8.

94 W.H. Dawson, *Cromwell's Understudy: The Life and Times of General John Lambert and the Rise and Fall of the Protectorate* (London, 1938), 309.

95 Thurloe, ii:19.

96 Signatories: Captain Henry Hedworth, Lieutenant John Braman, coronet John Toomes, John Loveland, quarter-master William Barford, quarter-master John Gregory, quarter-master John Waltridge, Mr Samuel Oates and Lieutenant Rawson (Thurloe, iii:206; Clarke MSS, 1/15, f. 26, 40).

97 Clarke MSS, 1/15, f. 41; *S & P*, 192.

98 *Clarke Papers V*, 234.

99 Thurloe, iii:45.

100 Gardiner, *C & P*, iii:267–9; Fraser, *Chronicles*, 409.

101 Nicoll, 144.

102 Lamont, 88; Row, *Life of Blair*, 319; Yullie, 31.

103 Thurloe, iii:46.

104 J[ohn] B[raman], *Calumny Condemned: Or, a True, Exact, and Sober Account of the Scotch Plot* (London, 1659), 4–6.

105 Nicoll, 145; Thurloe, iii:185.

106 Thurloe, iii:206.

107 Clarke MSS, 1/15: f. 34; Evans, *The Early English Baptists*, ii:215–18; *A Perfect Diurnall* (5–12 February 1655), 4143–4 [E479:22]; *Mercurius Politicus* (February 1–8, 1655), 5101; *Several Proceedings*, (1–8 February 1655), 4437; Hoy, 197.

108 Clarke MSS, 1/15: f. 35.

109 Clarke MSS, 3/2: f. 92.

110 Clarke MSS, 1/15: f. 49.

111 Thurloe, vii:335–6, 371, 554, 627.

112 Laurence, 70, 72, 74.

113 *Clarke Papers*, iii:52.

114 NLS, Wod.Qu.XXXVII, ff 21–39, f. 37.

115 J.Y. Akerman, ed., *Letters from Roundhead Officers Written from Scotland and Chiefly Addressed to Captain Adam Baynes* (Edinburgh, 1856), 114.

116 Underhill, *Records*, 164.

117 Row, *Life of Blair*, 333.

118 Nicoll, 147.

119 Brodie, 147.

120 Burnet, 14; Joseph Besse, *A Collection of the Sufferings of the People called Quakers*, 2 vols (London, 1753), ii:494.

121 Burnet, *Quakerism*, 14.

122 Besse, *A Collection of the Sufferings*, ii:494–5.

123 See chapter 4 of this volume.

124 Wariston, iii:35.

125 Baillie, *L & J*, iii:323.

126 Hew Wood was a nursery seedsman in the vicinity of Hamilton and also a gardener for the duke of Hamilton.

127 Torrance, 'The Quaker Movement in Scotland', 35.

128 NLS, 1.337. See p. 80 of this volume.
129 William Dundas make several references to Quakers he met in Scotland, as well as biographical information about Wood, but he makes no claim that Wood was a Quaker. Dundas, *A Few Words of Truth* (1673).
130 Nicoll, 39.
131 *The Faithful Scout* (No. 95. 5–13 Nov. 1652), 746 [E799(34)] and (No. 96. 12–19 Nov. 1652), 752 [E799(38)].
132 *To You the Parliament Sitting at Westminster* (1659).
133 Baillie, *L & J*, iii:323.
134 Penney, *Fox*, i:451 (290–2); Torrance, 'The Quaker Movement in Scotland', 32; Nickalls, *Fox*, 315n. Miller however, attributes the first meetings to 1656 (W.F. Miller, 'Notes on Edinburgh Meeting Houses', *JFHS*, 6 (1909), 27).
135 Robertson, *Lanark*, 101–2; Torrance, 'Quaker Movement', 35; Weare, *Doctrines*, 48; Baillie, *L & J*, iii:357.
136 Brodie, 178.
137 Burnet, *Quakerism*, 15; W.F. Miller, 'Stranger Friends Visiting Scotland, 1650–1797', *JFHS*, 12 (1915), 80; Hoy, 199.
138 Burnet, *Quakerism*, 26.
139 Thurloe, vi:708.
140 'Financial Statements sent to Swarthmore, 1654 and 1655', *JFHS*, 6 (1909), 50–1, 84–5, 127–8.
141 James Backhouse, *Memoirs of Francis Howgill, with Extracts from His Writings* (York, 1828), 50.
142 Thurloe, vi:811.
143 Burnet, *Quakerism*, 27.
144 Thurloe, iv:145–6, 162; Burnet, *Quakerism*, 26–7. Burnet gives the date incorrectly as 1658.
145 John Stalham, *Contradictions of the Quakers (so Called) to the Scriptures of God* (Edinburgh, 1655), 1.
146 Stalham, *Contradictions*, 2.
147 John Gilpin, *The Quakers Shaken, or, A Discovery of the Errours of That Sect* (London and Edinburgh, 1655); P. E., *A Serious Review of Some Principles of the Quakers* ([Edinburgh]: [Andrew Anderson], 1655).
148 Thurloe, iv:508; Ebenezer Hazard, *Historical Collections* (Philadelphia, 1792–4), i:630–2.
149 'Some Early Suffering in Scotland', *JFHS*, 21(1924), 68; NAS, CH10/1/66, 1.
150 Weare, *Doctrines*, 10–14.
151 CH10/1/66, 1.
152 'Some Early Sufferings in Scotland', 68.
153 *S & P*, 302–3; Dow, 142.
154 G. Davies, 'The Quarters of the English Army in Scotland in 1656', *SHR*, 21 (1924), 62–7.
155 Stephen Crisp, *Description of the Church of Scotland* (London, 1660), 4.
156 Burnet, *Quakerism*, 29.
157 NAS, CH10/1/66, 2. Justices of the peace will from henceforward be referred to as 'JP'.
158 'Some Early Suffering in Scotland', *JFHS*, 21 (1924), 70; *S & P*, 308–16.
159 Clarke MSS, 1/14: f. 170.
160 Dow, 146, 178–81. JPs were originally appointed in Scotland in 1610, but most scholars agree that the posts rapidly fell into disuse. Julian Goodare alone has challenged this assumption (J. Goodare, *The Government of Scotland 1560–1625* (Oxford, 2004), 203–7). For records pertaining to JPs under the Protectorate see: *S&P*, xxxviii, lix, 98, 106, 308–16, 321 and *n*, 403, 405 and *n*.
161 NAS, CH10/1/66, 2.
162 NAS, 'A Remembrance, or Record of the sufferings of some freinds of the trueth in Scotland', CH10/1/65, 3; CH10/1/66, 1–3; *S & P*, 308–16. Interestingly, the influence of the Independents in Aberdeen was reassured by the appointments of Alexander

Jaffray and Stephen Winthrop (son and grandson of governors of Massachussets) as JPs.

163 Robertson, *Lanark*, 103.

164 Weare, *Doctrines*, 14; Barry Reay, *The Quakers and the English Revolution* (London, 1985), 49; *To You the Parliament Sitting at Westminster* (London, 1659); Stephen Crisp, *A Description of the Church of Scotland*, 14.

165 Whitelocke, iii:385; *S & C*, 350.

166 Weare, *Doctrine*, 13–14.

167 Fox, 246.

168 *S & P*, 50, 314.

169 Thurloe, ii:167–8.

170 *S & P*, 350–1; Thurloe, vi:136, 167.

171 Thurloe, vi:162; *JFHS*, viii:158–9; Torrance, 'The Quaker Movement in Scotland', 33.

172 *S & P*, 352.

173 Reay, 51.

174 *S & P*, 350–2; 362–3.

175 Thurloe, 136.

176 Clarke MSS, 3/11: (unfoliated) 13 March 1657.

177 Clarke MSS, 3/11, April 22, 1657.

178 N. Penney, ed., *Extracts from State Papers Relating to Friends 1654 to 1672* (London, 1913), 29.

179 *Clarke Papers*, iii:122–3; *S & P*, 350–2, 362–3; Dow, 234, 328n; *Clarke MSS* 2/13: 2, 13, 27 March; 16, 22 April; 9, 15, 20, 25, 29 May; 16, 26, 27 Oct.; 20, 21 Nov.; 22 1657 Dec..

180 Dow, 328n; Reay, 50; J.F. McGregor and B. Reay, *Radical Religion in the English Revolution* (Oxford, 1984), 154.

181 *Clarke MSS* 2/13; Reay, 19.

182 Francis Howgill, *To All You Commanders and Officers of the Army of Scotland* (Leith,1657), 3

183 Fox, 247–8.

184 John Barclay, ed., *Journals of the Lives and Gospel Labours of William Caton, and John Burnyeat*, 2nd edn (London, 1839).

185 Burnet, *Quakerism*, 34; Fox, 239.

186 Fox, 239.

187 Burnet, *Quakerism*, 35; *To You the Parliament Sitting at Westminster* (1659), Stockdale, *Doctrines and Principles*, 2.

188 Fox, 239.

189 Robertson, *Lanark*, 101. Katherine Hamilton may have been the sister of Alexander Hamilton, which would put her among the first to be convinced in Lanarkshire.

190 Weare, *Doctrines*, 12–15, 45–6, 48; Robertson, *Lanark*, 101–2.

191 Weare, *Doctrines*, 1–2.

192 Weare, *Doctrines*, 10.

193 Weare, *Doctrines*, 13.

194 Weare, *Doctrines*, 12.

195 Penney, *Fox*, i:451 (292.3).

196 Clarke MSS, 3/11: 27 Oct. 1657.

197 Nickalls, *Fox*, 320n; Penney, *Fox*, i:452 (297.1); ii:434 (211.2).

198 Liu, *Discord in Zion*, 140–60.

199 *CSPD*, 1658–9:61.

200 Thurloe, vii:194.

201 Thurloe, vii:197.

202 Thurloe, vii:403, 527, 554.

203 Thurloe, vi:709.

204 Thurloe, vii:371.

205 Thurloe, vii:403.

206 Scott, (1926), 32; Scott, (1929), 183.

207 F.J. Grant, ed., *The Faculty of Advocates in Scotland, 1532–1943* (Edinburgh, 1944), 172.

208 Robert Pittillok, *A short brotherly examination of a sermon: At first preached by Mr Saloman Saffrey, and after published in print* (Leith: Evan Tyler, 1652). The tract is a response to: Salomon Saffery, *Part of a Discourse, Tending Only to Invite Those That Believe in Christ, to be Conformable to Him in Baptisme* ([s.l.]: [s.n.], 164?). Only one known copy survives: University of Aberdeen, King 231/53. Saffrey may have been distributing his work while in Edinburgh, as James Brown did with his book.

209 *Clarke Papers*, iv:271. The dating in this certificate is strange since it aserts that it was written in March 1659, but explains that Pittilloch continued to work until June 1659.

210 Robert Pittilloh, *The Hammer of Persecution: or, the Mystery of Iniquity In the Persecution of Many Good People in Scotland* (London: L. Chapman, 1659), 6.

211 Pittilloh, *Hammer of Persecution*, 7.

212 Pittilloh, *Hammer of Persecution*, 11; Dow, 200–1.

213 Dow, 58–61.

214 Dow, 206. For Broghill's Scottish ties see: Little, *Lord Broghill*, 93, 96–109.

215 Dow, 204.

216 Pittilloh, *Hammer of Persecution*, 13.

217 Pittilloh, *Hammer of Persecution*, 10.

218 Pittilloh, *Hammer of Persecution*, 12–13.

219 *S & P*, 317; Pittilloh, *Hammer of Persecution*, 12–14.

220 *S & P*, 317, 389.

221 David Pearsone (a schoolmaster), the son of the lord of Leyes and a Mr Malice all fled to England to avoid persecution (Pittilloh, *Hammer of Persecution*, 14).

222 Pittilloh, *Hammer of Persecution*, 12–13; Nicoll, 95, 207, 222.

223 *To You the Parliament Sitting at Westminster, Our Request Is to God That You Rule for His Honour. Here are Several of Our Names, Who Thus Suffers in the Behalf of Many More in the Nation of Scotland* (London, 1659). Only one surviving copy: British Library, 1865.c.15(9). Reay, *The Quakers and the English Revolution*, 49.

224 Dow, 241.

225 From the end of 1656, Wariston showed increasing compliance with the English. After being offered a salary of £300 to care for the public records of Scotland, he hailed Cromwell as 'the man whom thou hes providentially maid Thy depute on earth' (Wariston, iii:54). After serving in London as an envoy for the Protesters, Guthrie referred to him as 'our Independent' in London. In July 1657 he took the office of Public Register for Scotland; in November he became a Commissioner for the Administration of Justice; in January 1658 he sat in the newly formed upper house of Parliament; in January 1659 in Richard Cromwell's Parliament; at the restoration of the Rump Parliament he was appointed to the Council of State (*ODNB*, 'Johnston, Archibald, of Wariston'; Dow, 214, 221–2, 237, 240–3).

226 Wariston, iii:112; Row, *Life of Blair*, 338.

227 *Journals of the House of Commons*, vii, 664; Nicoll, 242–3; Holfelder, 284.

228 NLS, Wod.Fol.XXX.(27), f.105; *Some Sober Animadversions*, 1–2.

229 *Clarke Papers*, iv:51n; *S & C*, xxxix–xli; Dow, 242.

230 Row, *Life of Blair*, 338.

231 Maidment, *Historical Fragments*, 5:53; Baillie, *L & J*, iii:430; Douglas, William, *The Stable Trueths of the Kirk Require a Sutable Behaviour* (Aberdeen: J. B., 1660), 45.

232 NLS, Wod.Fol.XXX.(27), f. 106; Pittiloh, *Hammer of Persecution*, 12–13; *S & P*, 389.

233 The plight of Ireland is discussed below. For MacDowall of Garthland see pp. 112–13, 189 of this volume. For English see Peacey, *Politicians and Pamphleteers*, 81, 183, 267.

234 See pp. 112–13 of this volume. Wod.Fol.XXX.(27), f. 106; Row, *Life of Blair*, 253, 270. Abernethie was appointed a JP for 'Edinburgh Shire' in 1656, showing that he continued to be in favour with the regime (*S & P*, 312).

235 See pp. 112–13 of this volume. Nicoll, 52.

236 Wod.Fol.XXX.(27), f. 106. See chapter 4.

237 NAS, CH10/1/66, 1–3; CH10/1/65, 2–4; Robertson, *Lanark*, 101–3.

238 William Stockdale, *The Doctrins and Principles* (London, 1659), 3–6; Wod.Fol. XXX(27), f. 106.

239 Penney, *Fox*, i:451 (292.3), 452 (296.1). In 1662 Robeson was imprisoned in Duns for being a Quaker, during which time he produced a letter to the people of Scotland, the land of his 'nativitie' (NLS, MS. 2201, f. 99).

240 *S & P*, 390.

241 Pittiloh, *Hammer of Persecution*, 13.

242 Thurloe, vi:709.

243 *Journals of the House of Commons*, vii:736; Dow, 242; *Clarke Papers*, iv:51n; *Some Sober Animadversions*, 'to the reader,' 1; Wariston, iii:126.

244 Blair, *Life of Row*, 338. Nicoll affirms Gordon's involvement but makes no mention of Dundas (Nicoll, 244–5).

245 Dow, 242.

246 Wariston, iii:128.

247 Reid, *Andrew Hay of Craignethan's Diary*, 99.

248 Wod.Fol.XXX.(48), f. 157; NLS, Wod.Fol.XXX.(43) and (44). Concern over toleration in Galloway predated the petition. Sometime in the previous year, Earlstoun urged the synod of Galloway to condemn toleration: 'Will yow be exsamples and instruments to foment the division and distraction by your straining at an politick and only civil question, and will yow not scrouple to swallow so monstrous ane carnall as Tolleration, wherby covenants, o[a]thes, declarations and warnings are so openlie violatt to the ruine of religion and government evin in a moment' (Wod.Fol.XXXI. (62), f. 153).

249 Baillie, iii:392–5.

250 COS. *Presbytery of Edinburgh, A Testimony and Warning of the Presbyterie of Edinburgh, Against a Late Petition, Tending (in the Scope and Design Thereof) to the Overturning of the Ordinances and Truth of Christ in This Church. Octob. 5. Anno. Dom. 1659* (Edinburgh,1659); NLS, Wod.Qu.XXXVII, f.37.

251 COS. Presbytery of Edinburgh, *A Testimony and Warning*, 3.

252 COS. Presbytery of Edinburgh, *A Testimony and Warning*, 5.

253 COS. Presbytery of Edinburgh, *A Testimony and Warning*, 7; *Some Sober Animadversions, Humbly, and In All Meekness Offered to the Consideration of All Who Truly Fear the Lord, and Enquire in His Ways, in Scotland upon A Testimony and Warning, Emitted by the Presbytery of Edinburgh, Against a Petition Lately Presented to the Parliament, in Defence of the Said Petition* (London, 1659), 2.

254 *Some Sober Animadversions*, 25.

255 *Some Sober Animadversions*, 8.

256 *Some Sober Animadversions*, 2–3, 8.

257 *Some Sober Animadversions*, 6.

258 *Some Sober Animadversions*, 3.

259 For a comprehensive analysis of the closing months of the Interregnum see: Dow, chapter 12.

260 Richard Baxter, *Reliquiae Baxterianae* (London, 1696), 214.

261 Reid, ed., *Andrew Hay of Craignethan's Diary*, 169; Row, *Life of Blair*, 339; Heath, *A Brief Chronicle* (1676), 430; Dow, 251–3.

262 Adv.Ms.35.5.11, f. 58; *Clarke Papers*, iv:160–1.

263 *RHCA*, 579–80.

264 Adv.Ms.35.5.11, f. 62–4, 79, 83.

265 Parliament of Scotland, *Proclamation Against All Meetings of Quakers, Anabaptists, & c.* (Edinburgh: Evan Tyler, 1661).

266 Robert Baillie, *Anabaptism, the True Fountaine of Independency, Brownisme, Antinomy, Familisme, and the Most of the Other Errours* (London, 1647).

267 Fox, 240.

268 Fox, 241.

269 Kate Peters, '"The Quakers Quaking": Print and the Spread of a Movement', in Susan

Wabuda and Caroline Litzenberger, eds, *Belief and Practice in Reformation England*, St Andrews Studies in Reformation History (Aldershot, 1998), 250–67.
270 D.M. Butler, *George Fox in Scotland* (Edinburgh and London, 1913), 21.
271 NLS, MS. 2201, f. 100.
272 NLS, MS. 2201, f. 100.

Conclusion

1 Grainger, 42–58; Stevenson, *Counter-Revolution*, 149, 174; Dow, 11; Diane Rapaport, 'Scottish Slavery in 17th-Century New England', *History Scotland*, (5.1) 2005, 44–52.
2 W.S., *Presbyteries Triall*, 43–4.
3 Coffey, 188; J.C. Davis, 'Cromwell's Religion', in John Morrill, ed., *Oliver Cromwell and the English Revolution* (London, 1990), 198–208.
4 Worden, 'Toleration,' 210.
5 J. C. Davis 'Against Formality: One Aspect of the English Revolution', *TRHS*, 6th series, 3 (1993), 265–88.
6 Abbott, *Cromwell*, iii:459, 547, 586; iv:271; Worden 'Toleration', 211.
7 Geoffrey F. Nuttall, 'Presbyterians and Independents Some Movements for Unity 300 years ago', *JPHSE*, 10 (1952), 4–15; Geoffrey F. Nuttall, 'Relations Between Presbyterians and Congregationalists in England', *Studies in the Puritan Tradition*, (Dec. 1964), 1–7.
8 Thurloe, iv:557
9 Patrick Little, 'Putting the Protector back in the Protectorate', *BBC History*, 8.1 (2007), 12–16.
10 Whitelocke, iv:135.
11 Dow, 104–5, 146–7.
12 Francis Howgill, *To All You Commanders and Officers of the Army of Scotland* (Leith,1657), 2, 3.
13 Guthrie, *Some Considerations*, 65, 66; Hoy, 209. Moreover, one in a thousand is not an insignificant number in a country whose population in the mid-seventeenth century approached one million. Numbers need not be great for movements to have a significant influence. John Morrill has noted that even a generous estimate for the number of religious dissenters refusing to conform to the Restoration Church Settlement would be 3 per cent, and yet they profoundly affected Restoration Britain (John Morrill, review of *Deliver Us from Evil* by Richard L. Greaves, *The Journal of Modern History*, 60.4 (1988), 752–3).
14 Guthrie, *Some Considerations*, 85, 65.
15 Guthrie, *Some Considerations*, 68, 69.
16 Guthrie, *Some Considerations*, 69.
17 Macinnes, *The British Revolution*, 287 (44 n).
18 L.F. Brown, *The Political Activities of the Baptists and the Fifth Monarchy Men in England during the Interregnum* (Oxford, 1912), 134.

Bibliography

MANUSCRIPTS

Ayrshire Archives

CH2/751/3

National Archives of Scotland

CH10/1/65
CH10/1/66
CH10/3/35
GD1/389/6

National Library of Scotland (NLS)

Mf.114(1–17)
MS. 2201, f. 98–100

NLS, ADVOCATES' LIBRARY MANUSCRIPTS COLLECTION

Adv.Ms.16.2.21
Adv.MS.17.1.16
Adv.MS.33.4.1
Adv.Ms.35.5.11

NLS, WODROW COLLECTION

Wod.Fol.XXVI
Wod.Fol.XXX
Wod.Fol.XXXI
Wod.Fol.LXVI
Wod.Fol.LXVII
Wod.Qu.XXIX
Wod.Qu.XVII
Wod.Qu.XXXVII
Wod.Qu.XCVIII
Wod.Qu.XCIX

New College Library, University of Edinburgh

MSS Box 28.5
MSS CRA 1
MSS MYL
MSS PIT

University of Edinburgh Library, Special Collections

La.I.314
La.I.319
La.I.320
La.I.321
La.III.368

PRIMARY

A.B., *A Fight at Dunin in Scotland, Between the Scots Women and the Presbyterian Kirkmen* (Edinburgh, 1652).

A Large Relation of the Fight at Leith Neere Edenburgh. Wherein Major Generall Montgomery, Colonell Straughan, with Many More of Quality of the Scottish Party Were Slaine and Wounded (London: Ed. Griffin, 1650).

A Letter from Several Ministers in and About Edinburgh, to the Ministers of London, Concerning the re-Establishing of the Covenant (Edinburgh: Christopher Higgens, 1659).

A Letter from Some Officers of the Army at Whitehall, to the Chief Officers of the Several Regiments in Scotland, with a Copie of Their Agreement; Together with a Letter from the Officers of the Army in Scotland in Answer Thereunto (Edinburgh: C. Higgins, 1659).

A Letter To the Right Honorable William Lenthall Esq. Speaker of the Parliament of England. Giving a True Relation of a Late Great Victory Obtained by the Parliaments Forces Against the Scots Neer Dundee the Taking the Old Generall Lesley, Lord-Chancellour Louden, Lord Crauford Lindsey, Lord Ogleby, and 300 More, Whereof Divers of Qualit. (London: Francis Leach, 1651).

A Testimony to the Truth of Jesus Christ to the Doctrine, Worship, Discipline and Goverment of the Kirk of Scotland and to the National Covenant of Scotland and to the Solemn League and Covenant of the Three Nations, England, Scotland and Ireland and to the Work of Uniformity in Religion and Against the Errors, Heresies, Blasphemies and Diverse Practices of the Times, Especially Against the Vast Toleration Now on Foot in These Nations by Sundry Ministers of the Gospel in the Provinces of Perth and Fife (Edinburgh: Society of Stationers, 1660).

An Act for Discovering, Convicting, and Repressing of Popish Recusants. At the Parliament Begun at Westminster, the 17th Day of September, An. Dom. 1656 (Edinburgh: Christopher Higgins, 1657).

Akerman, J.Y., ed., *Letters from Roundhead Officers Written from Scotland and Chiefly Addressed to Captain Adam Baynes. July MDCL–JuneMDCLX* (Edinburgh, 1856).

Alured, Matthew, *The Case of Colonel Matthew Alured* (London, 1659).

B[raman], J[ohn], *Calumny Condemned: or, a True, Exact, and Sober Account of the Scotch Plot: for Which Many Worthy Officers Were Dismissed Their Commands, and Cashiered the Army* (London: J.C., 1659).

Baillie, Robert, *Anabaptism, the True Fountaine of Independency, Brownisme, Antinomy, Familisme, and the Most of the Other Errours, Which for the Time Doe Trouble the Church of England, Unsealed* (London: M.F. for Samuel Gellibrand, 1647).

Baillie, Robert, *A Dissuasive from the Errours of the Time* (London: printed for Samuel Gellibrand, 1646).

Baillie, Robert, *The Disswasive from the Errors of the Time, Vindicated from the Exceptions of Mr. Cotton and Mr. Tomes* (London: Evan Tyler, 1655).

Baillie, Robert, *Letters and Journals*, ed., Laing, D., 3 vols (Edinburgh, 1841–2).

Balfour, Sir James, *The Historical Works of James Balfour of Denmylne and Kinnaird, Knight and Baronet; Lord Lyon King at Arms to Charles the First, and Charles the Second*, 4 vols (Edinburgh, 1824).

Barclay, John, ed., *Journals of the Lives and Gospel Labours of William Caton, and John Burnyeat*, 2nd edn (London, 1839).

Baxter, C., ed., *Ecclesiastical Records. Selections from the Minutes of the Synod of Fife, 1611–1687* (Edinburgh, 1837).

Baxter, Richard, *Baxter: A Holy Commonwealth*, ed., Lamont, W., Cambridge Texts in the History of Political Thought (Cambridge, 1994).

Beverley, John, *Unio Reformantium. Or, The Presbyterian and Independent Vindicated, from the Contradictious Way of Free-Admission* (London: Ja. C., 1659).

Birch, T., ed., *A Collection of State Papers of John Thurloe*, 7 vols (London, 1742).

A Brief Narrative of The Great Victorie, Which it Hath Pleased God to Give to the Armie of This Common-Wealth Against the Scots Army, Near Dunbar, in Scotland, on Tuesdaie Morning, the Third of This Instant September, Related to the Council of State by an Express Messenger of the Lord General, Sent from the Armie, Which Messenger Was Present at the Action (London: William Du-gard, 1650).

Brodie, Sir Alexander, *Diary of Alexander Brodie of Brodie (1652–80)* (Aberdeen, 1863).

Brown, James, *Antichrist (in Spirit) Unmasked: or, The Leaven of the Sadduces (Lately Lying Hid Amongst the Ranters and Quakers) Laid Open to Publick View* (Edinburgh: Christopher Higgins, 1657).

Brown, James, *Scripture-Redemption Freed from Men's Restrictions: Being an Answer to a Book Lately Published by Mr. William Troughton* (London: J.C., 1653).

Brown, James, *Scripture Redemption Freed from Mans Restriction Being an Answer to a Book Published by Mr. William Troughton* (London: Francis Smith, 1673).

Burnet, Gilbert (Bishop), *Burnet's History of His Own Time* (London, 1875).

Burns, J., 'Memoirs by James Burns, Bailie of the City of Glasgow, 1644–1661', in J. Maidment, ed., *Historical Fragments* (Edinburgh, 1833).

Canne, John, *Emanuel, or, God with us. Werein Is Set Forth Englands Late Great Victory Over the Scots Armie, in a Battle at Dunbar, Septemb. 3. 1650* (London: Matthew Simmons, 1650).

Church of Scotland, *Causes of a Publick and Solemn Humiliation* (Edinburgh: Evan Tyler, 1650).

Church of Scotland, *The Confession of Faith of the Kirk of Scotland* (Edinburgh: Evan Tyler, 1650).

Church of Scotland, *Confession of Faith of the Kirk of Scotland* (Tot Rotterdam 1655).

Church of Scotland, *Directions of the Generall Assembly Concerning Secret and Private Worship, and Mutuall Edification, for Cherishing Piety, for Maintaining Unity, and Avoiding Schism and Division* (Edinburgh: Evan Tyler, 1650).

Church of Scotland, General Assembly, *Acts of the General Assembly of the Church of Scotland, 1638–1842*, ed., Pitcairn, T. (Edinburgh, 1843).

Church of Scotland, General Assembly, *A Declaration of the General Assembly of the Kirk of Scotland, in Answer to a Declaration, Intituled, A Declaration of the Parliament of England, upon the Marching of Their Army Into Scotland, and Concerning Present Dangers and Duties, in Reference Both to Sectaries and Malignants* (Edinburgh: Evan Tyler, 1650).

Church of Scotland, General Assembly, *Three Acts of the Generall Assembly, for Promoving [Sic] the Knovvledg of the Grounds of Salvation, and Observing the Rules of Discipline* (Leith, 1652).

Church of Scotland, General Assembly, *Warning and Declaration from the Generall Assembly. 30 of Iuly* (Aberdeen: James Brown, 1651).

Church of Scotland, General Assembly, Commission, *The Causes of a Publick Fast and Humiliation, To be Kept with All Convenient Diligence: By All the Members of This Kirk & Kingdom of Scosland* (Aberdeen: James Brown, 1650).

Church of Scotland, General Assembly, Commission, *Causes of an Humiliation Appointed by the Commission of the Generall Assembly, to be Observed through This Whole Kirk, on the Last Sabbath of March, and the First Sabbath of Aprile, 1653* ([Edinburgh?], 1653).

Church of Scotland, General Assembly, Commission, *For the Under-Officers and Souldiers of the English Army, from the People of Scotland* (Edinburgh: Evan Tyler, 1650).

Church of Scotland, General Assembly, Commission, *The humble representation of the Commission of the General Assembly to the Honourable Estates of Parliament upon their declareation lately communicate [sic] to us, Edinbuirgh, 28 Aprile, 1648* (London, 1648).

Church of Scotland, General Assembly, Commission, *A Seasonable and Necessary Warning Concerning Present Dangers and Duties, from the Commissioners of the Generall Assembly Unto All the Members of This Kirk* (Edinburgh: Evan Tyler, 1650).

Church of Scotland, General Assembly, Commission, *A Short Exhortation and Warning to the Ministers and Professours of This Kirk; from the Commission of the Generall Assembly. Perth, 20 March, 1651* (Aberdeen: James Brown, 1651).

Church of Scotland, General Assembly, Commission, *A Short Reply to the Army's Declaration* (Edinburgh, 1650).

Church of Scotland, General Assembly, Commission, *A Short Reply Unto a Declaration, Entituled, The Declaration of the Army of England, upon Their March Into Scotland. Together with a Vindication of the Declaration of the Army of England upon Their March Into Scotland, from the Unchari-table Constructions, Odious Imputations, and Scandalous Asperations of the General Assembly of the Kirk of Scotland, in Their Reply Thereunto* (London, 16 August 1650).

Church of Scotland, General Assembly, Commission, *A Solemn Testimony Against Toleration and the Present Proceedings of Sectaries and Their Abettors in England, in Reference to Religion and Government, with an Admonition and Exhortation to Their Brethren There, from the Commissioners of the General Assembly of the Kirk of Scotland* (Edinburgh: Evan Tyler, 1649).

Church of Scotland, General Assembly, Commission, *A Solemn Warning to All the Members of This Kirk, from the Commission of the Generall Assemblie with an Act for the Censuring Such as Act, or Comply with the Sectarian Armies* (Aberdeen: James Brown, 1651).

Church of Scotland, General Assembly, Commission, *West-Kirk the 13. Day of August, 1650* (Edinburgh: Evan Tyler, 1650).

Church of Scotland, Presbytery of Edinburgh, *A Testimony and Warning of the Presbyterie of Edinburgh, Against a Late Petition, Tending (in the Scope and Design Thereof) to the Overturning of the Ordinances and Truth of Christ in This Church. Octob. 5. Anno. Dom. 1659* (Edinburgh, 1659).

Clarke, William, *The Clarke Papers*, ed., Firth, C.H., Camden Society new Ser. 49, 54, 60, 62 (London, 1890–1, 1894–5, 1899).

Committee of Estates, Scotland, *An Answere from the Committee of Estates, To a Printed Paper Directed to the People of Scotland, and Signed in Name of L.G. Cromwel, and His Officers* (Edinburgh, 22 July 1650).

Committee of Estates, Scotland, *Declaration of the Committee of Estates. In Answer to The Declaration of the Parliament of England (18 June)* (Edinburgh: Evan Tyler, 1650).

Committee of Estates, Scotland, *Edinburgh, 4 Iune 1650. The Estates of Parliament Now Presently Conveened, Taking Into Consideration the Necessary Duty Lying upon Them to Use Their Best Endeavors for Securing of Religion and the Peace of the Kingdom* (Edinburgh: Evan Tyler, 1650).

Committee of Estates, Scotland, *Edinburgh, the Twentie Day of June, 1650. The Estates of Parliament Now Presently Conveened in This Fift Session of This Second Triennal Parliament, Taking to Their Consideration the Dangers Which Threatens Religion & This Kingdome* (Edinburgh: Evan Tyler, 1650).

Cramond, W., ed., *Extracts from the Records of the Kirk-Session of Elgin* (Elgin, 1897).

Cramond, W., ed., *Extracts from the Records of the Synod of Moray* (Elgin, 1906).

Cramond, W., ed., *The Records of Elgin, 1234–1800* (Aberdeen, 1898).

Cromwell, Oliver, *By His Excellency. Whereas it Hath Pleased God by His Gracious Providence and Goodnesse, to Put the City of Edinburgh and Towne of Leith Under My Power* ([Edinburgh]: [Evan Tyler], 1650).

Cromwell, Oliver, *A Declaration of Oliver Cromwell, Captain General of All the Forces of This Common-Wealth* (London: William Du-gard, 1653).

Cromwell, Oliver, *A Letter from the Lord General Cromwel from Dunbar; Containing a True Relation of the Proceedings of the Parliament Army Under His Command in Scotland* (London, 1650).

Cromwell, Oliver, *A Letter Sent to the Generall Assembly of the Kirke of Scotland* (London, 1650).

Cromwell, Oliver, *The Lord General Cromwell His March to Sterling. Being A Diary of All Proceedings in the Army from Their March Out of Edenburgh,* to the 25 of September 1650. Also, The Lord Generals Proclamation in Relation to Edenburgh and Leith (London: E.G., 1650).

Cromwell, Oliver, *Several Letters and Passages Between His Excellency, the Lord General Cromwel and the Governor of Edinburgh Castle, and the Ministers There, Since His Excellencies Entrance Into Edinburgh* (London: John Field, 1650).

Dell, Jonas, *Forms the Pillars of Antichrist; but Christ in Spirit the True Teacher of His People; and Not Tradition: for the Spirit of God Is Not Bound to Any Place, nor Time, nor Form; we May Not Limit the Holy One of Israel. The Spirits Teaching Doth Unmask and Unvail the False Prophet, or the Carnal Worshipper, and Discovers Them to be the Agents and Agitators of Antichrist. And the Kingdome of Antichrist Is Subdued to us, and Destroyed in us, by the Spirits Teaching. And to Him That Is Led by the Spirits Teaching Do I Commend These to be Received, and Not to the Naturall Mans Wisdom;. Written in Scotland in Opposition to Some People Who Do Imitate John the Baptist, by Dipping Themselves in Water, Holding Out Free-Will, and Falling from Grace, and Pretend That They are the Only Disciples of Christ, and Reject the Spirits Teaching, by One Who Waits to See the Downfal of the Kingdom of Antichrist, and the Prosperity of Sion, Jonas Dell Something in Answer to a Scandalous Paper Given Forth by W.P. to the Souldiers in the Garrison of Holmdell in Southerland* (London, 1656).

Dell, William, *Right Reformation: or, the Reformation of the Church of the New Testament Represented in Gospel-Light. In a Sermon Preached to the Honourable House of Commons, on Wednesday, November 25, 1646* (Edinburgh: Evan Tyler, 1650).

Douglas, Robert, *Short Information. A Short Information and Brotherly Exhortation to Our Brethren of England: From the Commissioners of the Generall Assembly of the Kirk of Scotland Convened at Forfarr. August 12, 1651* (Aberdeen: James Brown, 1651).

Douglas, William, *The Stable Trueths of the Kirk Require a Sutable Behaviour. Holden Forth by Way of a Sermon. Delivered by Mr. William Dowglas Professor of Divinity in Kings Colledge, in the University of Aberden [Sic]. April 18. 1659* (Aberdeen: J.B., 1660).

Dundas, William, *A Few Words of Truth from the Spirit of Truth* (1673).

Durham, James, *The Dying Man's Testament to the Church of Scotland* (Edinburgh: Christopher Higgins, 1659).

Edwards, Thomas, *Gangraena* (London, 1646).

England and Wales, Army, *A Declaration of the Army Concerning the Apprehending of Major Gen. Overton, and the Rest of the Officers of Scotland, Who Had a Design to Divide the Forces, and Stand in Opposition Against the Lord Protector, and the Present Government in England* (London, 1655).

England and Wales, Army, *Declaration of the Army of England, upon Their March Into Scotland* (Newcastle: S[tephen] B[ulkley], 1650).

England and Wales, Army, *A Declaration of the Army of England upon Their March Into Scotland as Also a Letter of His Excellency the Lord Generall Cromwell to the General Assembly of the Kirk of Scotland Together with a Vindication of the Aforesaid Declaration from the Uncharitable Constructions, Odious Imputations, and Scandalous Aspersions of the General Assembly of the Kirk of Scotland, in Their Reply Thereto and an Answer of the Under-Officers and Souldiers of the Army, to a Paper Directed to Them from the People of Scotland* (Edinburgh: Evan Tyler, 1650).

England and Wales, Army, *A Declaration of the Army of England upon Their March Into Scotland To All That are Saints, and Partakers of the Faith of God's Elect, in Scotland* (Edinburgh: Evan Tyler, 1650).

England and Wales, Army, *A Declaration of the Army of the Commonwealth of England, to the People of Scotland* (London, 1650).

England and Wales, Army, *A Declaration of the English Army Now in Scotland. [Sic] To the People of Scotland, Especially Those among Them, That Know and Fear the Lord; we the Officers and Souldiers of the English Army Do Send Greeting* (London, 1650).

England and Wales, Army, *A Declaration of the English Army Now in Scotland, Touching the Justness & Necessity of Their Present Proceeding in That Nation* (London, 1650).

England and Wales, Army, *A Declaration of the Officers of the Army in Scotland to the Churches of Christ in the Three Nations* (Edinburgh: C. Higgins, 1659).

England and Wales, Army, *Letters from the Head-Quarters of Our Army in Scotland: Being a Diary of All Proceedings in the Army to Octob. 30. 1650. An Accompt of Col. Kerr and Straughans Overture to the Lord Generall Cromwell, about Accomodation* (London: E.G., 1650).

England and Wales, Parliament, *An Act Against Vagrants, and Wandring, Idle, Dissolute Persons. At the Parliament Begun at Westminster the 17th Day of September, an. Dom. 1656* (Edinburgh: Christopher Higgins, 1657).

England and Wales, Parliament, *Declaration of the Parliament of England, upon the Marching of the Armie Into Scotland* (London: William Du-gard, 1650).

England and Wales, Parliament, *Proclamation Against All Meetings of Quakers, Anabaptists, & c.* (Edinburgh: Evan Tyler, 1661).

Farneworth, Richard, *The Scriptures Vindication Against the Scotish Contradictors. By One John Stalham, and as he Saith, Preacher of the Gospel at Edenborough in Scotland* (London, 1655).

Fergusson, James, *A Brief Refutation of the Errors Tolleration, Erastianism, Independency and Separation Delivered in Some Sermons from I Job. 4. I, Preach'd in the Year 1652 to Which are Added Four Sermons Preach'd on Several Occasions* (Edinburgh: George Mosman, 1692).

Firth, C.H., ed., *The Clarke Papers*, 4 vols (London, 1891–1901).

Firth, C.H., *Scotland and the Commonwealth* (Edinburgh, 1895).

Firth, C.H., *Scotland and the Protectorate* (Edinburgh, 1899).

Fox, George, *The Great Mistery of the Great Whore Unfolded* (London, 1659).

Fox, George, *The Journal*, ed., Smith, N. (London, 1998).

Fox, George, *The Journal of George Fox*, ed., Nickalls, J.L. (Cambridge, 1952).

Fox, George, *The Journal of George Fox*, ed., Penney, N. (Cambridge, 1911).

Fraser, James, *Chronicles of the Frasers*, ed., MacKay, W. (Edinburgh, 1905).

Friend to the Commonwealth, *A Declaration of the Commissioners for Visitation of Universities, and for Placing and Displacing of Ministers in Scotland; Against Praying, or Preaching for the Pretended King of Scotland: With Some Reasons Given by Some of the Ministers of Edinburgh, Why They Cannot in Conscience Omit to Pray for Him* (Leith,1653).

Friend to the Commonwealth of England, *The English Banner of Truth Displayed: or, The State of This Present Engagement Against Scotland* (London, 1650).

Gardiner, S.R., ed., *Letters and Papers Illustrating the Relations Between Charles the Second and Scotland in 1650* (Edinburgh, 1894).

Gillespie, Patrick, *Rulers Sins the Causes of National Judgments: or, a Sermon Preached at the Fast, upon the 26th Day of December, 1650* (Glasgow, 1718).

Gilpin, John, *The Quakers Shaken, or, A Discovery of the Errours of That Sect by John Gilpin* (Edinburgh, 1655).

Gough, James, *Memoirs of the Life, Religious Experience, and Labours in the Gospel of James Gough*, 3 vols (Lindfield, 1832).

A Great Victory God Hath Vouchsafed by the Lord Generall Cromwels Forces Against the Scots (London, 1651).

Green, M.A.E., ed., *Calendar of State Papers, Domestic Series 1651–1660*, 13 vols (London, 1877–86).

Guild, William, *An Ansvver to a Popish Pamphlet* (Aberdeen: James Brown, 1656)

Guild, William, *Anti-Christ Pointed and Painted Out in His True Colours* (Aberdeen: James Brown, 1655).

Guild, William, *The Noveltie of Poperied Discovered and Chieflie Proven by Romanists out of Themselves* (Aberdeen: James Brown, 1656).

Guthrie, James, *A Humble Acknowledgement of the Sins of the Ministery of Scotland* ([Edinburgh?], 1653).

Guthrie, James, *Protesters no Subverters, and Presbyterie no Papacie* (Edinburgh, 1658).

Guthrie, James, *Some Considerations Contributing Unto the Discoverie of the Dangers That Threaten Religion and the Work of the Reformation in the Church of Scotland* (Edinburgh, 1660).

Guthrie, James, *A Treatise of Ruling Elders and Deacons* (Edinburgh, 1652).

Guthrie, William, *The Christians Great Interest* (Glasgow: C. Higgins, 1659).

Hay, Andrew, *Andrew Hay of Craignethan's Diary, 1659–1660*, ed., Reid, A.G. (Edinburgh, 1901).

Hazard, Ebenezer, *Historical Collections: consisting of state papers and other authentic documents, intended as materials for an history of the United States of America* (Philadelphia, 1792–4).

Heath, James, *A Brief Chronicle of the Late Intestine War in the Three Kingdoms of England, Scotland and Ireland* (London: J.P., 1676).

Henderson, E., ed., *Extracts from the Kirk-Session Records of Dunfermline, from A.D. 1640 to 1689 Inclusive* (Edinburgh, 1865).

Henderson, F., ed., *The Clark Papers: Further Selections from the Papers of William Clarke*, Camden Fifth Series, vol. 27 (Cambridge, 2005).

Howgill, Francis, *To All You Commanders and Officers of the Army of Scotland* (Leith, 1657).

Hutcheson, George, *A Review and Examination of a Pamphlet Lately Published, Bearing the Title of Protesters no Subverters, and Presbyterie no Papacy, &c. By Some Lovers of the Interest of Christ in the Church of Scotland* (Edinburgh: C. Higgins, 1659).

Hutchinson, Thomas, *A collection of original papers relative to the History of the colony of Massachusets-bay* (Boston, New-England, 1769).

Innes, C. and Thomson, T., eds, *The Acts of the Parliament of Scotland*, 11 vols (Edinburgh, 1814–44).

Irving, Alexander, 'Protestation by Sir Alexander Irving of Drum Against the Presbytery of Aberdeen. 1652', *The Miscellany of the Spalding Club III* (Aberdeen, 1846), 205–7.

Jaffray, Alexander, *Diary of Alexander Jaffray*, ed., Barclay, John, 3rd edn (Aberdeen, 1856).

Johnston, Sir Archibald, of Wariston, *Causes of the Lords Wrath Against Scotland: Manifested in His Sad Late Dispensations; Whereunto Is Added a Paper, Particularly Holding Forth the Sins of the Ministery* (Edinburgh: by the heirs of Geo. Anderson, 1653.)

Johnston, Sir Archibald, of Wariston, *Diary of Sir Archibald Johnston of Wariston*, eds, Flemming, D.H. and Ogilvie, J.D., 3 vols (Edinburgh, 1919–40).

Jonas, A.C., 'Extracts from the Parish Records, 1644–1699', *Proceedings of the Society of Antiquaries of Scotland*, 46 (1911–12), 27–52.

Keith, George, *Help in Time of Need, from the God of Help* (Aberdeen, 1665).

Keith, George, *The Way Cast up, and the Stumbling-Blockes Removed from Before the Feet of Those, Who are Seeking the Way to Zion, with Their Faces Thitherward* (Aberdeen, 1677).

Kiffin, William, *A Confession of Faith, of Severall Congregations or Churches of Christ in London, Which are Commonly (Though Unjustly) Called Anabaptists*, Fourth impression, corrected. (Leith, 1653).

King, Daniel, *A Way to Sion Sought Out*, 2nd edn (Edinburgh: Christopher Higgins, 1656).

Laing, David, ed., *Correspondence of Sir Robert Kerr, First Earl of Ancram and His Son, William, Third Earl of Lothian*, 2 vols (Edinburgh, 1875).

Lamont, John, *The Diary of Mr John Lamont of Newton, 1649–1671*, ed., Kinloch, G.R. (Edinburgh, 1830).

Law, Robert, *Memorialls, or the Memorable Things That Fell Out within This Island of Britain from 1638 to 1684*, ed., Sharpe, C.K. (Edinburgh, 1818).

Leishman, M., ed., *The Works of the Rev. Hugh Binning*, 3rd edn (Edinburgh, 1851).

Letter of the Officers of the Army in Scotland (Oct. 22) (Edinburgh: C. Higgins, 1659).

Letter to the Lord Fleetwood, from an Officer in the Army (Edinburgh: C. Higgins, 1659).

Lockyer, Nicholas, *A Litle Stone Out of the Mountain. Church-Order Briefly Opened* (Leith: Evan Tyler, 1652).

Love the Precious Ointment, That Flowes Down from the Head Christ Jesus, to All His Members; and Makes Them Dwell Together in Unity (Leith, 1654).

MacTavish, D.C., ed., *Minutes of the Synod of Argyll, 1652–1661* (Edinburgh, 1944).

Maidment, James, ed., 'Diurnal of Occurences in Scotland', *The Spottiswoode Micellany* (Edinburgh, 1845), 75–208.

Mercurius Scoticus Giving the World Ground upon This Evident Truth, Videlicet, That the Scottish Rebels, the Presbyter, or Kirckfaction Never Intended That Charles the Second Should be Their King (Rotterdam: P.C., 1650).

Monck, George, *A Declaration of the Commander in Chief in Scotland, and the Officers Under His Command, in Vindication of the Liberties of the People, and Priviledges of Parliament* (Edinburgh: C. Higgins, 1659).

Munro, A.M., ed., *Records of Old Aberdeen*, vol. 2 (Aberdeen, 1909).

Nickolls, J., ed., *The Original Letters and Papers of State, Addressed to Oliver Cromwell* (London, 1743).

Nicoll, John, *A Diary of Public Transactions and Other Occurrences, Chiefly in Scotland, 1650–67*, ed., Laing, D. (Edinburgh, 1836).

Nimmo, James, *Diary, 1654–1709*, ed., Scott-Moncrieff, W.G. (Edinburgh, 1889).

Overton, Robert, *Two Letters from Major General Overton* (London: Livewell Chapman, 1655).

Owen, John, *The Advantage of the Kingdome of Christ, in the Shaking of the Kingdoms of the World: or, Providential Alterations, in Their Subserviencie to Christ's Exaltation. Opened in a Sermon Preached to the Parliament, Octob. 24. 1651. A Solemn Day of Thanksgiving for the Destruction of the Scots Army at Worcester, with Sundry Other Mercies; by John Owen, Minister of the Gospel* (Leith: Evan Tyler, 1652).

Owen, John, *The Branch of the Lord, the Beauty of Sion: or, The Glory of the Church, in Its Relation Unto Christ Opened in Two Sermons; One Preached at Berwick, the Other at Edinburgh* (Edinburgh: Evan Tyler, 1650).

Parker, Alexander, *A Discovery of Satan's Wiles. Lately Printed and Published in a Booke Entitled, Antichrist (in Spirit) Unmasked, Etc. Put Forth by One James Brown* (London, 1657).

P.E., *A Serious Review of Some Principles of the Quakers: Wherein Error Is Discovered, and Truth Defended* ([Edinburgh]: [Andrew Anderson], 1655).

Pittilloh, Robert, *Scotland Mourning: or, a Shorty Discovery of the Sad Consequences Which Accompanies the Delay of the Setling of Judicatories in That Nation* (London: L. Chapman, 1659).

Pittilloh, Robert, *The Hammer of Persecution: or, the Mystery of Iniquity In the Persecution of Many Good People in Scotland, Under the Government of Oliver Late Lord Protector, and Continued by Others of the Same Spirit; Disclosed, with the Remedies Thereof* (London: L. Chapman, 1659).

Pittillok, Robert, *A Short Brotherly Examination of a Sermon: At First Preached by Mr Saloman Saffrey, and After Published in Print; Intituted, Part of a Discourse, Tending Only to Invite Those That Believe in Christ, to be Conformable to Him by Baptisme. But Intending to Disswade from Infant-Baptisme* (Leith: Evan Tyler, 1652).

Prynne, William, *Sad and Serious Political Considersations, Touching the Invasive War Against Our Presbyterian Protestant Brethren in Scotland, Their Late Great Overthrow, and the Probable Dangerous Consequences Thereof to Both Nations and the Protestant Religion. Which May Serve as a Satisfactory Apology for Such Ministers and People, Who Out of Conscience Did Not Observe the Publike Thanksgiving, Against Their Covenant, for the Great Slaughter of Those Their Brethren in Covenant* (London, 1650).

Renwick, R., ed., *Extracts from the Records of the Burgh of Peebles, 1652–1714* (Glasgow, 1910).

Renwick, R., ed., *Extracts from the Records of the Royal Burgh of Stirling, A.D. 1519–1666* (Glasgow, 1887).

Robertson, J., ed., *Ecclesiastical Records. Selections from the Registers of the Presbytery of Lanark, 1623–1709* (Edinburgh, 1839).

Row, John, 'Diary', *Scottish Notes and Queries*, 7 (1894).

Row, John, *The History of the Kirk of Scotland, from the Year 1558 to August 1637 by John Row, Minister of Carnock: With a Continuation to July 1639, by His Son, John Row, Principal of King's College, Aberdeen* (Edinburgh, 1842).

Rushworth, John, *A True Relation of the Routing the Scottish Army Near Dunbar, Sept. 3. Instant: The Particulars of the Fight, Numbers Slain, and Prize Taken. With an Exact List of Names of the Prisoners* (London: John Field, 1650).

Rutherford, Samuel, *The Covenant of Life Opened: or, A Treatise of the Covenant of Grace* (Edinburgh: A. Anderson, 1655).

Rutherford, Samuel, *Letters of Samuel Rutherford*, ed., Bonar, A.A. (Edinburgh, 1863; 1984).

Rutherford, Samuel, *A Survey of the Spirituall Antichrist* (London, 1648).

Rutherford, Samuel, *A Survey of the Survey of That Summe of Church Discipline, Penned by Mr. Thomas Hooker* (London, 1658).

Saffery, Salomon, *Part of a Discourse, Tending Only to Invite Those That Believe in Christ, to be Conformable to Him in Baptisme* ([n.p.]: [n.p.], 164?).

Scobell, Henry, *A True Relation of the Proceedings of the English Army Now in Scotland, from the Two and Twentieth Day of July, to the First of August* (London, 1650).

Scotch man, *A Word of Advertisement & Advice to the Godly in Scotland. By a Scotch Man, and a Cordiall Wel-Wisher to the Interest of the Godly in Scotland, Both in Civils and Spirituals* (Edinburgh: Evan Tyler, 1651).

Scotland, Army, *To the Right Honourable the Lords and Others of the Committee of Estates, The Humble Remonstrance and Supplication of the Officers of the Army* (Edinburgh: Evan Tyler, 1650).

Scotland, Commissioners for Visitation of Universities and for Placing and Displacing of Ministers, *By the Commissioners. For Visiting and Regulating the Universities, and Other Affairs, Relating to the Ministery in Scotland* (Leith: Evan Tyler, 1652).

Scotland, Commissioners for Visitation of Universities and for Placing and Displacing of Ministers, *By the Commissioners for Visiting the Universities, Colledges, and Schooles of Learning in Scotland. Whereas by Our Former Proclamation, Bearing Date the Second Day of August, 1653. Whereas by Our Former Proclamation, Bearing Date the Second Day of August, 1653* (Edinburgh, 1655).

Servant of the Common-wealth of England, *An Examination of the Seasonable and Necessarie Warning Concerning Present Dangers and Duties, Emitted from the Commissioners of the General Assembly of the Kirk of Scotland, Unto All the Members of That Kirk. June 25 1650: Which Was Printed at Edinburgh* (London: William Du-gard, 1650).

Some Reasons Humbly Proposed to the Officers of the Army, for the Speedy re-Admission of the Long Parliament Vvho Setled the Government in the Way of a Free-State (Edinburgh, 1659).

Some Sober Animadversions, Humbly, and In All Meekness Offered to the Consideration of All Who Truly Fear the Lord, and Enquire in His Ways, in Scotland upon A Testimony and Warning, Emitted by the Presbytery of Edinburgh, Against a Petition Lately Presented to the Parliament, in Defence of the Said Petition. Published to Vindicate Truth, and Undeceive the Simple (London, 1659).

Stalham, John, *Contradictions of the Quakers (so Called) to the Scriptures of God, and to Their Own Scriblings and Vain Janglings. VVitnessed and Published by John Stalham, Preacher of the Gospel (for the Present) at Edinburgh in Scotland* (Edinburgh, 1655).

Sterry, Peter, *England's Deliverance from the Northern Presbytery, Compared with Its Deliverance from the Roman Papacy* (Leith: Evan Tyler, 1652).

Stockdale, William, *The Principles and Doctrines* (London, 1659).

Sydenham, Cuthbert, *The False Brother, or, A New Map of Scotland. The*

Grounds of the Entrance of Our Army Into Scotland Cleared, from Their Own Principles and Actings; Their Main Pleas Impleaded, and Answered (London: R.W., 1651).

T.B. *A Message from the Lord General Crumwel to the Communalty of the Kingdom of Scotland* (London, 1650).

The Fifth Monarchy, or Kingdom of Christ, in Opposition to the Beasts, Asserted, by the Solemn League and Covenant, Several Learned Divines, the Late General and Army (Viz.) in Their Declaration at Muslebrough, August 1650 (London, 1659).

The Humble Representation of Some Officers of the Army, to the Right Honourable Lieutenant General Fleetwood. Delivered, November 1. 1659 (Edinburgh: Christopher Higgins, 1659).

The King of Scotlands Negociations at Rome for Assistance Against the Common-Wealth of England, As Also Severall Letters of the Chancellour of Scotland to the King Since His Coming Into Scotland, Taken in His Cabinet at the Late Fight Neer Dunbar (Edinburgh: Evan Tyler, 1650).

The Lord Gen. Cromwel's Letter: With a Narrative of The Proceedings of the English Army in Scotland, and a Declaration of the General Assembly, Touching the Dis-Owning Their King and His Interest (London: Edward Husband and John Field, 1650).

The Sum of Saving Knowledge (Edinburgh, 1650).

To the Generals, and Captains, Officers and Souldiers of This Present Army; The Just and Equal Appeal, and the State of the Innocent Cause of us, Who Have Been Turned Out of Your Army for the Exercise of Our Pure Consciences, Who are Now Persecuted Amongst Our Brethren, Under the Name of Quakers (London, 1658).

To the Very Honorable the Representative of the Common-Vvealth. The Humble Petition and Remonstrance of Such in Scotland (Leith: Evan Tyler, 1652).

To You the Parliament Sitting at Westminster, Our Request Is to God That You Rule for His Honour. Here are Several of Our Names, Who Thus Suffers in the Behalf of Many More in the Nation of Scotland (1659).

Turner, James, *Memoirs of His Own Life and Times, 1632–1670*, ed., T. Thomson (Edinburgh, 1829).

Tweedie, W.K., ed., *Select Biographies*, vol. 1 (Edinburgh, 1845).

Two Declarations of the Parliament of the Commonwealth of England. Together with Several Proceedings of the Commissioners Appointed by the Parliament for Ordering and Managing Affairs in Scotland (London: John Field, 1652).

Urquhart, Thomas, *Ekskybalauron: or, The discovery of a most exquisite jewel* (London, 1653).

Vicars, John, *A Caveat for Covenant-Contemners and Covenant-Breakers* (Edinburgh: Evan Tyler, 1650).

Weare, George, *The Doctrins & Principles of the Priests of Scotland, Contrary to the Doctrine of Christ and the Apostles Here All May See, the Priests of Scotland, and Their Church, and Their Persecution, Against the Saints, and Lambs, Servants, and Children of God, Which the Lord Moved to go among Them, to Visit the Seed of God, in That Dark Wildernesse Country, Who Has Been as Sheep among Wolves* (London, 1657).

Whitelocke, Bulstrode, *Memorials of the English Affairs*, 4 vols (Oxford, 1853).

Wood, James, *A Little Stone Pretended to be Out of the Mountain, Tried and Found to be Counterfeit. Or An Examination & Refutation of Mr. Lockyers*

Lecture, Preached at Edinburgh, Anno 1651. Concerning the mater of the Visible Church: And Afterwards Printed with an appendix for Popular Government of Single Congregations. Together with an Examination, in Two Appendices, Of What Is Said on These Same Purposes in a Letter of Some in Aberdene, Who Lately Have Departed from the Communion and Government of the Church (Edinburgh: Andro Anderson, 1654).

Wood, Thomas, *The Dead-Man's Testament: or, A Letter Written to All the Saints of God in Scotland, Fellow-Heirs of the Blessing with Those in England* (Leith: Evan Tyler, 1651).

W.S., *Presbyteries Triall* ([Douai?],1657).

SECONDARY

Abbott, W.C., ed., *The Writings and Speeches of Oliver Cromwell*, 4 vols (Cambridge, MA, 1937–47).

Aldis, H.G., *List of Books Printed in Scotland Before 1700, Including Those Printed Furth of the Realm for Scottish Booksellers, with Brief Notes on the Printers and Stationers* (Edinburgh, 1970).

Anderson, P.J., ed., *Fasti Academiae Mariscallanae Aberdonensis: Selections from the Records of the Marischal College and University, 1593–1860*, 2 vols (Aberdeen, 1898).

Anson, Peter F., *Underground Catholicism in Scotland 1622–1878* (Montrose, 1970).

Backhouse, James, *Memoirs of Francis Howgill, with Extracts from His Writings* (York, 1828).

Barratt, David B., *Sects,'Cults' and Alternative Religions* (London, 1996).

Beattie, J., *History of the Church of Scotland during the Commonwealth* (Edinburgh, 1847).

Berry, W.G., *Scotland's Struggles for Religious Liberty*, Eras of Nonconformity, VIII, ed., Horne, C. Silvester (London, 1904).

Besse, Joseph, *A Collection of the Sufferings of the People Called Quakers*, 2 vols (London, 1753).

Bissett, John, 'The Bibliography of Samuel Rutherford', *Records of the Glasgow Bibliographical Society*, 6 (1920), 79–83.

Blagden, C., *The Stationers' Company: A History, 1403–1959* (London, 1960).

Bower, A., *The History of the University of Edinburgh*, 2 vols (Edinburgh, 1817).

Brailsford, M.R., *A Quaker from Cromwell's Army: James Nayler* (London, 1927).

Brown, L.F., *The Political Activities of the Baptists and the Fifth Monarchy Men in England During the Interregnum* (Oxford, 1912).

Brown, P. H., ed., *Register of the Privy Council of Scotland* (Edinburgh, 1689–1707).

Buckroyd, J., 'Lord Broghill and the Scottish Church, 1655–1656', *JEH*, 27 (1976), 359–68.

Bulloch, J. M., *A History of the University of Aberdeen 1495–1895* (London, 1895).

Bulloch, James, 'Conformist and Nonconformists', *Transactions of the East Lothian Antiquaries and Field Naturalists' Society*, 8 (1960), 70–84.

Burnet, G.B., *The Story of Quakerism in Scotland 1650–1850* (London, 1952).

Butler, D.M., *George Fox in Scotland* (Edinburgh, 1913).

Calderwood, David, *The History of the Kirk of Scotland*, ed., Thomson, T., 8 vols (Edinburgh, 1842–9).

Capp, B.S., *The Fifth Monarchy Men: A Study in 17th Century English Millenialism* (London, 1972).

Carlyle, Thomas, ed., *Oliver Cromwell's Letters and Speeches with Elucidations*, 3rd edn (London, 1888).

Caton, William, *Journals of the Lives and Gospel Labours of William Caton and John Burnyeat*, ed., Barclay, John, 2nd edn (London, 1839).

Chalmers, George, *The Life of Thomas Ruddiman* (London, 1794).

Chambers, Robert, *Domestic Annals of Scotland from the Reformation to the Revolution*, 3rd edn (Edinburgh, 1874).

Clyde, W.M., *The Struggle for the Freedom of the Press from Caxton to Cromwell*, St Andrews University Publications, no. 37 (London, 1934).

Coffey, J., *Politics, Religion and the British Revolutions: The Mind of Samuel Rutherford.* (Cambridge, 1997).

Couper, W. J., *The Origins of Glasgow Printing* (Edinburgh, 1911).

Craven, J.B., *History of the Church in Orkney, 1558–1662* (Kirkwall, 1897).

Crippen, T.G., 'Nicholas Lockyer: A Half-Forgotten Champion of Independency', *TCHS*, 9 (1929–32), 64–77.

Davidson, J., *Inverurie and the Earldom of the Garioch* (Edinburgh, 1878).

Davies, G., 'The Quarters of the English Army in Scotland in 1656', *SHR*, 21 (1924), 62–7.

Davis, J.C., 'Against Formality: One Aspect of the English Revolution', *TRHS*, 6th Series, 3 (1993), 265–88.

Dawson, W.H., *Cromwell's Understudy: The Life and Times of General John Lambert and the Rise and Fall of the Protectorate* (London, 1938).

Devine, T.M., 'The Cromwellian Union and the Scottish Burghs: The Case of Aberdeen and Glasgow, 1652–60', in Butt, J. and Ward, J.T., eds, *Scottish Themes: Essays in Honour of S.G.E. Lythe* (Edinburgh, 1976), 1–16.

Dickinson, W.C. and Donaldson, G., eds, *A Source Book of Scottish History*, vol. 3 (London, 1954).

Dobson, D., *Scottish Quakers and Early America: 1650–1700* (Baltimore, MD, 1998).

Donald, P., 'Archibald Johnston of Wariston and the Politics of Religion', *RSCHS*, 24 (1991), 123–40.

Donaldson, G., 'The Emergence of Schism in Seventeenth-Century Scotland', in Donaldson, G., ed., *Scottish Church History* (Edinburgh, 1985), 204–19.

Douglas, D., *History of the Baptist Churches in the North of England from 1648 to 1845* (London, 1846).

Douglas, W.S., *Cromwell's Scotch Campaigns: 1650–1651* (London, 1899).

Dow, Frances, *Cromwellian Scotland: 1651–1660* (Edinburgh, 1979, 1999).

Dunlop, A.I., *The Kirks of Edinburgh 1560–1984* (Edinburgh, 1988).

Emerson, E.H., 'Calvin and Covenant Theology', *Church History*, 25 (1956), 135–44.

Escott, H., *A History of Scottish Congregationalism* (Glasgow, 1960).

Evans, B., *The Early English Baptists*, 2 vols (London, 1862–4).

Firth, C.H., ed., *The Last Years of the Protectorate, 1656–1658* (New York, 1964).

Firth, C.H., *Oliver Cromwell and the Rule of the Puritans in England*, The World's Classics, 536: Oliver Cromwell (London, 1956).

Firth, C.H. and Davies, G., *The Regimental History of Cromwell's Army*, 2 vols (Oxford, 1940).

Furgol, Edward M., *The Regimental History of the Covenanting Armies 1639–1651* (Edinburgh, 1990).

Gardiner, S.R., *History of the Commonwealth and Protectorate 1649–1656*, 4 vols (London, 1903).

Gentles, I., *The New Model Army in England, Ireland and Scotland, 1645–1653* (Oxford, 1992).

Goldwater, E.D., 'The Scottish Franchise: Lobbying During the Cromwellian Protectorate', *The Historical Journal*, 21 (1978), 27–42.

Goodare, J., *The Government of Scotland 1560–1625* (Oxford, 2004).

Goodare, J., *State and Society in Early Modern Scotland* (Oxford, 1999).

Grainger, J.D., *Cromwell Against the Scots: The Last Anglo-Saxon War, 1650–1652* (East Linton, 1997).

Grant, F.J., ed., *The Faculty of Advocates in Scotland, 1532–1943* (Edinburgh, 1944).

Greaves, R.L. and Zaller, R., eds, *Bibliographical Dictionary of British Radicals in the 17th Century*, 3 vols (Brighton, 1982–4).

Gribben, Crawford, 'Defining the Puritans? The Baptism Debate in Cromwellian Ireland, 1654–56', *Church History*, 73.1 (2004), 63–89.

Gribben, Crawford, 'Robert Leighton, Edinburgh Theology and the Collapse of Presbyterian Consensus', in Boran, E. and Gribben, C., eds, *Enforcing Reformation in Ireland and Scotland, 1550–1700*, St Andrews Studies in Reformation History (Aldershot, 2006), 183.

Guizot, F.P.G., *Memoirs of George Monk*, trans., Wortley, J.S. (London, 1838).

Hannen, R.B., 'Cupar, Fife, 1652–1659', *BQ* 10 (1940–1), 45–9.

Hardman Moore, S., 'Arguing for Peace: Giles Firmin on New England and Godly Union', in Swanson, R.N., ed., *Unity and Diversity in the Church*, Studies in Church History, 32 (Oxford, 1996), 251–61.

Hay, M.V., *The Blairs Papers, 1603–1660* (London, 1929).

Henderson, G.D., 'The Idea of Covenant in Scotland', *Evangelical Quarterly*, 27 (1955), 2–14.

Henderson, G.D., *Religious Life in Seventeenth Century Scotland* (Cambridge, 1937).

Henderson, G.D., 'Some Early Scottish Independents', *Transactions of the Congregational Historical Society*, 12 (1933–6), 67–79.

Hewison, J.K., *The Covenanters*, 2 vols (Glasgow, 1913).

Hirsch, E.F., 'John Cotton and Roger Williams: Their Controversy Concerning Religious Liberty', *Church History*, 10 (1941), 38–51.

Historical Manuscript Commission, *Report on the Laing Manuscripts Preserved in the University of Edinburgh*, ed., Paton, Rev. Henry, 2 vols (London, 1914).

Horle, C.W., 'Quakers and Baptists 1647–1660', *BQ*, 26 (1975–6), 344–62.

Howie, J., *The Scots Worthies: Their Lives and Testimonies* (Edinburgh, 1876).

Hoy, W.I., 'Entry of Sects Into Scotland: A Preliminary Study', *Reformation and Revolution*, ed., Shaw, D. (Edinburgh, 1967).

Hughes, Ann, 'Approaches to Presbyterian Print Culture', in Anderson, J. and Sauer, E., eds, *Books and Readers in Early Modern England* (Philadelphia, 2002), 97–116.

Hughes, Ann, '"Popular" Presbyterianism in the 1640 and 1650s: The Cases of Thomas Edwards and Thomas Hall', in Tyacke, N., ed., *England's Long Reformation: 1500–1800*, The Neale Colloquium in British History (London, 1998, 2000), 235–260.

Hughes, Ann, 'Public Disputations, Pamphlets and Polemic, 1649–60', *History Today*, 41 (1991), 27–33.

Hughes, Ann, 'The Pulpit Guarded: Confrontations Between Orthodox and Radicals in Revolutionary England', in Laurence, A., Owens, W.R. and Stuart, S., eds, *John Bunyan and His England, 1628–88* (London, 1990), 31–50.

Innes, C., ed., *Fasti Aberdonenses* (Aberdeen, 1854).

Irons, J.C.c *Leith and Its Antiquities*, 2 vols (Edinburgh, 1897).

Johnson, B., 'On Church and Sect', *American Sociological Review*, 28 (1963), 539–49.

Kendall, J. and Tompkins, J., *Piety Promoted*, 8 vols (London, 1789).

Kennedy, W, *Annals of Aberdeen*, 2 vols (London, 1818).

Kenyon, J., Ohlmeyer, J. and Morrill, J., eds, *The Civil Wars: A Military History of England, Scotland and Ireland 1638–1660* (Oxford, 2002).

Kinloch, G.R., ed., *Ecclesiastical Records of the Presbyteries of St. Andrews and Cupar 1641–1698* (Edinburgh, 1837).

Knox, R.B., 'A Scottish Chapter in the History of Toleration', *Scottish Journal of Theology*, 41 (1988), 49–74.

Korbin, D., 'The Expansion of the Visible Church in New England: 1629–1650', *Church History*, 36 (1967), 189–209.

Laing, Malcolm, *The History of Scotland*, 4 vols (London, 1801).

Landsman, Ned C., *Scotland and its First American Colony 1683–1760* (Princeton, 1985).

Laurence, Anne, *Parliamentary Army Chaplains, 1642–51* (London, 1990).

Little, Patrick, *Lord Broghill and the Cromwellian Union with Ireland and Scotland* (Woodbridge, 2004).

Liu, Tai, *Discord in Zion: The Puritan Divines and the Puritan Revolution 1640–1660*, International Archives of the History of Ideas: 61 (The Hague, 1973).

Lomas, S.C., ed., *The Letters and Speeches of Oliver Cromwell*, 3 vols (London, 1904).

Lynch, Michael, ed., *The Oxford Companion to Scottish History* (Oxford, 2001).

Macinnes, A.I., *The British Revolution, 1629–1660* (Houndsmill, 2005).

Macinnes, A.I., *Clans, Commerce and the House of Stuart, 1603–1788* (Edinburgh, 1996).

Macinnes, A.I., 'Covenanting Ideology in the Seventeenth Century Scotland', in Ohlmeyer, J.H., ed., *Political Thought in Seventeenth Century Ireland* (Cambridge, 2000), 191–200.

Macinnes, A.I., 'The Impact of the Civil Wars and Interregnum: Political Disruption and Social Change within Scottish Gaeldom', in Mitchison, R. and Roebuck, P., eds, *Economy and Society in Scotland and Ireland* (Edinburgh, 1988), 58–69.

Maclehose, James, *The Glasgow University Press 1638–1931* (Glasgow, 1931).

Maidment, James, ed., *Historical Fragments, Relative to Scottish Affairs, from 1635 to 1664.* (Edinburgh, 1833).

Makey, W.H., *The Church of the Covenant: Revolution and Social Change in Scotland* (Edinburgh, 1979).

Mann, A.J., *The Scottish Book Trade 1500–1720: Print Commerce and Print Control in Early Modern Scotland* (East Linton, 2000).

Masson, D., ed., *The Registry of the Privy Council of Scotland* (Edinburgh, 1896).

Matthews, D.H., 'The Glass House and Glaziers' Hall: Two Seventeenth-Century Baptist Meeting Houses – or One?', *BQ*, 34 (1991–2), 124–6.

McCoy, F.N., *Robert Baillie and the Second Scots Reformation* (Berkeley, 1974).

McCrie, T. and Thomson, T., *Lives of Alexander Henderson and James Guthrie with Specimens of Their Writings* (Edinburgh, 1841).

McGregor, J.F. and Reays, B., eds, *Radical Religion in the English Revolution* (Oxford, 1984).

Mehl, Roger, *The Sociology of Protestantism*, trans., Farley, James H. (London, 1970).

Meikle, James, *The History of Alyth Parish Church* (Edinburgh, 1933).

Miller, W.F., 'Financial Statements Sent to Swarthmore, 1654 and 1655', *JFHS*, 6 (1909), 49–52, 82–5, 127–8.

Miller, W.F., 'Notes on the Early Records of Friends in the South of Scotland from 1656 to about 1790', *JFHS*, 1 (1903), 69–73, 117–130.

Miller, W.F., 'Notes on the Meeting Houses of Edinburgh', *JFHS*, 6 (1909), 27–33.

Miller, W.F., 'Stranger Friends Visiting Scotland, 1650–1797', *JFHS*, 12 (1915), 79–83.

Mitchell, A.F. and Christie, J., eds, *Records of the Commission of the General Assembly*, 3 vols (Edinburgh, 1890–1909).

More, Ellen S., 'Congregationalism and the Social Order: John Goodwin's Gathered Church, 1640–60', *JEH*, 38 (1987), 210–35.

Morrill, John, *The Nature of the English Revolution* (London, 1993).

Morrill, John, ed., *Oliver Cromwell and the English Revolution* (New York, 1990).

Morrill, John, ed., *Revolution and Restoration: England in the 1650s* (London, 1992).

Morrill, John, ed., *The Scottish National Covenant in its British Context* (Edinburgh, 1990).

Morrill, John, 'Seventeenth-Century Scotland', review of Walter Makey, *The Church and the Covenant* (1979), Frances Dow, *Cromwellian Scotland* (1979), J. Buckroyd, *Church and State in Scotland 1660–1681* (1976), in *JEH*, 33.2 (1982), 266–71.

Mullan, David G., *Religious Controversy in Scotland 1625–1639* (Edinburgh, 1998).

Mullan, David G., *Scottish Puritanism, 1590–1638* (Oxford, 2000).

Murray, T., *The Life of Samuel Rutherford* (Edinburgh, 1828).

Naismith, R., *Stonehouse: Historical and Traditional* (Glasgow, 1885).

National Register of Archives (Scotland), *City Churches, Edinburgh* (Edinburgh, 1999).

Nelson, C. and Seccombe, M., *British Newspapers and Periodicals, 1641–1700* (New York, 1987).

Norman, J.G.G., 'The Relevance and Vitatlity of the Sect-Idea', *BQ*, 27 (1977–8), 248–258.

Nuttall, Geoffrey F., 'Presbyterians and Independents: Some Movements for Unity 300 years ago', *JPHS*, 10 (1952), 4–15.

Nuttall, Geoffrey F., 'Relations Between Presbyterians and Congregationalists in England', *Studies in the Puritan Tradition* (1964), 1–7.

Nuttall, Geoffrey F., *Visible Saints: The Congregational Way 1640–1660* (Oxford, 1957).

Ogilvie, J. D., 'A Bibliography of the Resolutioner–Protester Controversy, 1650–59', *Transactions of the Edinburgh Bibliographical Society*, 14 (1930), 57–86.

Ogilvie, J. D., 'Papers from an Army Press, 1650', *Edinburgh Bibliographical Society Transactions*, 2 (1938–45), 420–3.

Orme, William, *Memoirs of the Life, Writings, and Religious Connexions of John Owen, D.D.* (London, 1820).

Paterson, J., *History of the Counties of Ayr and Wigton*, 2 vols (Edinburgh, 1864).

Peacey, Jason, 'Cromwellian England: A Propaganda State?', *History*, 91 (2006), 176–99.

Peacey, Jason, *Politicians and Pamphleteers: Propaganda During the English Civil Wars and Interregnum* (Aldershot, 2004).

Penney, N., ed., *Extracts from State Papers Relating to Friends 1654 to 1672* (London, 1913).

Peterkin, Alexander, ed., *Records of the Kirk of Scotland* (Edinburgh, 1838).

Peters, Kate, *Print Culture and the Early Quakers*, Cambridge Studies in Early Modern British History (Cambridge, 2005).

Peters, Kate, '"The Quakers Quaking': Print and the Spread of a Movement", in Wabuda, S. and Litzenberger C., eds, *Belief and Practice in Reformation England*, St Andrews Studies in Reformation History (Aldershot, 1998), 250–67.

Pope, R.G., *The Half-Way Covenant: Church Membership in Puritan New England* (Princeton, 1969).

Pottinger, M., 'Cromwellian Soldiers in Cannesbey, 1652 to 1655', *Caithness Field Club Bulletin*, 11 (1993), 5–8.

Rait, R. S., *The Universities of Aberdeen: A History* (Aberdeen, 1895).

Rapaport, Diane, 'Scottish Slavery in 17th-Century New England', *History Scotland*, 5.1 (2005), 44–52.

Reay, Barry, *The Quakers and the English Revolution* (London, 1985).

Rigney, James, '"To Lye upon a Stationers Stall, Like a Piece of Coarse Flesh in a Shambles": The Sermon, Print and the English Civil War', in Hughes, A., Milton, A. and Lake, P., eds, *The English Sermon Revised: Religion, Literature and History 1600–1750*, Politics, Culture and Society in Early Modern Britain (Manchester, 2000).

Rogers, P.G., *The Fifth Monarchy Men* (London, 1966).

Ross, James, *A History of Congregational Independency in Scotland* (Glasgow, 1900).

Row, W., *The Life of Mr Robert Blair*, ed., McCrie, T. (Edinburgh, 1848).

Sachse, W.L., 'The Migration of New Englanders to England', *American Historical Review*, 53 (1948), 251–78.

Schmidt, L.E., *Holy Fairs: Scottish Communions and American Revivals in the Early Modern Period*, 2nd edn (Grand Rapids, MI, 2001).

Scott, H, ed., *Fasti Ecclesiae Scoticanae*, 7 vols (Edinburgh, 1915–28).

Scott, J., 'Baptists in Scotland during the Commonwealth', *Records of the Scottish Church History Society*, 3 (1929), 174–85.

Scott, J., 'Baptist Witness during the Commonwealth', in Yullie, G., ed., *History of the Baptists in Scotland* (Glasgow, 1926), 24–35.

Scott, Jonathon, 'What were Commonwealth Principles?', *The Historical Journal*, 47.3 (2004), 591–614.

Seebass, Gottfried, 'The Importance of Apocalyptic for the History of Protestantism', *Colloquium*, 13 (1980), 24–35.

Sessions, W.K., *Stephen Bulkley, Newcastle's First 'Long-Stay' Printer*, History of the Book Trade in the North (York, 1997).

Shepherd, Christine, 'University Life in the Seventeenth Century', in Donaldson, G., ed., *Four Centuries: Edinburgh University Life, 1583–1983* (Edinburgh, 1983), 1–15.

'Sir William Lockhart of Lee', *North British Review*, 36 (1862), 88–117.

Smith, C. Fell, *Stephen Crisp and His Correspondents* (London, 1892).

Smith, David L., 'New Perspectives on Britain's Civil Wars', *The Historical Journal*, 46.2 (2003), 449–61.

Smith, David L., 'Oliver Cromwell, the First Protectorate Parliament and Religious Reform', *Cromwell and the Interregnum*, Blackwell Essential Readings in History (Oxford, 2003), 167–81.

Smith, J., *The Church in Orkney* (Kirkwall, 1907).

Smith, Lesley M., 'Sackcloth for the Sinner or Punishment for the Crime? Church and Secular Courts in Cromwellian Scotland', *New Perspectives on Politics and Culture in Early Modern Scotland* (Edinburgh, 1982), 116–32.

'Some Early Sufferings in Scotland', *JFHS*, 21 (1924), 68–72.

Spalding, John, *Memorialls of The Trubles in Scotland and England. A.D. 1624–A.D. 1645*, 2 vols (Aberdeen, 1829–51).

Sprott, G.W., *The Doctrine of Schism in the Church of Scotland* (Edinburgh, 1902).

Sprott, G.W., *Worship of the Church of Scotland During the Covenanting Period, 1638–1661* (Edinburgh, 1893).

Stark, W. *The Sociology of Religion*, vol. 2, Sectarian Religion (London, 1967).

Stephen, W., *History of the Scottish Church*, 2 vols (Edinburgh, 1896).

Stephen, W., ed., *Register of the Consultations of the Ministers of Edinburgh and Some Other Brethren of the Ministry*, 2 vols (Edinburgh, 1921–30).

Stevenson, D., 'Conventicles in the Kirk, 1619–37. The Emergence of a Radical Party', *Records of the Scottish Church History Society*, 18 (1974), 99–114.

Stevenson, D., 'Deposition of Ministers in the Church of Scotland, 1638–1651', *Church History*, 44 (1975), 321–35.

Stevenson, D., ed., *The Government of Scotland Under the Covenanters* (Edinburgh, 1982).

Stevenson, D., *Revolution and Counter-Revolution in Scotland, 1644–1651* (London, 1977; 2003).

Stevenson, D., 'A Revolutionary Regime and the Press: The Scottish Covenanters and Their Printers, 1638–51', *Union, Revolution and Religion in 17th-Century Scotland* (Aldershot, 1997).

Stevenson, D., *St Machar's Cathedral and the Reformation*, Occasional Papers No. 7 (Aberdeen, 1981).

Stewart, Laura A.M., *Urban Politics and the British Civil Wars: Edinburgh, 1617–53*, The Northern World (Leiden, 2006)

Stuart, J., ed., *Extracts from the Presbytery Book of Strathbogie, 1631–1654* (Aberdeen, 1843).

Stuart, J., ed., *Selections from the Records of the Kirk Session, Presbytery, and Synod of Aberdeen* (Aberdeen, 1846).

Taft, Barbara, 'The Humble Petition of Several Colonels of the Army: Causes, Character, and Results of Military Opposition to Cromwell's Protectorate', *The Huntington Library Quarterly*, 42 (1978–9), 15–41.

Terry, C.S., ed., *The Cromwellian Union* (Edininburgh, 1902).

Todd, Margo, *The Culture of Protestantism in Early Modern Scotland* (London, 2002).

Tolmie, M., *The Triumph of the Saints: The Separate Churches of London 1616–1649* (Cambridge, 1977).

Toon, P., *God's Statesman: The Life and Work of John Owen* (Exeter, 1971).

Torrance, J., 'The Early Quakers in North-East Scotland', *Transactions of the Banffshire Field Club* (1936), 67–87.

Torrance, J., 'The Quaker Movement in Scotland', *Records of the Scottish Church History Society*, 3 (1929), 31–42.

Trevor-Roper, H.R., 'Scotland and the Puritan Revolution', *Religion, the Reformation and Social Change*, 2nd edn (London, 1972).

Troeltsch, Ernst, *The Social Teaching of the Christian Churches* (Chicago, 1981).

Underhill, E.B., *Records of the Churches of Christ Gathered in Fenstanton, Warboys and Hexham, 1644–1720* (London, 1854).

Underwood, T. L., *Primitivism, Radicalism, and the Lamb's War: The Baptist–Quaker Conflict in Seventeenth-Century England*, Oxford Studies in Historical Theology (Oxford, 1997).

Walker, Edward, *Historical Discourses, upon Several Occasions* (London, 1705).

Walker, J., *The Theology and Theologians of Scotland* (Edinburgh, 1872).

Walsham, Alexandra, *Providence in Early Modern England* (Oxford, 1999).

Watson, James, *James Watson's Preface to the History of Printing 1713* (Greenock, 1963).

Wheeler, J.S., 'The Logistics of the Cromwellian Conquest of Scotland 1650–1651', *War and Society*, 10.1 (1992), 1–18.

Wheeler, J.S., 'Sense of Identity in the Army of the English Republic, 1645–51', in Macinnes, A.I. and Ohlmeyer, J., *The Stuart Kingdoms in the Seventeenth Century* (Dublin, 2002), 151–68.

White, B.R., *The English Baptists of the Seventeenth Century*, vol. 1 of Roger Hayden, ed., *A History of the English Baptists* (Didcot, 1996).

White, B.R., 'The Organisation of the Particular Baptists, 1644–1660', *JEH*, 17.2 (1966), 209–226.

Whitley, W.T., *A History of British Baptists* (London, 1923).

Wilson, J., *Dunning: Its Parochial History, with Notes, Antiquarian, Ecclesiastical, Baronial, and Miscellaneous*, 2nd edn (Crieff, 1906).

Wilson, J.F., *Pulpit in Parliament: Puritanism during the English Civil Wars 1640–1648* (Princeton, 1969).

Wodrow, Robert, *Analecta: Or Materials for a History of Remarkable Providences; Mostly Relating to Scotch Ministers and Christians*, 4 vols (Glasgow, 1842–3).

Wood, M., ed., *Extracts from the Records of the Burgh of Edinburgh 1642 to 1655* (Edinburgh: Oliver and Boyd, 1938).

Wood, M., ed., *Extracts from the Records of the Burgh of Edinburgh 1655 to 1665* (Edinburgh, 1940).

Worden, B., 'Providence and Politics in Cromwellian England', *Past and Present*, 109 (1985), 55–99.

Worden, B., 'Toleration and the Cromwellian Protectorate', in Sheils, W.J., ed., *Persecution and Toleration: Papers Read at the Twenty-Second Summer Meeting and the Twenty-Third Winter Meeting of the Ecclesiastical History Society* (London, 1984), 199–233.

Wright, S., *The Early English Baptists, 1603–1649* (Woodbridge, 2006).

Young, John R., 'The Scottish Parliament and National Identity from the Union of the Crowns to the Union of the Parliaments, 1603–1707', in Broun, D., Finlay, R.J. and Lynch, M., eds, *Image and Identity: The Making and Re-making of Scotland through the Ages* (Edinburgh, 1998).

THESES

Carter, R. B., 'The Presbyterian–Independent Controversy with Special Reference to Dr. Thomas Goodwin and the Years 1640–1660', 2 vols (PhD Thesis, University of Edinburgh, 1961).

Chatfield, D.F., 'The Congregationalists of New England and Its Repercussions on England and Scotland, 1641–2' (PhD Thesis, University of Edinburgh, 1964).

Holfelder, K.D., 'Factionalism in the Kirk during the Cromwellian Invasion and Occupation of Scotland, 1650 to 1660: The Protester–Resolutioner Controversy' (PhD Thesis, University of Edinburgh, 1998).

Seymour, M.J., 'Pro-Government Propaganda in Interregnum England, 1649–1660'(PhD Thesis, University of Cambridge, 1987).

Thompson, G.L.S., 'The Origins of Congregationalism in Scotland' (PhD Thesis, University of Edinburgh, 1932).

Yeoman, L.A., 'Heart-Work: Emotion, Empowerment and Authority in Covenanting Times' (PhD Thesis, University of St Andrews, 1991).

Index

263